ENGLISH G

access 3

Jasper Lauterbach

Cornelsen

English G Access · Band 3

Im Auftrag des Verlages herausgegeben von
Jörg Rademacher, Mannheim

Erarbeitet von
Laurence Harger, Wellington, Neuseeland
Cecile Niemitz-Rossant, Berlin

unter Mitarbeit von
Dr. Annette Leithner-Brauns, Dresden
Birgit Ohmsieder, Berlin
Mervyn Whittaker, Bad Dürkheim

in Zusammenarbeit mit der Englischredaktion
Dr. Philip Devlin (koordinierender Redakteur), Gareth Evans, Bonnie Glänzer, Stefan Höhne, Dr. Christiane Kallenbach (Projektleitung), Uwe Tröger *und beratend* Filiz Bahsi, Christiane Bonk, Gwendolyn Düwel, Solveig Heinrich, Renata Jakovac *und* Lothar Teworte (digitales Schülerbuch)

Beratende Mitwirkung
Peter Brünker, Bad Kreuznach; Anette Fritsch, Dillenburg; Uli Imig, Wildeshausen; Thomas Neidhardt, Bielefeld; Wolfgang Neudecker, Mannheim; Dr. Andreas Sedlatschek, Esslingen; Sieglinde Spranger, Chemnitz; Marcel Sprunkel, Köln; Sabine Tudan, St. Georg; Friederike von Bremen, Hannover; Harald Weißling, Mannheim

Illustrationen
Tobias Dahmen, Utrecht/NL; Burkhard Schulz, Düsseldorf *sowie* Stefan Bachmann, Wiesbaden, Christian Bartz, Berlin und Roland Beier, Berlin

Fotos
Nigel Wilson Photography, Bristol

Umschlaggestaltung und Layoutkonzept
kleiner & bold, Berlin
hawemannundmosch, Berlin
klein & halm, Berlin

Layout und technische Umsetzung
zweiband.media, Berlin

Begleitmaterial zu English G Access 3	
9783060328062	Workbook mit Audio-CD
9783060331062	Workbook mit Audio-CD und interaktiven Übungen
9783060323814	Vokabeltaschenbuch
9783060330829	Wordmaster
9783060330881	Klassenarbeitstrainer
9783060330782	*Jerry* (Lektüre)

www.cornelsen.de

Druck: Mohn Media Mohndruck, Gütersloh

1. Auflage, 3. Druck 2017
broschiert
ISBN 978-3-06-032804-8

1. Auflage, 3. Druck 2017
gebunden
ISBN 978-3-06-032805-5

E-Book
ISBN 978-3-06-033363-9

PEFC
PEFC/04-31-1033

PEFC zertifiziert
Dieses Produkt stammt aus nachhaltig bewirtschafteten Wäldern und kontrollierten Quellen.
www.pefc.de

English G Access 3 enthält folgende Teile:

Units	die fünf Kapitel des Buches
Text File (TF)	eine Sammlung englischer Gedichte, Geschichten und Sachtexte
Skills File (SF)	eine Beschreibung wichtiger Lern- und Arbeitstechniken
Grammar File (GF)	eine Zusammenfassung der Grammatik jeder Unit
Vocabulary	das Wörterverzeichnis zum Lernen der neuen Wörter jeder Unit
Dictionary	alphabetisches Wörterverzeichnis zum Nachschlagen (Englisch-Deutsch und Deutsch-Englisch)

In den Units findest du diese Überschriften:

Background file	Informationen über Land und Leute
Looking at language	Beispiele sammeln und sprachliche Regeln entdecken
Language help	Hilfe in Form von sprachlichen Regeln
Practice	Aufgaben und Übungen
Writing course	englische Texte besser schreiben
The world behind the picture	vom Bild in den Film – Videoclips mit Aufgaben
Text	eine spannende Geschichte oder ein informativer Text

Du findest auch diese Symbole:

	Texte, die du dir anhören kannst: *www.englishg.de/access*
www	zusätzliche Materialien, die du unter *www.englishg.de/access* finden kannst
	Landeskundliche Informationen zu Großbritannien und Irland
	deinen Alltag mit der Alltagskultur anderer Länder vergleichen
	Übungssequenz: neue Grammatik intensiv üben und dann anwenden
Early finisher	zusätzliche Aktivitäten und Übungen für Schüler/innen, die früher fertig sind
More help	zusätzliche Hilfen für eine Aufgabe
You choose	eine Aufgabe auswählen
EXTRA	zusätzliche Aktivitäten und Übungen für alle
My Book	schöne und wichtige Arbeiten sammeln
Study skills	Einführung in Lern- und Arbeitstechniken
Your task	Was du in einer Unit gelernt hast, kannst du in einer Lernaufgabe zeigen.
	Hören Sprechen Lesen Schreiben Hör-Seh-Verstehen
	Mediation (zwischen zwei Sprachen vermitteln)
	Partnerarbeit Partnercheck Gruppenarbeit Kooperative Lernform

Inhalt

Dylan

Gwen, Morgan, Gareth

Die hier und auf den Folgeseiten aufgeführten Angebote sind nicht obligatorisch abzuarbeiten. Die Auswahl der Übungen und Übungsteile richtet sich nach den Schwerpunkten des schulinternen Curriculums.

Lauren

1 Unit

This is London

London

8 million people

611 square miles

300 languages

Europe's biggest street festival

…

1 London pictures

Think: Do you recognize any of the places, people, signs … in the pictures?
Make notes on what you know.

Pair: Exchange information with a partner.

- I think that's …
- Do you know what that is?
- That must/could be … What do you think?

If you still have questions about any pictures, write them down.

Share: Join another pair and try to find answers to your open questions.

2 London sounds

Listen to these sounds of London.
Match as many as you can to the pictures.

3 London and you

Do you know London?
Yes? When were you there? What did you do?

I went to London in … — *We visited … and I saw …* — *The best thing about my trip was …*

No? Tell your group what you would like to see and do there.

I'd really like to see … — *I've always wanted to see …* — *One thing that I'd really like to do is …*

→ Workbook *1 (p. 8)*

A
B
C
D
E
G
TAXI
UNDERGROUND
H
K
L
M
MIND THE GAP
N
390
King's Cross
Euston
Oxford Street
MARBLE ARCH
O
P
Q
R

1 Up on the roof

"Here we are," Mo said to his friend Luke and pointed to a huge glass building.
"You want to take photos of One New Change?" Luke asked. "But why? It's just a shopping centre."
"Oh – have you been here before?" Mo asked.
"Yeah, I came with Dad a few months ago. We bought Mum's birthday present here."
"So, have you been up on the roof too?"
"The roof? No. Why?"
"Well, you'll see. That's where I want to take some photos."

❖

"Just one more photo, Luke," Mo said. "As soon as these people move out of the way."
There were lots of tourists on the roof. Mo and Luke could hear all the different languages.
"St Paul's Cathedral ist mehr als 350 Jahre alt," a man said.
"Hey, that's German!" Mo said to Luke.
"Buckingham Palace'ı görebiliyor musun?"
"And what language is that, Mo?" asked Luke.
Mo didn't know.
"Beth ydi enw yr adeilad yna?" said a woman, and pointed to the Shard.
"Please don't speak Welsh, Mum," a girl replied.
"You have to practise your Welsh for your new school, Emily. I'm only trying to help."
The girl was quiet. A man looked up from a map.
"The building is called the Shard, Emily. It's the tallest building in Europe."
"No, it isn't!" Mo whispered. Then he couldn't stay quiet. "Excuse me. The Shard is only the tallest building in western Europe. There are two taller buildings in Moscow."
"Oh, I see," said the man, and smiled at Mo.
"But," Mo went on, "the Shard is 306 metres high.

It has 87 floors, 44 lifts, and amazing views from the top."
"Oh, have you been up there?" the man asked.
Mo shook his head. "It's much too expensive."
"So how do you know all about it?" Emily asked.
"I put a post about it on my blog last weekend," Mo explained. For a moment nobody said anything. Then Luke asked:
"Are you here on holiday?"
"Yes, we are," said the man. "But we only arrived yesterday evening, so we haven't seen much yet."
"But we have a lot of plans," the woman said.
"Mum wants to visit lots of museums," Emily said. "But I'd really like to do something different."
"Well," said Luke. "Notting Hill Carnival is this weekend."
"And the England–Australia test match!" Mo went on.
"I'm not into cricket," Emily replied, "but the carnival sounds fun."
"Yes, it is," said Mo. "Well, I hope you enjoy your holiday. And now I must take my photo."
"Er … wait a minute," said Emily. "Your blog – could you give me the address?"
"Sure," said Mo. "Just give me your number and I'll text you. Oh … and I'm Mo, by the way. And this is my friend Luke."

2 Who is this?

a) Take turns to say who the people are.
This person …
1 has been to *One New Change* before.
2 wants to take photos.
3 can understand German.
4 says something in Welsh.

b) Write four more sentences like the ones in a).

c) Read your sentences to your partner.

This person doesn't want to speak Welsh.

I think that's …

➔ Workbook 2 (p. 9)

3 Mo's blog

SOUTH LONDON BLOGGER

ABOUT ME | CRICKET | LONDON IN FILM

LONDON IN FILM

- Harry Potter
- Star Trek Into Darkness
- Notting Hill
- James Bond
- Sherlock Holmes

Star Trek Into Darkness

Year 2013

Director J. J. Abrams

Story It's the year 2259. A man called Khan attacks the Starfleet Archive in London. Captain Kirk and the *Enterprise* have to catch him.

Guess what city this is. Here's a clue. There is one building in both pictures. What is it? Is this how the skyline will look in 200 years?

Say what this page on Mo's blog is about. Which photo did he take at One New Change, and why? Which other pages on Mo's blog would you like to read? What information might you find there?

4 Mo sends a link

Listen to a conversation between Emily Evans and her parents.

a) Listen. Then say which parts of Mo's blog they talk about. What else do you learn about Mo?
b) Read the statements below. Listen again. Are they true or false? Correct the false statements.

1. Mr Evans gets a text message.
   That's false. Emily gets a text message.
2. Mrs Evans explains why Mo took a photo of St Paul's Cathedral.
3. Emily knows all about the film *Notting Hill*.
4. Mr Evans wants to tell Emily about the film *Notting Hill*.
5. The *About me* page has lots of information about Mo.
6. Mr Evans wants to see Mo's cricket page.
7. Mo and Luke play cricket for a London team.
8. Emily wants to watch the England–Australia match.

www Find out about London in Mo's other films. Find out about cricket.

1 WORDS City holidays

TIP
When you practise vocabulary, it helps to learn verbs and nouns that go together.

a) Write down verb/noun combinations like this:
go by bus, take the bus, wait for the bus, get on …

go by go on take get on wait for	bus · the bus car +Tube · the Tube +underground · the underground a tour · a boat trip

go to +stay at have look at queue at visit walk around	a hotel · a bed & breakfast a map · a website · a +timetable a cathedral · a museum · a +gallery the theatre · the cinema a café · a +restaurant · a carnival a park · a shopping centre lunch · a cup of tea · a drink

More help → p. 116

\+ new words

b) What do you do on holiday in a big city? Correct the silly sentences.
You don't queue at a cup of tea. You queue at a …

1 You go to a drink.
2 You visit a map.
3 You wait for a park.
4 You stay at the bus.
5 You walk around a tour.
6 You take a gallery.
7 You go on a drink.
8 You look at lunch.
9 You have a café.
10 You go by a hotel.

Early finisher Make three more silly sentences.

→ Workbook 3 (p. 9)

2 REVISION Your holidays (Simple past)

a) Write questions like these for a partner:
Did you stay at home or go away?
Did you go to a city / to the coast / … ?
Where did you stay? What … ?

More help → p. 116

When you're finished, go to a bus stop.

A bus stop is a place in the classroom where you meet a partner to work with.

b) Take turns to ask and answer questions. Take notes on your partner's answers.
A: What did you do in Dresden?
B: We walked around the city centre and went on a boat trip.

c) Go to another bus stop. Tell your new partner about your last partner's holiday.
A: Jan went on a boat trip in Dresden. He …

→ GF 1.1: Simple past (p. 155) → Workbook 4 (p. 10)

3 REVISION Have you ever …? (Present perfect)

Find out if you have both done the same things in your lifetime. Each make a window for the answers.

Have you ever been to London?
Have you ever eaten shark?
Yes I have. / No, I haven't.

WE HAVE BOTH … *eaten shark.* …	ONLY I HAVE … *visited another country.*
WE HAVEN'T … *played cricket.*	ONLY MY PARTNER HAS … *been to Darmstadt.* …

Early finisher → p. 126

→ GF 1.2: Present perfect (p. 156)

4 REVISION A message from London (Simple past or present perfect?)

Complete Emily's message with the correct tenses: simple past or present perfect.

Hey Amelia,
Hi from London. I [1]... (arrive) on Friday evening (with Mum and Dad), so we [2]... (already do) a few things. Yesterday morning we [3]... (go) up to the roof of a building where we [4]... (have) a great view. On the roof we [5]... (meet) two boys – Luke and Mo. They [6]... (give) us some tips. Luke [7]... (tell) us about a carnival at a place called Notting Hill.
After lunch we [8]... (visit) St Paul's Cathedral and then we [9]... (take) a red London bus to Hyde Park. It [10]... (be) beautiful there, and the park is really huge. [11]... you [12]... (ever be) there?
There are lots of places that we [13]... (not be) to yet – like Buckingham Palace, so I [14]... (not have) tea with the Queen either (LOL). And we [15]... (not visit) any museums yet, but Mum has plans! [16]... you [17]... (enjoy) your trip to France last week? What [18]... (be) the weather like there? In London it [19]... (not rain) yet! Hugs, Emily xxx

More help → p. 116 → GF 1.3 Present perfect or simple past? (pp. 156 – 157) → Workbook 5 (p. 10)

5 Pronunciation (Different stress in German and English words)

a) Write down the German and English words. Underline the stressed vowel in each word.

interessiert	interested	Palast	palace
Familie	family	Programm	programme
Kathedrale	cathedral	Tourist	tourist
Moment	moment	traditionell	traditional

TIP
Check the stress marks [ˈ] in the Dictionary.
interested [ˈɪntrəstɪd]
cathedral [kəˈθiːdrəl]

b) Listen and check.

→ True and false friends (p. 248) → Workbook 6 (p. 11)

6 Everyday English: Small talk

a) Two people meet at *One New Change*. Read their dialogue. Put the orange sentences in the right order. Then listen and check.

A: It's a great view of the cathedral, isn't it?
B: Thanks. Have a nice day.
A: Have you been here before?
B: I'm John. Nice to meet you, Sandy.
A: Well, I work near here, so I come here often. By the way, my name is Sandy.
B: Just for a long weekend.
A: How long are you staying in London?
B: No, this is my first time. I'm a tourist.
A: Well, enjoy the rest of your visit. Bye.
B: Oh, yes, it's amazing.

b) Practise the dialogue.

c) Act out your own dialogue.
Partner A → p. 132 Partner B → p. 135

Access to cultures

In Britain and in other English-speaking countries, people often have short, friendly conversations with people they don't know – for example, at a shopping centre or a bus stop. Then they say goodbye and don't expect to meet again.
What about your country? Is it the same there?

→ Workbook 7 (p. 11)

1 London attractions

Say what the headings and pictures tell you about each of the four attractions.

2 The Evans family's plans

a) Listen to Emily and her parents. Which attraction would each of them like to visit?

b) Why do you think Emily and her parents have chosen "their" attractions?
Read texts A–D. Then say what their reasons could be.

I think Emily's mum wants to go to … because …

I'm sure Emily likes … because …

c) Listen to Emily and her parents.
What are their arguments ***for*** and ***against*** the attractions?
What do they decide to do today?
What are they going to do tomorrow?

3 Your plans

Make plans for a day in London. Talk about arguments for and against the four attractions. Then agree on two attractions you would like to visit.

A

LOVELY PLANET **London** *and its treasures*

NATURAL HISTORY MUSEUM

This cathedral of science is THE place for everyone who is interested in the history of our planet.

Open every day – 10:00 – 17:50

Entry free

37

B

Inside **Big Ben** Inside **Big Ben**

Everyone calls this famous clock tower 'Big Ben', but its real name is the Elizabeth Tower. Big Ben is in fact the name of the largest bell inside it.
The bell rang for the first time on 11th July 1859. Today, not only Londoners hear the clock every hour; around the world millions of people also hear it on BBC radio. Most people who visit London see Big Ben from the outside. Why don't you climb the tower and see the inside too?

Tour times
December–May, Mon–Fri: 9:15, 11:15, 14:15
May–September, Mon–Fri: 9,11,14 and 16
Tours are only for people who live in the UK.
Tours are free, but please reserve your place early.

What will you see?
The tour will take you up 334 stone steps to hear Big Ben ring out the hour. You'll have an amazing view over London – and a chance to walk behind the clock faces and see the clock wheels at work.

C

THE LONDON EYE
FACTS AND FIGURES

1 The London Eye travels at less than 1 km an hour. That's as fast – or slow – as a tortoise. This means that a ride takes about 30 minutes and you have lots of time to enjoy the sights.
2 The London Eye is 135m high. That is like 64 red telephone boxes on top of each other.
3 From the top of the Eye you can see around 40 km on a clear day. There is a great view of famous sights like Buckingham Palace, the Houses of Parliament, the Shard and St Paul's Cathedral.
4 800 people can travel in the Eye at one time, as many as in 11 big red London buses.

Opening times
The London Eye is open every day except Christmas Day.
The first ride starts at 10:00am, and the ticket office opens at 9:30am.
Check the website for more details.
www.londoneye.com

Tickets & Prices	on the day	online
Adult (16+)	£19.95	£17.96
Child (4–15 yrs)	£14.00	£12.60
Child (under 4)	FREE	FREE
Family of four	£67.91	£54.33

London Eye: Conceived and designed by Marks Barfield Architects

D

TOWER OF LONDON *Over 900 years of history.*

During its long history, the Tower of London has been a palace, a prison, and even a zoo.
When you take the tour with one of the Beefeaters who guard the Tower, you'll hear many stories and legends from the past. One legend is that six ravens must always live at the Tower. If they leave, the king will fall. The Beefeaters look after the ravens and feed them 'bird biscuits', full of blood!
The Tower is also home to the Crown Jewels.
School classes which visit the Tower education centre can try on a copy of the Crown.

Opens	9 am Tues to Sat 10 am Sun and Mon	**Closes**	17:30 (16:30 Nov to Feb)	**Adult**	£21.45	**Child** (under 16)	£10.75

1 Learn how

Good sentences give your readers a clearer picture of what you want to say.

a) Read the tips on the right.
   Think of more examples for each tip.

You can use terrible or awful instead of bad.

Five years ago or during the holidays are examples of time phrases.

TIP

1. Use different adjectives (*bright, fantastic, dark, …*) to describe people, things and places – not just *good, bad* and *nice*.
   Use adverbs (*quietly, slowly, …*) for actions.
   Use *really, very, a bit* etc. (*really slowly, very quietly, a bit dark*) to be more exact.
2. Use time phrases (*last week, tomorrow, …*) to tell your reader when things happened.
3. Use linking words (*and, but, because, …*) and relative clauses to link short sentences.

b) Read the first draft of Leon's text. Then look at his corrections.
   Say how he has followed the tips.
   Suggest other ways to make his text better.

My trip to London — Leon Schmidt

My family and I were in London from Friday night to Saturday. We stayed at a hotel. It was near London Bridge. I had a nice view of the River Thames from my window.

We visited the Natural History Museum. The exhibits were very good. There were also lots of people there. The queue for the dinosaurs was long. We waited over an hour. It was worth it! There was a big model of T. Rex. It moved and roared. We also went to the Tower of London. We went on a tour there. I didn't like it. The tour guide spoke too fast. His jokes weren't funny.

We had dinner at an Indian restaurant. I had vegetable curry. It was good. I ate too much. I felt sick.

London is a nice city. Two days aren't enough.

There are so many places to visit.

My trip to London — Leon Schmidt

My family and I were in London *for the weekend* ~~from Friday night to Saturday~~. We stayed at a hotel. ~~It was~~ near Lo… Bridge. I had a *fantastic* ~~nice~~ view of the River Tham… window.

On Saturday ~~We~~ visited the Natural History Museum. The … were *really amazing. It was also very crowded.* ~~very good. There were also lots of people there.~~

The queue for the dinosaurs was *really* long. We waited over an hour, *but* ~~It~~ it was worth it! There was a *huge* ~~big~~ model of T. Rex, *which* ~~It~~ moved and roared. We also went ~~to~~ *of* the Tower of London. We went on a tour there. I didn't *enjoy* ~~like it~~ *because* ~~The~~ the tour guide spoke too fast *and* ~~His~~ his jokes weren't funny.

On Sunday ~~We~~ we had dinner at an Indian restaurant. I had vegetable curry. It was good, *but* I ate too much. I felt *a bit* sick *in the evening*.

London is a *great* ~~nice~~ city, *but* ~~Two~~ two days aren't enough.

There are so many *exciting* places to visit.

adjectives:
+ beautiful
great
fantastic
amazing
– silly
boring

➔ SF 10: Good sentences (p. 144) ➔ Workbook 8 (p. 12)

2 Now write …

You choose — Choose a), b) or c).

a) Describe a place that you visited in the summer holidays.
b) Write a short story about a person that you met in London.
c) Describe the loudest/quietest/strangest / most dangerous / … place in your hometown.

➔ Workbook Wordbank 1–2, 5, 7

1 Study skills: Giving feedback on a text

With good feedback, you can improve your writing. On this page you will learn to
- check another student's text.
- give good feedback to another student.
- react to the feedback that you get.

a) Checking a text

Give your partner the text you wrote for 2 on p. 16.
Look back at the writing tips on p. 16.
Read your partner's text and enter your feedback in a copy of the checklist on p. 256.

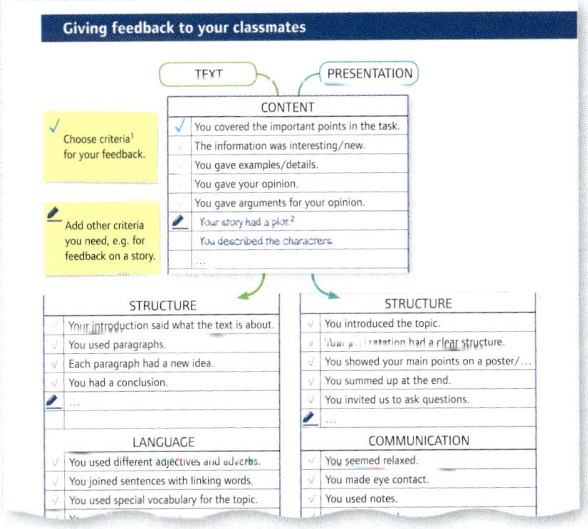

Make notes on how your partner can improve his/her text. Check spelling and grammar too.

b) Giving feedback

Make comments, suggestions and corrections on your partner's text. Follow these steps:

1 Tell your partner what he/she did well:
- I really liked what you wrote here because ...
- The details were interesting and ...
- I liked it when you used the word ...
- This was really fun to read because ...
- My favourite part was ... because ...

2 Say what you think your partner didn't do well. Say what he/she could do better.
- Your sentences are really short. Maybe you could link these two sentences with ...
- It's hard to understand *when* something happens. Why don't you use ...
- You use the same adjective more than once. You could use a different adjective here.
- Why don't you use an adverb with this verb?

3 Point out grammar and spelling mistakes.

c) Revising your text

Think about what your partner has said. Decide what to change.

My Book Write your final text.

Workbook 9–10 (p. 13)

Study skills

Giving feedback on a text

Wenn ich jemandem eine Rückmeldung zu einem Text gebe ...
- sollte ich zuerst sagen, was ...
- dann sollte ich erklären, was ...
- ...

Vergleiche deine Ideen mit dem Abschnitt im Skills File:

SF 14: Feedback – writing (p. 146)

2 REVISION How can I get there?

a) Find these places on the map of London on the front inside cover of your book:

- the British Museum
- the Millennium Bridge
- the London Eye
- Piccadilly Circus

Then explain where they are. Take turns.

It's in .... Street/Road · It's near ... <name of tube station> · It's on the corner of ... Street and ... · It's between ... <names of tube stations/ roads/other places>

b) You're at Russell Square tube station. Ask the way to other places on the map.

How can I get to the British Museum, please?

Walk along Southampton Row. Then turn right into ...

More help → p. 117

Early finisher Find a partner. Give directions to places in your town.

→ Workbook 11 (p. 14)

3 Go by tube

a) You're staying near Marble Arch. You want to go by tube to Big Ben. Practise this dialogue. Take turns.

A: How do we get from here to Big Ben?

B: Big Ben? That's Westminster tube station. We take the Central line eastbound from Marble Arch to Bond Street. And then we change to the Jubilee line southbound.

take the ... line · change to the ... line · northbound · southbound · eastbound · westbound

b) Choose other sights from the map on the inside cover. Find the nearest tube station. Act out more dialogues like the one in a).

→ Text File 1 (p. 98) → Workbook 12 (p. 14)

4 WORDS German *gehen*

Some German words like *gehen* have lots of different meanings in English.
Choose eight sentences that match the pictures. Translate them into German. Use a form of *gehen*.

1 They're going for a walk.
2 I don't feel well.
3 The clock is slow.
4 How are you?
5 Can you answer the phone?
6 We've missed it! Let's walk.
7 I'm fine, thank you.
8 It's too cold to go swimmning.
9 This torch doesn't work.
10 You can't do that!
11 What's the book about?
12 Just head for the church.

Early finisher Look at the four sentences that didn't go with a picture. Translate them into German.

5 A station announcement

a) You're at a train station on your way to Bonn. You hear an announcement. Listen carefully.

b) A British family doesn't understand. Act out a dialogue to answer their questions. Take turns at playing the British speaker.
1 We're going to Bonn. Was that announcement for our train?
2 What's the problem?
3 When and where does it leave now?

TIP

The most important thing about mediation is the *message*. You don't have to translate every word. If you don't know *Gleis* in English, try to explain it.

➜ Workbook 13–14 (pp. 14–15)

The adventures of Morph

1 Watching the cricket

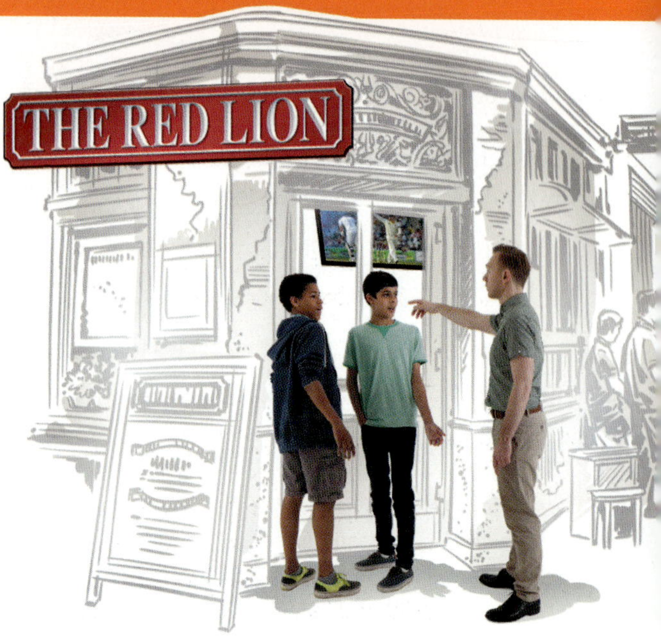

On Sunday morning Luke rang Mo's doorbell. When Mo opened the door, Luke said, "It's 10:30, Mo. The cricket is on TV."
In the living room, Mo's big sister Mishal was on the sofa. She was watching a music show. The music was so loud she didn't notice the two boys.
"Can we watch the cricket, Mishal?" asked Mo, but Mishal didn't answer. So Mo shouted, "Mishal! The cricket is on. Can we watch the test match?"
Mishal looked over at the two boys: "No way!"
"You've been watching TV for hours," Mo said.
"No, I haven't," his sister said. "I've been watching since 10, when Mum went out. Remember? And anyway, the cricket lasts all day. You can watch it later."
"But we're going to Notting Hill Carnival later, Mishal," Luke said and smiled at her. "Please, can we watch the cricket before we go? Please?"
"Nice try, Luke," Mishal said, "but no."
Then she picked up the remote and turned the volume up even louder.
Luke and Mo looked at each other. Mo made a face at his sister, then he said, "OK, Luke, let's just go to the carnival."

Five minutes later the two boys were walking towards the tube station when they passed a pub. Luke pointed through the door to a big TV screen. "Look, the cricket is on. Let's watch it for a while."
"But we can't go into a pub," Mo said. "We're not old enough."
"But we *can* watch through the door."
The boys stood at the door of the pub and looked in. After a while, Mo felt a tap on his shoulder. He turned round. A man shook his head at them. "I've been waiting here for five minutes, boys. Do you think I can go in now?"
"Sorry," Mo and Luke both said. They moved to the side and the man went in.
The match was getting very exciting and the boys slowly moved a bit closer to the TV. In a few minutes, they were just inside the door of the pub. They could hear the TV now too: **"The English team has been playing much better since the break,"** the commentator's voice said.
When England made a breakthrough, Mo shouted "Yes!" and Luke clapped his hands and sang, "England! England!"
Suddenly they heard another voice.
"All right, you two," said the barman. **"I've been watching you since you came in. You're** too young to be in here, you know that. Off you go now."
Luke and Mo turned round and left the pub.
"Notting Hill, here we come!" Mo shouted and they ran off together towards the tube station.

2 Follow the story

Take turns to explain:

1 why Luke goes to Mo's house.
2 what Mo and Luke's plans for they day are.
3 why they can't do what they want to at home.
4 where they go instead.
5 what happens there.

3 Have a go

Say how long you have been doing these things:

sit on this chair
*I've been sitting on this chair for **25** minutes.*
go to this school
learn English
use this book
work on this page

for

... minutes
... hours
... days
... weeks
... months
... years

Looking at language

Look at these sentences from p. 20. Then complete the explanation.

You've been watching TV for hours.
I've been waiting here for five minutes.
The English team has been playing much better since the break.

The **present perfect progressive** has three parts:
have/has + ________ + ____-form

We use this tense to say that something started in the past and is still going on now.
I've been watching TV since 3 o'clock.
= I started at 3:00 and I am still watching TV now.

3 o'clock ——————— now - - - - - - ▸

In German we use
1 the ... tense in situations like this.
2 ... for the English for and since.

➜ GF 1.4: Present perfect progressive (pp. 157–158)

1 I've been waiting for the bus ...

(Present perfect progressive)

Complete each sentence in two ways: with for and since.

1 I ... (wait) for the bus ...
I've been waiting for the bus for 20 minutes.
since nine o'clock.
2 You ... (watch) TV ...
3 It ... (rain) ...
4 She ... (feel) ill ...
5 I ... (learn) maths at school ...
6 We ... (have) lessons in this classroom ...

for	since
20/45/... minutes a few hours two/three/... days a year/two years/... ...	8:30/nine o'clock/... yesterday evening last week/January/... 2010/2011/... ...

➜ Workbook 15 (p. 15)

2 I've been living here ...

(Present perfect progressive)

Complete Mo's sentences.

I'm a Londoner.
I've been living here ...

Use the verb in brackets and for and since.

1 I'm a Londoner. I ... (live) here ... I was three.
2 I like languages. I ... (learn) German at school ... three years.
3 My sister Mishal loves music. She ... (sing) in a band ... over a year.
4 I have a blog. I ... (write) posts ... last March
5 My friend Luke and I love cricket. We ... (play) in the same team ... a long time.
6 Luke is a big fan of Notting Hill Carnival. He ... (go) there ... he was twelve.

More help ➜ p. 117
➜ Workbook 16 (p. 16)

3 How long ...?

a) Make a profile like this about yourself.

Name:	Daniel		
Hometown:	Berlin	Languages:	English/...
Address:	...straße 14	Sports:	football/...
School:	... Gymnasium	Hobbies:	choir/...

b) Meet a partner at a bus stop. Swap profiles. Then ask and answer like this:

How long have you been living in Berlin?
I've been living in Berlin for thirteen years.
How long have you been going to ... Gymnasium?

More help ➜ p. 117

c) Go to another bus stop. Tell your new partner about your last partner.

Daniel has been singing in a choir since last May.

Early finisher ➜ p. 126 ➜ Workbook 17 (p. 16)

1 A bus tour of London

The number 11 bus passes lots of famous sights. You can get on and off as often as you like and walk to sights near the route too.

a) Look at the London map on your inside cover.
Make a list of sights like the one below.
Put a star beside *your* five favourites.

On the bus route	Near the bus route
St Paul's Cathedral	The Tower of London ★
...	...

b) Watch the film.
Tick (✓) the places on your list that you see.

c) Watch again and listen for information about your favourites.
Write captions for each one that you see.
1 The royal family lives here.
2 ...

d) Read your captions to your partner.
Can he/she say what your favourites are?

The royal family lives here.

That's easy! Buckingham Palace.

2 Making the film: Time

a) Watch the film again. Think about *time*.
How long was the film?

How long do you think the tour really was?
Give reasons for your opinion.
You can check the distances on the map.

b) Think about *speed*.
The film-maker often speeds up the film.

Where in the film does he do this?
What could his reasons be?
Do you think it's a good idea?

c) Say which statement you agree with.

I liked the film because I had the feeling I was sitting on the bus.

It was a pity that we didn't see the person who was speaking.

What else did you like/not like about the film?

➜ Text File 2 (p. 100)

London for free

Big cities can be very expensive, but in London there's lots that will cost you nothing at all!

1 Museums and galleries
Most of London's most famous museums and galleries are free! See Van Gogh's *Sunflowers* at the National Gallery. Or admire the Rosetta Stone in the **British Museum** and find out how modern people learned to read Egyptian hieroglyphics.

2 Bridges over the Thames
If you have all the time in the world, you can walk across 27 of 34 bridges over the River Thames. They are great places to see life on the water or London's beautiful buildings.
With some bridges, like **Vauxhall Bridge** or Tower Bridge, the view *of* the bridge is at least as good as the view *from* it.

3 London's parks
London is one of the greenest cities in the world. Escape from the noise and traffic and crowds at the Diana, Princess of Wales Memorial Fountain in Hyde Park. Or imagine you're really in the country and watch the deer in **Richmond Park**, the largest in London.

4 Architecture and music
You have to pay to get into London's two most famous churches, St Paul's Cathedral and **Westminster Abbey** – unless you go to a service there. Then you can admire the majestic buildings and listen to their wonderful choirs.

5 Fabulous views
So the Shard is too expensive? Don't worry! There are many great free views in London. If you're in the City, take the lift to the roof of *One New Change*. Or in North London take a walk on Hampstead Heath and climb **Parliament Hill** with all of London below you.

Think of the five best free attractions in your town or region.
Which are similar to the free attractions in London? Which are different?

Workbook *18 (p. 17)*

1

2

3

4

5

The Notting Hill Carnival Parade

"Hurry," said Emily, "or I'll miss Mo and Luke."
"Don't be silly, Emily," her mum replied, "There'll be thousands of people at the carnival. There's no way you'll see those two boys there."
The platform at the tube station was full. When the train came in, everyone moved to the doors.
"Dad!" said Emily and pointed to two free seats. "You and Mum sit there. I can stand."
But more and more people got onto the train at each station, and they pushed Emily further and further away from her parents.
At Notting Hill Gate, everyone got off. Emily tried to wait for her parents, but the crowd pushed her along the platform and up the stairs. Out in the street, she held onto a lamppost. She scanned the sea of faces, but her parents didn't appear.

◆

Dancers in bright costumes moved along the street. Caribbean music filled the air. On the crowded pavement, Mo held his camera high and took as many photos as he could. Luke tried to move to the front of the crowd.
"Where are you going?" Mo shouted.
"I want to see my cousins. They're in the parade with my Uncle Ray. They're drummers!"

◆

Emily tried to call her parents.
"The number you are calling is not available at the moment. Please try again later."
All around Emily, it was getting louder. The sound of drums filled her ears. People were shouting wildly and blowing whistles. The crowd danced to the music and everyone was pushing against her. She started to panic. Then she took out her phone again. "Just do it!" she said to herself. A moment later she tapped 'Call Mo'.

◆

"Who?" said Mo. "Oh, right, Emily – I remember. … You're at Notting Hill Carnival? Cool, I'm here too, with Luke. … Oh! … Don't worry. Tell us where you are! We'll come and find you. … Well, can you see a street sign? … Westbourne Grove? Where exactly? … Emily? Oh no, … I've lost her."
He called back, but Emily didn't answer.
"Maybe she's in trouble, Luke," he said. "We have to find her. She's in Westbourne Grove."

◆

Emily bent down between someone's dancing legs and picked up her phone.
"Oh no!" she cried. "It doesn't work." She decided to go back to the tube station but it was impossible to move on the crowded pavement.
"I'll have to walk with the parade," she thought.
She climbed under the rope onto the road. Suddenly she was in the middle of a group of dancers. On their backs were huge wings in all the colours of the rainbow. They turned in circles, faster and faster, and sang:
"Chiga-lee-a-chiga-lee-chiga-lee-bom!"
Emily started to feel dizzy. Suddenly she felt a pair of hands on her waist.
"Come and dance with me," said a voice. Emily turned and looked into a strange painted face.
"Aaaaaah," she screamed. "Don't touch me!"

◆

"It's too crowded here," said Mo. "If we want to find her quickly, we'll have to join the parade."
"But we're not wearing costumes." Luke replied.
"We just have to dance to the music – like this."
Mo started to move his hips in a little circle.
"That's not how you dance, Mo!" Luke laughed.
"You have to have rhythm, man. Watch me!"
And the two boys danced their way towards Westbourne Grove as fast as they could.

"Sorry if I scared you," said the man with the painted face. "When I saw you with the dancers, I thought you wanted to take part."

"No," said Emily. "I was looking for my parents. I've lost them. And …"

Suddenly, a loud voice filled the air.

"Hello, Notting Hill! How are you feeling?"

The crowds in the street clapped and roared. Emily looked up and saw a red bus. On the open roof was a man with a loudspeaker, and drummers and dancers in bright orange costumes.

"Come on," said the man with the painted face. "Let's take that bus. Ray won't mind. You can sit downstairs and rest for a bit. And then we'll look for your mum and dad."

There was no sign of Emily in Westbourne Grove.

"Man, my eyes are tired," said Luke. "I can't look at any more faces!"

"And my legs are tired," Mo replied.

"Hello, Notting Hill! Do you want to dance?" said a voice over a loudspeaker.

"No, thanks," said Mo under his breath.

Luke looked up. "Mo! That's Uncle Ray's bus."

"Your uncle has a bus?" asked Mo.

"That's him with the loudspeaker. And my cousins are playing the drums."

Luke took Mo's arm and ran towards the bus. "Come on," he said. "Let's go up to the top. I'm sure we'll see Emily from there."

"Are you feeling better now?" asked the man with the painted face.

"Yes," smiled Emily. "I'm sorry I screamed at you."

"Don't worry," said the man. "Let's go to Ray."

Upstairs, the dancers were dancing to the drums. Emily started tapping her foot to the rhythm. The man with the painted face went over to Ray and whispered in his ear. Then Ray took his loudspeaker and spoke:

"Hello, Notting Hill! Hello, Mr and Mrs Evans from Cardiff. Can you hear me? Your daughter Emily is waiting for you here, so please come up!"

"What?" said Mo. The two boys looked around. And there was Emily behind them.

"Mo! Luke!" she said. "How did you get here?"

"The question is: How did *you* get here?" Mo replied. "And who is that man?"

1 How did they feel?

Say how Emily, Mo and Luke felt at different points in the story. You can use these words:

angry · excited · lonely · happy · scared · shocked · surprised · unhappy · worried

I think Emily felt excited when she was on the train.

I think Mo was worried when …

2 The end of the story

How does Emily find her parents? What happens when they meet?

You choose Choose a), b) or c).

a) Write an ending of about 10 to 15 lines.

b) Make a cartoon. One partner can draw pictures. The other can write the speech bubbles.

c) Write a dialogue and act it out.

→ Workbook 19 (p. 17)

Workbook Checkpoint (pp. 18–21)

3 EXTRA A British Isles album

Each student will make one page for the album.

a) Choose your topic, e.g.
London museums, Big cities, Ireland north and south, The rivers and lakes of the British Isles, …

www You can watch the video clips again to get ideas.
Agree with your teacher when your page should be ready.

b) Now follow these steps:
- Collect information and pictures.
- Write your text(s).
- Make your page for the class album.

→ *SF 22: Putting a page together (p. 152)*

1 A first look

a) Look at the map and the key. What do they tell you about the British Isles?
Talk about countries, cities, mountains, water …

b) Watch the first video clip.
Say what you've learned about the British Isles.

2 Land and people

a) Look at the eight captions.
Say what you already know about the topics.

1 London

2 City highlights

5 Sport

6 Music

3 Land and water

4 Languages

7 Food

8 History

b) Watch the other video clips.
Note down the three topics you liked most.
Which country would you like to know more about?
Compare your ideas. Give reasons why you are interested in a topic or a country.

- UK/Ireland border
- UK country border
- Belfast capital city
- cities by population:
  - over 5 million
  - over 1 million
  - over 500,000
  - over 100,000
  - under 100,000
- railway lines
- important roads
- ferry links
- ▲ 1045 metres above sea level

Lewis McCray's trip around Ireland

Welcome to Snowdonia

1 Welsh countryside

a) Make a list of words to describe the picture.

b) Compare your lists and add words.

c) Take turns to describe the picture.

In the background, I see mountains with shadows on them.

On the left, there's a …

d) Imagine you're in the picture.
Choose a place and describe what you can see, hear, smell or feel there.
Can your partner guess where you are?

I can see some birds in a tree and hear a river behind it.

OK … are you in the field in the middle of the photo?

➜ Workbook 1 (p. 22)

2 A long journey

a) ➜ pp. 26–27 Look at the map and find Cardiff and Caernarfon. Describe the route between them (mountains? big cities? …?)

b) Listen and find out who the people are and the reason for their journey.

c) Listen again. Say how the girl feels and how she shows her feelings.

More help ➜ p. 118

➜ Text File 3 (p. 101)

EXTRA Imagine the family's arrival in Caernarfon.

You choose a) or b).

a) Draw a picture story about it.
b) Write a mail from the girl to a friend in Cardiff.

Your task

At the end of this unit:
Imagine you're moving to Wales. Write about how your life would change.

1 Everything is wrong

As Emily walked down the long path to her new home, her legs felt heavy and tired. The house was dark and empty. Then she remembered that her mum was out at sea. Mrs Evans was a scientist who studied sea animals and plants.

Emily walked across the garden to her dad's workshop. There was music in the air – someone was singing a Welsh song. She walked through the workshop door and turned the radio off. "If I hear one more word of Welsh, I'll scream!" she said.

Emily's dad was building a table. He was a carpenter and made all kinds of beautiful furniture. His workshop smelled of wood and special oils.

"Someone has had a bad day," he said.

"I just don't like that music – that's all," said Emily. She picked up a hammer from the table.

"What's happened?" Mr Evans asked.

"I don't want to talk about it." Emily started hitting an old piece of wood with the hammer.

"But if you talk about it, you'll feel better. And put that hammer down! It's making me nervous."

"Sorry!"

"So, tell me what's wrong?"

"What's wrong? Everything is wrong! Seven hours of school and then Welsh lessons at the learning centre. I have to work harder than all the others! And my Welsh still sounds funny – kids laugh when I speak. *And* it's hard to understand the teachers – they speak so fast!"

"Which language do your classmates speak at the breaks: English or Welsh?"

"Breaks are the worst! Today at lunch, we were talking about the class trip to Snowdon. Then this boy came over. Dylan. He *never* stops telling jokes. He said something in Welsh and everybody laughed except me. I asked a girl what was so funny, and she said, 'Oh forget it, you probably don't want to know.' Then the bell rang for the end of break. I know that boy was making fun of me."

"Well, if you laugh with the others, you won't feel so bad."

"That's silly, Dad. How can I laugh at their jokes if I don't understand them?"

"Give it more time. You'll soon speak Welsh as well as the others … if you don't give up."

"Yeah, right, Dad," said Emily. She picked up the hammer again. "When will Mum be back?"

"She won't be back till tomorrow. So I'll make my famous vegetable curry for dinner."

"Hmm… If you don't mind, Dad," said Emily, "I'll cook tonight. I'm *really* hungry, and …"

"You don't like my curry?" he said in a sad voice. Then he laughed. "Just a little joke. Let's have pizza instead then."

2 Understanding the story

a) Look at lines 1–22 again. Describe Emily's feelings. How does she show them?

b) Read lines 24–47 again. Then describe Emily's relationship with her classmates.

c) Choose a part of the text and show it as a freeze frame.
Your partners describe the scene and guess which part of the text it is.

1 WORDS Jobs

a) Complete each sentence with the right word.

actor • +architect • artist • +astronaut • carpenter • dentist • farmer • +hairdresser • +musician • +painter • scientist

1 Astronauts travel to the moon or other planets.
2 … study plants, animals or other things in the natural world.
3 … paint pictures or people's houses.
4 … play an instrument.
5 … draw plans for new buildings.
6 … cut other people's hair.

b) Write sentences for the other jobs in the box.

1 … in films or plays or TV shows.

More help ➔ p. 118

c) Write down the jobs from a) in a list.
Add other jobs that you know.

d) Act out a job from your list. The others say what you're doing and guess the job.

A: You're playing an instrument.
B: Yes, right!
C: You're a musician.

➔ Workbook 2 (p. 22)

2 REVISION Tom thinks he'll be an astronaut (*will*-future)

a) What do you think you'll be or do in the future? Copy the table and add ideas.
Then make appointments with three classmates and interview them.

What we will be/do	Me	Partner A	Partner B	Partner C	
in 5 years					
in 10 years					
in 20 years					

More help ➔ p. 118

b) Report interesting ideas to the class.
- Tom thinks he'll be an astronaut in 20 years.
- Dilek thinks she'll work in Hollywood in …

c) Write sentences about what you *won't* do.
I'm sure I won't be in Germany in 10 years.
I'm sure I won't play for Chelsea in …

➔ GF 2: Future (pp. 159–160) ➔ Workbook 3 (p. 23)

3 REVISION If I don't go to bed … (Conditional 1)

a) CHAIN GAME Look at the sentences in the game. Think of endings for the last sentence.

A: *If I don't go to bed, I won't get enough sleep.*
B: *If I don't get enough sleep, I'll be tired tomorrow.*
C: *If I'm tired tomorrow, I'll play badly in the match.*
D: *If I play badly in the match, our team won't win.*
E: *If our team doesn't win …*

b) Play the if-sentence game. You can use these ideas:

If we work hard for the English test, …
If you eat too much, …
If the weather is nice tomorrow, …
If you don't wear warm gloves, …

Early finisher ➔ p. 127
➔ GF 3.1: Conditional 1 (p. 161)
➔ Workbook 4 (p. 23)

4 Study skills: Using an English-German dictionary

When you read English texts, try first to understand a new word from the context.
Thinking about what kind of word it is (noun, verb, adjective, etc.) can help you to understand it.
If you really need to check the meaning, you can use a dictionary.

a) Write down what you think the underlined words mean. Check on the right.
Compare your results.

1 That's not your pen, it's mine!
2 My grandfather worked in a coal mine.
3 They mine the gold deep underground.
4 The navy dropped mines in the enemy harbour.

headword · part of speech · example · translation · context

mine¹ [maɪn] *Pronomen*
1 meine(r, -s): ***Your bike is newer than mine.*** Dein Rad ist neuer als meins. • ***It's mine.*** Es gehört mir. • ***some friends of mine*** ein paar Freunde von mir
2 at mine *umg* bei mir zu Hause

mine² [maɪn] *Substantiv*
1 ≈ *Zeche* Bergwerk, Mine
2 MILITÄR Mine

mine³ [maɪn] *Verb* (**mining**): *auch* **mine for** *Bodenschätze* abbauen

b) Say what the underlined words below mean.
Use a dictionary if you need to.

1 He didn't want to sit on the ground because it was wet.
2 My parents will ground me if I'm late.
3 Welsh is one of the country's two official languages.
4 He works as a city official.

c) Words like *for, on, up, away, ...* can change the meaning of a verb. Say what the underlined verbs mean in German.
Use a dictionary if you need to.

1 Let's look for a good place to have lunch.
2 I look after my baby sister every Sunday.
3 He looked around the room to see if he knew anyone.
4 Please look up the meaning of that word.
5 We're looking forward to your visit next week.
6 The police are looking into the fire at the hotel.

d) Translate these sentences into German.
Use a dictionary if you need to.

1 Nicholas came up with a new idea.
2 He came down the stairs at 9 am.
3 Her aunt came down with malaria.
4 Can you come over to my house tomorrow?
5 We came across an old church on the moor.
6 Chelsea came back well in the second half.

→ Workbook 5 *(p. 24)*

e) Find a partner and open a dictionary at any page. Each write down the answers to these questions.

1 What is the first headword on the page?
2 What is the longest headword on the page?
3 Which word has the most different meanings?
4 How many words do you already know?

Compare your answers.

Study skills

Working with an English-German dictionary

Wenn ich ein Wort nicht verstehe, ...
- sollte ich zuerst versuchen, ...
- dann sollte ich überlegen, ...
- ...

Vergleiche deine Ideen mit dem Abschnitt im Skills File:

→ *SF 5: English-German dictionaries (p. 141)*

Facts about Wales

- A country in the UK
- Population (2011): 3.06 m
- Area: 20,779 square km
- Capital: Cardiff (Caerdydd)
- Languages: English, Welsh
- Highest point: Snowdon, 1085 m

The capital city

Cardiff, the capital, is Wales's largest city (346,000). With over 300,000 tourists a year, it is one of Britain's favourite cities. People go there to see its old castle or watch the Welsh Parliament at work.
Or they visit the Welsh National Museum or the famous *Doctor Who Experience*.

www Find out more about Cardiff's attractions.

Steel, coal and rugby: the Valleys

Wales was once a land of steel and coal. In 1945, 30 per cent of all Welsh men worked in these industries in the valleys of south Wales. But today, steel and coal are no longer important. The last coal mine closed in 2008.
One million people still live in the Valleys, but today they work in manufacturing or health and social services.

The Valleys are still a centre of Welsh culture, and rugby, the "national sport" of Wales, is very popular. There are rugby grounds in most of the towns and villages.

The National Eisteddfod (Eisteddfod Genedlaethol Cymru)

The Eisteddfod is the biggest festival in Wales and takes place in a different town every year. 150,000 visitors come for a mix of music, dance and theatre. There are competitions for everything from disco dancing to large choirs, many of them for young kids and teens.
The Eisteddfod goes back to 1176. It promotes Welsh language and culture and all official events are in Welsh. But everyone is welcome, even if they can't speak Welsh.

Two languages

Welsh and English are official languages in Wales. That's why road signs are bilingual. Everyone in Wales speaks English, but about 20 per cent of the population also speak Welsh, the country's original Celtic language. In the north-west, the number of Welsh speakers is higher. There, many people use Welsh in everyday life and at school.

a) Compare Wales with your *Bundesland*. Think about size, population, languages, sport, culture, festivals, the capital, …

b) Watch the video and find out more about Wales.

c) Write six questions for a quiz on Wales.
Ask your partner your questions.

➜ Workbook 6 *(p. 24)*

1 Climbing Mount Snowdon

On Friday morning, Emily's class travelled by bus to Snowdonia National Park. When they arrived, their teacher, Mrs Grant, spoke to the group, first in Welsh, then in English. "Before we start, please choose a partner. You should know where he or she is all the time. The walk to the top of Mount Snowdon isn't easy and I don't want any accidents or lost children." Mrs Grant scanned the students' faces to make sure they were listening. She went on: "We'll stop for lunch in about two hours, when we get to the waterfalls. Altogether, the walk will take eight hours, so we won't be back here at the hostel till 6 pm. OK?"

"OK, Miss!" the students shouted, and hurried around to find their partners.

"Will anyone choose me?" Emily wondered. She studied the ground and wished she could disappear into it. Then someone tapped her on the shoulder. It was Dylan. "He wants to make fun of me again," she thought.

"*Wyt ti wedi dewis partner?*"

Emily pretended not to understand.

"Sorry?" she asked.

"Have you chosen a partner, Emily?" he repeated.

"Not really," she answered.

"Good, me neither. Is this your first time here?"

Emily nodded.

"Well, I've been here lots of times."

"Really?" said Emily in a bored voice.

"Yes. If you gave me a pound for every trip, I would be rich." Dylan started talking about his last trip, but Emily wasn't listening any more.

"Why did it have to be him?" she thought.

They started walking. Everyone was excited. Some of the boys climbed and jumped off the big rocks along the path, until Mrs Grant stopped them. Time went by quickly, and they were soon at the waterfalls.

"See that waterfall?" Dylan said. "If I had a kayak, I'd paddle right down from the top to this pool."

"That's a stupid idea, Dylan," said a boy called Philip. "If you did that, you would die. If I were you, I'd go down inside a great big beach ball. That way, you wouldn't hit the rocks!"

"Let's test your idea, then," said Dylan. "See this water bottle? I'm going to write a note and put it

inside. Then I'm going to run to the top, and drop it into the water. Does anyone have a pen?"

Emily gave Dylan her pen. He wrote something on a piece of paper and put it into the bottle.

"You wait here at the pool and catch the bottle before it goes downstream," Dylan said, and started to climb up the side of the waterfall. Emily looked around nervously. "I hope Mrs Grant doesn't see," she whispered.

"Ready?" Dylan shouted down from the top of the waterfall. He held up the bottle with the note inside. Then he threw it into the waterfall. The bottle sailed down, crashed against a rock, flew up in the air again, and then dropped back into the water. Emily and the others waited by the pool. As the bottle came nearer, Emily tried to fish it out, but it was too far from the edge. Mrs Grant blew her whistle. The break was over and it was time to go on. Emily tried to reach the bottle with a stick, but she only pushed it towards Philip.

"I've got it!" he shouted. Dylan ran over to Philip, grabbed the bottle, and gave it to Emily.

"This is for you," he smiled. "If Philip read it, he could get the wrong idea."

Then Mrs Grant blew her whistle again. The others were already on their way. "I'll read it later," she said under her breath, and put the bottle into her rucksack.

As they went on up the mountain, the path became steeper.

"How much further is it to the top?" asked Philip. "We've been walking for hours!"

"Let's sing a song," said Dylan. "An English one that Emily knows." Emily went bright red. Dylan thought for a moment. "What about *If I had a hammer?*"

Emily knew the song. "If I had a hammer, I'd hammer in the morning …" She and her dad often sang it together. Dylan started singing and the others sang along with him. Then Emily joined in. They sang song after song. Before long, they were at the top of Mount Snowdon.

"Wow, what a view!" Philip shouted. "Amazing!"

Emily looked across the countryside. Yes, the view was amazing. But she was only thinking one thing: what was the message in the bottle?

2 On the walk

a) Choose the correct answer to each question: a, b or c.

1 Before the walk, Mrs Grant tells the students not to
a) lose their partners
b) be late for lunch
c) get back to the hostel too early.

2 When Dylan asks Emily about her partner, she
a) doesn't understand him
b) says that she already has one
c) doesn't give a clear answer.

3 Dylan tells Emily that
a) he always gets money for climbing Snowdon
b) she should give him some money
c) he has climbed Snowdon many times before.

4 Dylan says he'd like to go down the waterfall in a
a) kayak
b) beach ball
c) big water bottle.

5 The message in the bottle is for
a) Mrs Grant
b) Philip
c) Emily.

6 Emily puts the bottle in her rucksack because
a) there is no time to read the message
b) she wants to join in the singing
c) she isn't interested in the message.

b) What do you think Dylan's message in a bottle says? Write your idea down on a piece of paper. Collect all the ideas in class and read them out. Vote for your favourite.

3 Similar words

The word *partner* is the same in Welsh, English and German.

Think of a language that you speak at home or at school, or a language that you learn (Latin, German, Turkish, French, …).
Write down five words that are similar to English words and mean the same.
But be careful – similar words *can* have different meanings, e.g.
English: map – German: Landkarte (not Mappe!)

➜ *True and false friends (p. 248)*

4 Have a go

Say what you would do if you were alone on a small island.

If I were alone on a small island, I would …

collect wood •
make a fire •
talk to the fish •
climb a tree •
look for food •
…

Looking at language

a) Complete these sentences from pp. 34–35.

if-clause	main clause
If you ... me a pound for every trip,	I ... be rich.
If I ... a kayak,	I... paddle right down ...
If I ... you,	I... go down inside a ...
If Philip ... it,	he ... get the wrong idea.

b) Say how we form conditional 2 sentences.

- In the *if*-clause, the verb is in the ... **past**.
  With the verb *be*, we often say *If I ...* instead of *If I was*.
- In the main clause, we use ... or ... + infinitive.

c) Look at this German sentence.

Wenn der Bus schneller fahren würde, kämen wir früher an.

Which translation is correct?

If the bus would drive faster, we would arrive earlier.

If the bus drove faster, we would arrive earlier.

Now make a rule to help you to form *if*-clauses correctly.

→ *GF 3.2: Conditional 2 (pp. 161–162)*

1 If I had ... (Conditional 2)

a) Finish five of the sentences with the best idea from the box. Use *would* or *could*.

do more at weekends · have more fun in breaks · not know the time · often visit them · paddle across the lake

1 If I had a kayak ...
If I had a kayak, I could ...
2 If we had a climbing wall at school ...
3 If I had friends in Wales ...
4 If we had a sofa in our classroom ...
5 If we didn't have clocks or watches ...
6 If we didn't have school on Mondays ...
7 If I had eyes in the back of my head ...

Early finisher Think of as many endings as you can for the other two sentences.

b) Read the first verse of the song. Then listen. What else do the singers say they would do?

If I had a hammer (Hays & Seeger)

If I had a hammer,
I'd hammer in the morning,
I'd hammer in the evening,
All over this land.
I'd hammer out danger,
I'd hammer out a warning,
I'd hammer out love between
my brothers and my sisters,
All over this land.

EXTRA Use these ideas to write another verse.

dance · drum · flag · torch · pen · poem

dance · fly · light · play · say · write

If I had a drum, I'd play it in the morning.

2 If I were a police officer ... (Conditional 2)

Think of six jobs. Write a sentence about what you could or would do in each job.

If I were a police officer, I'd catch lots of thieves.
If I became a cameraman, I could film action movies.

More help → *p. 119*

EXTRA Read your sentences.
Say which job would be best for you, and why.

→ Workbook 7 *(p. 25)*

3 What would happen if …? (Conditional 2)

a) Emily doesn't feel at home in North Wales. Sometimes she wants to

- run away to London
- shout at Dylan
- walk alone in the hills
- invite classmates home
- stop speaking Welsh
- ask a teacher for help

Are Emily's ideas good or bad? Make notes like this:

Idea	+	–
run away to London:	see Mo and Luke	no place to live
…		

More help ➔ p. 119

b) Say what would happen.

If Emily ran away to London, she could see Mo and Luke.

Yes, but if she ran away, she wouldn't have a place to live. So that's not a good idea.

➔ Workbook 8–9 (p. 25)

4 If I were the head teacher …

a) Which of these things would you do if you were the headteacher? Make a list. Then add more ideas.

- buy more whiteboards
- allow mobiles in class
- have a school uniform
- start dancing lessons
- send students that fight home
- give students free sweets

Yes	No
– more whiteboards	– …
– …	

b) On a different piece of paper, make notes about your reasons.

- more whiteboards: students would learn better.
- mobile phones: …

c) You're a reporter. Interview the headteacher. Use your partner's list from a) to ask questions. Then swap roles.

You say you would buy more whiteboards. Why?

Well, students would learn better if we had more whiteboards.

➔ Workbook 10 (p. 26)

5 A conservation project

a) You want to work for a project in Wales. But will your parents agree to take you there? Take notes about the project in German.

b) Use your notes to explain what the project is about and what you will need. Take turns.

TIP
Give only key information when you mediate. The Skills File can help you to take good notes.
➔ SF 16: Mediation (p. 148); SF 8: Taking notes (p. 143)

Volunteer for a conservation project in Wales!
The Snowdonia Project needs you!

"This was the best week in our whole college course. It was a real honour to work at the hostel and on the footpaths on Snowdon!"
Gemima, 16

We are working so that future generations can enjoy Snowdonia's beautiful countryside and amazing wildlife. When we do practical conservation work, we invite local people and visitors to take part in our workdays.
Join us. Remember: It's your Snowdonia.

Why volunteer?
You can see more of Snowdonia, meet new friends, keep fit and active, get training and experience and feel that you have done something special.

General information
You will need warm work clothes, waterproofs and strong boots or wellies. Trainers are not acceptable.
We provide tools, gloves, training, insurance, first-aid kit.
Travel expenses to/from work sites: 25p/mile, maximum £15
We do a full risk assessment before each activity and a First Aider is always present.
A responsible adult must accompany all under 18-s.

➔ Workbook 11–13 (p. 26–28)

1 Learn how

People don't think in paragraphs.
When you write, ideas often come all at once.
But paragraphs and topic sentences help you to organize ideas more clearly for your reader.

A paragraph is a group of sentences that are all connected to one main idea.

A topic sentence tells your reader what the main idea of a paragraph is. Try to start each paragraph with a topic sentence.

A trip to the top of Snowdon
by Philip Nash

On Friday our class walked to the top of Mount Snowdon. It's 13 km and a 1,085 metre climb to the summit. It was a long, hard walk up and back down again, but all 24 kids in our class managed it.
At 10 am, we started walking on the Watkin Path. The first part of our walk was easy. We walked for two hours through a beautiful forest and stopped at some amazing waterfalls for lunch. We stayed there until it was time to continue our walk. The second part of our walk was hard. The path was rocky and steep. Sometimes we had to use our hands – like real mountain climbers. We reached the summit at 2 pm. At the top of Snowdon the sky was clear, so we had a great view of Snowdonia National Park. We saw a great big lake and mountain after mountain. The trip back was fun because it was all downhill. We even ran down some parts of the path. But we still needed energy: our class ate a total of 59 chocolate bars on the way down! We reached our hostel at 6 pm. We were really tired, but we all felt like heroes!

a) Read Philip's report. On a copy, mark where other paragraphs should start. Underline the topic sentence for each paragraph.

b) Compare *where* you marked paragraphs. Did you choose the same first sentences? Explain your reasons.
- I started the paragraph here because …
- I think this is the topic sentence and these sentences go with it.
- I think this sentence goes in the next paragraph.

2 Now write …

You choose a) or b).
Write at least four paragraphs about:
a) a walk through a big city, a forest, in the mountains, or by the sea.
b) a film you have seen

→ Workbook *Wordbank 1, 5, 7*

TIP
1 Before you start writing, make a mind map or table to collect and organize your memories and ideas.
2 The 5 ***Ws*** (When? Where? What? Who? Why?) can help you to find ideas.
3 Start a new paragraph for every new idea.
4 Use a topic sentence in each paragraph. In the other sentences add details or examples.

3 … and revise

a) Give feedback. Read your partner's text and make notes to answer these questions:
- Does it have clear paragraphs?
- What is the topic sentence in each paragraph?
- Do you get information about the 5 Ws?

Take turns to make comments, suggestions and corrections.

b) Think about what your partner has said. Decide what to change and write a second draft.

→ *SF 12: Paragraphs (p. 145)*
SF 14: Feedback – writing (p. 146)
SF 15: Revising texts (p. 147)

→ *Unit 1 (p. 17): Feedback*

→ Workbook *14 (p. 28)*

1 Adam's video blog

Watch the blog. Say what you learn about Adam.

One thing I've learned is that Adam speaks …

Another thing is that he …

2 Adam and Welsh

Watch the video again. Choose the right answer for each question: a or b.

1 Adam says the number of Welsh speakers is
a) 500,000 b) 3,000,000

2 He says his first school was
a) English-speaking b) Welsh-speaking

3 He says that, for him, changing from one language to the other is
a) sometimes difficult b) always easy

4 In English, the Welsh word for *goodbye* means
a) big carrot b) big fun

3 Making a video

a) Adam is a blogger who talks about his everyday life. Tell your partner about other bloggers you know. Say what you think about them.

I've seen a blogger who talks about …

I think he's really funny because …

b) Plan a video blog like Adam's. Complete the table with ideas from the box. Add more ideas of your own.

things I need	before I start	while I'm filming
a good place to film	think of a good topic	…
…	…	

a good place to film · computer · look at the camera · look friendly/angry … · make notes · smile · speak clearly · think of a good topic · use captions · use music/sounds/… · wear something interesting

Early finisher → p. 127

EXTRA Choose a topic and make your blog.

The adventures of Morph

Snowdonia at night

Look at the pictures in the story. Where are Dylan and Emily? Who are the other people in the pictures and what are they doing? Say in a few sentences what you think the story is about.

When the class got back to the hostel, Emily ran to the toilet and closed the door behind her. She pulled the bottle out of her rucksack and tried to shake out the note, but the neck of the bottle was too narrow. With a pencil, she pressed hard against the note and tried again and again to pull it towards her. Finally, she had the note in her hand and was able to read the message:

Meet me at the last door on the 2nd floor at 8 pm.
I want to show you something! Dylan.

Emily put the note back into her rucksack and hurried downstairs. The kitchen and dining room were noisy and crowded. A large choir group from Bangor was staying at the hostel too. Emily entered the kitchen, where the kids from her class were preparing the evening meal.

During dinner, Emily kept checking the time on the big clock over the dining room door. At five to eight, she looked across the table at Dylan. He nodded, pointed to the stairs, pressed his finger against his chest, and silently said: "I'll go first." Then he left the table and disappeared up the stairs.

A few minutes later, Emily stood up to follow him.

"Where are you going, Emily?" said Mrs Grant. "We haven't had dessert yet."

"I'm really tired, Miss," replied Emily. "I think I'll go to bed early."

"All right. Good night, then."

❖

Emily ran up the stairs. It was dark on the first floor, but she didn't turn on the lights. She walked to the end of the corridor and almost screamed as a hand touched her shoulder.

"Shshsh … it's only me!" said Dylan. "Come, it's this way – Look! These stairs go to the roof!"

"The roof? Are you sure we can go up there? I mean, won't Mrs Grant be angry?"

"Don't worry, Emily. It's all right. I've done this before," said Dylan. "Come on!"

Emily followed him up. At the top of the stairs, there was another door. Dylan pushed it open. They walked out onto the roof and looked out. The trees were full of dark shadows, and behind the trees, a large lake shimmered in the moonlight. The night sky was clear and full of stars.

"Welcome to Snowdonia!" Dylan said.

"It's magical," whispered Emily.

"Come on," Dylan said. "We can lie down here and look up at the stars."

"Lie down?" she asked, "but …"

"Don't worry. It's all right. No one will find us."

❖

Back downstairs it was as busy and noisy as before. Emily's classmates were clearing dishes from the table. In the living room area, the choir group were sitting in a circle, laughing and talking. One of the girls whispered to her neighbour.

"Morgan, let's go upstairs and get our guitars."

"Good idea, Gwen. I want to play a new song for you. Gareth and I wrote it together."

At the top of the stairs, they felt a cool breeze.

"Brrr … it's cold up here!" said Gwen.

"Of course it's cold! Someone has left the door to the roof open," said Morgan. "Look!"

"Hey, can you really go up to the roof?" Gwen asked. "Let's go and have a look, then!"

"But what if someone finds out? We'll get into trouble, I'm sure," said Morgan.

"Oh, come on. We'll just say that we went through the wrong door," said Gwen, and pushed Morgan up the stairs.

❖

"What was that sound?" Emily whispered to Dylan.

"What sound?"

"I heard something."

"It's probably just the trees. You always hear those kinds of sounds in the country," said Dylan.

"Wow!" Emily whispered. "A shooting star!"

"I think you *were* right," whispered Dylan.

"What do you mean?"

"Someone *is* coming up the stairs," he said.

Emily sat up like a wooden puppet, her eyes wide open in the dark. Two figures appeared on the roof. A girl spoke:

"Look, Morgan. We're not alone. Hey, can we join you?" she asked, and walked towards Emily and

Dylan. "My name's Gwen, and this is Morgan."

"Hi! I'm Dylan and this is Emily."

❖

"What a great place," said Morgan. "So many stars! You can even see the Milky Way."

Dylan pointed up at the sky. "See that bright light there?" he said. "That's the planet Venus. If you lie down and look up, the view is amazing."

"Right! Good idea," Gwen said, and they all lay on their backs.

"Wow! It's so beautiful!" said Gwen.

She took out her harmonica and played a few notes. Morgan started to sing a song:

Cold star, you're such a cold star.
Why are you so far, cold star, cold star?
Why are you so far away-ay-ay-ay?
Never calling me, never touching me. Cold star.

❖

"Wow, you sing really well! What's the name of that song?" Emily asked. "It's really nice."

"The name?" Morgan asked. "Oh, I don't know. I've just made it up. Let's try again. This time, all of us join in, OK? One, two, three: Cold star..."

The four kids sang the song again and again. They changed the words and sang louder each time. And then, as they looked up into the night, a shadow moved slowly over their heads. There was something behind them.

"What, may I ask, are you doing up here?" asked a voice that Emily and Dylan knew very well.

"We're looking at the stars, Mrs Grant," said Dylan. "We've learned a lot about stars this year in science and we thought ..."

"That's enough, Dylan. The party is over. Go downstairs, please. It's very dangerous up here and it's against the rules."

"But, Mrs Grant ..." started Dylan.

"Don't argue, Dylan," Mrs Grant said.

They stood up and walked back down the stairs. Nobody said another word.

"Please go to your rooms," said Mrs Grant.

"Are we going to be in trouble, Miss?" asked Emily.

"We'll talk about that tomorrow. It's been a long day and now it's time to get some sleep."

❖

Emily and Dylan didn't sit together at breakfast, but more than once their eyes met between spoonfuls of cornflakes and bites of toast. Mrs Grant wasn't there yet.

"I hope she won't come," Emily thought.

But Mrs Grant did come. "Follow me," she said, and went towards the hostel director's office.

"What you both did last night is not only against the rules, it's very dangerous!" Mrs Grant began. "We've given Mr Smart, the hostel director, a very bad picture of our school. He could send the whole class back home. Do you understand that?"

Emily and Dylan nodded.

2 Text

"He isn't going to do that," Mrs Grant went on. "But we have to show him that our students know how to behave. It will be your job, Emily and Dylan, to wash the floors in the corridors, in the toilets and in the living room each day for the rest of our weekend. Mr Smart will show you where the mops are. Any questions?"

"No, Mrs Grant," said Emily and Dylan.

"Good. Then you can start work now."

❖

"Careful," laughed Emily as Dylan wildly mopped the corridor floor, "you're splashing me!"

"Oops!" said Dylan. Then he started to sing: "Have you seen the mopping man, the mopping man, the mopping man…?"

"Good song," said Emily, "but I know a better one." Quietly, she began to sing: "Cold star, you're such a cold star …"

Dylan put his mop down and joined in: "Why are you so far, cold star … "

1 The story

a) Were your ideas about the story and the people in it correct?

b) Match these headings to the right part of the story.

We aren't alone
Door to the roof
Looking up at the stars
The note in the bottle
The dark shadow
You've broken the rules
Welcome to Snowdonia

c) Make groups of four.
Each student chooses two parts of the story and sums up each part in one or two sentences.
Then put all the sentences together to tell the story.

2 A fair punishment?

a) What do you think about Dylan and Emily's punishment? Make notes like this:

fair because	not fair because
roof dangerous	kids only wanted to see stars
…	

More help ➔ p. 119

b) Discuss your ideas in a double circle.

3 Points of view

You choose a) or b)

a) Imagine you're Emily or Dylan.
In four or five sentences, write about what you think about the other.

b) Imagine you're Dylan or Mrs Grant.
Write one part of the story again from that person's point of view.

EXTRA Find other classmates who chose the same task. Compare your ideas.

➔ Workbook 15–16 (p. 29)

Workbook Checkpoint (pp. 30–33)

Your task

Imagine you had to move to Wales with your family.
Write a short text for an online magazine about how your life would change.

Step 1
Look through Unit 2 again and note down the important things that you have learned.
Think about topics, vocabulary, skills, …

Step 2
Read the task again carefully.
Then discuss which things that you have learned in Unit 2 will help you with your text.
Present your group's ideas to the class.

Step 3
Think about why you could have to move.

One student writes down *one* idea on a piece of paper. Then another student adds an idea.
Go on like this for two minutes.

Step 4
Decide where you would move to.

Step 5
Think about how your life would change. What would you miss about Germany?
Make notes. Then write your text.

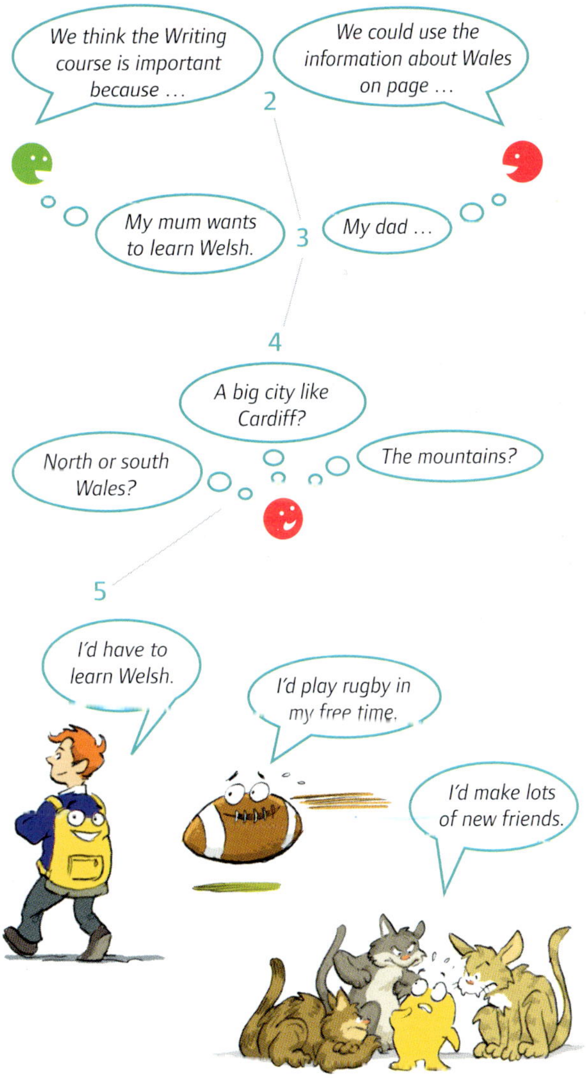

Step 6
Swap texts. Your teacher will give you a checklist. Use it to give your partner feedback.

Step 7
Think about the feedback from your partner.
Then revise your text.

➔ *SF 15: Revising texts (p. 147)* ➔ Workbook *Wordbank 7*

A weekend in Liverpool

1 We're going on a trip

a) Say what the people are doing. Who do you recognize from Unit 2? Say what you remember about them.

b) Describe the route from Bangor to Liverpool.

They travel east from Bangor.

First the road goes along the coast.

2 The city of Liverpool

a) Imagine you are on the boat in the picture. Write a short message to a friend and describe what you see.

b) Compare the view of Liverpool with your hometown. What's different? What's similar?

c) → pp. 26–27 Find Liverpool and name the nearby towns. How far away is London?

www Find out more about Liverpool.

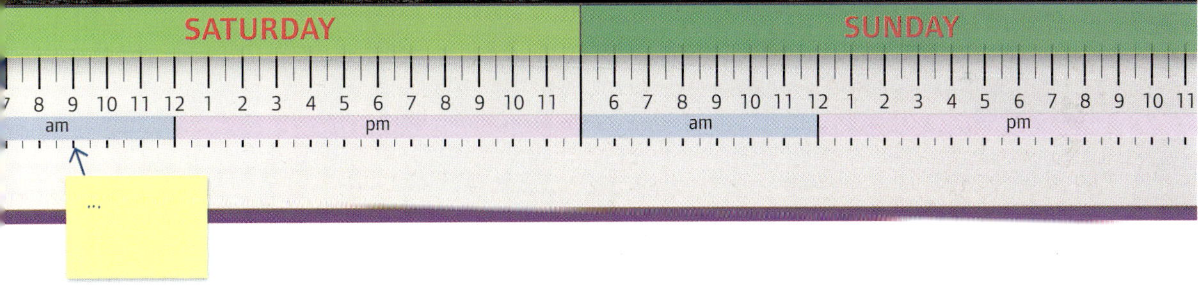

3 The Liverpool programme

a) Copy the timeline. Then listen to Mr Edwards, the choir leader, and take notes.
Complete the timeline with the times for everything in the box.

arrive back in Bangor • explore Liverpool • Beatles show at the Cavern Club • free afternoon • River Mersey cruise • International Slavery Museum • concert • leave Liverpool

b) Compare and check your timelines.

Your task

At the end of this unit:
Write about the person behind the name of a street or building near your home.

→ Workbook 1 (p. 34)

If you visited a city for the first time, would you explore by yourself or go on a guided tour? Give reasons.

1 Morgan's plan

Morgan: We have three hours. Let's go to the waterfront at Albert Dock.
Gareth: OK, we can go through Mathew Street on the way.
Gwen: Mathew Street? The street that's full of tourist shops?

Gareth: For tourists who like the Beatles – like me!
Gwen: But I want to see the real Liverpool.
Morgan: OK, here's the plan. We walk to the waterfront and go along Mathew Street on the way. So you see all the Beatles stuff that you want to.
Gareth: Maybe I'll buy some John Lennon sunglasses. He's the Beatle I like best.
Morgan: And *Gwen* decides what we do after that.
Gwen: I'd like to go to Greaty.
Morgan: Greaty?
Gwen: It's a market which sells food and clothes, and things normal people buy.
Gareth: The real Liverpool!
Gwen: It's in *Great* Homer Street. Greaty. Get it?
Morgan: OK, that's what we'll do if no one protests.

2 A city walk

Read the picture story.
Then take turns to describe the scenes.
Did the kids keep to Morgan's plan?

A: In the first picture, the kids are walking along Mathew Street.
B: Right. That's where Gareth wanted to go. And it's part of Morgan's plan.

3 The real Liverpool

a) Listen to the dialogue between the choir kids and two local kids, Grace and Charlie Hill. Say which of these topics they talk about.

Chinatown • drinks • a drumming workshop • football • James Clarke Street • Liverpool Cathedral • the real Liverpool

Write them in a list.

b) Listen again. Take notes about each of the topics in your list.

c) Take turns to say what you found out about the topics in your list.

➜ Text File 4 (p. 103)

1 Telephone information for tourists

a) You're in Liverpool.
Partner A: You phone *The Beat Museum of Liverpool*. Listen and take notes on Message 1.
Partner B: You phone *The Merseyside Football Museum*. Listen and take notes on Message 2.

TIP
Before you listen, write down the main things that you want to find out.
You can use English or German for your list and for your notes.

b) Tell your partner in German what you have found out.

➔ Workbook 2 (p. 34)

2 WORDS John Lennon was a famous musician

a) Use the ideas below to make six sentences like this:
John Lennon was a famous musician who wrote *Imagine* and other songs.

Cate Blanchett	brilliant	actor	build	*Imagine*
Gustave Eiffel	famous	architect	+design	the Boy Scouts
John Lennon	great	+engineer	+found	the Eiffel Tower
Norman Foster	+well-known	musician	+invent	the thermometer
Steffi Graf	…	scientist	play (in)	*The Hobbit*
Galileo Galilei	Australian	+sportsperson	win	the *Reichstag* building
Robert Baden-Powell	British	+soldier	write	the Wimbledon Singles
…	French	…	…	…
	Italian			
	…			

More help ➔ p. 120

b) Use your own ideas to write three more sentences like the ones in a).

Early finisher ➔ p. 128

3 REVISION Crossword clues (Relative pronouns)

Write clues for the crossword.
Use relative pronouns, e.g.

1 A thing which you can see in the sky at night.
2 A person who works with you in class.

More help ➔ p. 120

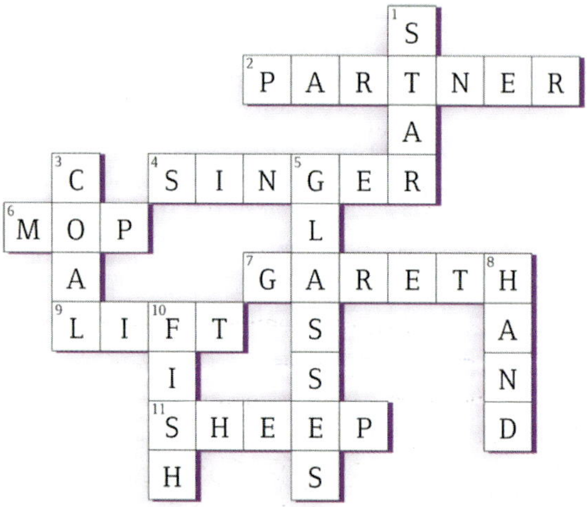

Early finisher ➔ Go to a bus stop and find a partner. Play this game.

The part of your body that has fingers.

That's easy! 8.

➔ GF 4.1: Relative clauses (p. 162) ➔ Workbook 3 (p. 35)

Language help

When a relative pronoun is the **object**, you can leave it out.

He's the Beatle who I like best.
... *der Beatle, den ich am liebsten mag.*
... the Beatle ~~who~~ I like best.

Remember the plan that we made!
... *den Plan, den wir gemacht haben!*
... the plan ~~that~~ we made!

When a relative pronoun is the **subject**, you cannot leave it out.

He's the Beatle who wrote the best songs.
... der Beatle, der die besten Songs schrieb.

We need a plan that will work.
... *einen Plan, der funktioniert.*

Relative clauses without relative pronouns are called *contact clauses*.

➜ *GF 4.2: Contact clauses (p. 163)*

4 What was the name of that place ...? (Contact clauses)

In the evening, Gareth tells other choir members about the walk, but he has forgotten lots of details.

a) Write down Gareth's other questions to Gwen. Use contact clauses.

What was the name of the ...

1 town • see on the other side of the Mersey
What was the name of the town we saw ... ?
2 Chinese gate • see
3 church • would like to sing in
4 market • not find
5 green bananas • see outside that shop
6 girl and boy • meet at the shop

b) Find the answers to Gareth's questions. Then act out a dialogue.

What was the name of the town we saw ... ?

Birkenhead!

5 Gwen's photos (Contact clauses)

Gwen talks about the photos she took.

Make sentences with contact clauses if possible. If not, use a relative pronoun in the sentence.

1 shops • wanted to see.
These are the shops Gareth wanted to see.
2 the shop • sells John Lennon sunglasses
This is the shop that sells ...
3 the sunglasses • bought there
4 one of the ferries • crosses the Mersey
5 the Chinese gate • saw on our walk
6 the kids • gave us tickets for the match
7 the shop • work in
8 the fruit • looks like green bananas

More help ➜ p. 120 Early finisher ➜ p. 128

➜ Workbook 4 (p. 35)

The Beatles – a Liverpool band

The band

The Beatles are the best-selling band in history, with over 600 million records sold. From their first meeting in 1957 to their 1970 album *Let It Be*, they changed the history of pop music.

The beginnings

The Beatles' success story started in 1960, when the young musicians (George was only 17!) played in clubs in Liverpool and Hamburg. They made their first record, *Love Me Do*, in London in 1962.

A new sound

The band from Liverpool was the first British group to take the world by storm with a new sound in rock music. Two guitars, a bass, drums and two or three singers may not seem new now, but in those days, it was a revolution. In the early 1960s, the "Fab Four" toured the world and "Beatlemania" was born.

Second revolution

In 1966, the Beatles gave their last concert. Because of their great success in the years before, they were able to experiment and change their style. On their later albums like *Sgt. Pepper's Lonely Hearts Club Band* or *Abbey Road*, they mixed many musical styles and created a whole new sound. These albums started another pop music revolution.

The solo careers

So far, the ex-Beatles have recorded 64 solo albums since they stopped recording together.

John Lennon – who some people have called **the "soul" of the Beatles** – became a fighter for freedom and peace, but he was murdered in 1980. His song *Imagine* is still well known all over the world:

Imagine all the people, living life in peace …
You may say I'm a dreamer, but I'm not the only one …

Paul McCartney – **the "heart" of the Beatles** – still attracts thousands to his concerts today. He sang *Hey Jude* at the opening of the 2012 London Olympics.

George Harrison – **the "spirit" of the Beatles** – was influenced by Indian culture and made music to raise money for people in poor countries. He died in 2001.

Ringo Starr – **the one "who played the drums"** – worked on musical projects and films and still performs with different artists.

a) My Book Choose a Beatles song and find out more about it (who wrote it, when; which album it was on; what it is about; …) Write a short info box about your song.

b) GALLERY WALK Hang up the info boxes, walk around and read them all.

Bring your Beatles song to class. Present it and play it to your classmates.

1 Learn how

A text is easier to follow when it has an introduction, a body and a conclusion.

- In the **introduction**, you tell your reader what your text is about.
- In the **body**, you go into detail about your topic. You usually use several paragraphs.
- In the **conclusion**, you can give your opinion, or end with an interesting or funny fact about the topic.

a) Read these five paragraphs about the Beatles and Hamburg. On a copy, label the paragraphs *introduction*, *body* and *conclusion*. Decide on the right order.

A On their second trip they played in better clubs like the Kaiserkeller, the Top Ten and the Star Club, but the schedule was still very hard. Sometimes they started playing at 7pm and didn't finish until 7 am the next morning! In 1961 they played every night for 98 nights without a day off!

B They didn't earn much for their concerts, but their Hamburg experience was an important part of their training as musicians and as a band. As John Lennon said: "I might have been born in Liverpool – but I grew up in Hamburg."

C Many people say that the Beatles invented the modern rock band, but not everyone knows that their success began in Hamburg. Between August 1960 and December 1962, they made five trips to the city, and performed 281 times.

D If you go to Hamburg today, you can visit the Beatles Platz on the corner of the Reeperbahn and Große Freiheit streets. It's a popular monument to the famous band's experience in Germany.

E On their first trip, the Beatles performed in the Indra Club – a small and dirty place in the Reeperbahn area of Hamburg. They played four one-hour concerts each night.

b) Compare your labels. Did you label the text in the same way? Do you agree on the right order? Explain your reasons.

2 Now write …

Write about your favourite band or sports team.

TIP

1 Organize your ideas and plan your paragraphs. (See the TIPS on p. 38.)
2 Write your text. Remember:
- say what the text is about (first paragraph)
- use topic sentences in the body of the text
- find a good way to end your text.

3 Read your text. Check your topic sentences and decide if the paragraphs are in a good order.
4 Change the order of the paragraphs if necessary.

3 … and revise

a) Give feedback. Read your partner's text and make notes to answer these questions:
- Is there a good introduction to the topic?
- Do the paragraphs in the body of the text give more information about the topic? Are they in a good order?
- Does the conclusion end the text in a funny or interesting way?

Take turns to make comments and suggestions.

b) Think about your partner's feedback. Decide what to change and write a second draft.

➜ *SF 10: Good sentences (p. 144); SF 14: Feedback – writing (p. 146)*
➜ **Workbook** *5–6 (pp. 36–37), Wordbank 1, 7*

1 At the slavery museum

The guide led the choir group into the first gallery. "This museum was founded to tell the story of slavery," she began. "But it also tells us about life in West Africa before the slave trade. And that's what we'll learn about in the first gallery."

"We'd have much more fun at the Beatles Story!" said Gareth under his breath.

"Sssh!" said Gwen and Morgan together.

❖

In the gallery, the guide pointed to a mask. Gareth jumped in front of Morgan and Gwen. He held his hands on his head like horns and rolled back his eyes to look like the mask. Gwen had to laugh, but Morgan didn't find it funny. "Come on, you two. Do you have to behave like little kids?"

The guide smiled. "So you like the goat's face?"

"Sorry?" said Gareth.

"This mask is a goat's face. It was made in West Africa a long time ago. Similar masks are worn in Nigeria today, at the festivals of the Ogoni people."

"Who wears them?" Morgan asked.

"Boys and young men wear masks with animal faces at festivals and parties."

❖

"Is that a drum?" Gwen asked.

"Yes," said the guide."It's an udu - an instrument of the Igbo people. Udus are made of clay, not wood. And they have a funny shape, like water pots. In fact, they are also called water pot drums because first they were used to carry water. And then one day someone found that they could also make music. It was probably a woman. Carrying water is a woman's job and, usually, udus are played by women."

"What about that drum there?" Morgan asked.

"That's a djembe, a drum of the Bamana people. It has a great sound, probably because it's played with bare hands, not with sticks. It's used at special events, like family celebrations."

"My cousin has a drum like that," Gareth said. "Are they really from Africa?"

"Yes," said the guide, "but they're very popular in Britain now."

"I'd like to try it," Gareth said.

"Maybe you can in your workshop ... Ah, here's your workshop leader now. So I'll leave you, and see you later for our tour of the second gallery."

A tall man with dreadlocks walked towards them.

"My name is Gordon Skeefe," he said and shook hands with everyone.

2 In the first gallery

a) When Gareth made a face like the mask, Gwen, Morgan and the guide reacted differently. Describe their reactions.

b) Say what you think about how Gareth behaved.

- I think he didn't show enough respect.
- It was only a joke. He didn't want to hurt anyone.
- In my opinion, it's OK to have fun in a museum.
- I agree. / I don't agree.

...

3 The drumming workshop

Listen to Mr Skeefe. Take notes on:

- what he says about Jamaica
- where his ancestors come from
- why he has travelled to western Africa
- what he says about the drums
- why he says Gareth is like a baby

EXTRA **Say how you think Gareth feels after the workshop. Is he still sorry that he couldn't go to the Beatles story?**

4 After the second gallery

Look at the picture of Morgan, Gareth and Gwen and say how they feel.
Why do you think they feel like this?

5 The slave trade

a) Make groups of four.
Each partner chooses one of the texts on pp. 133–134. Read your text and take notes.

> **TIP**
> The 5 ***Ws*** (When? Where? What? Who? Why?) can help you to find the important information when you take notes.

b) Use your notes to say what you have read. When everyone has spoken, say what was new to you, or what surprised or shocked you.

c) Tell the class how your group reacted.

We didn't know about Britain and the trade triangle.

We were very shocked about …

6 Have a go

The mask on p. 52 was made in West Africa. Say where other things were made. You could talk about your pencil, your computer, your mobile, your family car, your T-shirt …

My dad's car was made in Germany.

Our car was made in France.

> **Access to cultures**
> You can visit national museums everywhere in the UK for free.
> What about museums in your country?
> What are the advantages of free museums?

Looking at language

a) Look at these sentences:

1 Similar masks are worn in Nigeria today.
2 Boys and young men wear masks with animal faces.

Which sentence tells us *who* wears the masks?
That sentence is *active*. The other sentence is *passive*.

How many of these sentences have a passive verb form?
This museum was founded to tell the story of slavery.
Udus are made of clay, not wood.
A tall man with dreadlocks walked towards them.

b) To make the passive, we use a form of *be* + the past participle.

Complete these sentences from p. 52.
This mask ... made in West Africa.
In fact, they ... also called water pot drums.
First they ... used to carry water.
It... played with bare hands.

Say what tenses the sentences are in.

➜ *GF 5: The passive (pp. 164–165)*

1 Building an Igbo house (Passive sentences: simple present)

Complete the sentences with a verb in the passive.

1 First, a good place ... (choose), usually on land that ... (own) by the family.
2 Then the land ... (clear) to make room for the building.
3 After that the building materials ... (collect).
4 Different materials ... (need): mud, wood and grass.
5 The mud ... usually (make) with clay and water, but sometimes sand ... (add) too.
6 The floors and walls ... (build) with the mud.
7 Sometimes wood ... (use) with the mud to make the walls stronger.
8 The finished walls ... (paint) with special designs.
9 The roof ... (cover) with grass.
10 Heavier work ... (do) by men. Easier jobs ... (do) by women and children.

➜ Workbook *7 (p. 37)*

2 They aren't worn at Igbo festivals (Passive: simple present)

Correct the wrong information in each sentence. You can check the facts on p. 52.

1 Goat face masks are worn at Igbo festivals.
 – No, they aren't worn at Igbo festivals.
 They're worn at Ogoni festivals.
2 Goat face masks are worn by young women and girls.
 – No, they ...
3 An udu is made of wood.
 – No, it ...
4 Udus are played by men and older boys.
5 Djembe drums are also called water pot drums.
6 The djembe is used every day.
7 The djembe is played with sticks.

More help ➜ *p. 121*

Early finisher Look at exercise 1 again. Make three wrong sentences about Igbo houses. Find a partner to correct your sentences.

3 Which is oldest? (Passive: simple past)

a) Look at the pictures and read the dialogue.

A: Which one was built first?
B: I think Chinatown Arch was built first.
A: Sorry, that's wrong. The Chinatown Gate was built in 2000. The Brandenburg Gate was built in the 18th century. OK, it's your turn.

b) Partner A: Continue on p. 132.
Partner B: Continue on p. 135.

→ Workbook 8 (p. 38)

4 Oliver Twist was written by … (Passive with *by*)

a) Make sentences like the ones in the examples.

Oliver Twist was written by Charles Dickens.

The 2014 World Cup was won by Germany.

TIP
With the passive, we use *by* … if we want to say who did something.

Romeo and Juliet	build	by …
Treasure Island	paint	
The 1966 World Cup	sing	
The 2010 Eurovision Song Contest	win	
Imagine	write	
We Are the Champions		
Hadrian's Wall		
The Eiffel Tower		
The *Mona Lisa*		

b) Compare your answers.

More help → p. 121

5 Liverpool quiz

Liverpool football

- Liverpool has two famous football teams. Liverpool FC was founded in 1892. Everton was founded in 1878.
- The football goal net was invented by an Everton fan in 1889. This made it easier to see when a goal was scored.

Liverpool buildings

- Liverpool's Anglican cathedral is the UK's largest, and the fifth largest in the world. It was designed by Sir Giles G. Scott.
- The name of Liverpool's airport was changed to John Lennon International Airport in 2002.

Liverpool culture

- Liverpool is the city with most galleries and national museums in the UK outside London.
- John Lennon was born in Liverpool in 1940.
- Over 250 bands are invited to perform in the Liverpool International Music Festival every year.

Liverpool firsts

- Europe's first Chinese community was founded in Liverpool in the 1850s.
- Britain's first mosque opened here in 1889.
- The UK's first Nobel prize was won here in 1902 by Sir Ronald Ross for his work on malaria.

a) Make groups of four. Each student reads *one* fact sheet and makes questions.
When was … founded/born/… ?
Where is/was … ? • How many … ?
What was … in 1889? • …

b) Read the other three fact sheets.

c) Ask your questions to the group.

→ Workbook 9–10 (pp. 38–39)

1 The match at Anfield

a) Look at the scenes in pictures A–E and say what is happening.

b) You will hear the five scenes in the right order. Listen and match each scene to a picture.

I think scene 1 is picture A. — *No, scene 1 is picture …*

c) Listen again. Take notes about each scene.
Scene 1: Choir kids wait, G + C arrive late.
Scene 2: ...

d) Compare your notes.
Change or add information if necessary.

2 The match on the radio

Listen to a report about the match. Find out
- which of these players scored:
  Barnes • Bates • Beedle • Jezzard • Oscar
- the score at half-time
- the final score.

Add the information to your notes.

TIP
We talk about football scores like this:

1:0	one nil	1:1	one all
2:1	two one	2:2	two all

YOU'LL NEVER WALK ALONE
(Rogers & Hammerstein)

When you walk through a storm
Hold your head up high
And don't be afraid of the dark
At the end of the storm
Is a golden sky
And the sweet silver song of the lark
Walk on through the wind
Walk on through the rain
Though your dreams be tossed and blown
Walk on walk on with hope in your heart
And you'll never walk alone

3 A great afternoon

a) You choose Imagine you are one of the five kids at the match. Use the notes you took in 1 and 2 to write about *your* afternoon there.

b) Swap texts.
Read your partner's text and give feedback.
Say what is good about it:

- ✓ It has an introduction, a body and a conclusion.
- ✓ It has all the important information.
- ✓ The information is in a good order.
- ✓ The sentences are linked well.
- ○ …

➔ *SF 14: Feedback – writing (p. 146)*
➔ *Inside back cover: Giving feedback*

4 The fan song

Read the lyrics of the Liverpool fan song and choose what you think its message is:

1 Don't walk alone in bad weather.
2 Never give up your dreams.
3 Everyone needs sunshine after a rainy day.

EXTRA Listen to the song and sing along.

1 WORDS Grace and Charlie's favourite sport

Match the words in the box to the picture of the football match.

football • football fan • player • goal • shirt • +referee • +goalkeeper • socks • +shin guards • goalkeeper's glove

➜ Workbook 11 (p. 39)

2 Study skills: Ordering and structuring topic vocabulary

Before you write a text, it helps to order and structure vocabulary for your topic.

a) What equipment do football players need?
Add as many words as you can to the *equipment* umbrella.

b) When you order topic words, you can use a tree diagram.
Look at this diagram and say where you would add your equipment umbrella.

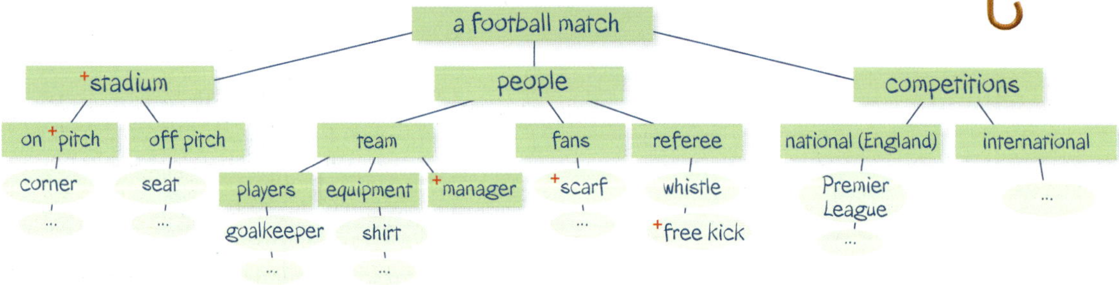

c) Add words from 1 and from the right to a copy of the diagram in b).
More help ➜ p. 121

d) Now make a tree diagram for one of these sports:
basketball • hockey • tennis • volleyball
➜ *Sports words (pp. 136–137)*

Study skills

Ordering and structuring topic vocabulary

Wenn ich einen Text zu einem bestimmten Thema schreibe, sollte ich zuerst ...

Vergleiche deine Ideen mit dem Abschnitt im Skills File.
➜ *SF 1: Structuring vocabulary (p. 139)*

➜ Workbook 12–13 (p. 40)

1 The story

There's only one Jimmy Grimble is a film about a boy who gets a pair of football boots from an old woman. The old woman says the boots are magic, but Jimmy throws them away.

Say why you think he doesn't want the boots.

2 The bullies

a) You can't see Jimmy's face in this still. But can you guess how he feels? Discuss your ideas.

b) Watch part 1. Then say
- what happens to Jimmy's boots
- why this is a problem
- how Jimmy solves the problem.

c) Say what you think of the way the other boys behave.

→ Text File 5 *(p. 104)*

3 The match

a) Look at the still. Discuss what you think has happened to Jimmy.

b) Watch part 2.
Then say how Jimmy's feelings change.

At first he feels very … | *Then he is …* | *At the end, he feels …*

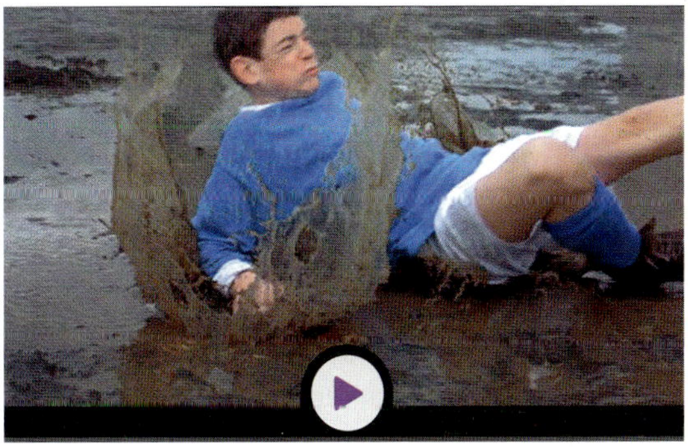

4 The language of film

a) Watch part 2 without sound.
Say how Jimmy's face and body language tell us about his feelings.

The way he closes his eyes and looks down tells us … | *The way he jumps up and down shows that …*

b) Now watch with sound. Say what happens
- when the music is playing
- when the music stops
- in the slow motion scenes.

EXTRA Say what effect the music and slow motion have.
I think the music makes the film more …

A Liverpool hero

Look at the the man in the pictures. Why do you think he is remembered?

On hot summer's days, kids like to be near the water, and it was no different over a hundred years ago in Liverpool. One hot summer's day in 1911, a group of children from Vauxhall, a poor area of the city, walked from Scotland Road over to the Leeds & Liverpool Canal. The sun shone strongly from a blue sky and they wanted to cool off in the deep, cold water. The canal is still there today but no one swims in it now.

That afternoon, over 100 years ago, the children played happily next to the water. People who crossed the bridge on Eldonian Way could hear the children's screams and laughter as they passed. The swimmers jumped in and out of the canal; those who couldn't swim sat on the edge with their legs in the water.

Little Willy was one of the boys who sat on the edge. The cool water felt good on his feet, but the sun was so hot on his face and arms. "If only I could just put some cold water on my face," he thought. "Then I'd feel much better."

He started to bend down and moved his arms towards the water. His fingers touched the surface and disappeared and then, with a great big splash, Willy's whole body followed and he fell in. He seemed to go down in the canal for ever. He didn't know where was up and where was down. The cold, dirty water burned his open eyes and he could see nothing in the dark canal. When his head came up, he opened his mouth and screamed, but he couldn't reach the side. He screamed again and again and tried to hold his head out of the water but he kept going under. His mouth was full of water. He was so scared he couldn't really think any more. His friends in the water were scared too. They didn't want to go near him and be pulled under. Those on the canal's edge were too far away to reach him. Like many others before him, Willy was going to drown.

Then, suddenly, out of nowhere, a man appeared. He was big and strong and he ran to the canal and dived in. He soon reached Willy and swam quickly back to the side with him. Willy was saved. The big, strong man who saved him was James Clarke.

Today, almost everyone in Liverpool, almost everyone in Britain, learns to swim when they're young, often at school. But it wasn't always like that, and James Clarke, a champion swimmer from Liverpool, was one of the people who helped to change things.

JAMES CLARKE

- Born in 1886 in Georgetown, British Guyana, South America.
- He arrived in Liverpool as a stowaway at the age of 14.
- He was found in the city and went to live with an Irish family in Vauxhall.
- In 1914 he married a young Irish woman. They had 13 children together.
- He worked in the docks.
- He loved swimming and started his career at Wavertree Swimming Club.
- He became a swimming champion there and later at other clubs in Liverpool.
- For 40 years he performed in swimming shows in many parts of Britain. His favourite trick was to put a bucket over his head and sit under water and sing "Oh my darling, Clementine".
- He saved many children, sailors and dock workers from drowning in the River Mersey and the Leeds & Liverpool Canal. He helped the police to find the bodies of people who had drowned.

- He believed that all children should be able to swim, so he started to give lessons at his local pool. His idea spread until there were swimming lessons in schools all over the city.
- He was a local hero. When he died in 1946, children lined the streets from his home to the church where his funeral took place.
- In 1986, "James Clarke Street" became the first street in Liverpool that was named after a black man.

1 Did you get it?

Choose the right ending for each sentence: a, b or c.

1 Little Willy fell into the water because he wanted to …
a) cool his face. b) disappear. c) swim.

2 James Clarke came to Liverpool in …
a) 1886. b) 1900. c) 1914.

3 His swimming career started in the …
a) Leeds and Liverpool Canal.
b) River Mersey.
c) Wavertree Swimming Club.

4 He often saved people from drowning …
a) all over Britain.
b) in the canal and in the River Mersey.
c) in the Wavertree Swimming Club.

5 This gave him the idea to …
a) call the police.
b) start swimming lessons for children.
c) work in swimming shows.

2 What do you think?

Name the thing about James Clarke that most makes him a hero in your eyes. Tell the class.

3 Local hero

a) Work in groups of four.
Make a placemat on an A3 piece of paper.
Think how someone could become a hero in your area.
Write your ideas in your corner of the placemat.

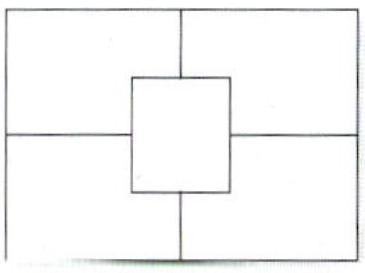

b) Turn the placemat and read the others' ideas. Discuss the ideas and agree on the best one. Write it in the middle of the placemat.

c) Present your idea to the class.

EXTRA Imagine you interviewed the local hero who carried out this idea.
Write the interview.

➔ Workbook *14 (p. 41)*

Workbook Checkpoint (pp. 42–45)

Your task

The story behind a name

My Book Imagine a British school has asked students from your school to write a text for its magazine. Like James Clarke Street in Liverpool, lots of German streets and buildings have a story behind them. Write a text about the person behind the name of a building or street in your area.

STEP 1

Choose a bridge, street, school, theatre … in your area.
Take a photo of the name sign and the building or street.

STEP 2

Get information from the internet or a library. Here are some ideas about what you could find out:

- a few important facts about the place you choose (e.g. when the bridge/school/… was built)
- some facts about the person and why he or she is famous
- when the building or street was named after the person
- why it is important to remember the person or event

Take notes and organize your information in a mindmap or table.

STEP 3

Write a first draft of your text. Organize your information in paragraphs.
Your text should have:

- an introduction, e.g.
  In Germany, lots of places are named after people. Not far from my house is a bridge which is called …
- a body: remember to start each paragraph with a topic sentence.
  - The Carl-Schurz-Brücke was built in … /
  - Carl Schurz is famous because he was the first German who … Schurz was born in …
- a conclusion
  It is important to remember people like Schurz because …

STEP 4

Go to p. 63 to check your first draft. Then revise it.

STEP 5

GALLERY WALK Hang up your text and photos in the classroom.
Walk around, read the other texts and look at the photos.

EXTRA Use your text to make an audio guide for British visitors.

→ Workbook *Wordbank 1–3, 7*

How did you do?

Answer these questions about your text.

How can you do better?

If your answer is "no", follow the tips below.

How did you do?	Tips
Content	
Have you given enough information about the person behind your street name?	• Check your mindmap or table: Highlight information that is not in your text. • Decide what information to add to your text.
Structure	
Have you used paragraphs to organize your information?	• Read the text again and look for places where you could start a new paragraph.
Does your first paragraph say what you are going to write about?	• Read your paragraphs again and make notes about their content. • Use your notes to revise your introduction.
Does your conclusion go well with the rest of the text?	In this text, you are writing about two things: • a building or a street • a person Your conclusion should bring these ideas together. For example, you could say how you think the person would feel, if he or she knew that a place was named after them. ➜ *p. 51, Structuring a text*
Language	
Could you find the right words to describe your person and what he or she did?	• Look at the table in exercise 2 a) on page 48. Decide what kind of words you need: adjectives, nouns or verbs. If you can't find the words you need in the table look them up in a dictionary.

Did you use the passive to talk about the history of places? For example: The school was named after Max Planck in 1947.	• Go back and check where you can use a passive sentence to improve your text. ➜ *p. 55 ex.3*

My trip to Ireland

A

B

D

E

1 Impressions of Ireland

Look at the photos for two minutes. Then close your books and say what you remember.

A: There's a picture of huge cliffs by the sea. Two people are lying at the edge of the cliff. Scary!
B: OK. My turn. I remember some signs …

→ pp. 26–27 Look at Ireland on the map. Say what you notice about the island.

2 Lewis's trip

Lewis McCray from Edinburgh is visiting his Aunt Mary and Uncle Frank in Belfast. They're taking him on a tour of Ireland.

→ pp. 26–27 Find Lewis's route around Ireland.

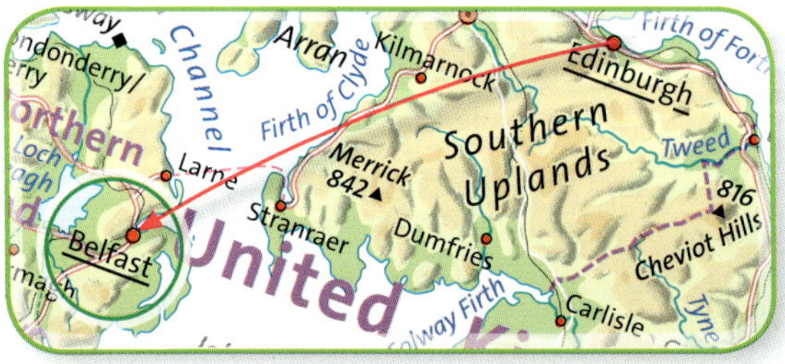

C

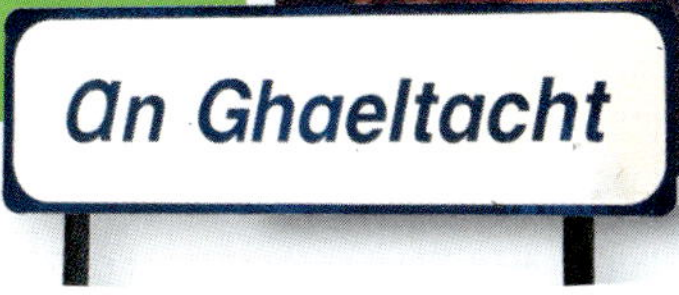

H

G

F

3 Attractions

a) You will hear about three attractions.
→ pp. 26–27 Listen and find where they are on the map.
Say what you can do at each one.

b) Choose one of the attractions.
Explain why you would like to go there.

Your task

At the end of this unit:
In a team, make a brochure with practical tips for Irish students who want to visit Germany.

→ Workbook *1 (p. 46)*

1 Belfast and the northern coast

Uncle F.: Can you pass the coffee?
Lewis: May I have some too, please?
Aunt M.: Of course not! You mustn't drink coffee at your age! Is that what you do at home?
Lewis: Er … sometimes.
Aunt M.: Well, it's not good for you. But what you can do, is help me to clear the table.
Lewis: Where are we going today?
Uncle F. To the Giant's Causeway, about an hour in the car from Belfast. But it might as well be the other side of the moon.
Lewis: I don't understand.
Uncle F. You will … Now go and help your aunt!

❖

Uncle F. Don't drive so fast, Mary. I want to read this to Lewis. "The cliffs are made of tall stone columns. In some places, the columns rise up nearly 30 metres from the water, while in others, they are like steps that form a wide stone path down to the sea."
Lewis: What's so special about cliffs?
Uncle F.: You'll see!

❖

Lewis: Wow! This *is* like being on the moon! Who built this place?
Aunt M.: There's a legend that it's the work of an Irish giant called Finn McCool.
Lewis: McCool? Sounds like the name of a DJ.
Aunt M.: Does it now? But no, he was a giant, and a proud one too, who couldn't say no to a challenge.
Lewis: That sounds more like me.

Aunt M.: Well, to go on with my story: One day a Scottish giant challenged Finn McCool to a fight. Finn of course agreed. But because he couldn't swim, he built a stone path all the way to the Scottish coast. The giants met in the middle, fought fiercely, and Finn won. After the fight, the Scottish giant was so scared that Finn would follow him to Scotland, he pulled up the stones as he ran back home. What you see is all that is left.
Uncle F.: Where did you hear *that* story? I know a different legend. Shall I tell you?
Lewis: Later. Right now I'd like to explore.
Aunt M. Careful or you'll fall and break your neck!

❖

Uncle F.: What about some music?
Aunt M.: It's only adverts.
Uncle F.: That advert is about the Titanic museum. It's where we're going tomorrow.
Lewis: Really? Fantastic.

2 Sounds like me

Say which adjectives best describe Lewis. Find lines in the text which show this.

careful · curious · excited · impolite · nervous · polite · proud · shocked · shy

Early finisher Describe the character of Aunt Mary or Uncle Frank.

3 Legends

Did someone really build the Giant's Causeway? Say why you think legends say so.

I think people tell legends because …

If you want to explain something …

www Find out how the Giant's Causeway was really formed.

➜ Text Files 6 and 7 (pp. 106–111) ➜ Workbook 2 (p. 46)

Moments in Irish history

Read about some key moments in Irish history.

1801

The Act of Union made Ireland part of the United Kingdom, with one parliament for all its countries. 121 years later, in 1922, southern Ireland left the UK. It became a republic in 1949. Northern Ireland chose to stay in the UK.

Irish flag before 1801

GB flag before 1801

UK flag from 1801

www Find out more about the long history of Ireland's relationship with Britain.
Why did southern Ireland leave the UK?
Why did the North keep its link with Britain?

1909 to 1911

The Titanic, the world's largest passenger ship at that time, was built in Belfast.
In April 1912, it sailed for the first and last time.

Building the Titanic in Belfast

www Find out about the Belfast shipyards and what happened to the Titanic. ➜ Text File 7

1998

The Belfast Agreement ended a 30-year conflict between supporters and opponents of Northern Ireland's union with Britain. Northern Ireland will now stay in the UK, but it will also have closer links with the Republic. During the conflict, over 3,000 people were killed.

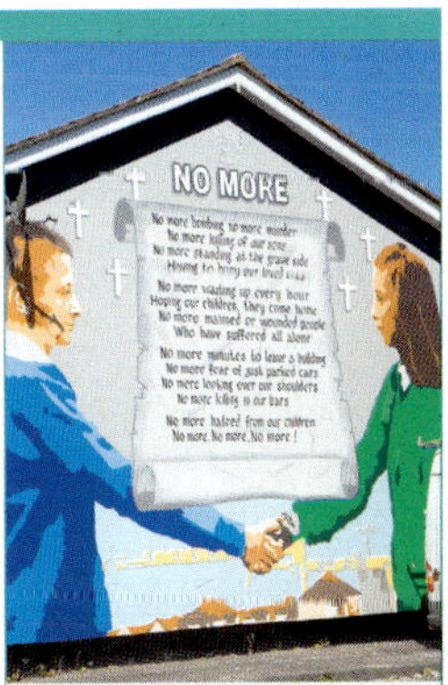

Wall painting, Belfast

www Find out about four people who won the Nobel Peace Prize for their work on bringing peace to Northern Ireland.

1845 to 1849

The Great Famine started when a potato disease hit the country. Potatoes were then the main food for half the population, so millions of people went hungry. About a million died, and over a million left Ireland for ever.

Deserted village from the time of the Great Famine

www Find out why so many people died. Learn more about emigration from Ireland.

1973

The EEC (now the **EU**) welcomed the UK and Ireland as new members. Membership has been good for both parts of Ireland, but especially the Republic, which is now much richer than it was in the 1970s.

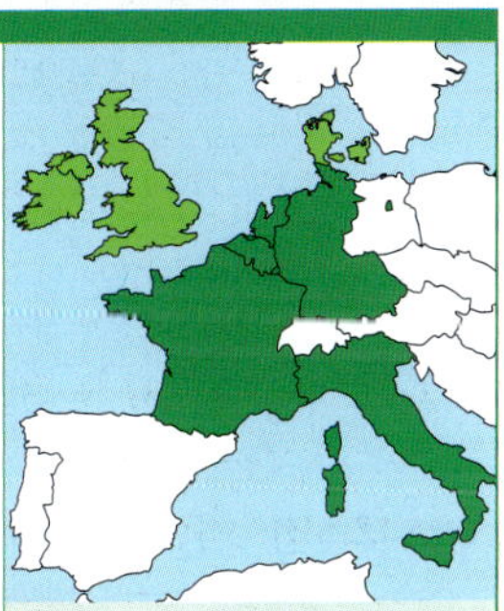

EEC members 1973

www Find out how the republic of Ireland has become a richer country.

2003

Google opened its European headquarters in Dublin. This continued the 1990s boom that made Ireland a big world centre for high-tech companies.

Dublin Docklands, where many big IT companies have their offices.

➜ Workbook 3 (p. 47)

1 WORDS Countries

You choose Choose one way to order these words: a, b or c. Then choose 25 words and try it out.

battle · beautiful · +border · +change money · coast · county · crown · culture · +currency · defend · demonstration · enemy · +EU · +euro · Europe · flag · +ID card · invade · island · king · land · language · mayor · +nation · navy · parliament · +passport · +peace · peaceful · police officer · +police station · +population · pound · +president · queen · +republic · royal · +state · traditional · travel · UK · village · +visa · visit

a) Copy the table and add the nouns from the box. Then add the verbs or adjectives that go with the nouns. Think of more words for each noun, e.g. *passport* + *show*.

noun	verb	adjective
battle		
border		

b) Write the words in a mind map.

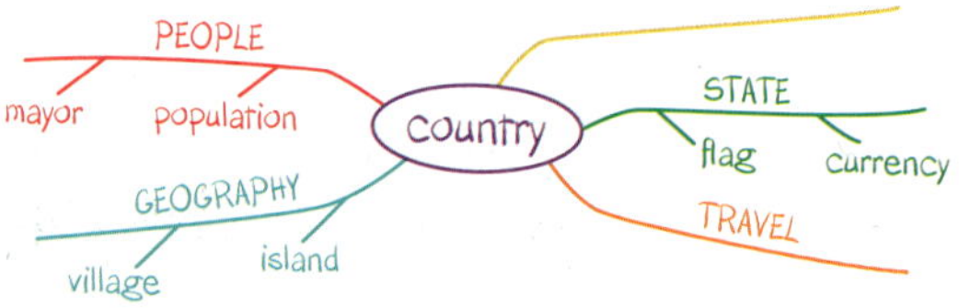

c) Draw a picture with the words and label them.

➔ Workbook 4 (p. 48)

2 REVISION Travelling to other countries (Modal verbs)

a) Choose a country and write six rules for travelling there. Use *can*, *can't*, *must*, *mustn't* or *needn't*.

carry a knife in your bag · change money · get a visa · pay in euros · see a doctor · show your ID card · show your passport · take your pet/laptop/… · visit a police station

1 If you travel to the UK or Ireland, you must show your ID card or passport.
2 If you travel to Spain, you needn't ...

More help ➔ p. 122

b) Give advice to someone who is going to another country. You can use ideas from the table.

If you lose your passport/ID card	you could	buy some in a shop
If you don't have the right currency	you should	ask if they speak English
If you don't speak the language	you must	go to a police station
If you don't have the right clothes		go to a bank
If your money is stolen		have a problem at the airport
…		…

Early finisher ➔ p. 129 ➔ GF 6.1: Modal verbs (p. 165) ➔ Workbook 5 (p. 48)

3 Study skills: Teamwork

This page will show you how to work in a team.

a) When you work in a team, everyone has a special job. Match these four jobs to the speech bubbles.

1 coordinator

2 writer

3 picture and layout editor

4 language watchdog

A *I do research. When I find the information we need, I write the texts.*

B *I look for pictures, or I draw them. Then I put the pictures and the texts together so that our results look good.*

C *I check all the texts and make sure there are no mistakes. I also suggest how we can improve our text.*

D *I plan our discussions and take notes on our decisions. I also check that everyone does their job at the right time.*

b) Work in teams of four. Choose one of these topics and make a brochure on it.

1 The Titanic
2 Irish writers
3 Horse riding in Ireland
4 Dublin for kids

Decide who will do what job and make a timetable for all the work. Then make your brochure.
www Find more information. You can also get information about the Titanic in the *Text File*.

Text File 7 *(pp. 110–111)*

c) Swap brochures with another team. In your team, say what you think about the other brochure.

d) **Think**: Think of at least two reasons why teamwork helped you, and write them down.
Pair: Compare your reasons. Number them 1 *(most important)*, 2, 3, etc.
Share: Join two other pairs and agree on the four most important reasons.

e) In your team, talk about your teamwork. Did each member of the team have the right job? Did the team do the task successfully?

Study skills

Teamwork

Wenn wir im Team arbeiten, kann ich folgende Aufgaben übernehmen: ...
Ein Team kann ...

→ *SF 19: Teamwork (p. 151)*

→ Workbook 6–7 *(p. 49)*

1 Lewis's travel posts

30 minutes ago

Lewis McCray I've just heard angels singing!

Chloe Carr Where? Are you in heaven?

Lewis McCray Not yet! ;)))) I was in St Patrick's Cathedral. Uncle Frank and Aunt Mary took me there to hear the boys' choir. We weren't allowed to take photos inside, but I found this on the Internet. And I talked to one of the boys after the service. He told me the 21 choir boys go to the cathedral school. They're allowed to miss lessons because they have to sing at two services every day! It's a real job and they get paid!

Chloe Carr I'd love to have a job like that! Could I join the choir?

Yesterday

Lewis McCray Check this video out! I've been to lots of these places!

… and here's Dublin at night. This area is called Temple Bar.

Music and dancing is EVERYWHERE!

Chloe Carr I wish I could see you doing an Irish dance, Lewis!

Lewis McCray Irish dance? No way! I wanted to go into a nightclub! There are hundreds of them. But Uncle Frank was like: "Stop. You aren't allowed in there!" I'll have to wait till I'm 18 … Unfair! : (((

Jack Boyd Who wants to go to nightclubs? There are better things to look forward to. Like when I'm 18, I'll be allowed to ride my brother's motorbike!

Yesterday

Chloe Carr I'm listening to U2 songs and thinking about you. ❤
Have you seen any leprechauns yet?

Lewis McCray Yes! Here's one of the little people!

Luke Reid I thought leprechauns wore green suits and hats, funny shoes and smoked a pipe! That one looks like a little girl!

Chloe Carr Looks like she wasn't able to climb onto the chair!

Lewis McCray I had to help her. And she thanked me with a pot of gold!
PS This photo is REAL! (2 hours ago – National Leprechaun Museum)

Two days ago

Lewis McCray Today we crossed the border into southern Ireland. We stopped at a shop, but I wasn't able to pay for this chocolate. Welcome to the eurozone!

Luke Reid Hey, Lewis. We learned all about Ireland in geography last year! Maybe you were ill that day? ;))))

Jack Boyd So you won't be able to buy any cool souvenirs!

2 In Dublin

a) Copy and complete the table.

place	what Lewis did	what he didn't do
St Patrick's Cathedral	heard choir …	take photos
Temple Bar	…	

b) Add a comment to each one of Lewis's posts. Read one of your comments to the class.

c) Watch the video Lewis posted for his friends.

3 Have a go

Talk about what you will be allowed to do after your eighteenth birthday.

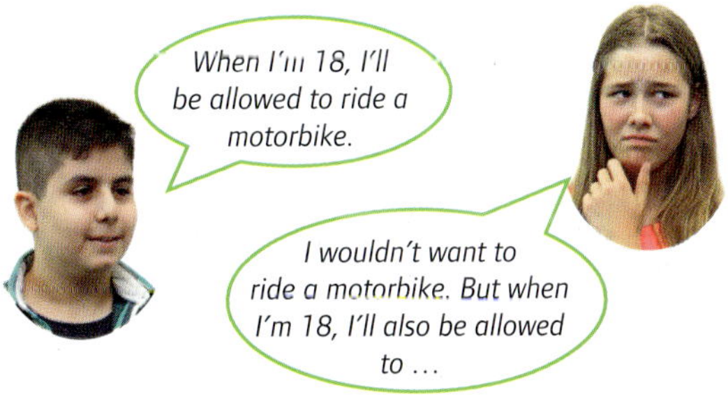

Looking at language

a) In the present tense, you can use *have to* or *must*.

*We **have to** be at the station at 7:45. / We **must** be at the station at 7:45.*

In the past and future, you can only use a form of *have to*.
Complete these sentences from 1 on pages 70–71:

Simple past: *I ... help her onto the chair.* Future: *I'... wait till I'm 18.*

b) In the past and future, *be able to* or *be allowed to* are used instead of *can*.
Complete these sentences from 1 on pages 70–71:

Simple past: *We ... to take photos.*
I ... to pay for this chocolate.

Future: *When I'm 18, ... to ride my brother's motorbike!*
So you ... to buy any cool souvenirs.

Choose the right answer:

For German *können*, we use *be able to / be allowed to*.
For German *dürfen*, we use *be able to / be allowed to*.

➜ GF 6.2: Modal substitutes (pp. 166–167)

1 Hostel from hell (*have to, be allowed to*: Simple past)

On holiday, you stayed at an awful hostel.
Read the hostel rules and write sentences.

We had to be in bed by 8 pm.
We were only allowed to sleep till ...

Early finisher Think of more awful rules and write similar sentences.

We had to clean our rooms with a toothbrush.

➜ Workbook 8 (p. 50)

1 You must be in bed by 8 pm.
2 You can only sleep here till 5.30 am.
3 You must have a cold shower every morning.
4 You must clean your room before breakfast.
5 You can only have one piece of bread for breakfast.
6 You must leave the building to use your mobile.
7 You can only play games between 6:30 pm and 6:40 pm.
8 You must use earphones when you listen to music.

2 You'll have to revise ...

(*have to, be able to, be allowed to*: Future)

A new classmate has some questions about next week's English test. Write answers.

1 Will I have to revise for the test?
Yes, you'll have to revise the last unit.
2 What about dictionaries?
You will/won't be allowed to use ...
3 And electronic dictionaries, mobile phones?
No, you won't ... / Yes, you will ...
4 Will I have to arrive early?
5 Will we be able to work together?
6 Will I be allowed to sit where I want?
7 Will I have to bring my own paper for the test?
8 Will I be able to leave when I'm finished?

More help ➜ p. 122 ➜ Workbook 9–10 (pp. 50–51)

3 I won't be able to go swimming

a) Choose one of these places to visit.
Make notes on advantages and disadvantages.

Ireland · a small island in the Atlantic · Greenland · the moon · ...

the moon: + good view of the earth, a ...
– no swimming, ...

More help ➜ p. 122

b) Say which place you've chosen.
Talk about the advantages and disadvantages.

I've chosen the moon. I'll be able to get a great view of the Earth.
But I won't be able to go swimming.
And I'll have to ...

Early finisher ➜ p. 130

1 Yu Ming is ainm dom

a) Look at the stills from the film.
Say what you think it might be about.

b) Watch the film and say where the action is:
1 at the beginning
2 after the plane lands
3 at the end of the film

c) There are a lot of misunderstandings in the film. Explain what these people think at first.
1 Yu Ming: when he learns Irish at the beginning.
2 The blond man: in the hostel.
3 Yu Ming: when nobody understands him.
4 The barman: when Paddy talks to Yu Ming.

d) Say which three languages you hear in the film. Explain what you find out about Irish (Gaelic) in Ireland.

e) It's not always easy to understand each other across cultures. Explain:
1 how people react when they cannot understand Yu Ming.
2 why the man at the hostel asks another Asian guest for help with Yu Ming.

f) **EXTRA** What's your favourite scene in the film? Explain why.

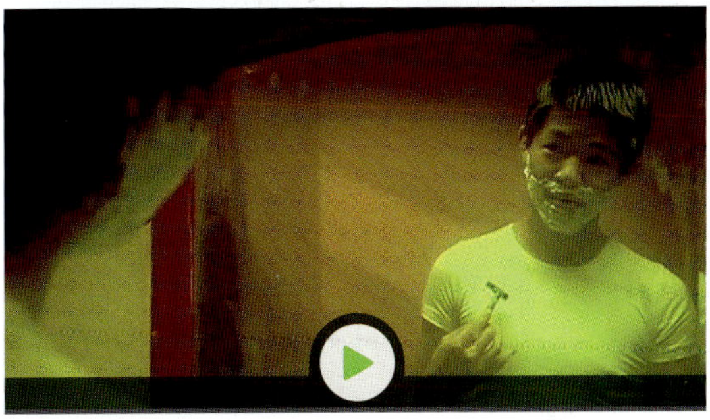

2 Making the film: Feelings

a) Say how you think Yu Ming feels ...
1 in his job at the beginning of the film.
2 when he is learning Irish (Gaelic).
3 when he arrives at the airport.
4 when he is walking around Dublin.
5 when people don't understand him.
6 at the end of the film.

Access to cultures

Irish is spoken as an everyday language in some parts of the west coast.
Name countries where different languages are spoken in different regions, e.g. Canada.
Are there regions with different languages in your country?

b) Work in groups of five.
Here are five ways that film-makers can show their characters' feelings:
1 music
2 colour
3 facial expressions
4 body language
5 interaction with other people.

Each student chooses one of these five ways.

Look carefully at the parts 1–6 from 2a).
Watch the film again.
Say where you saw the way of showing feelings which you chose.

1 Arrival in the Burren

5 minutes ago

Lewis McCray We're at the horse-riding centre on the west coast. Aunt Mary fell asleep in the car just outside Dublin and only woke up when we arrived!
The owner's weird daughter showed us our cottage. She looks just like a VAMPIRE. Black hair, black clothes and a very white face! She's taking us on the horse ride tomorrow. SCARY!
We have to be up EARLY (6 am!!!) for the ride. Help! I've never been on a horse. ☹

Chloe Carr Be careful. If you're in Countess Dracula's castle, I hope you'll still be alive for the ride tomorrow!! ☺

TUESDAY 15 APRIL 127 days since Dad died

Mum says that I have to go on the horse ride with her tomorrow because it's a big group and she can't do it on her own. I had planned to ride Raven down to the beach, so we had a big argument. That never happened when Dad was alive. I miss him so much!

The worst thing is that I have to be friendly to the guests too. "They're here to have a good time, Ashling," Mum always says. Yeah, Mum, right. But what about me? I'm not having a good time! I can't even listen to my music. "It's too loud. Think of our guests, please!" Guests, guests, It's all about the guests here. I can't do anything I want to at home – and the people who live round here stare at me as if I'm mad. If we lived in the city, people wouldn't care what I looked like. But I'd miss the horses ...

When the last guests arrived, Mum had already gone to bed. So I showed them their cottage and their sandwiches and drinks. They were starving because they hadn't had anything to eat since lunch. They had travelled all the way from Dublin. They sound funny, but not like Dubliners. I think they're from Northern Ireland. The boy wanted to talk about the ride tomorrow – but I just said goodnight and left them to unpack.

When I got back to my room, I saw a blue light in the cottage. I think it was that boy on his computer. Was he writing, like me? No, I'm sure he talks more than he writes. He was probably chatting or playing a game ... The lights are out now, so he must be asleep. I hope he doesn't talk too much tomorrow. Oh, God – I hope they know how to ride! The worst thing is guests who don't know how to ride ...

2 Lewis and Ashling

Make groups of four.
Each student does one of the following:

a) Explain why Lewis calls Ashling a vampire.
b) Say what you have learned about Ashling and her family from her diary.
c) List what Ashling likes and dislikes about her life in the Burren.
d) Say what Ashling thinks of the new guests.

3 On the horse ride

Imagine Lewis and Ashling talk during the horse ride. What might they say?
Write a dialogue.

Early finisher Find another early finisher. Act out each other's dialogues.

1 Pronunciation (Consonants)

a) Look at the word pairs below. Then listen. For each pair, write down the word you hear.
Compare your answers.

1 white – wide
2 feed – feet
3 God – got
4 side – sight
5 bang – bank
6 docks – dogs
7 cheap – jeep
8 pick – pig
9 card – cart
10 nod – not
11 choose – juice
12 thing – think

b) Listen and write down the missing word.

1 the red ...
2 with a red ...
3 a lovely ... beach
4 lots of lovely ... beaches
5 all the different ... in Dublin
6 on different ... in the match
7 put it in the ... of the car
8 put your ... in the car
9 on your own two ...
10 time to ... her
11 and then it went ...
12 we went to the ...

More help → p. 123

→ Workbook 11 (p. 51)

2 At the hotel

At a hotel, you hear some conversations between a tour guide and some tourists.

Listen to the four conversations.
Take turns to explain in German why there are misunderstandings.

→ Workbook 12 (p. 52)

TIP
Don't translate every detail. Think about what is important and interesting: in these conversations what the people understand and don't understand.

3 Regional accents

a) Listen to seven tour guides.
Say where they are giving their tours.
Which one speaks standard English?

b) Listen to how the standard English speaker says these words:

everyone · guide · here · name · tour · thirty

Then listen to the first guide again, and try to say the words like he does.

c) Listen again to the other tour guides and to how they say the same six words.
Say which accent you find easiest to understand. Which one is the most difficult?

→ Workbook 13–14 (p. 52)

Access to cultures

In the UK and Ireland, people often speak with **regional accents**, so a Londoner can sound very different from someone from Liverpool. And in Scotland, Wales and Ireland, they also have their own English accents.

A regional accent isn't always easy to understand, but everyone in the UK and Ireland understands standard English. You often hear standard English on the BBC, and you also learn it in this book.

Say if the situation in your country is the same.
Say which accents you find harder to understand.
Is there a standard accent?

4 REVISION I had a weird dream (Simple past)

Complete Chloe's message. Use the simple past of the verbs in the box.

Chloe Carr Last night I [1]... this weird dream. You and I [2]... on our way up a rocky hill with other kids from our class. Our German teacher Miss Kunzel [3]... already at the top. She [4]... angry and [5]... at us to hurry. I [6]... to get into trouble, so I [7]... up the hill like mad. When I [8]... the top, I [9]... around but you [10]... there. Then I [11]... you at the bottom of the hill. You had fallen all the way down. I [12]... you, but you [13]...You [14]... hurt, and I was sure you had broken your leg. Lewis, tell me you're OK.

(not) answer · be (3 x) · (not) be · call · have · look (2 x) · reach · run · see · shout · (not) want

More help ➜ p. 123

➜ Workbook 15 (p. 53)

Language help

We use the simple past to say what happened in the past.
To say what happened before this time, we use the past perfect.
I saw you at the bottom of the hill. You had fallen all the way down.
You were hurt. I was sure you had broken your leg.

We form the past perfect with <u>had + past participle</u>.

➜ *GF 1.5: Past perfect (p. 158)*

5 After the class trip (Past perfect)

Say how the students felt after their class trip.
Use the past perfect for the earlier action.

1 Susan ... (be) happy to be back because she ... (miss) her parents.
Susan was happy to be back because she had missed her parents.
2 Dan ... (be) unhappy because he ... (lose) his mobile.
3 Sam ... (feel) tired because he ... (not sleep) very well.
4 Peter ... (feel) sick because he ... (eat) too many biscuits.
5 Jill ... (look) worried because her boyfriend ... (not phone) her.
6 Tom ... (be) all red because he ... (stay) in the sun too long.
7 Ben ... (look) excited because he ... (meet) a nice girl at the hostel.

➜ Workbook 16 (p. 53)

6 At the farm in the Burren (Past perfect)

Link the two sentences with the word in the brackets. Use the past perfect for the earlier action.

1 Aunt Mary fell asleep.
The car arrived at the farm. (when)
Aunt Mary had fallen asleep when the car ...
2 Ashling's mum went to bed.
Ashling welcomed the guests. (so)
3 The guests were hungry.
They didn't eat on the journey. (because)
4 Ashling tried to be friendly to the guests.
Her mum told her to. (because)
5 Lewis couldn't find Ashling.
She went to her room. (because)
6 Lewis's room was dark.
He turned off the lights. (because)

Early finisher ➜ p. 130

➜ Workbook 17 (p. 54)

1 Learn how

a) Make a table like this. On a copy of the story, underline all the time markers. Then put them in the correct column of your table.

when sth. happened	what happened first, second, etc.	how much time passed
the Easter holidays	First	for about five minutes
…	…	…

b) Add these time phrases to your table too.

after that · next · last Monday · for two weeks · in the beginning · a few hours ago · for a while · two weeks later · later

c) Now look at these two sentences:
The guests went horse riding.
Ashling's mother prepared their lunch.

Link the sentences in as many ways as you can with phrases from the box.

before · after · as soon as · while · shortly after that · earlier · First … then

- While the guests went horse riding, Ashling's mother prepared their lunch.
- The guests went horse riding after …
- …

2 Now write …

Write a short story. Use time markers to show the order of events. Remember to start a new paragraph for every new idea.

➜ *SF 12: Paragraphs and topic sentences (p. 145)*
➜ Workbook *Wordbank 7*

3 … and revise

a) Give feedback. Read your partner's text and make notes where it is clear/unclear to you when things happened.

Take turns to make comments and corrections.

TIP
1 Use time markers to help your reader to see
– when something happened
– what happened first, second etc.,
– how much time passed
2 Use time markers to link sentences.

The view from my window

It was the Easter holidays and I had nothing to do because all of my friends were away. Early one morning, I was watching TV, but the show was silly and I soon got bored. So I sat by the window to watch the people go by.

Our flat is on the fifth floor of a corner building at a busy junction, so there are always lots of cars and pedestrians.

First I watched a woman who was walking three little dogs. They had very short legs which moved very quickly and it looked like they were taking her for a walk instead.

Then I watched a little boy and his father. The boy didn't want to walk any more and sat down on the pavement. At first his father waited, but then he became angry and started shouting. This continued for about five minutes. Finally the father picked up the boy and carried him like a baby. The boy kicked and screamed.

Suddenly a white sports car raced down the street. It was going really fast! The traffic light turned red as the car reached the junction and BAM! It drove into a green van. The white car spun around, while the green van hit a parked car. Glass flew everywhere.

Seconds later, I saw a man in a black hat jump out of the white car and run away. I called the police immediately. Five minutes later I heard the siren and ran down to the street. But it was too late – the man in the black hat was gone. I had to wait for an hour while they cleared the road. Finally I had the chance to tell a policeman what I had seen.

b) My Book Think about your partner's feedback and what you've learned on this page. Decide what to change and write a final draft.

➜ *SF 13: Time markers (p. 146); SF 14: Feedback – writing (p. 146)*
➜ Workbook *18 (p. 54)*

The horse ride

Part 1

It was just as Ashling had expected. Nine guests and none of them could ride very well. At least the four old couples had ridden before, but the boy had never sat on a horse – ever.

"Still," she thought, "he's not so bad for a city boy from Edinburgh."

They were on a four-hour ride into the Burren. It was starting to rain a little and the old couples were so slow. The ride would take five hours like this. Or even longer! Why did these city folk come here? They were like fish out of water on horseback in the country.

At least she hadn't had to talk very much yet. She was at the front of the group while her mother moved from person to person along the line and chatted happily with them all. She showed them the views and told them why the area was so rocky. But now, as they were passing some old stone walls, her mother said, "We'll come to a very interesting area later. Ashling will tell you all about it. She knows more about the history of the Burren than I do."

"Thanks, Mum," Ashling thought.

❖

The rain was getting heavier when Ashling's mother called out to her, "Wait, please, Ashling." Ashling stopped and turned her horse. "What's up?"

"Well," her mother started, "it's like this ..."

One of the old men went on. "Some of us old folk are feeling a bit cold in this rain, dear, so ..."

"So we're going to take the short trail back," her mother finished.

"Oh, OK," Ashling said and began to walk her horse back towards the others.

"No, Ashling, wait. I'll take most of us back on the short trail but Lewis would like to go the long way round. So he'll go with you."

The boy from Edinburgh smiled up at Ashling. She sighed, turned her horse round again and with a "Come on, then," started back up the long trail.

Part 2

"We can go a bit faster if you like," Lewis said. "Now that we haven't got the old folk with us."

Ashling stopped her horse and turned round to look at Lewis. Her black hair and clothes, her black horse and the dark clouds behind her made her face seem whiter than ever. Lewis suddenly felt cold.

"So you want to go faster, do you?" Ashling asked. "Well, these rocky trails get very slippery in the rain. Have you seen all the green ditches next to the trail? Some of them have holes in them, big holes. If you're not careful you'll fall off the rocks into a ditch and disappear down a big hole, horse and all. No one will ever find you again."

For a moment Lewis didn't know what to say. Was that a smile on Ashling's lips?

"She's just trying to scare me," he thought. He smiled back at her and said, "Nice story! You should be on the stage. Anyway, that's good. If we go slower, we'll have more time to talk."

As they went up the hill, Lewis talked and talked. Ashling thought he would never stop. He told her about his visits to Belfast and Dublin. She had only been to Dublin twice, when she was much younger and her dad was still alive. She had never been to Belfast.

Lewis was full of questions too. "Who built all these stone walls?"

"Farmers," Ashling answered. "A long time ago. A lot more people lived in the Burren in the old days. Some of these walls are 4,000 years old."

"So where did all the people go?"

"Er ... well, that's a long story, but I'll show you something on the other side of the hill."

At the top of the hill, Ashling stopped her horse and pointed. Looking down, Lewis could see the ruins of an old church with some gravestones.

"That's where they buried lots of people who died in the Great Famine," Ashling told him.

"The Great Famine?"

"Yes, you know, in the 19th century, when the potatoes had a disease and didn't grow. A million people died and another million emigrated. Because potatoes were all that poor people in Ireland had to eat."

"Was there no other food in Ireland?" Lewis asked.

"There was enough food. But the farmers sold it. Lots of it was sold in Britain. And the British government did nothing to stop the exports."

For the second time that day, Lewis didn't know what to say.

Part 3

On the way down the hill, Ashling suddenly stopped and got off her horse.

"Can you just wait here for a minute?" she said and started walking off the trail towards a stream.

"I'll come with you," said Lewis.

"No, no," Ashling turned round and held her hand up. "There's something I have to do – alone."

Lewis watched as Ashling walked over the rocks to the stream. She knelt down and scooped up some water in her hands then let it fall slowly back into the stream. She stayed there a few minutes, turned round and came back to the horses.

As they went on down the hill towards the end of the trail, Lewis asked, "What was that all about? Back at the stream?"

For a while it seemed as if Ashling didn't want to answer. Then she suddenly looked at Lewis and said: "It was about my dad. He loved that stream, so we threw his ashes into it after he died. I like to talk to him there. I really miss him."

It was the third time that Lewis didn't know what to say – and now, for the first time, Ashling asked him a question: "So, what's Edinburgh like?"

"Edinburgh?" Lewis said in surprise. He had a lot to say on that topic and was glad to forget about death and dying in the Burren for a while.

"It's a great city," he began, "especially in the summer when the Edinburgh Festival is on. One thing I like to do at the festival is ..." and he talked all the way to where Ashling's mother and the others were waiting. This time, Ashling was surprised that she didn't mind listening.

1 The ride across the Burren

Say who the riders are in each part of the story and what they talk about.

More help → *p. 123*

2 Ashling and Lewis

Work in groups of four. Each student reads *one* of these parts of the story again:
ll. 50–62 • ll. 71–93 • ll. 95–114 • ll. 115–126
Then explain to the others what you find out about Ashling and/or Lewis in your part.

3 Silent thoughts

You choose Choose a, b or c.
Write a few sentences about

a) what Ashling thinks about Lewis before and after the ride.

b) what Lewis might think when he hears about the Famine.

c) what Lewis might think when Ashing tells him about her father.

→ Workbook *19 (p. 55)*

Workbook Checkpoint (pp. 56–59)

4 Unit

Your task

A brochure for students from Ireland

Students at your partner school in Ireland want to visit your area.
Work in a team with four students. Make a brochure with tips for the visit.

STEP 1

Make a checklist with the main points. Think of what you could say about each point, for example:

- tips on travel
  - If you fly from Belfast you'll have to change in London. But if you travel from Dublin …
  - If you live in the Republic, you won't have to …
- suggestions about where to stay
  - There's a very good hostel in …
  - The *Pension* in the old town is cheap and …
- attractions and activities in your area
  - The countryside around … is very beautiful.
  - Our local chocolate museum is a big attraction.
- what your guests will be able to do, see, …
  - Why not pack some strong boots? Then you'll be able to …

STEP 2

Choose your team roles: writer, picture and layout editor, language watchdog or coordinator.
Then the coordinator asks each member to do one of these jobs and suggests the best order for them.

- get information and write the texts
- check the language
- find good pictures that go with the brochures

The coordinator says when each job must be done before the next meeting.

➜ *SF 19: Teamwork (p. 151)*

STEP 3

Before the meeting, each team member checks his/her own work so far.

How am I doing? Answer the questions about your role.	**How can I do better?** Follow these tips if you need to.
Writer • Have I found all the information we need? • Have I organized the information clearly in my texts?	• Read through the checklist from Step 1 and make sure you have all your main points. • Check that you have enough information for each point. Add more information, if necessary. • Check the tips on writing paragraphs.
Picture and layout editor • Have I found good pictures for the brochure?	• Use the checklist from Step 1 to make sure that you have pictures for the main points. • Ask the writer to show you his/her text and check that your pictures go with it. ➜ *p. 38*
Language watchdog • Have I checked everything I need to?	• Make sure that the writer has used the right travel vocabulary. ➜ *p. 68, ex. 2* • Check if the writer has used phrases like *you'll be able to, you'll have to, you won't have to*, etc. If not, make suggestions about where to use them. • Look out for spelling and grammar mistakes.
Coordinator • Have I prepared everything for the meeting?	Remember, before the meeting you should • check that the writer has given his/her texts to the language watchdog • check that the picture editor has a copy of the pictures for everyone to see. • make a list of discussion points, e.g. headings for the texts, order of the texts in the brochure, position of the pictures, etc. • have a plan for the next steps, e.g. printing or writing the final version

STEP 4

At the team meeting, the coordinator leads the discussion.
The team agrees on the final steps, who does what, and when the brochure must be ready.
When your brochure is finished, swap with another group and read theirs.

EXTRA Give feedback to the other group about their brochure.

➜ *Inside back cover: Giving feedback*
➜ **Workbook** *Wordbank 4–5, 7*

5 Unit

Extraordinary Scotland

Access File Edit View History

1

Skye Hunter is performing in the Edinburgh Fringe Festival. I met Skye on the Royal Mile, where she was promoting her new show with the rest of the cast.

2

Listen to my interview with Angus MacLeod from Glasgow and find out how bagpipes work!

3

LOOK OUT!!!! The Fringe Festival is coming!

4

A girl and her dog: Lauren Reid and her dog Shadow compete in sheepdog trials in the Scottish Highlands.

5

On board the yacht *Wee Lass* Katie MacNeil, Iain Ferguson and the rest of their class from the Isle of Barra learn how to identify dolphins.

1 Social media and you

Talk about the kind of information, photos and videos you post or watch on the internet. Then report to the class.

2 Lewis's social media page

a) Describe the photo you like most. Say why you like it and what you'd like to find out about the people or situation.

b) → *pp. 26–27*
Find Edinburgh and the other places Lewis writes about in his captions.
Say what part of Scotland they're in.

c) Listen to Lewis and write down his questions to Angus, Skye, Lauren and Katie.

Listen again and take notes on the answer to the questions. Use your notes to describe their hobbies.

What else would you like to know? Write down other questions you'd like to ask.

3 The Fringe

Watch the film about the Edinburgh Fringe. Take notes about the kind of performers you see.

Say which performers or show you found the most interesting. Give reasons.

→ Workbook *1 (p. 60)*

Your task

At the end of this unit:
Interview someone who plays an instrument or has an unusual hobby.
Make a poster about the interview and present it to the class.

1 Extraordinary west coast

Dolphin watching near Barra

A team of students from Castlebay Community School is helping the Western Isles Dolphin Trust's (WIDT) research on Barra's dolphins

When the WIDT was looking for volunteers to make dolphin sightings near the Isle of Barra in the Western Isles, students from the island's community school put their hands up.

Classroom at sea

On the Trust's yacht, the Wee Lass, Castlebay students learned how to watch, photograph and identify dolphins.

"Scientists don't know much about the dolphins on Scotland's west coast," said Katie MacNeil, 14, "so sightings are important for research."

Katie explained: "Pollution is a huge problem for dolphins. And fishing – they get caught in the nets of big fishing boats. So if we know where they spend their time and what they do there, we can protect them better. They can't protect themselves from us."

"I've seen dolphins around Barra before," said Katie's classmate Iain Ferguson, 15, "but I couldn't identify them. You can't teach yourself to do that. Someone has to show you. You identify each dolphin by its dorsal fin, so you need photos. Taking good photos of fins is one thing I've learned to do."

Teamwork

Other students learned how to record the exact locations of the sightings. "So we can monitor a dolphin's movements over time and see where it goes," said Katie. "It's all about teamwork. When we help each other we can make exact sightings."

New skills and hard work

With their new skills, the students continue their work on their island home. "When the sea is rough, I look for dolphins from land," Iain explained. "And when I make a sighting, I can identify the dolphin and record its exact location, all on my own."

In calm weather, the students go out together in small sailing boats or kayaks to look for dolphins.

"We phone each other first before we go out in boats," Katie said. "You shouldn't do that alone. You have to look after yourself at sea. We don't often see dolphins. It's hard work and I get seasick sometimes. But I tell myself it's worth it to protect these beautiful animals."

2 Understanding the article

a) Make notes on what you learned about:

1 the west coast of Scotland
2 the WIDT
3 dolphins
4 the students of Castlebay Community School.

b) Use your notes to compare your ideas. Take turns.

3 EXTRA Our English lesson

Your parents ask you and your friend what you did in English today.
Tell your parents about the article on dolphins. Use your notes from 2 to explain the main points in German.

→ Workbook 2 (p. 60)

1 Looking for dolphins

a) Think of all the sounds you might hear if you were on the *Wee Lass*. Write them down. Then listen and check if you hear them.

b) Listen again. Say which of these things happened on the boat. Say what you can remember about them.
The Castlebay students …

listened to music | listened to dolphins | saw dolphins | swam with dolphins | got seasick | fell off the boat | took photos of each other | took photos of dolphins | got wet | arrived back later than planned

c) Would you like to go on a trip on the *Wee Lass*? Give reasons.

2 After the boat trip (Reflexive pronouns)

a) Finish the sentences with the right pronoun.

myself · yourself · himself · herself · ourselves · yourselves · themselves

1 When Iain got home, he made himself a cup of tea.
2 "I'm hungry," said Iain's dad. "Let's cook … something for dinner."
3 "Be careful with that knife, Dad," said Iain, "or you'll cut …"
4 "Too late," said his dad, "but I haven't hurt … badly."
5 When the food was ready, Iain and his dad got … something to drink.
6 "Shall we keep some food for Mum?", asked Iain. "Or will she look after …?"

b) In English, not as many verbs need a reflexive pronoun as in German.
Read the dialogue.
Decide where you need pronouns.

Mrs M: Sit [1]… down, Katie. You must be tired.
Katie: Don't worry [2]…, Mum. I feel [3]… fine.
Mrs M: You just relax [4]… Katie. Here's some soup. It's hot, so don't burn [5]….
Katie: Mmm, thanks. Delicious!
Mrs M: So you heard dolphins today. I can't imagine [6]… what they sound like.
Katie: Mum, they're amazing! And we really have to help them, because they can't help [7]…

➜ *GF 7.1: Reflexive pronouns (pp. 167–168)*
➜ **Workbook** *3–4 (p. 61)*

3 Katie and Iain help each other (*each other*)

TIP

They looked at …

themselves. | each other.

Make sentences with each other which show that Katie and Iain are good friends.

help give send phone invite buy miss argue with look after	parties presents texts homework

1 Katie and Iain help each other with their homework.
2 They usually phone each other at weekends.
3 They never …

➜ *GF 7.2: themselves or each other (p. 168)*
More help ➜ *p. 124* **Early finisher** ➜ *p. 131*
➜ **Workbook** *5 (p. 61)*

This is Scotland

The Highlands

Scotland has some of the world's most beautiful countryside. Maybe the best place to enjoy it is in the Highlands with their snowy mountains, green glens, wonderful lochs (one even with a monster!), and lots of wild animals.

Urquhart Castle, Loch Ness

Rival cities

Scotland's two main cities, only 60 km away from each other, have long been rivals.

Edinburgh, the capital, with its stunning historical centre, is a UNESCO World Heritage Site and home to the world's biggest arts festival.

Glasgow, the largest city and Edinburgh's "ugly sister", was once a centre of shipbuilding and other industries. These have declined, but the city now offers great museums and exciting nightlife.

National Gallery, Edinburgh, with the UK and Scottish flags

Cycle Arc Bridge, Glasgow

Traditions

Kilts are traditional clothing for men. They're worn at weddings and céilidhs or on fun nights out.

A **tartan** is the pattern on kilts and other clothes. It shows the family or clan of the man who is wearing it.

Bagpipes are played every day in towns and cities all over Scotland – by street musicians, at weddings, at Highland dancing and at many other events.

Shop window, Edinburgh

Street piper, Edinburgh

www Find out more about Scottish traditions.

Scotland and England

In 1314, the Scots defeated the English at Bannockburn. The battle is still celebrated in Scotland today.

In those days, the two countries were often at war. But in 1603, Scotland's King James also became king of England. A century later, the two countries formed the kingdom of Great Britain.

But the Scots have always seen themselves as a different nation. From the late 20th century, many Scots wanted to be independent again. However, in a 2014 referendum, 55.3% of the population decided that it was better to stay in the UK.

Bannockburn celebration, 2014

Compare Scotland with your region.
Think about the countryside and cities, traditions and important historical events.

→ Workbook 6 *(p. 62)*

1 Escape to … Scotland

a) Look at the film stills. Describe each one.
Take turns. Agree on captions for each still and write them down.

b) Watch the film and put your captions in the right order.

c) The film will be shown in four parts.
Your teacher will say which part each pair should watch.
Take notes while you watch your part.

d) Use your notes to write a short voice-over for your part of the film. You should:
- describe what the film shows, e.g.
  Here an old train is crossing a bridge.
- make a comment, e.g.
  I'd love to travel through Scotland by train.

Make sure your voice-over is not too long.

e) Join pairs who watched the other parts of the film.
Your teacher will play the whole film again.
Each pair reads the voice-over for their part.

f) Now watch a version of the film with a voice-over.
Compare your voice-over to the film's.
What else did you learn?

2 Making the film: Split screen and music

Partner B: Go to page 132.

Partner A:

a) Watch the film again (first version, without voice-over).
Take notes about where the film
- has a split screen
- shows one picture on top of another.

Think of why the film-maker does this. Make notes about your ideas.

b) Talk to your partner. Use your notes to say what you noticed about the split screen.
Then listen to what your partner tells you about music changes in the film.

1 Star performers

2 At the rehearsal

a) Say who these people are and how they feel:
Lewis · Sandra · Skye

Lewis is the boy we met ...

I think ...

b) Look at the first picture again. What do you think the play is about? What will happen next?

Write the next few lines of dialogue and stage directions.

3 Time for a chat

edinlew: Hey Ash! Are you online?

nightmaid: Hey Scottie! Yes, I'm free. Mum isn't home yet.

edinlew: I've just got back from rehearsal – wow, it was tough!

nightmaid: What happened?

edinlew: Skye started to cry. She said she didn't want to be in the play any more.

nightmaid: Skye? Your star perfomer? Did you tread on her toes again?

edinlew: No, she didn't come in on her cue. So Sandra gave her a hard time.

nightmaid: Sandra?

edinlew: Our director. She said we'd never get it right if Skye couldn't remember her cues.

nightmaid: What then?

edinlew: Well, they had a bit of an argument. Skye said it was too noisy backstage, so she couldn't hear the cue. Then Sandra told her that she had to concentrate – you know, this is for the Edinburgh Festival. It's not a school play. Stuff like that.

nightmaid: So did Skye leave then?

edinlew: No, she calmed down. I told her that Sandra was just nervous, that we were all nervous.

nightmaid: So *you* calmed her down! Hey, you're a hero.

edinlew: Well, I just told her that she was our star performer and that we needed her.

nightmaid: 👍 ★★★★★

edinlew: What's up in the Burren?

nightmaid: Not much. Mum said there would only be a few guests on Saturday's ride, so I wouldn't have to go with her. And Mike is going with her on the Sunday ride. So I'll be able to ride Raven along the beach at the weekend, and scare all the tourists!

edinlew: In your black clothes, on your black horse. They'll think you're a witch.

nightmaid: I'm not a witch – I'm a fairy. Witches ride broomsticks not horses, silly! Anyway, I'll fly off now. Mum is calling me. It's time for dinner. Bye!

4 Good friends?

a) What are the real names of *edinlew* and *nightmaid*? Explain how you know. Say what you know about them.

b) Say which of these sentences you think best describes the relationship between *edinlew* and *nightmaid*. Give reasons for your opinion.

1 They really like each other now.
2 They know a lot more about each other now.
3 Edinlew still talks, nightmaid listens.

I think sentence number … is the best description because …

Sorry, but I don't agree. In my opinion …

More help → p. 124 → Text File 8 (pp. 112–115)

5 Have a go

Report what *nightmaid* said to *edinlew*.

1 *I'm free.*
2 *Mum isn't home yet.*
3 *You're a hero.*
4 *I'm not a witch.*
5 *It's time for dinner.*

Nightmaid told *Edinlew* that
1 she was free.
2 her Mum wasn't …
3 he …
4 she …
5 it …

Looking at language

Look at sentence 1 to see how the verb changes when you report what somebody said. Then read the other speech bubbles and write the sentences in indirect speech. Say how the verb changes. You can check on p. 89.

	Direct speech	Indirect speech	
1 *Skye:*	*It's too noisy backstage.*	Skye said it was too noisy backstage.	Simple present > simple ...
2 *Lewis:*	*You're our star performer.*	Lewis told Skye that she ... their star performer.	...
3 *Skye:*	*I don't want to be in the play any more.*	Skye said that she ... to be in the play any more.	...
4 *Skye:*	*I can't hear the cue.*	Skye said that she ... hear the cue.	can't > ...
5 *Ashling's mum:*	*There will only be a few guests.*	Ashling's Mum said there ... only be a few guests.	will > ...

➔ *GF 8: Indirect speech (pp. 168–169)*

1 Skye said she was nervous (Indirect speech)

Imagine you're Lewis. Report to Ashling what these people said on the first night of the play.

Skye

I'm so nervous.

So many people will be there.

I have a funny feeling in my stomach.

Sandra

You look great in your costumes.

I'm really proud of you all.

I can't understand why everyone is so nervous.

We'll have a party on the last night.

Mr McCray

It's a great play.

I'll have to see it again.

I can't wait to see you on stage.

Skye said she was so nervous.
She said so ...

Sandra said we ...
She said she ...

Dad said ...

More help ➔ *p. 125* ➔ Workbook *7 (p. 62)*

2 Jana said she could speak Chinese (Indirect speech)

Work in groups of three.
Take turns to play A, B and C.

A: I can speak Chinese.
B: What did Jana say?
C: She said she could speak Chinese.

Use the sentences on the right.

I'm a Hertha fan.
I can speak Chinese.
I can't do my homework today.
There's a snake near the board.
I live in a palace.
Hamburgers cost 50 cents in the school shop.
Beyoncé is my friend on Facebook.
I'll be 18 on my next birthday.
It will be quite warm tomorrow.
Partner B can't hear very well.
These exercises are easy.
I like Scottish music.
Our teacher won't give us homework today.
The window is broken.

➔ Workbook *8 (p. 63)*

3 An interview about the internet and social media

a) Ask your partner these questions and write down his/her answers.

1 Can you use the internet at home? Are you allowed to use it whenever you want?
2 Do you use social media
  - on your home computer?
  - on your phone?
  - at school?
3 What is your favourite social media site?
4 Do you have a blog? What kind of posts do you write?
5 Do you chat online with your friends? When?
6 How often do you watch online videos?
7 Do you listen to music online? On what sites?
8 Which is your favourite online activity?
  - writing posts on a social media platform
  - watching videos
  - listening to music

b) Work with students from other pairs. Say what you learned about your partner in a).

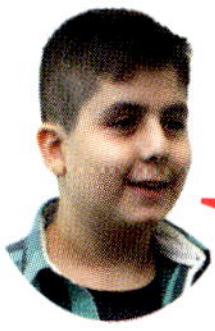

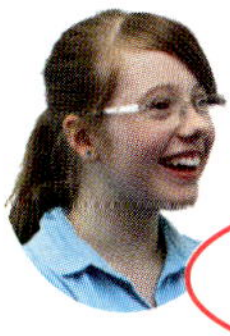

Early finisher → p. 131
→ Workbook 9–10 (pp. 63–64)

4 WORDS Music and entertainment

a) Start a table. Add words from the box under the right heading. Be careful! Some words don't go under any of the headings.

b) Add other words you know to the lists. Compare your list with a partner's.
More help → p. 125

c) Write five sentences about a musical event you have seen or would like to see. The 5 *Ws* (*When? Where? What? Who? Why?*) can help you to find ideas.

verbs	instruments	events	people
…	…	…	

band · bus · choir · chorus · +comedian · comedy · concert · drums · +entertainment · festival · flag · guitar · musical · musician · pedestrian · perform · piano · play an instrument · poster · rhythm · shop · show · sing (along) · singer · song · telephone

→ Workbook 11 (p. 64)

5 An arts festival in Dresden

You are visiting Dresden with a British friend. You hear a report on the *Elbhangfest*. Listen, then tell your friend what you could do there.

TIP
Concentrate on things that interest you and your friend and give information about them.

→ Workbook 12 (p. 65)

6 Study skills: A good presentation

The Western Isles Dolphin Trust works to protect dolphins. This page will help you to prepare and give a good presentation about a place, animal, river, … that needs protection in your area.

Preparing and giving your presentation

1 **Do your research.**
- Find out more about your place/animal/…
- Make notes on the points you want to talk about.

2 **Look up words you need in a *German-English dictionary*.**
- Explain the meaning of important words in your presentation on a handout – or write them on a transparency or the board.
- Don't just use the first translation you find.
- Make sure you find the right translation for your context.
  For example, what English word do you need for Beute in this sentence:

Das Reh ist die bevorzugte **Beute** des Luchses.

➜ *SF 6: German-English dictionaries (p. 142)*

3 **Write down your presentation and make notes on cards with numbers.**

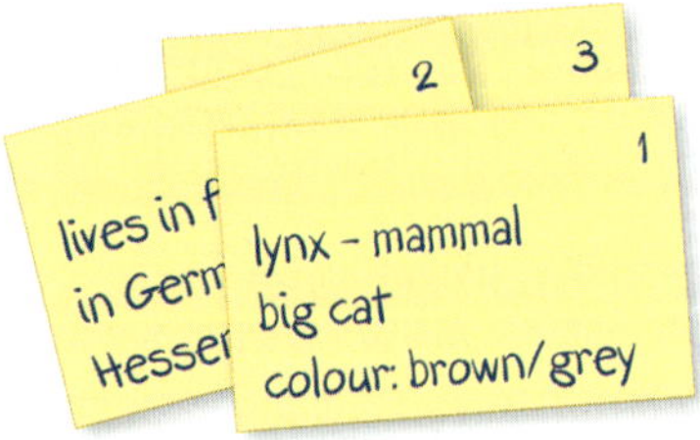

4 **Practise your presentation in front of a mirror, your family, a friend, …**

5 **Give your presentation.**
- before you begin, make sure you have everything ready (cards, handout, …)
- wait till your classmates are quiet then tell them what your presentation is about
- use your cards, but look at your classmates when you speak, not at your notes
- speak slowly, loudly and clearly
- finish your talk and ask for questions

➜ *SF 23: Presentations (p. 153)*
➜ Workbook *13 (p. 65)*

Beute
1. *(Diebesgut)* loot; haul; *(im Krieg)* booty; spoils *(of war) (pl)*; **reiche** *o.* **fette Beute machen** make a big haul; **eine Beute von mehreren Millionen Euro** a multi-million-euro haul
2. *(von Tieren; auch übertragen: Opfer)* prey; **leichte Beute sein (für)** be (an) easy prey (to/for)

The Eurasian lynx *(Lynx lynx)*

KEY VOCABULARY
lynx – Luchs
habitat – Lebensraum
coat – Fell
predator – Raubtier

Study skills

A good presentation
Für eine gute Präsentation muss ich Folgendes beachten:
– …
– …

➜ *SF 23: Presentations (p. 153)*

1 Learn how

You've learned different writing skills in this school year. Here you will learn how to choose which skills you need and how to combine them when you write a longer text.

2 Now write …

a) Decide what you're going to write about: you can write about a film, a game or a book. Or you can write a story.

b) Read the tips and choose the ones that might help you. Make notes on these tips. Then write a first draft of your text.

➜ Workbook *Wordbank 7*

3 … and revise

a) Read your text again carefully. Look at the tips you wrote down. Can you use them to improve your text more? Correct any grammar or spelling mistakes.

b) Give feedback. Read your partner's text and make notes. Take turns to make comments and corrections.

c) Think about your partner's feedback and what you've learned on this page. Decide what to change and write a second draft.

EXTRA Put together a class magazine with all the reviews for each member of your class.

➜ *SF 10: Good sentences (p. 144); SF 11: Structuring texts (p. 145); SF 12: Paragraphs (p. 145); SF 15: Revising texts (p. 147)*

➜ Workbook *14 (p. 66)*

TIPS - UNIT 2

1 Before you start writing, make a mind map or table to collect and organize your memories and ideas.
2 The 5 ***Ws*** (When? Where? What? Who? Why?) can help you to find ideas.
3 Start a new paragraph for every new idea.
4 Use a topic sentence in each paragraph. In the other sentences add details or examples.

TIPS - UNIT 3

1 Organize your ideas and plan your paragraphs.
2 Write your text. Remember to
- say what the text is about (first paragraph)
- use topic sentences in the body of the text
- find a good way to end your text.

3 Read your text. Check your topic sentence and decide if the paragraphs are in a good order.
4 Change the order of the paragraphs if necessary.

TIPS - UNIT 1

1 Use different adjectives (*bright, fantastic, dark,* …) to describe people, things and places – not just *good, bad* and *nice*. Use adverbs (quietly, slowly, …) for actions. Use *really, very, a bit,* etc. (*really slowly, very quietly, a bit dark*) to be more exact.
2 Use time phrases (*last week, tomorrow,* …) to tell your reader when things happened.
3 Use linking words (*and, but, because,* …) and relative clauses to link short sentences.

TIPS - UNIT 4

1 Use time markers to help your reader to see
- when something happened
- what happened first, second, etc.
- how much time passed.

2 Use time markers to link sentences.

Missing

Look at the pictures and say what the characters are thinking or feeling. Discuss what the pictures tell you about the story.

1

Lauren looked across the green field where the sheepdog trials were taking place. On the right, a mountain of brown heather and grey rock rose up. On the left, the field ended at the edge of a high cliff. Far below, she could see the dark waters of Loch Ness with the ruins of Urquhart Castle next to it. She wondered why there was no fence or wall at the edge of the field. That cliff was dangerous …
When it was Lauren's turn, one black sheep moved away from the group of four and stood next to some rocks at the edge of the cliff.

"I'll lose some points for that," Lauren thought. She could feel the tension in her arms and throat. She wanted to win this trial. She took a deep breath and gave a short whistle. Her black and white sheepdog, Shadow, raced off towards the black sheep. But Lauren could see that he was getting too near to the nervous animal. The sheep turned, panicked, and ran over the edge of the cliff. She imagined its body falling, falling, falling … then, while she watched in horror, Shadow followed it. He jumped over the rocks into the air. Lauren screamed "Shadow!!!"
In the bed next to her, Beth heard her sister make a strange noise: "Aaaahooww!" She reached over, touched Lauren's face softly with her fingers and whispered, "Wake up! You're having a bad dream." Lauren opened her eyes and looked at Beth. Then she sat up in bed and looked out of the window at the barn where the dogs slept. Shadow was in there, warm and dry. "But," she thought, "a dream like that could be a bad sign …"

2

Lauren got off the bus outside her school in Inverness. Two boys, Callum Macdonald and Ross Fraser, followed her. All three lived on farms in the same valley.
"Do you think your dad will beat Lauren at the trials on Saturday?" Callum asked Ross.
"Aye, of course he will," Ross answered with a smile. "Believe me, I know."
"How do you know?"
"Och, I just know."
"I think her dog Shadow can read her mind," Callum continued. "That's why they're such a good team."
"My dad has been a shepherd for 25 years. Lauren's just a wee girl."
"But she beat a lot of older shepherds last time," Callum said. "I think you're just jealous because you weren't good enough to get into the main trials."
"Don't be stupid. I'm not really interested in sheepdog trials any more. And anyway," Ross went on, "why do you care? I didn't know you liked Lauren. What's that all about, eh? I think …"
Callum pushed Ross away and walked quickly in through the school gates.

3

When Lauren got on the school bus the next morning, the seat next to Callum was empty, so she sat down next to him.
"Where's Ross?" she asked.
"He's not coming to school. His mother said he wasn't well," Callum told her.
"I feel ill too. I hate Thursdays."
"Aye, I'm sure you'd just love to stay at home with Shadow, right? And practise for Saturday's trials?"
"Aye," Lauren nodded, "but Mum and Dad wouldn't let me."

4

That afternoon, the school bus stopped at the farm gate and Lauren got off. Where was Shadow? She didn't understand. He was always there when she came home from school – he heard the bus and ran to the gate. She called his name but there was still no sign of him, so she started to walk slowly from the road to the farmhouse.
"He must be in the fields with Dad," she thought, but when she reached the house, she found her dad in the kitchen with her mum and sister.
No one knew where Shadow was.

5

When the sun went down at twenty past ten that evening, Lauren was still outside. She had walked around the whole farm and looked everywhere for Shadow. She was still walking and calling his name when her mum and dad came to pick her up.
"The poor girl's so worried," Lauren's mum said.
"I know, but it'll be dark soon," said her dad.
He opened the car window and called to his daughter: "Come on, Lauren. We'll have to go home now. We can look again in the morning."
Lauren looked at her dad, then down at the ground and burst into tears.

6

As they arrived at their farm gate, another car stopped – a police car. A policeman and a policewoman got out.
"It's not about our dog, is it?" Lauren's dad asked.
"Your dog?" the policewoman shook her head. "No, it's about Ross Fraser. Have you seen him? Has he been at your house today?"
"Ross? No. Why, what's happened?"
"He's missing."
Lauren opened the door and got out of the car.
"Ross wasn't at school today," she told the police officers. "His mum said he was ill."
"Aye," the policeman said. "He was at home in bed this morning but then he just, well, disappeared. No one has seen him since then."
Lauren's mouth fell open as she stared at the police officers. "My dog Shadow has disappeared too!"
"Is that right?" the policewoman asked. "OK, now tell us all about it."

7

From her window Lauren watched the lights on the mountain above the farm. About forty police officers and volunteers were looking for Ross in the dark night. She wanted to go too – maybe she would find Shadow up there – but no children were allowed. She watched until her eyes got heavy and the lights started to dance.
Then she was running through the heather. She saw something in front of her. It was running fast. It was Shadow, she was sure, but she couldn't reach him. She called him and suddenly, there he was, just a few metres away. He turned and barked, but the bark sounded wrong: bang, bang, bang.
Her mother shook her gently awake. Lauren opened her eyes.
"I knocked but you were asleep," her mother said. "They've found Ross. He's hurt his foot, but he's all right. And guess what … Shadow was with him!"

8

On Friday evening, Callum sat next to Ross's bed in the Ross Memorial Hospital.
"I see they named this place after you," he said.
Ross smiled but didn't say anything.
"So what happened?" Callum asked. "I thought you were ill in bed."
"Well, I wasn't really ill, you see … it was like this."
And he told Callum his story.

9

"And in second place, with 137 points, from down the road in Beauly, Lauren Reid, just 15 years old, with Shadow."

The crowd cheered, and Lauren and Shadow went to get their prize. Next came the winner, Mr Fraser, Ross's dad. He held up the trophy and then he spoke to the crowd.

"I know you've all heard that we had a bit of an adventure this week down in Beauly. My son Ross was missing – and Lauren's dog Shadow too. Well, Ross fell and hurt his foot out on the mountain and Shadow stayed with him till he was found in the middle of the night. Shadow and Lauren, thank you for that. And this morning, Ross told me a story. I'm not going to repeat that here, but what it means is that, actually, Lauren and Shadow are the real winners of the trial today. So this trophy here, Lauren … this trophy is yours."

Access to cultures

Sheepdogs are trained to help people with their work. Sheepdog trials test how well the people and the dogs work together. They take place all over the British Isles.

Talk about ways that animals help people with their work in your country.
Are there competitions like sheepdog trials?

1 Understanding together

a) Compare the ideas you had before you read the story with what really happens.

b) Give each part of the story a title, e.g. **1 A bad dream**.
Then think of two questions about each part and write them down.

c) Compare your titles with another pair. Then answer the other pair's questions. Make sure that you all understand the story.

2 Ross's story – Part 1

My Book: Write the story Ross tells Callum at the hospital. You could write about:

1 why Ross was out on the mountain
2 why Shadow was with him
3 how he hurt his foot
4 how he was found.

More help → p. 125

3 Ross's story – Part 2

a) Listen and take notes on what Ross tells Callum. Use points 1–4 from the last task. Compare your notes and agree on what happened.

b) Compare the story you have just heard with the story you wrote in 2.
Explain which you like better and why.

4 What would they say?

You choose Do a), b) or c).

What would these people say? Write one or two sentences. Find a partner who has chosen the same task and read out your sentences.

a) Lauren when she meets Ross at school.
b) Mr Fraser when he takes Ross home.
c) Ross when he next sees Shadow.

→ Workbook 15–16 (pp. 66–67)

Workbook Checkpoint (pp. 68–71)

Your task

A UK music channel is preparing a programme about the hobbies of young people.
They have asked viewers from around the world to send in their stories or film clips.
Interview someone who plays an instrument, sings in a choir, band, etc. <u>or</u> who has an unusual hobby.

You choose a) or b)

a) Make a poster about your interview and present it.

b) Make a film presentation about your interview.

Step 1

Brainstorm ideas about people you could interview. Discuss what questions you could ask.

Step 2

Write down your questions. Remember you will do the interview in the language of your interview partner.

2 Warum wolltest du Flöte spielen?
3 ...

3 Wann hast du mit deinem Hobby angefangen?
4 ...

Step 3

Do your interview. Take notes on the answers to your questions or record them.

Step 4

Take photos of the person and things they use, e.g an instrument, equipment for a hobby, etc.

<u>or</u>

Film the person and show them while they are playing an instrument, doing their hobby, etc.

Step 5

Prepare texts for your poster <u>or</u> a script for your film presentation.
Use your German notes to write your texts in English. ➜ SF 16: Mediation, (p. 148)
Use a dictionary to look up key words you don't know. ➜ p. 92, 6 Study skills, 2

Step 6

Put your poster together. Use text and photos.

<u>or</u>

Make a film presentation about your interview. Use some of the scenes you filmed.

Step 7

Give a presentation of your poster in class.
➜ p. 92, 6 Study skills

<u>or</u>

Show your film clip to the class.

Step 8

Use the checklist on the inside back cover to give feedback on one of the presentations or film clips.

Text 1 Underground etiquette

a) Look at the illustrations in each tip.
Describe the situation in each one.
Then listen to the rhymes.
For each rhyme, sum up the tip in one short sentence.

b) Choose your favourite rhyme.
Say why you like it.
Learn it by heart and say it to the class, or read it aloud.

---

yet [jet] aber **certainly** ['sɜːtnlɪ] sicherlich

c) Tips No. 2 and No. 5 are missing.
Say what you think they could be.
Think of as many tips as you can about how to behave on trains or buses.

d) Is it a good idea to use rhyme to give people tips about how to behave?
Give reasons for your opinion.
Write a rhyme for another tip.

destination [ˌdestɪˈneɪʃn] Ziel **plain** [pleɪn] deutlich, offensichtlich **delay** [dɪˈleɪ] Verspätung **rather** [ˈrɑːðə] ziemlich **please sb.** [pliːz] jm. eine Freude machen

Text 2

London shapes

a) Listen to the poems. Then read them aloud.

b) Think of London shapes you could write a poem about.

Tower Bridge! *A policeman's helmet.* …

c) My Book Choose one shape. Then write a shape poem.

---

whispering gallery *ein Ort, an dem sich Personen über eine große Entfernung in normaler Lautstärke unterhalten können*
spy [spaɪ] erspähen **gherkin** [ˈɡɜːkɪn] Gewürzgurke **steeple** [ˈstiːpl] Kirchturm **wind its way** [waɪnd] sich schlängeln
sweeping [ˈswiːpɪŋ] weit ausholend

Text 3

Jerry

by Laurence Harger and Cecile Rossant

Chapter 5 The magic hit

Paige walked along to the big COMPANY shop and set up her table in front of the shop window with all its adverts. ONE PHONE FOR THE WHOLE WORLD. NO MORE LONELY DAYS OR NIGHTS – WITH PERFECT PAL, YOU'LL ALWAYS HAVE COMPANY.

She put her sign on the table: Matches' Magic Show. Then she placed her hat for money in front of it and got everything else that she needed out of her bag: the cards, the coins, the small cups and larger boxes.

When she started on her magic routine, a few people stopped to watch: an old man with a walking stick, a young boy with his mother.

"Look, Mummy. She's doing magic like on TV!"

Soon five or six people, a small crowd, stood in front of her table. At the end of every trick the little boy clapped, the old man smiled kindly and a teenage boy in a bright blue jacket, with a COMPANY phone in his hand, shook his head and rolled his eyes.

"OK," Paige thought and gave him a hard look. "I know I'm not very good yet, you tosser[1], so why don't you just …"

Suddenly Paige felt that someone was standing behind her. She turned round quickly to see Knuckles. He was dressed as usual in an army pullover and trousers. He moved his face towards her and gave her a horrible smile. She saw the big gap in his front teeth and felt his hot breath on her face.

Knuckles pulled a five-pound note out of his trouser pocket and held it up.

"See this?" he said.

"Yes," Paige nodded at him. "It's a five-pound note."

"Right," Knuckles agreed. "I bet you a fiver[2] I can work out how you do your next trick. If I'm right, I win a fiver from you. If you win, you get this." He waved the money around for everyone to see.

Paige looked at the coins in her hat and said, "All right."

She took a pack of cards and spread them across her table so that everyone could see they were normal playing cards. She picked them up and began to shuffle[3] them. Then she held them out to Knuckles. "Pick a card," she said to him, "any card."

Knuckles picked a card from the pack.

"Now, don't let me see the card, but show it to everyone else, so they can see what it is."

As Paige went on with her trick she thought, "This is the easiest trick in the world, but I don't think Knuckles will get it …"

At the end of the trick, Paige placed one card after another on the table. "Not that one," she said. "Not that one. Not that one …"

Finally she looked up at Knuckles as she placed the Queen of Spades[4] on the table for everyone to see.

"Was that your card?" she asked. "The Queen of Spades?"

Everyone in the crowd began to clap and Paige smiled at the big boy in his army clothes.

Knuckles didn't smile back.

---

[1] **tosser** ['tɒsə] *(infml)* Vollidiot/in [2] **I bet you a fiver.** [bet], ['faɪvə] Ich wette mit dir um 5 Pfund. [3] **shuffle** ['ʃʌfl] *(Kartenspiel)* mischen [4] **Spades** [speɪdz] *(Kartenspiel)* Pik

"No," he said. "That wasn't my card."
The crowd booed him. "Don't be a cheat[1]," the old man said. "Give the young lady her fiver."
"Don't you call me a cheat," Knuckles threatened[2]. "She's the only cheat here."
"Cheat, cheat, cheat," the crowd began to chant and Knuckles went wild. He put his hands under Paige's table and threw it into the air. Her cards, her hat, coins and boxes flew everywhere. Suddenly everyone was shouting. The noise was so loud that all the customers[3], the shop assistants and a security guard[4] came out of the COMPANY shop to find out what was happening.
"Oi!" the guard shouted at Knuckles as he stood over Paige, who was picking her things up off the ground. "Get lost, will you! You're scaring our customers away."
"You get lost!" Knuckles shouted. He walked over, grabbed the guard's hat and ran off along the street. The security guard started to run after him but soon stopped. He turned back to Paige.
"Hurry up," he told her. "Pack up and get out of here. And don't let me catch you here again, or I'll call the police."
Then he spoke to the big crowd of customers outside the shop.
"Sorry about that, ladies and gents, but the show's over now, so if you'd like to go back inside …"
Slowly, the crowd of COMPANY customers started to move into the shop again. The security guard followed them, and as he entered the shop his hand flew up to his mouth.
"What the …? Who did that?"
Paige had all her things together again now and went to look in the shop too. Across the walls, and the counters, she could see slogans in big, bright red letters: "EVERY TEXT YOU SEND, EVERY CALL YOU MAKE, WE'LL BE WATCHING YOU! THE COMPANY" the slogans said. "YOUR PERFECT PAL IS THE COMPANY'S PERFECT SPY[5]!" And "DUMP[6] YOUR COMPANY PHONE! DO IT TODAY! THE GROUP"
A big smile spread across Paige's face. "Yes!" she said under her breath, clenched her fist[7] and started to walk away. She stopped when the teenager in the bright blue jacket stood in her way. He held out a five-pound note to her. She took it automatically.
"Here," the boy said, "you won this. That kid had no idea how you did that trick."
Then he turned round and walked quickly away before Paige could say a word. She just stood there and watched him with her mouth open. When he disappeared round a corner she looked down at the note in her hands. Next to the picture of the Queen was a telephone number and a smiley face.

a) Say …
- how Knuckles behaves towards Paige
- what Paige thinks when she sees the slogans on the walls of COMPANY

b) You've read one chapter of *Jerry*.
Say what you think the book is about.

---

1 **cheat** [tʃiːt] Mogler/in 2 **threaten sb.** ['θretn] jm. drohen 3 **customer** ['kʌstəmə] Kunde/Kundin 4 **security guard** [sɪ'kjʊərətɪ ˌgɑːd] Wachmann 5 **spy** [spaɪ] Spion/in 6 **dump sth.** [dʌmp] etwas wegwerfen 7 **clench your fist** [klentʃ] die Faust ballen

Text 4

A Liverpool street

PENNY LANE *(John Lennon and Paul McCartney)*

In Penny Lane there is a barber showing photographs
Of every head he's had the pleasure to know
And all the people that come and go
Stop and say hello

On the corner is a banker with a motorcar
The little children laugh at him behind his back
And the banker never wears a mac in the pouring rain
Very strange

Penny Lane is in my ears and in my eyes
There beneath the blue suburban skies
I sit and meanwhile back in

Penny Lane there is a fireman with an hourglass
And in his pocket is a portrait of the Queen
He likes to keep his fire engine clean
It's a clean machine

Penny Lane is in my ears and in my eyes
A four of fish and finger pies
In summer meanwhile back

Behind the shelter in the middle of a roundabout
A pretty nurse is selling poppies from a tray
And though she feels as if she's in a play
She is anyway

Penny Lane, the barber shaves another customer
We see the banker sitting waiting for a trim
Then the fireman rushes in from the pouring rain
Very strange

Penny Lane is in my ears and in my eyes
There beneath the blue suburban skies
I sit and meanwhile back

Penny Lane is in my ears and in my eyes
There beneath the blue suburban skies
Penny Lane

Penny Lane is the name of a Liverpool street near where two of the Beatles, John Lennon and Paul McCartney, grew up. In the song *Penny Lane*, the two young musicians describe the kind of people that they saw while they were waiting for a bus to take them into the city centre.

a) Read or listen to the song and make a list of the people, what they're doing and what else you learn about them.
barber
...
Say what other people you think might live in this part of town.

b) Think of a street you know where you can see lots of different people. What kind of people are they and why do they come to this street?

c) Tell your partner about the street you chose and the people you can see there.

barber ['bɑːbə] (Herren-)Friseur **pleasure** ['pleʒə] Vergnügen **mac** [mæk] Regenmantel **pouring** ['pɔːrɪŋ] strömend **beneath** [bɪ'niːθ] unter **suburban** [sə'bɜːbən] vorstädtisch **meanwhile** ['miːnwaɪl] unterdessen **hourglass** ['aʊəglɑːs] Sanduhr **fire engine** ['faɪər_endʒɪn] Feuerwehrauto **pie** [paɪ] Pastete **shelter** ['ʃeltə] Wartehäuschen **roundabout** ['raʊndəbaʊt] Kreisverkehr **nurse** [nɜːs] Krankenschwester **poppy** ['pɒpɪ] Mohn(blume) **tray** [treɪ] Tablett **(to) shave** [ʃeɪv] rasieren **customer** ['kʌstəmə] Kunde, Kundin **trim** [trɪm] Schnitt **(to) rush in** [rʌʃ_'ɪn] hineinstürzen

Text 5

Juggling with Gerbils

a) Listen to the poems. Then read them to yourself.

When you are called names, remember

If bullies mock and reject you
Repeat after the poet, please:
A cat's a wonderful creature
That does not converse with its fleas

Mr Ifonly

Mr Ifonly sat down and he sighed,
I could have done more if only I had tried
If only I had followed my true intent
If only I had done the things that I meant
If only I had done the things that I could
And not simply done the things that I should
If only a day had lasted a year
And I had not lived in constant fear
Mr Ifonly sat down and he cried:
I could really have lived if only I had tried!
Now life has passed me by and it's such a crime,
Said Mr Ifonly who had run out of time

The Panther's Heart

Although he still pads about behind
The bars of his solitary cage,
Although he still looks up nightly
At the moonstruck mountains
And the falling snow,
The panther's heart
Stopped long ago.

call sb. names jn. beschimpfen **mock** verspotten **reject** [rɪˈdʒekt] zurückweisen **flea** [fliː] Floh **mean** beabsichtigen **fear** [fɪə] Angst **run out of time** keine Zeit mehr haben **although** [ɔːlˈðəʊ] obwohl **pad about** herumtappen

My Neighbours' Rabbit

On the wall between my neighbours' garden and mine
a rabbit is sitting, shivering with cold.
They've been away some days now.
They've left out water and dry food
(though the rain's put paid to that).
What they haven't left behind is love.
They've asked no one to call in,
to stroke it, to make sure it's OK.
Having made it dependent upon them
they've abandoned it.
I take it from the wall,
feed it some apple, feel
how warm it grows, a furry volcano,
as warm as my absent neighbours are cold.
I marvel at how many sizes
the human heart comes in.
Some hearts have room inside them for a hutchful of rabbits,
some are so small
not even one rabbit would fit inside.
Perhaps my neighbours possess such hearts –
hearts that keep on shrinking,
that grow smaller and smaller until finally
nothing will fit inside, not even
the breath of a solitary rabbit.

b) Say which poems are about
 – how cruel people can be
 – unhappy people
 Which poems give the reader advice?
 Give reasons for your answers.

c) Say which poem you like most and why.

The poet and writer **Brian Patten** was born in Liverpool in 1946. He left school at 15 and worked for a local newspaper, where he wrote articles on pop music.
In the 1960s he was one of the group of three "Liverpool Poets" (the others were Adrian Henri and Roger McGough). The "Liverpool Poets" wanted to make poetry more popular in everyday life. In 1967 they published a book of poems called *The Mersey Sound*, which became a bestseller.
Brian writes for adults and children. He often reads his poems on stage. The poems above are from *Juggling with Gerbils*, a book of poetry for children which came out in 2000.

put paid to sth. etwas zunichtemachen **stroke** [strəʊk] streicheln **dependent upon sb./sth.** [dɪˈpendənt] von jm./etwas abhängig **abandon** [əˈbændən] im Stich lassen **furry** [ˈfɜːrɪ] kuschelig **marvel at sth.** [ˈmɑːvəl] staunen über etwas **hutchful of** [ˈhʌtʃfʊl] Käfig voller

Text 6 *Finn McCool*

The legend of Finn McCool, an Irish giant, tells how Finn builds a bridge or causeway between Ireland and Scotland so that he can fight a Scottish giant. There are two versions of this legend. In the one you read about on page 67, the two giants fight in the middle of the causeway. Finn is the winner, and the Scottish giant runs home as fast as he can. On his way he pulls up all the stones and destroys the bridge. He is so afraid of Finn that he never wants to fight him again.
The second version of the legend tells a different story. You can read it below.

Long ago, there was a giant called Finn McCool. He lived on the northern coast of Ireland with Oonagh, his wife. At 54 foot[1], he was half as tall as the tallest oak tree. He was, people said, the tallest giant in the British Isles.
Finn was strong too. He could lift rocks the size of elephants and throw them for 50 miles and more. People said he was the strongest giant in the whole of the British Isles.
And Finn was handsome[2]. He had thick yellow hair that shone like gold in the morning sunshine. His nose was as noble as the nose of a king, and his eyes bluer than the blue, blue sea between Scotland and Ireland. Nowhere in the British Isles was there a giant more handsome than Finn, people said.

❖

One morning, as Oonagh was preparing breakfast, Finn called to her and spoke:
"I forgot to tell you, but I'll be away for a few days."
"And where are you going?" Oonagh asked.
"To Carlingford. The giant Ruscaire has challenged me to a fight."
Oonagh frowned. "You could say no."
"Are you mad?" said Finn. "If I didn't accept a challenge, people would think I was afraid. They might even think Ruscaire is stronger than me."
"Would that matter[3]?" Oonagh asked.
"Would that *matter*? Of course it would matter. Anyway, I'll only be gone for a few days."
"Exactly," said Oonagh. "A few days this week, a few days next week. Week in, week out, you walk from one end of Ireland to the other. And why? To fight with other giants! Well, I'm tired of it, Finn McCool. You're like a little boy. It's time you stopped fighting and grew up."
"Oonagh," said Finn. "People say I'm the strongest giant in the British Isles. I have a reputation[4], and I mean to defend it."
"There are other ways to defend a reputation, Finn McCool," Oonagh replied.
"You can keep them to yourself," said Finn. "*I* don't want to know." And he picked up his sword and his club[5] and walked out of the house.

❖

When Finn arrived in Carlingford, Ruscaire was waiting for him. They fought for three days. On the first day, they fought with clubs. On the second day, they fought with swords. And on the third day, they fought with their bare hands.
"All right, Finn, you win," said Ruscaire, as he lay face down on the ground with Finn's knee pressing against his back. "But there'll be another day."
"There will!" said Finn. "Another day, another fight, another victory[6]."
With that, he left Ruscaire and made his way home.

❖

[1] **54 foot** [fɪə] 54 Fuß groß *(ca. 16,5 m)* [2] **handsome** [ˈhænsəm] gut aussehend [3] **Would that matter?** Wäre das schlimm?
[4] **reputation** [ˌrepjʊˈteɪʃn] Ruf [5] **club** Knüppel [6] **victory** [ˈvɪktərɪ] Sieg

When Finn got back to the northern coast, it was already dark. Oonagh was fast asleep. Finn climbed into bed and, soon, he was dreaming of the battles he had fought and the victories he had won. Then suddenly, in the early hours, he was torn from his sleep by a terrible roar:

"Finnnnn … Finn McCool," cried a voice like an erupting volcano. "Finnnnn …"

Oonagh woke up too.

"Is that thunder?" she asked.

"No", said Finn. "It's somebody calling me."

"Finnnnn …" roared the voice.

A moment later, there was a loud bang outside. Finn ran to the door. In front of the house he saw a huge rock with a message carved[1] into it. He read it out loud:

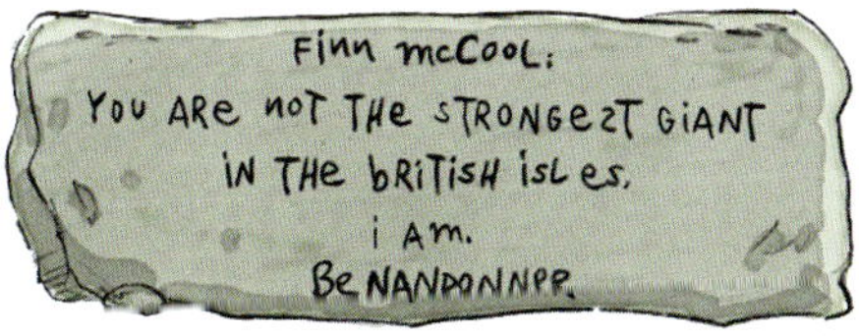

"Benandonner – the Scottish giant!" said Finn. "He *can't* be stronger than me."

"Well," said Oonagh. "With a voice like thunder that carries across the sea, he must be quite big. And if he's big, he's probably quite strong. And who knows? He might be a handsome fellow, too."

"I must challenge him to a fight," said Finn.

"Must you really?"

"Of course I must," growled[2] Finn. "But first I'm going to finish my sleep."

And with that, he went back to bed.

❖

The next day, Finn carved a message into a rock:

Then he hurled[3] the rock over the sea to Scotland. Before long, a rock with Benandonner's answer came flying through the air. Finn caught it in one hand and read out loud:

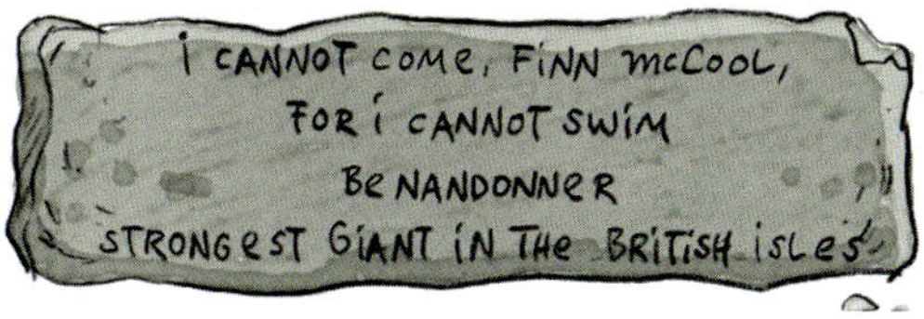

"Well," said Oonagh. "That solves that problem."

"It solves nothing," shouted Finn. "Do you really believe that he cannot swim? In truth, he is afraid. He wants to call himself the strongest giant, but without a fight."

"Let him," said Oonagh. "It does no harm[4]."

"He's bluffing, said Finn, "but I will call his bluff[5]. Of that you can be sure."

"I'm sure you know best what to do, Finn McCool," Oonagh sighed. "And now, if you'll excuse me, I'll have to go. King Cormac has invited me to lunch."

❖

When Oonagh returned from lunch with the king, she could hardly believe her eyes. In front of her house was a pile[6] of rocks 40 foot high, and at least a mile long

"Finn!" she called angrily. "What in heaven's name have you been doing?"

"Collecting rocks," Finn replied.

"I can see that," said Oonagh "but I don't want to have a huge wall of rocks in front of my house."

Finn smiled. "They'll be gone soon. Don't worry."

For the next six days, Finn walked all over Ireland, collecting the biggest rocks he could find.

With each day, the pile became longer and higher.

"Finn," cried Oonagh. "I thought you said the rocks wouldn't be here for long."

"They won't be," Finn answered.

"What are you going to do with them?"

---

1 **carved** [kɑːvd] gehauen 2 **growl** [graʊl] knurren, brummen 3 **hurl** [hɜːl] schleudern 4 **It does no harm.** [hɑːm] Es schadet nichts. 5 **call sb's bluff** [blʌf] jn. auf die Probe stellen 6 **pile** [paɪl] Stapel, Haufen

"I'm going to build a causeway, Oonagh," Finn explained. "Between Ireland and Scotland, so that Benandonner can come over here and accept my challenge."

Once Finn had collected enough rocks, he began to build the bridge to Scotland. One after the other, he hurled the rocks into the sea and day by day the bridge grew until finally it was complete.

"So," said Finn to Oonagh, "you'll be pleased to see that the pile of rocks in front of the house has disappeared. It now forms a causeway across the sea to Scotland."

"Aye," said Oonagh with a smile. "The Giant's Causeway."

"And now," said Finn, "I'll tell Benandonner that he can cross the water." He picked up a rock and carved a message into it. Then he threw the rock across the sea to Scotland.

❖

It was a fine day. Finn stood on the Irish side of the causeway, waiting for Benandonner to arrive. In the distance[1] he could hear footsteps, each as loud as a clap of thunder. Then suddenly, the Scottish giant came into view. Finn shuddered[2]. "He must be 75 foot!" he thought.

Quickly, he picked up his sword and his club and hurried back to his house.

Oonagh was surprised to see him.

"Have you beaten Benandonner already?"

"There's no time for joking, Oonagh. "I wouldn't have a chance against Benandonner. He's huge. And he'll be here any minute. What can I do?"

"You aren't afraid of a Scottish giant, Finn McCool?" Oonagh asked.

"Of course not," Finn replied. "It's just … er …"

"Never mind[3]," said Oonagh. "Take this."

"A bonnet[4]?" said Finn in surprise.

"Yes, a bonnet. Now put it on your head and lie down on that bed over there."

Finn did as Oonagh said. Oonagh then fetched some blankets and covered Finn with them. Then she went to a cupboard and took out a rattle[5].

"Hold this in your hand," she said.

Finn did as he was told. Moments later there was a loud knock on the door.

❖

Oonagh opened the door and looked up. Benandonner was indeed much taller than Finn, and probably much stronger. But there was nothing handsome about him at all. His red stringy hair fell over a face which was covered in pimples the size of apples. His eyes were greener than poison[6] and his huge nose was like a parrot's beak. Through his open mouth Oonagh could see a long row of sharp, crooked, yellow teeth.

"Good morning, sir," said Oonagh. "And what can I do for you?"

"My name is Benandonner," said the giant. "I'm looking for Finn McCool."

"Benandonner!" said Oonagh. "Finn is expecting you. He's out now, but he'll be back soon. Won't you come in and sit down while you're waiting?"

Benandonner came in and took a seat.

"I hope you don't mind if I work at the stove[7]," said Oonagh. "I'm making the baby's breakfast," she added, pointing to Finn in the bed in the corner.

"That's a fine big baby," said Benandonner.

"He is indeed." Oonagh replied. "And just like his father. Finn is very proud of him, of course."

"He must be," said Benandonner.

---

[1] **distance** ['dɪstəns] Ferne [2] **shudder** ['ʃʌdə] erschaudern [3] **Never mind.** [maɪnd] Mach dir nichts draus. [4] **bonnet** ['bɒnɪt] Haube [5] **rattle** ['rætl] Rassel [6] **poison** ['pɔɪzn] Gift [7] **stove** [stəʊv] Herd

"Anyway," said Oonagh. "I'm making steak and pancakes. Would you like some yourself?"

"Yes, please," said Benandonner.

At the stove, Oonagh made two huge pancakes. Into the second one she threw a handful of stones. When it was cooked, she put it on a plate and gave it to Benandonner. Then she took the other pancake and began to feed it to Finn."

"Ouch!" cried Benandonner.

"What's the matter?" Oonagh asked.

"I've just broken a tooth," said the giant.

"On a pancake so soft?" cried Oonagh. "Oh, dear! I *am* sorry. But don't worry, I'm sure you'll enjoy your steak."

Oonagh went back to the stove. With a sharp knife she cut a pocket into one of the steaks and pushed a plank[1] of oak into it. Then she put it on a plate and gave it to Benandonner.

"Thank you," said the giant. "It smells delicious."

Benandonner closed his mouth on the steak and his sharp teeth sank into the plank of oak."

"Mmmmmmmmmmmm," he whined[2].

"I'm glad you're enjoying it," Oonagh smiled.

Benandonner shook his head wildly and pointed at the steak between his teeth. It was clear that he couldn't open his mouth.

"Good heavens," said Oonagh. "Your teeth are stuck – in such a tender piece of steak! Sure it was no problem at all for Baby Finn."

Benandonner pulled and grunted[3] until finally he managed to free his teeth. Then he put the steak back onto his plate. "I'm sorry," he said, "but I can't eat this."

"No need to worry," said Oonagh. "I can give it to Baby Finn for his lunch."

"What a strong little baby he is," said Benandonner.

"Yes," said Oonagh. "He's going to be just as strong as his father when he grows up."

Benandonner stood up.

"Well," he said. "It doesn't look as if Finn will be back very soon."

"You don't want to go, surely?" cried Oonagh. "Finn will be here very soon, and he'll be disappointed[4] if he doesn't see you."

"To be honest[5]," said Benandonner, "I have some important business back in Scotland. I really must be on my way."

With that, he ran out of the house as fast as his feet could take him.

❖

"Well," said Finn, "You saved me."

Oonagh smiled. "Why don't we go out for a walk? You can show me the causeway you built. I've not seen it yet, you know."

They walked down to the sea.

"So where is it?" Oonagh asked.

"I don't believe it," said Finn. "Look, there's the beginning of the causeway," he said, and pointed to the Giant's Causeway as we know it today. "But the rest has disappeared. Benandonner must have destroyed it on his way back to Scotland."

"He must be scared of you, Finn," said Oonagh. "Very scared."

a) Work in threes. Each partner takes one character – Finn, Oonagh or Benandonner. Choose three adjectives to describe your character. Explain your choice.

b) Explain why Benandonner destroyed the Giant's Causeway.

c) You choose Do i) or ii).
   i) Draw a picture of a scene from the story.
   ii) The legend explains the origins of the Giant's Causeway, but it also has a moral. Explain what you think the moral is.

[1] **plank** [plæŋk] Brett [2] **whine** [waɪn] heulen, jammern [3] **grunt** [grʌnt] grunzen [4] **disappointed** [ˌdɪsəˈpɔɪntɪd] enttäuscht [5] **honest** [ˈɒnɪst] ehrlich

Text 7

The Titanic

Crossing the Atlantic

When people travel to New York from Frankfurt or London today, they usually go by plane. The flight takes between six and nine hours. But in the early 1900s, there were no planes. Back then, millions of people left Europe and crossed the Atlantic Ocean to go to America. They all crossed the Atlantic by ship. It took about a week.

In 1911, a new steamer[1] was built in Belfast for a Liverpool company, White Star Line. It was bigger and more comfortable than any other ship in the world. That ship was the Titanic, and in April 1912 it was ready for its first transatlantic journey.

early 20th century
➤ about 7 days

early 21st century
➤ 6 to 9 hours

1 How has travelling across the Atlantic changed since the early 20th century? Use phrases from the box.

> today / these days / in the early 1900s / back then / …
> It takes/took … hours/days/weeks … to go by plane/ship …
> The journey by plane/ship takes/took …

A big ship

The White Star Line wanted people to believe that their ship was not only the biggest, but also the strongest and safest[2] ship in the world. They named it Titanic. Newspapers called the ship "unsinkable". The Titanic was like a big hotel on water with restaurants, a swimming pool and comfortable rooms for first and second-class passengers[3]. It also had space for hundreds of third-class passengers who couldn't pay much for a ticket. This was a time when large numbers of emigrants were leaving Great Britain and Ireland and other parts of Europe for political and economic[4] reasons. They were hoping for a better life in America.

The Titanic's dimensions

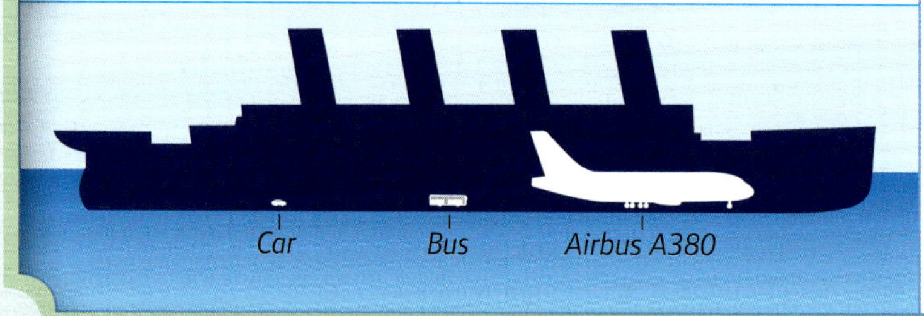

The Titanic in numbers

Length	269 m
Width	28 m
Height	53 m
Passengers	about 2,200

2 Look at the text, diagram and table above. Talk to a partner about the Titanic's dimensions. The phrases in the box can help you.

> This diagram shows … / gives information about …
> From the diagram you can see that …
> The Titanic was (about) as big as three …
> It was … metres long/wide/high.
> It could carry … passengers.

[1] **steamer** ['stiːmə] Dampfschiff [2] **safe** [seɪf] sicher [3] **passenger** ['pæsɪndʒə] Reisende(r) [4] **economic** [iːkə'nɒmɪk] wirtschaftlich

3 Read *The Titanic's first and last journey* and sum up the events in 5–6 sentences. Compare with a partner.

The Titanic's first and last journey

On 10 April 1912, the Titanic left Southampton for New York with about 2,200 people on board. On the journey, there were warnings from other ships about icebergs, but the captain didn't take them seriously[1]. On the night of 14 April, people suddenly saw an iceberg in front of the ship, but it was already too late. The ship hit the iceberg. The collision left six small holes in the ship's hull[2]. Water began to fill the bow[3] of the ship. At first the people were calm because they didn't believe that the Titanic could sink. But soon everyone knew that the ship was in trouble.

The Titanic only had enough lifeboats for about half of the people on board. The captain said that women and children must go first. Many lifeboats left the ship only half full because no one knew how many people they could take.

Two and a half hours later, the Titanic broke into two parts, filled with water and sank. There were still over 1,000 people on board. In the end, about 1,500 people drowned or froze to death in the ice-cold water.

Illustration of the sinking Titanic

The ship's captain, Edward Smith

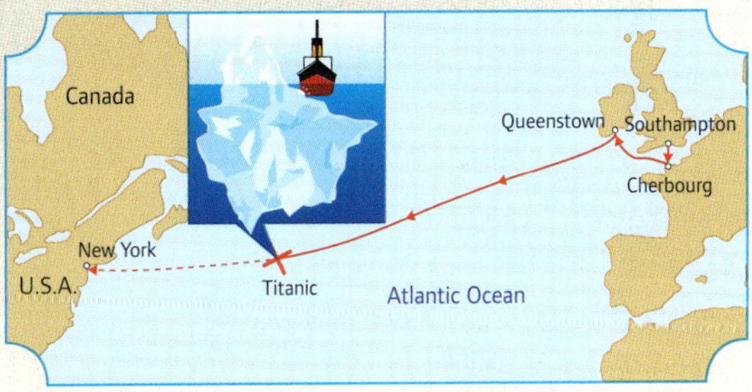

Diagram: Position of the Titanic and the iceberg

Passengers

Most of the passengers on the Titanic were travelling third-class. They were not allowed to visit the parts of the ship that were for first-class and second-class passengers only.

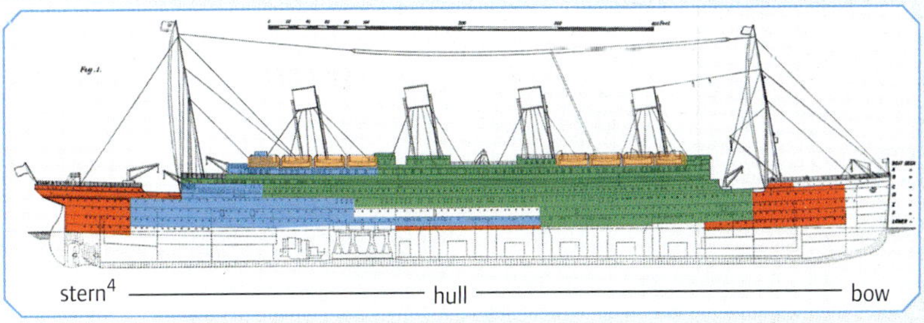

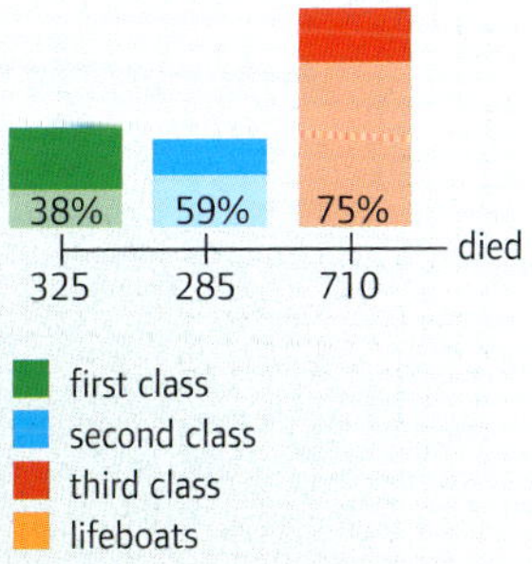

Diagram of the classes and the lifeboats of the Titanic

4 Look at the diagrams. Say why you think so many third-class passengers died. The language box can help you.

The green/blue/red part is …
…-class passengers were near / far from the lifeboats.
… passengers were in the first/… class.
… per cent of the first-class/… passengers died/survived.

[1] **take sth. seriously** ['sɪərɪəslɪ] etwas ernst nehmen [2] **hull** [hʌl] Rumpf [3] **bow** [baʊ] Bug [4] **stern** [stɜːn] Heck

Text 8

The Off-side Trap[1] by Mary Colson

a) Describe the pictures on pp. 112-115. Say why you think the characters look different in grey than in colour.

b) Read the play. Choose three examples of where the characters say something different from what they think.
Compare your examples.

EXTRA Act out the play.

List of characters

Maxine, Maxine 1 *(her thoughts)*
Paul, Paul 1 *(his thoughts)*
Dave *(Paul's friend)*
Shelly *(Maxine's friend)*

Setting

Football club disco.

Maxine really fancies Paul and he quite likes her. They're thirteen years old. He's hugely into football – she knows nothing about it but has to pretend she does in order to make conversation. While their thoughts are being spoken, Maxine and Paul are experiencing awkward silences, looking ill at ease and searching for something to say. There is a prevailing embarrassed awkwardness throughout their dialogue. ➔ *Text in English and German (p. 197)*

Maxine	Hi, Paul.
Maxine 1	OK, done it. Made contact.
Paul	All right, Maxine.
Maxine 1	He doesn't sound very pleased to see me.
Paul	What you up to?
Paul 1	Tell me I didn't say that – talk about stating the blinking obvious![2]
Maxine	Oh, you know, nothing much.
Paul	Right.
Pause.	
Maxine 1	Come on, come on. Say something.
Paul 1	What do I say now?
Pause.	
Paul	So … um …
Maxine	*(at the same time)* What did you … Oh, sorry.
Maxine 1	Oh no – how clumsy[3] was that?
Paul	No, you first.
Paul 1	Come on, man, be cool.
Maxine	I was just going to ask what you did today. Did you play?
Maxine 1	That's better. More confident. Dead cas[4].
Paul	Yeah. Well, I was sub[5].
Paul 1	I sound like a half-wit! I haven't said a normal sentence yet. What's she going to think?
Maxine	I see. Whereabouts did you play, then? On the wing?

[1] **off-side trap** ['ɒfsaɪd træp] Abseitsfalle [2] **Talk about stating the blinking obvious!** ['blɪŋkɪŋ] *(infml)*, ['ɒbvɪəs] Musste ich etwas so Offensichtliches sagen?! [3] **clumsy** ['klʌmzɪ] ungeschickt [4] **dead cas** [ded 'kæʒ] *(infml)* (= **casual**, ['kæʒjʊl]) total locker [5] **sub** [sʌb] *(infml)* (= **substitute**, ['sʌbstɪtjuːt]) Ersatzspieler/in

Maxine 1 Did that sound technical enough? Do you even have wings in footie? I wish I'd listened to our Stuart when he used to go on.

Paul No, I went on for[1] Dave in midfield.

Paul 1 A sentence! At last!

Maxine Good match, was it?

Maxine 1 Smooth[2].

Paul Not really, we lost 3–1.

❖

Maxine Oh, sorry.

Maxine 1 Why'd I have to put my foot in it[3]?

Paul 1 Oh God! What now?

Maxine So do you play in a league or something?

Maxine 1 This is awful.

Paul Yeah, but it's nothing great or anything. It's just a local Saturday league.

Paul 1 Is she as bored as I am?

Maxine 1 This has to be the most boring conversation I've ever had.

Maxine So do you want to dance? I like this one.

Maxine 1 Anything to avoid[4] talking!

Paul I'm not much good at dancing, actually.

Paul 1 I can't dance at all – nightmare[5]. I'm not having Gav and that lot laughing at me – no way.

Maxine Neither am I[6] really – Shelly always says I've got one dance that I do whatever the song is. I don't think that's true but she says it is.

Maxine 1 I really like this one – I might just go and join Shell and Rach anyway if he won't dance with me.

❖

Maxine What sort of music do you like?

Maxine 1 He must like some music – even if it's heavy metal.

Paul I like rap, you know, Eminem and such.

Paul 1 That sounds pretty cool.

Maxine Isn't he the one who's been done for[7] attacking somebody?

Maxine 1 Oh, I can't stand[8] rap! Even heavy metal would've been better than rap.

Paul Yeah, but that's just the way it is in America – you just have to accept it.

Paul 1 She must think I'm pretty cool now.

Maxine What? You have to accept people killing each other?

Maxine 1 I can't believe he's saying this.

Paul 1 Oh here we go – what is it with girls and violence[9]? It's not as if it's really happening, is it?

Paul It's just the way it is in the States, Maxine, it's the law[10] of the gun[11].

Paul 1 She'll soon see I'm right.

Maxine I'm sorry, Paul, but I don't think it's fun to point guns at people or beat them up. It's barbaric.

Maxine 1 How naïve can he be?

[1] **go on for sb.** für jn. eingewechselt werden [2] **smooth** [smuːð] cool [3] **put my foot in it** ins Fettnäpfchen treten
[4] **avoid** [əˈvɔɪd] vermeiden [5] **nightmare** [ˈnaɪtmɛə] Albtraum [6] **Neither am I.** Ich auch nicht. [7] **be done for doing sth.** wegen etwas bestraft werden [8] **stand sth.** etwas ertragen, etwas aushalten [9] **violence** [ˈvaɪələns] Gewalt [10] **law** [lɔː] Gesetz
[11] **gun** [gʌn] Schusswaffe

Paul 1 — Oh God.

Paul — So you don't ever watch anything violent at all?

Maxine 1 — No, I don't.

Paul — I expect you watch *EastEnders* and *Neighbours*[1] and stuff though, don't you?

Maxine — Yeah, who doesn't?

Paul — What about the explosions they had at the car yard[2] and all the slagging off[3] they do?

Maxine 1 — What's he getting at? What's he saying?

Maxine — Well, yeah, but it's only a story, isn't it? It's not real.

Paul 1 — Is she thick[4] or what?

Paul — But it's supposed to[5] reflect society[6] so it seems like it's real.

Maxine — I suppose so[7].

Paul 1 — At last! She's starting to get the picture. Cor, took her a while.

Maxine 1 — I don't get this. Does he think it's real people? And when you think about it, they've had murders[8], crimes[9], assaults[10], drugs – all the things that happen in real life.

Maxine — Yeah, so?

Paul — So it's not just in America that it's violent – it's here too, it's just we don't have as many guns.

Paul 1 — Made it!

Maxine 1 — Wow, that's a really thoughtful thing to say.

Maxine — You've got a really mature[11] attitude[12] towards things, Paul.

Paul 1 — I'm in here.

Maxine 1 — He's so nice and mature – not like those silly boys who talk about gangs and guns all the time.

Paul — Yeah, well, you've got to, haven't you?

Paul 1 — Go on, my son!

Maxine — Yeah.

Maxine 1 — He's gorgeous[13].

Paul 1 — She's all right is Maxine. Dave'll be dead jealous[14].

Maxine 1 — I've got to tell Shell, she'll be so envious[15]!

Maxine and Paul — I've just got to . . .

Paul — Oh, sorry. After you.

Maxine 1 — He's such a gentleman!

Maxine — I was just going to ask you if you could hold my coke whilst I go to the loo.

Maxine 1 — How embarrassing[16]! I hate my bladder[17].

Paul — Oh yeah, sure.

Maxine — I'll be back in a sec.

Paul — Right.

Maxine leaves Paul and walks over to Shelly who's standing near the girls' toilets. Paul remains where he is and his friend Dave comes over.

Maxine — Oh, Shell, I spoke to him! He's absolutely gorgeous!

Shelly — What'd he say? It looked like you were getting on[18] really well.

---

[1] ***EastEnders, Neighbours*** *beliebte britische TV-Serien* [2] **yard** [jɑːd] Hof [3] **slag sb. off** [slæg] *(infml)* jn. runtermachen [4] **thick** [θɪk] dumm [5] **be supposed to do sth.** [səˈpəʊzd] etwas tun sollen [6] **society** [səˈsaɪəti] die Gesellschaft [7] **I suppose so.** [səˈpəʊz] Das nehme ich an. [8] **murder** [ˈmɜːdə] Mord [9] **crime** [kraɪm] Straftat, Verbrechen [10] **assault** [əˈsɔːlt] Körperverletzung [11] **mature** [məˈtjʊə] reif [12] **attitude** [ˈætɪtjuːd] Einstellung, Haltung [13] **gorgeous** [ˈɡɔːdʒəs] fantastisch, traumhaft [14] **dead jealous** [ˈdʒeləs] *(infml)* total neidisch [15] **envious** [ˈenviəs] neidisch [16] **embarrassing** [ɪmˈbærəsɪŋ] peinlich [17] **bladder** [ˈblædə] Blase [18] **get on** sich verstehen

Maxine: Oh, you know, we just talked about telly and stuff.

Shelly: Well? Are you going out with him or what?

Maxine: Well he hasn't asked me yet but …

Dave: How's it going with the lovely Maxine, then?

Paul: All right, actually. She is pretty stunning[1], isn't she?

Dave: I'll say, she's a babe. What were you talking about? You've been chatting for ages.

Paul: Oh, you know, footie, telly – the usual sort of stuff.

Dave: Get in[2] there, my man!

Paul: Shut up[3], Dave, she's coming back.

Dave: See you later, Romeo.

Maxine: Hiya.

Maxine 1: He looks different somehow.

Paul: Hi.

Paul 1: Dave's right; she *is* a babe.

Maxine: Thanks for holding my drink.

Paul: No worries.

A beat[4].

Paul: So … uh … Do you want to dance? I'm not very good, like I said, but if you want to …

Paul 1: Oh God, please say no!

Maxine: No, that's OK. I'm happy just talking.

Paul: Well, if that's what you want, that's fine with me.

They smile happily at each other.

Maxine: I think we're really similar, don't you?

Paul: Yeah, I suppose we are.

Maxine: I mean, we've got similar friends, like the same sorts of things, music and stuff. We even hang around the same places.

Paul: Yeah.

A beat.

Um … Maybe we could um … go out some time – to the cinema – um … There's a really good new film out – the one with Leonardo DiCaprio and um … Jennifer Aniston, I think.

Maxine: I'd love to go.

Maxine 1: Leo's so sweet!

Paul: Great.

Paul 1: Jennifer Aniston's such a stunner[5].

Maxine: I've wanted to see it for ages.

Paul: But it's only been out about a week.

Maxine: Oh, well, I've read loads about it – it sounds really good.

Maxine 1: I can't believe he wants to see this film. Most lads hate Leo.

Paul: Yeah, I think it's good to see all sorts of different films.

Maxine: Mm. When do you want to go?

Paul: How about tomorrow night?

Maxine: Great.

Maxine 1: Fantastic a night with Paul and Leo!

Paul 1: I can't believe it – I get to see Jennifer Aniston and Maxine at the same time! And I get to see Leonardo DiCaprio looking a right idiot pretending to be an ugly midfielder – I bet he can't even kick the ball straight. I'm a genius[6]!

Maxine 1 and Paul 1: Cool.

---

[1] **stunning** ['stʌnɪŋ] atemberaubend [2] **Get in!** *(infml)* Mach doch! [3] **Shut up!** [ʃʌt‿'ʌp] Halt die Klappe!
[4] **beat** [biːt] Pause [5] **stunner** ['stʌnə] *(infml)* Wucht [6] **genius** ['dʒiːnɪəs] Genie

Part A Practice

1 WORDS City holidays

p. 12

Can you find the verb-noun combinations in the snakes?

2 REVISION Your holidays (Simple past)

p. 12

Make questions for a partner.

Did you	stay at home / go away? make new friends? do any sports? visit friends/family?

What did you	do/see/play there?
Where did you	go/stay?
How did you	travel/get there?

Go back to c) on p. 12.

4 REVISION A message from London (Simple past or present perfect?)

p. 13

Complete Emily's message with the correct tenses. Look closely at the signal words for the **simple past** or the **present perfect**. They can help you to choose the right tense.

Hey Amelia,
Hi from London. I [1]... (arrive) on Friday evening (with Mum and Dad), so we [2]... (already do) a few things. Yesterday morning we [3]... (go) up to the roof of a building where we [4]... (have) a great view. On the roof we [5]... (meet) two boys – Luke and Mo. They [6]... (give) us some tips. Luke [7]... (tell) us about a carnival at a place called Notting Hill.
After lunch we [8]... (visit) St Paul's Cathedral and then we [9]... (take) a red London bus to Hyde Park.
It [10]... (be) beautiful there, and it's really huge. [11]... you [12]... (ever be) there?
There are lots of places that we [13]... (not be) to – like Buckingham Palace, so I [14]... (not have) tea with the Queen yet! (LoL) And we [15]... (not visit) any museums yet, but Mum has plans!
[16]... you [17]... (enjoy) your trip to France last week? What [18]... (be) the weather like there? In London it [19]... (not rain) yet! Hugs, Emily xxx

Part B Practice

1 REVISION How can I get there?

p. 18

b) You're at Leicester Square tube station.
Ask the way to other places on the map.
You can use these phrases to answer your partner's questions.

Go along … Street.
Cross … Road near the …
Turn left between the … and the …
Turn right behind the church/…
Go past the hotel/…
Go straight on until you get to …

How can I get to Covent Garden Market, please?

Walk along Cranbourn Street. Then turn right into …

Part C Practice

2 I've been living here … (Present perfect progressive)

p. 21

Complete Mo's sentences with *for* or *since*.

I'm a Londoner. I've been living here …

1 I'm a Londoner. I've been living here … I was three.
2 I like languages. I've been learning German at school … three years.
3 My sister Mishal loves music. She's been singing in a band … over a year.
4 I have a blog. I've been writing posts … last March.
5 My friend Luke and I love cricket. We've been playing in the same team … a long time.
6 Luke is a big fan of Notting Hill Carnival. He's been going there … he was twelve.

3 How long … ?

p. 21

b) Swap profiles.
Ask and answer like this:

How long have you been living in Berlin?

I've been living in Berlin for thirteen years.

How long have you been going to … Gymnasium?

Here are some example answers to questions about hobbies and sport.

I've been

learning the piano
playing the drums
playing computer games
playing football
going swimming
doing judo
collecting comics
taking photos

for
ten months.
a long time.
three years.
my whole life.

since
April.
Year 5.
last summer.
I was little.

Lead-in

2 A long journey

p. 28

c) Listen again. Say how the girl feels and how she shows her feelings when:

- her parents speak about her when they think she's asleep.
- her mother asks her if she wants to stop for lunch.
- her mother wants to listen to the weather report.
- her father asks her to explain some Welsh words.
- her father asks if she'd like to go on a train.
- her mother asks her the name of a lake.

You can find ideas in the box.

- She feels angry/bored/sad/unhappy.
- She speaks loudly / in an angry voice.
- She shouts.
- She makes a funny sound.
- She says she doesn't want to …
- She says her mother/father can/can't/should …

Part A Practice

1 WORDS Jobs

p. 31

b) Write sentences for the other jobs in the box.

1 … in films or plays or TV shows.
2 … draw or paint pictures.
3 … work on a farm.
4 … are doctors for people's teeth.
5 … make furniture.

actor · +architect · artist · +astronaut · carpenter · dentist · farmer · +hairdresser · +musician · +painter · scientist

2 REVISION Tom thinks he'll be an astronaut (*will*-future)

p. 31

a) What do you think you'll be or do in the future? Copy the chart and add ideas.
Then make appointments with three classmates and interview them.

You can use these ideas about your future.

live in another town/country · be a star · have a family · become a farmer/teacher/… · go on a bike tour across the Sahara · travel to Mars … · be rich and famous

What we will be/do	Me	Partner A	Partner B	Partner C
in 5 years				
in 10 years				
in 20 years				

Part C Practice

2 If I were a police officer … (Conditional 2)

p. 36

Think of six jobs. Write a sentence about what you could or would do in each job.
If I were a police officer, I'd catch lots of thieves.
If I became a cameraman, I could film action movies.

Match the ideas in the boxes to make more sentences.

If …	I would / I could …
architect	be nice to my students.
artist	grow vegetables in my fields.
carpenter	paint pictures of famous people.
designer	build the highest building in the world.
hairdresser	play songs in the pedestrian zone.
farmer	make a desk for my room.
musician	make beautiful clothes.
teacher	cut my friends' hair for free.

Workbook 1–2 (p. xxx)

3 What would happen if …? (Conditional 2)

p. 37

a) Make notes like this. You can use the ideas from the list.

Idea	+	–
run away to London	see Mo and Luke	no place to live
shout at Dylan		
walk alone in the hills		
invite classmates home		
stop speaking Welsh		
ask a teacher for help		

- laugh at her
- shout back
- feel sad
- lose her way
- be more friendly
- become her friends
- give her some good tips
- have time to think
- not learn the language
- not feel at home in North Wales

Text

2 A fair punishment

p. 42

a) What do you think about Dylan and Emily's punishment?
Read the statements below. Choose the five that you agree with most and write them down.

FAIR BECAUSE …
- It's very dangerous on the roof.
- They knew that they weren't allowed to go up.
- They're lucky that they didn't fall.
- Mrs Grant was right to be angry. She's responsible for a lot of students.
- Mrs Grant didn't send Dylan and Emily home. They only had to wash the floors.

NOT FAIR BECAUSE …
- The kids only looked at the stars and sang. They didn't do anything dangerous.
- The door to the roof was open.
- Mrs Grant didn't listen when Dylan tried to explain why they were on the roof.
- It isn't right to tell children to clean toilets.
- It would be enough to wash the corridor floors.

Part A Practice

2 WORDS John Lennon was a famous musician

p. 48

a) Match six of the people from the column on the left with things that they did on the right to make six sentences like this: John Lennon was a famous musician who wrote *Imagine* and other songs.

John Lennon was a famous musician		**wrote** *Imagine*.
Cate Blanchett is an Australian actor		**built** the Eiffel Tower.
Galileo Galilei was an Italian scientist		**designed** the *Reichstag* building.
Gustave Eiffel was a French engineer	… who …	**founded** the Boy Scouts.
Norman Foster is a British architect		**invented** the thermometer.
Robert Baden-Powell was a British soldier		**played** in *The Hobbit*.
Steffi Graf is a German sportsperson		**won** the Wimbledon Singles.

3 REVISION Crossword clues (Relative pronouns)

p. 48

Use these ideas and relative pronouns to write clues for the crossword.

1 thing • you see • sky at night
– A thing which you can see in the sky at night.
2 person • works • with you • class
– A person who works with you in class.
3 black thing • people use • make fire
4 person • sings
5 things • people wear • nose • see
6 thing • you use • clean the floor
7 Welsh boy • likes • Beatles
8 something • at the end • arm
9 thing • takes people • upstairs
10 animal • swims • river or sea
11 white animal • you see • countryside

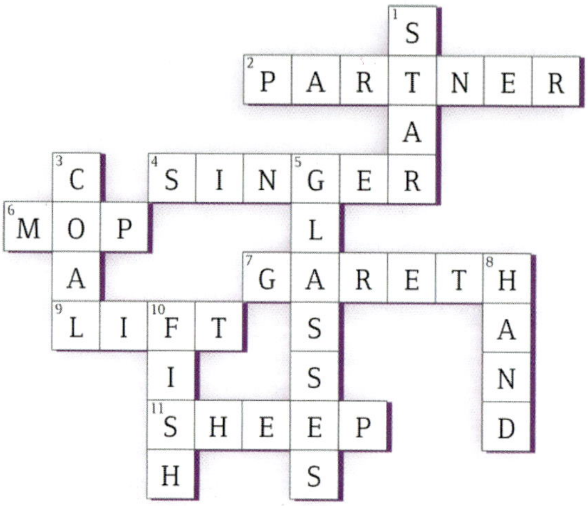

5 Gwen's photos (Contact clauses)

p. 49

Decide if you can make sentences **without** a relative pronoun or if you have to use which or who.
TIP: Never leave out who or which if they come directly before the verb.

1 These are the shops ~~which~~ Gareth wanted to see.
2 This is the shop which sells John Lennon sunglasses.
3 These are the sunglasses ... Gareth bought there.
4 This is one of the ferries ... crosses the Mersey.
5 This is the Chinese gate ... we saw on our walk.
6 These are the kids … gave us tickets for the match.
7 This is the shop ... they work in.
8 This is the fruit ... looks like green bananas.

Part B Practice

2 They aren't worn at Igbo festivals (Passive: simple present)

p. 54

Correct the wrong information in each sentence and complete the sentences.

1 Goat face masks are worn at Igbo festivals.
– No, they aren't worn at Igbo festivals.
They're worn at Ogoni festivals.

2 Goat face masks are worn by young women and girls.
– No, they ... by young women and girls.
They ... by boys and young men.

3 An Udu is made of wood.
– No, it ... of wood. It ... of clay.

4 Udus are played by men and older boys.
– No, they ... by men and older boys.
They ... by women.

5 Djembe drums are also called water pot drums.
– No, they ... water pot drums.
Udus ... water pot drums.

6 The djembe is used every day.
– No, it ... every day. It ... at special events.

7 The djembe is played with sticks.
– No, it ... with sticks. It ... with bare hands.

4 Oliver Twist was written by ... (Passive with *by*)

p. 55

a) Make sentences like the ones in the examples.
Use the verb in the correct form and choose the correct name on the right.

Oliver Twist • write • Charles Dickens
The 2014 World Cup • win • Germany

Oliver Twist was **written** by Charles Dickens.
The 2014 World Cup was **won** by Germany.

Romeo and Juliet Treasure Island	write
The 1966 World Cup The 2010 Eurovision Song Contest	win
Imagine *We Are The Champions*	sing
Hadrian's Wall The Eiffel Tower	build
The Mona Lisa	paint

Lena (Germany) · Emperor Hadrian · England · Gustave Eiffel · Queen · John Lennon · Robert Louis Stevenson · William Shakespeare · Leonardo da Vinci

Part C Practice

2 Study skills: Ordering and structuring topic vocabulary

p. 58

c) Add these words to a copy of the diagram in b).
They can go under these headings, but you decide where to put them exactly.

STADIUM
goal
penalty area
refreshment stalls
terrace
ticket office

PEOPLE
cards
defender
flag
foul
gloves
midfielder
penalty
shin guards
shirt
shorts
socks
song
striker
substitute
watch

COMPETITIONS
FA Cup
FIFA World Cup

Part A Practice

2 REVISION Travelling to other countries (Modal verbs)

p. 68

a) Complete these rules for travelling. Use can, can't, must, mustn't or needn't.

If you travel	to the UK or Ireland,	you	must	show your ID card or passport.
	to Spain,		...	change money.
	by plane,		...	carry a knife in your bag.
	to the USA,		...	pay in euros.
	to Austria,		...	take your pet.
	to India,		...	get a visa.

Part B Practice

2 You'll have to revise ... (*have to, be able to, be allowed to*: Future)

p. 72

On the left are some questions from a new classmate about next week's English test. Match the answers (a–h) to the questions and complete them with will or won't.

1 Will I have to revise for the test?
2 What about dictionaries?
3 And electronic dictionaries, mobile phones?
4 Will I have to arrive early?
5 Will we be able to work together?
6 Will I be allowed to sit where I want.
7 Will I have to bring my own paper for the test?
8 Will I be able to leave when I'm finished?

a) No, you ... be able to get it from the teacher.
b) No, you ... be allowed to use dictionaries.
c) No, you ... be allowed to use things like that.
d) No, you ... have to sit where the teacher says.
e) No, you ... have to work on your own.
f) Yes, you ... have to revise the last unit.
g) You ... have to be there just before the test.
h) You ... have to stay until everybody is finished.

3 I won't be able to go swimming

p. 72

a) Choose one of these places to visit.

Ireland · a small island in the Atlantic · Greenland · the moon · Mallorca · Berlin · Africa

Choose advantages and disadvantages from the lists on the right or use your own ideas.

the moon:
\+ good view of the earth:
I'll be able to have a good view of the earth
\- no swimming: I won't be able to ...

Advantages	Disadvantages
see wild animals	too cold to have fun
beautiful countryside	dangerous alone
cheap	dirty
friendly local people	expensive
good for swimming	full of tourists
good for walks	too hot to have fun
good music	lonely
good view of the earth	far from home
museums	no swimming
practise my English	rainy
tasty food	mobile phone problems

Part C Practice

1 Pronunciation (Consonants)

p. 75

b) Listen. Which of the words in brackets do you hear? Write it down.

1 the red ... (card/cart)
2 with a red ... (card/cart)
3 a lovely ... beach (white/wide)
4 lovely ... beaches (white/wide)
5 all the different ... in Dublin (sides/sights)
6 on different ... in the match (sides/sights)
7 put it in the ... of the car (back/bag)
8 put your ... in the car (back/bag)
9 on your own two ... (feed/feet)
10 time to ... her (feed/feet)
11 then it went ... (bang/bank)
12 we went to the ... (bang/bank)

1 card
2 cart
3 ...

4 REVISION I had a weird dream (Simple past)

p. 76

Complete Chloe's message. Use the simple past of the verbs in brackets.

Chloe Carr Last night I [1]... (have) this weird dream. You and I [2]... (be) on our way up a rocky hill with other kids from our class. Our German teacher Miss Kunzel [3]... (be) already at the top. She [4]... (look) angry and [5]... (shout) at us to hurry. I [6]... (not want) to get into trouble, so I [7]... (run) up the hill like mad. When I [8]... (reach) the top, I [9]... (look) around but you [10]... (not be) there. Then I [11]... (see) you at the bottom of the hill. You had fallen all the way down. I [12]... (call) you, but you [13]... (not answer). You [14]... (be) hurt, and I was sure you had broken your leg. Lewis, tell me you're OK.

1 had
2 were
3 ...

Text

1 The ride across the Burren

p. 79

Say who the riders are in each part of the story and what they talk about.
Find these key words in the story:

PEOPLE	
Ashling	old people
Lewis	Ashling's mother

TOPICS	
Burren	cold
Great Famine	big holes
rain	Dad's ashes

Use the words in sentences when you talk to your partner.

Part A Practice

3 Katie and Iain help each other *(each other)*

p. 85

TIP

The sentences below show that Katie and Iain are good friends. Complete the sentences with verbs from the box and each other.

give · help · send · miss · phone · argue · invite

1 Katie and Iain help each other with their homework.
2 They usually … at weekends.
3 They never … with …
4 They always … to their parties.
5 They … texts every day.
6 They … presents on their birthdays.
7 They … when they're on holiday with their families.

Part B

4 Good friends?

p. 89

b) Say which of these sentences you think best describes the relationship between *edinlew* and *nightmaid*.

1 They really like each other now.
2 They know a lot more about each other now.
3 Edinlew still talks, nightmaid listens.

Sorry, but I don't agree. In my opinion …

I think sentence number … is the best description because …

Give reasons for your opinion.
Look at the information in the boxes below.

What Lewis thought about Ashling:

The owner's weird daughter looks just like a VAMPIRE. Black hair, black clothes and a very white face! SCARY! (p. 74)

Her black hair and clothes, her black horse and the dark clouds behind her made her face seem whiter than ever. Lewis suddenly felt cold. (p. 78)

Ashling asked him a question: "So, what's Edinburgh like?" "Edinburgh?" Lewis said in surprise. (p. 79)

"She's just trying to scare me," (p. 78)

What Ashling thought about Lewis:

He was probably chatting or playing a game … I hope he doesn't talk too much tomorrow. (p. 74)

As they went up the hill, Lewis talked and talked. Ashling thought he would never stop. (p. 78)

He talked all the way to where Ashling's mother and the others were waiting. This time, Ashling was surprised that she didn't mind listening. (p. 79)

Part B Practice

1 Skye said she was nervous (Indirect speech)

p. 90

Imagine you're Lewis. Report to Ashling what these people said on the first night of the play. You always need to change the verb. Often you need to change the pronoun too, e.g. I → she.

Skye said she was so nervous. She said so many people ... be there. She said ... ... a funny feeling in ... stomach.	Sandra said ... ... great in ... costumes. She said ... ... really proud of ... all. She said ... ... understand why everyone ... so nervous. She said we ... have a party on the last night.	Dad said ... ... wait to see ... on stage. He said it ... a great play. He said ... ... have to see it again.

4 WORDS Music and entertainment

p. 91

b) Add more words from this box to the lists you started in a). Add any more that you know. Compare your lists.

verbs	instruments	events	people
...	...	...	

act · actor · artist · audition · author · cameraman · carnival · cheer · dance · dancer · director · disco · drum · drummer · drums · edit · film · fun park · guitar · juggle · juggler · model · New Year's Eve · parade · piano · play · reader · recorder · sleepover · star · street artist · theatre · winner · writer

Text

2 Ross's story – Part 1

p. 96

Write the story Ross tells Callum at the hospital. Here are some ideas, but you can use your own too.

1 I was out on the mountainside because I wanted to
- kill/sell/hurt/… Shadow.
- find a doctor because I felt so ill.
- write Lauren a love-letter because I'm jealous of Callum and I want Lauren for myself.

2 Shadow was with me because
- I stole him from the farm.
- he likes me and enjoys long walks in the countryside.
- he wanted to leave the farm and live somewhere else.

3 I hurt my foot
- because it was dark.
- because Shadow bit me.
- because the Loch Ness monster bit me.

4 They found me when
- Shadow barked and told the volunteers where we were.
- I phoned the police on my mobile.
- I was taking the Loch Ness monster to the police station.

Hidden words

p. 12, 3 REVISION Have you ever …?

a) Copy the grid.

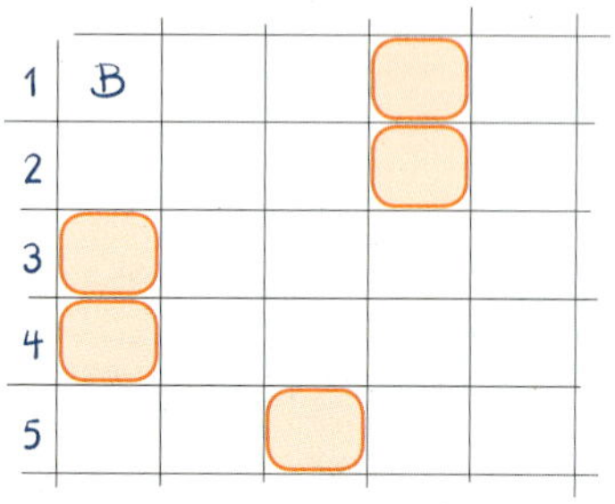

Write in the simple past of these verbs.

1 BEGIN
2 CHOOSE
3 DRIVE
4 HEAR
5 THROW

Use the letters in the orange boxes to make the name of a famous London building.

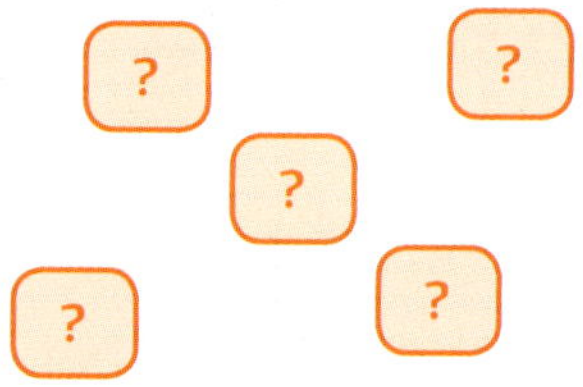

b) Copy the grid.

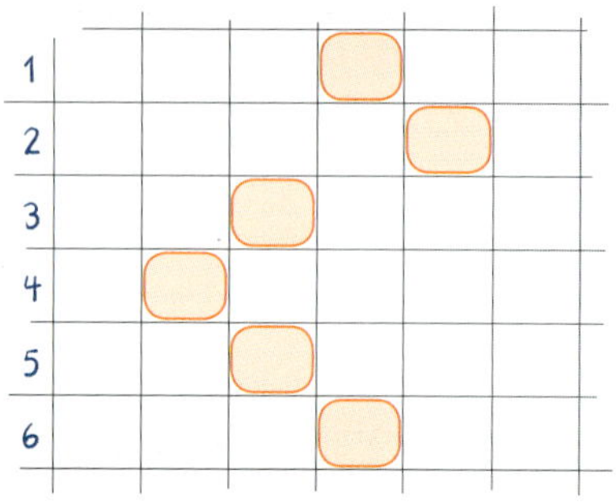

Write in the past participle of these verbs.

1 AGREE
2 BECOME
3 CHOOSE
4 DRIVE
5 JUMP
6 PLAY

Use the letters in the orange boxes to make the name of a game.

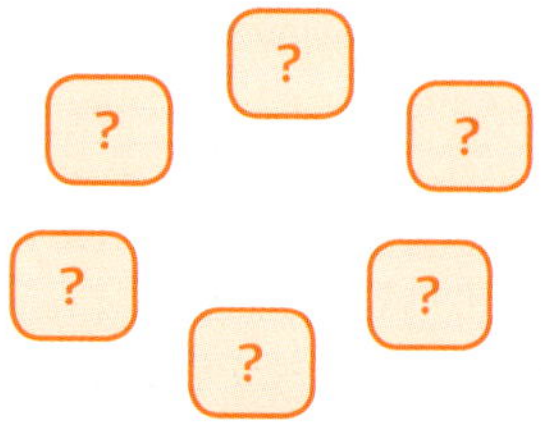

True or false?

p. 21, 3 How long …?

Read the black sentences. Then decide if the green sentences are true or false.
Correct the false sentences.

1 We moved here in 2010. Our neighbours moved here one year after us.
a) Our neighbours have been living here since 2009.
b) We have been living here longer than our neighbours.
c) Our neighbours have been living here for two years.

2 I got up at 7 o'clock and had breakfast at 8. It started raining during breakfast.
It's 3 o'clock in the afternoon now and it is still raining.
a) It has been raining for 8 hours.
b) It has been raining since 7 o'clock.
c) It has been raining since breakfast.

3 Mrs Adams got to the bus stop at 10:10. Mrs Bell got there 5 minutes before Mrs Adams.
When Mrs Crown got to the bus stop, nobody was waiting there.
After 10 minutes Mrs Bell came. It is now 10:15.
a) Mrs Crown has been waiting the longest.
b) Mrs Bell has been waiting for the bus since 10 o'clock.
c) Mrs Crown has been waiting for 15 minutes.

Answers p. 250

Word games

p. 31, 3 REVISION If I don't go to be

Do a) or b).

a) Find the fourth word

1

music	musician
science	???

2

guitar	instrument
table	???

3

cloud	cloudy
???	rocky

4

farmer	farm
teacher	???

5

drive	car
???	plane

6

carpenter	furniture
???	pictures

7

hairdresser	hair
???	teeth

8

April	spring
October	???

9

shoe	foot
???	hand

b) Words from a Welsh village

A village in Wales has the longest place name in Europe:
Llanfairpwllgwyngyllgogerychwyrndrobwllllantysiliogogogoch.
It also has a shorter name: *Llanfairpwll*. Make as many words as you can from the shorter name.

Number memory game

p. 39, 3 Making a video

These numbers are all in Philip's report on page 38.
Can you remember what they are?
Match them to the phrases on the right.

13 2 1,085

10 2 59

24 6

- the number of students in the class
- the time they started the walk
- the walk through the forest in hours
- the walk in kilometres
- the climb to the summit in metres
- the time the students reached the summit
- the time they arrived at the hostel
- the number of chocolate bars they ate

Strange answers

p. 48, 2 WORDS John Lennon ...

Gareth, Gwen and Morgan are walking through Liverpool. Gareth is listening to music. So he can't hear the others very well and gives some strange answers.

Gareth thinks Gwen said: "What are you listening to?"

Read these dialogues. Say what Gareth thinks Gwen and Morgan said.

1 *Morgan:* Who's your favourite Beatle?
Gareth: I don't really like any of our teachers.

Gareth thinks Morgan said: "..."

2 *Gwen:* When are we meeting the others?
Gareth: Back at the hostel.

...

3 *Gwen:* Do you like it here?
Gareth: What a silly question. You know I live in Bangor.

...

4 *Morgan:* I'm thirsty.
Gareth: Don't be silly. You're only sixteen.

...

5 *Gwen:* Take your earphones out!
Gareth: I'm not shouting – you are.

...

What am I?

p. 49, 5 Gwen's photos

Try and answer these puzzles. If you need help, match them to the answers below.

1 I'm a place that begins with P and ends with E and has thousands of letters.
2 I'm a five-letter word which becomes shorter if you add two letters.
3 I am something people answer, but I never ask them questions.
4 I am something everyone has. I go up but I never go down.
5 I am something you can't use until somebody breaks me.
6 I am something that has a neck but no head.

A egg | B phone | C bottle | D short | E post office | F age

Answers p. 251

The right words

p. 68, 2 Travelling to other countries

Do a) or b).

a) Country words

Match a word in a yellow box to a word in a green box.

coast
travel
currency
president
mayor
queen
navy

crown
pound
city
cliff
republic
passport
ship

coast — cliff
currency — ...

b) In English-speaking countries

Choose the best word to finish the sentence below.

perfect *polite* *poor* *practical* *pretty* *purple*

When you visit English-speaking countries, it's important to be ... and friendly.

Now do this quiz to find out what kind of person you are.
How would you answer in these situations? Choose a), b) or c).
Then work out your result on page 251.

1 A: Thank you for your help.
You: a) OK.
b) That's OK.
c) You're welcome.

2 B: Have a good weekend.
You: a) Thank you. You too.
b) I will.
c) Thanks.

3 C: What would you like to drink?
You: a) I want a glass of water.
b) Can I have glass of water?
c) I'd like a glass of water, please.

C: Here you are.
You: a) That's a very small glass.
b) Thanks.
c) OK.

4 D: Hello, can I help you?
You: a) Yes. Where is the post office?
b) Yes, please. Can you tell me where the post office is?
c) I want to find the post office.

D: Go along this road and it's on the left.
You: a) Thank you very much.
b) Is it?
c) OK.

5 E: Are you feeling tired?
You: a) What do you think?
b) Yes, I am a little tired actually.
c) Of course I am. I've been walking for hours.

6 F: Sorry I'm late.
You: a) I've been waiting for 20 minutes.
b) That's OK.
c) Don't worry – I've only just arrived.

The right verbs

p. 72, 3 I won't be able to go swimming

a) First choose the correct verb for phrases 1–8.

1 *hear / listen* to the radio	1 listen
2 *put / take* off your coat	2 …
3 *do / make* your homework	
4 *carry / wear* a bag	
5 *drive / ride* a motorbike	
6 *make / take* photos	
7 *say / tell* your friends	
8 *clean / wash* your hair	

b) Use letters from the correct verbs to make the name of a country.

1 last letter	liste(n)	N
2 first letter	…	
3 second letter		
4 first letter		
5 third letter		
6 second letter		
7 third letter		
8 third letter		

When is Tina's birthday?

p. 76, 6 At the farm in the Burren

Complete this text with the correct prepositions and you will find out when Tina's birthday is. Use at, in or on.

Tina's birthday isn't in the shortest month of the year. It isn't in one of the longest either. That means it must be [1]… April, June, September or November. But when is it? Her birthday isn't [2]… the autumn, so it must be [3]… the spring or the summer. When Tina was 'sweet sixteen' she had a big party. She didn't have one the year before because her 15th birthday was [4]… a Thursday, and [5]… Friday morning she had a test at school. She couldn't have a party [6]… the weekend because her father had planned dinner in a restaurant [7]… Friday evening to celebrate her mother's 40th birthday. And her mother had already organized a big party for her friends [8]… Saturday. But this year Tina started planning very early. She decided to have a garden party because the weather is usually good [9]… her birthday. And it doesn't get dark very early. The party started [10]… 5 o'clock [11]… the afternoon and finished late [12]… night. The last friends left [13]… 4 o'clock [14]… the morning!

Now you should know the month, but what date is Tina's birthday? Is it [15]… the 5th, 6th, 7th or 8th? Count how many times you used the preposition ***on*** and you will know! And if you need a bit more help, the month and the date are the same!

Answers p. 251

Work it out

p. 85, 3 Katie and Iain help each other

Do a) or b).

a) Are you good friends?

Complete these questions. The scrambled letters will help you to find the missing verbs.

Do you and your best friend
1 ... each other every weekend?
2 ... each other's birthdays?
3 ... to each other about problems at home?
4 ... or ... each other every day?
5 ... each other ... at Christmas?

Mere berm
ESE
KEASP
pen the tox
spy beer Nuts

b) Where do they live?

Copy the map of the street.

Then read the text and work out where A, B, C, D, E and F live.
Write the letters on your drawing of the map.

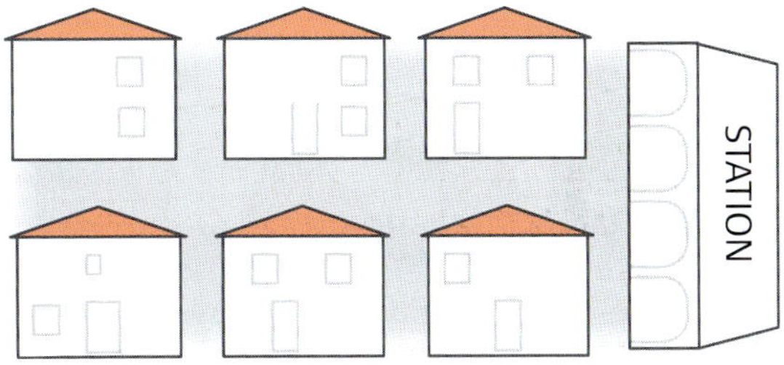

When **A** comes out of his house in the morning, **D** comes out of her house opposite and they say hello to each other. **A** turns right and goes past **C**'s house on the way to the station, but they never see each other because **C** works at night. **C** and **E** met each other when they were students and lived together for five years. But they argued with each other so much that **E** moved to the other end of the street. **E** and **D** became friends and they often talk to each other over the garden fence. **D** and **B** have lived next to each other for ten years but they have never spoken to each other. Nobody knows why. **F** and **A** both have cats so they look after each other's cats when one of them is on holiday.

A game without a name

p. 91, 3 An interview about the internet ...

This game is like the German game *Stadt, Land, Fluss*.
You can play it alone or with another Early Finisher.

1 Make a table like this: →

CITY or COUNTRY	HOBBY	SINGER or GROUP	ACTOR	FOOD or DRINK
...	...	...	...	...

2 Take the first letter of your name or the name of somebody in your family.

3 Give yourself three minutes and see if you can complete the table.

If you play with another person,
- take turns to choose a letter
- see who can complete the table first.

There is no name for this game in English. Try to think of a good name.

6 Everyday English: Small talk

p. 13

c) Partner A:
You're at a tourist sight in London (choose your sight).
You want a photo of yourself at the sight and ask a person who is standing there. He/she takes the photo and starts to talk to you.
Have a nice conversation with him/her.

3 Which is oldest? (Passive: simple past)

p. 55

b) Partner A: Ask the questions about 1, 3 and 5.

When was Liverpool Cathedral started?

Liverpool Cathedral

start
finish

1

Mona Lisa

paint
1503–1507

2

Berlin Underground

open

3

Treasure Island

write
1881–1883

4

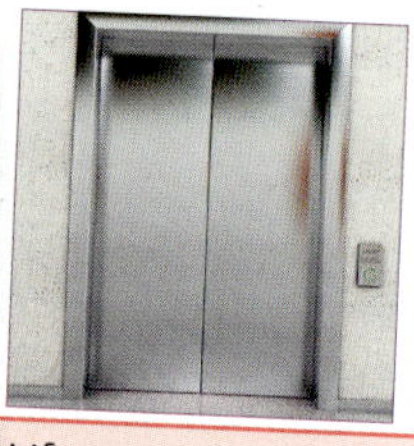

Lift

invent

5

Cologne Cathedral

start
finish

Portrait of Ludwig van Beethoven

paint
1820

London Underground

open

Oliver Twist

write
1837–1839

Escalator

invent

2 Making the film: Split screen and music

p. 87

Partner B:

a) Watch the film again (first version, without voice-over).

Take notes on the places where the music changes.
Think about the effect these changes have on the film.
Make notes about your ideas.

b) Listen to your partner. He or she will tell you about how the film uses a split screen.
Then tell your partner your ideas about the music changes in the film.

5 The slave trade

p. 53

Each partner chooses one of the texts on this page or page 134.

1 *The trade triangle: Selling people to get rich*

In the 17th and 18th centuries, millions of Africans were taken from their homes and sold into slavery. This is how the triangle worked:

1 British traders exported goods to West Africa.
2 In West Africa, many of these traders took African people as captives, sometimes with the help of other Africans. Why? Because they wanted to take them across the ocean and sell them as slaves.
3 When they sold their captives in America, the traders often got products like sugar or coffee instead of money. Back in Europe, they could sell these products and, in this way, they became very rich.

The captive Africans lived the rest of their lives far from their homes. They had to work very hard, but they earned nothing. The slave trade was one reason why Britain became such a rich and strong country.

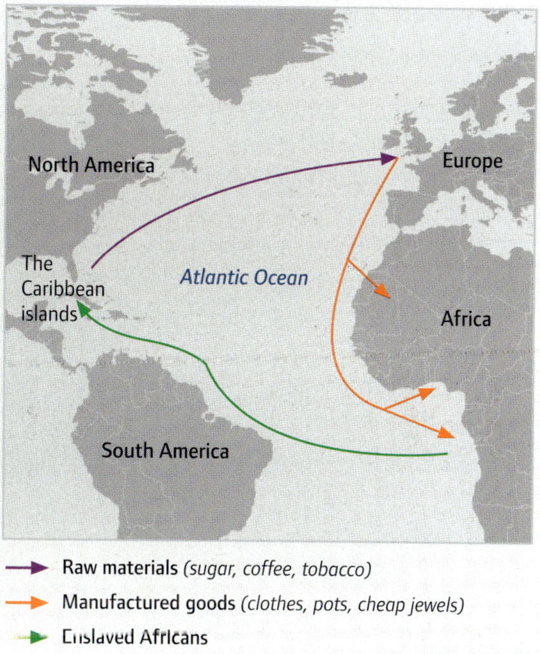

2 *From West Africa to America: The captives' journey*

The journey from Africa to America took about eight weeks. During that time the captives lived in terrible conditions. Hundreds of men, women and children had to stay in a tiny area below deck. They travelled like goods, not like people. It was hard to sit and impossible to stand. Many died during the journey, and the sea was their grave. Those who arrived had to work as slaves on big plantations for the rest of their lives.

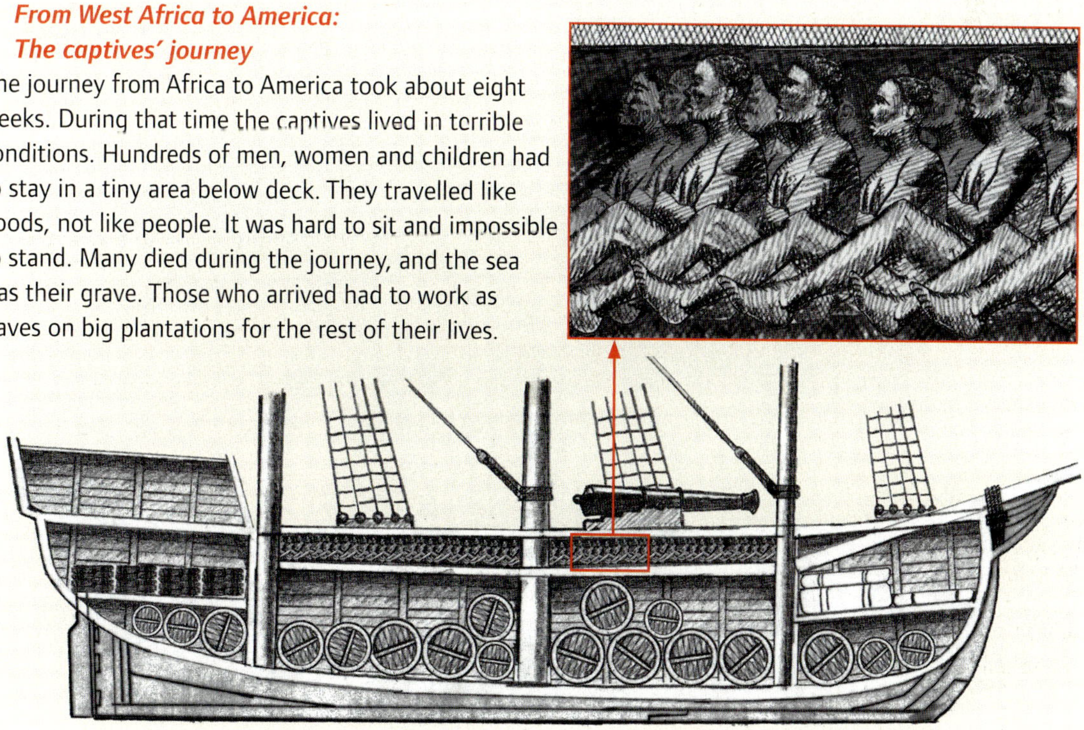

5 The slave trade

p. 53

Each partner chooses one of the texts on this page or page 133.

3 Life on the plantations

Plantations were big farms. The farmers were white Europeans who used slaves because they didn't want to pay people to work.

Life for slaves was hard and cruel:
- They had long working days.
- Usually, they didn't get enough food.
- Living conditions were awful.
- There were often brutal punishments.
- All of this meant that they often became ill.

All slaves had to work – children, men and women. Many of them died young because of this terrible life.

4 The battle against slavery

Protest on the plantations

Captive Africans protested against slavery in many ways. Some worked slowly or pretended to be sick. Some rebelled against their European masters. Many tried to hold onto their culture and sang traditional songs or told old African stories.

Protest in Britain

In 18th century Britain, people began to change their ideas about slavery. One key figure in this change was Olaudah Equiano (c. 1745–1797).
Equiano's master sent him to Britain while he was still a slave. There he learned to read and write and, later, bought his freedom. He wrote a book about the cruel life of slaves and gave talks on the topic all around Great Britain and Ireland. His book became a bestseller.

First steps to freedom

In 1807, the UK parliament prohibited the slave trade, and the British navy tried to stop ships which carried slaves. In 1833, parliament prohibited slavery completely. These were important steps, but the fight was not over. In many other countries, slavery was still allowed.

6 Everyday English Small talk

p. 13

c) Partner B:

You're from Britain. At a tourist sight in London (your partner will tell you which sight) you meet a visitor from Germany.

You start talking to him/her and have a nice conversation.

3 Which is oldest? (Passive: simple past)

p. 55

b) Partner B: Ask the questions about 2 and 4.

Liverpool Cathedral was started …

Liverpool Cathedral

start 1907
finish 1978

Mona Lisa

paint

Berlin Underground

open 1902

Treasure Island

write

Lift

invent
1852

1

Cologne Cathedral

start 1248
finish 1880

2

Portrait of Ludwig van Beethoven

paint

3

London Underground

open 1863

4

Oliver Twist

write

5

Escalator

invent
1895

Basketball

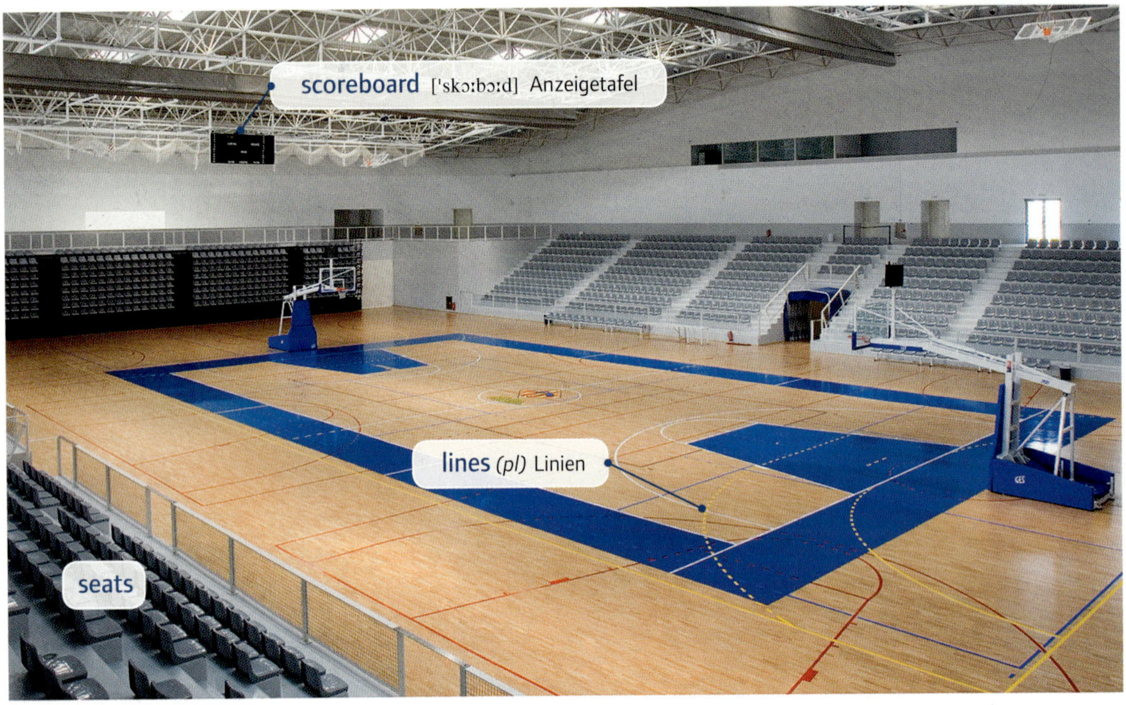

court [kɔːt] Spielfeld • **referee** [ˌrefəˈriː] Schiedsrichter/in

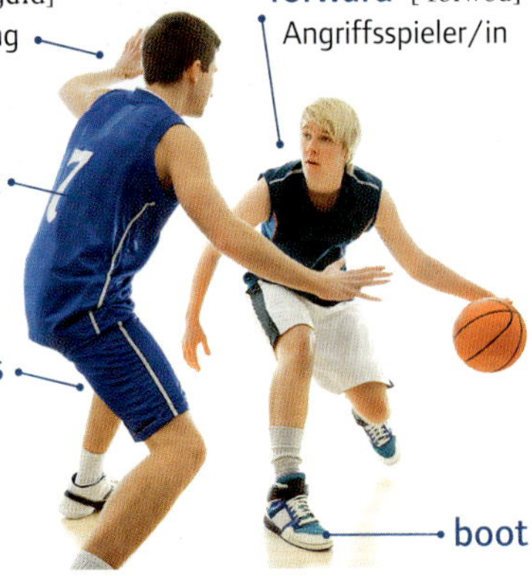

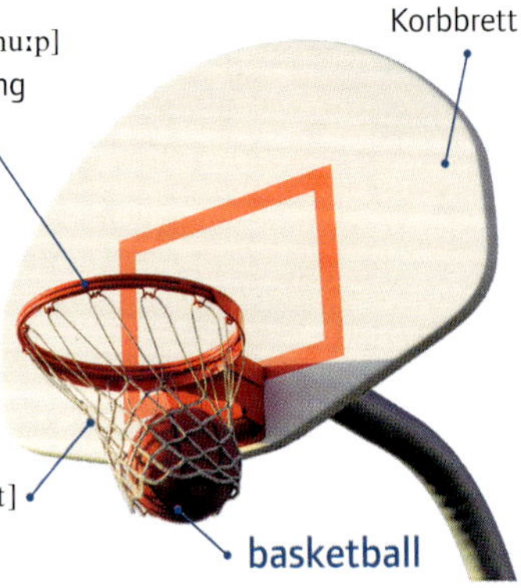

Tennis

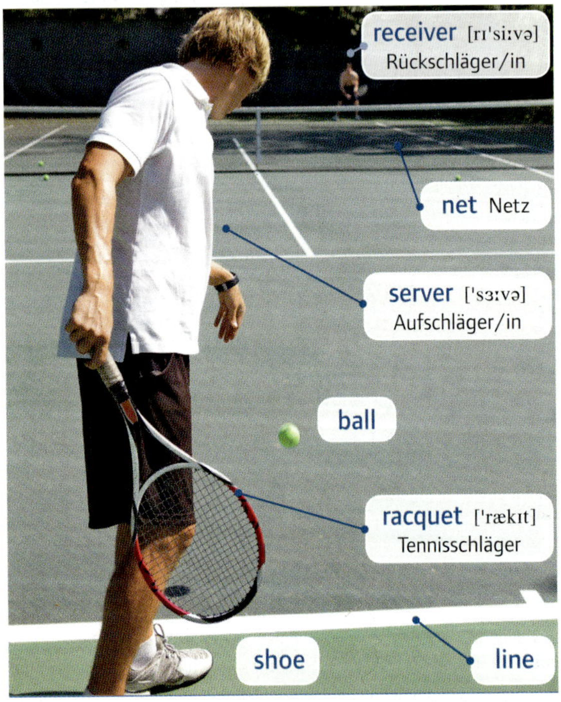

court [kɔːt] Spielfeld • **umpire** ['ʌmpaɪə] Schiedsrichter/in

Volleyball

court [kɔ:t] Spielfeld • **referee** erste(r) Schiedsrichter/in • **left/centre/right forward** linke(r)/mittlere(r)/rechte(r) Netzspieler/in • **left/centre/right back** linke(r)/mittlere(r)/rechte(r) Abwehrspieler/in • **server** Aufgeber/in

Hockey

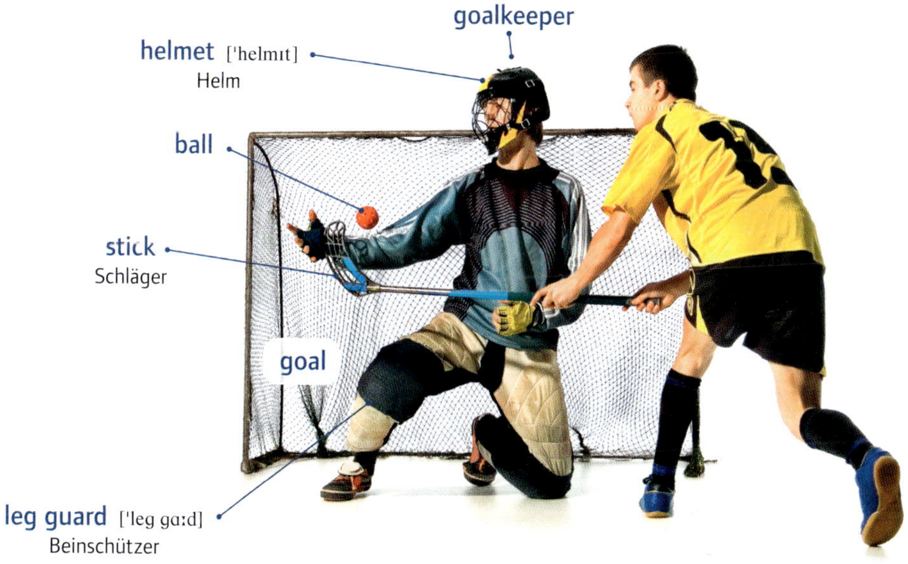

pitch [pɪtʃ] Spielfeld • **referee** Schiedsrichter/in • **centre forward** [ˌsentə‿'fɔ:wəd] Mittelstürmer/in • **left/right wing** linke(r)/rechte(r) Flügelspieler/in • **left/right inner** linke(r)/rechte(r) Innenfeldspieler/in • **left/right half** linke(r)/rechte(r) Mittelfeldspieler/in • **centre half** Mittelfeldspieler/in • **left/right back** linke(r)/rechte(r) Verteidiger/in

Skills File – Inhalt

In diesem **Skills File** findest du **Lernhilfen und Methoden,** die dir z.B. den Umgang mit Texten erleichtern, beim Schreiben von eigenen Texten und bei der Sprachmittlung helfen oder Tipps zum Vorbereiten von Präsentationen geben.

Alles, was du auf den *Study skills*- und *Writing course*-Seiten in den Units gelernt hast, wird hier nochmal aufgenommen und erläutert.

Einige der Einträge wie z.B. **Study posters** kennst du schon aus Band 1 oder 2. Sie sollen dich an das schon Gelernte erinnern. Du erkennst sie am Zusatz **(Revision)**.

STUDY SKILLS

SF 1 Ordering and structuring topic vocabulary

➜ p. 58

Warum soll ich Wortschatz sammeln und strukturieren?

Wenn du einen Text zu einem bestimmten Thema schreiben sollst, kann es dir helfen, vorab Vokabeln dazu zu sammeln und zu ordnen, damit dein Text einen abwechslungsreichen Wortschatz hat und sich gut liest. Oft wird auch schon beim Sammeln eine Gliederung des Themas erkennbar. Dadurch merkst du auch schnell, welche Wörter du ggf. noch in einem Wörterbuch nachschlagen musst.

Diese Art, Wortschatz zu sammeln und zu ordnen, hilft dir auch Vokabeln zu lernen oder zu wiederholen und sie zu vernetzen, so dass sie besser in deinem Gedächtnis bleiben.

Wie strukturiere ich den Wortschatz?

Für das Ordnen der Wörter gibt es verschiedene Möglichkeiten. Du solltest unterschiedliche Formen ausprobieren und dann diejenige verwenden, die am besten zu dir oder der Aufgabe passt.

Einige der Formen, die du nutzen kannst, sind:

- Tabellen (***tables***)
- Diagramme (z.B. ***tree diagrams***)
- Mindmaps

Wenn du Wortschatz zusammenstellst, um damit einen Text zu einem bestimmten Thema zu schreiben, solltest du unbedingt daran denken, dass du für einen guten Text nicht nur Nomen, sondern auch Verben, Adverbien, Adjektive etc. brauchst, sowie Varianten für Ausdrücke, die häufig vorkommen.

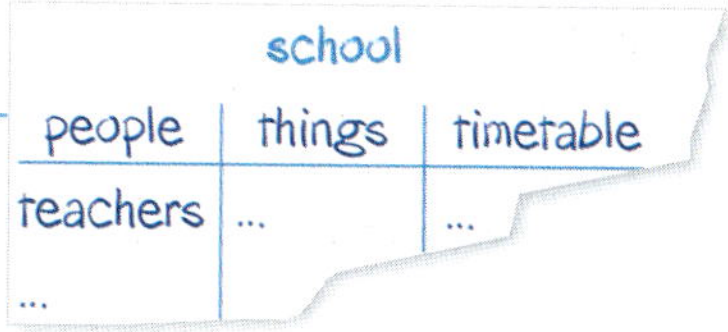

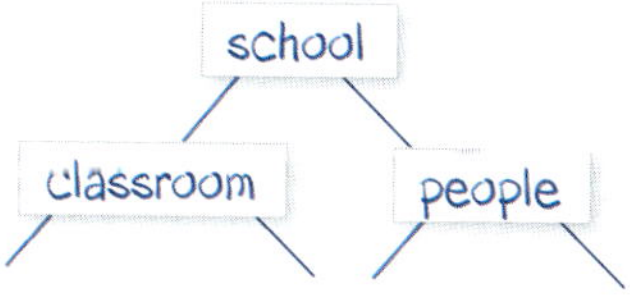

SF 2 REVISION Study posters

Lernplakate sind ein gutes Hilfsmittel, um Informationen darzustellen, die du dir merken möchtest wie z.B. Grammatikregeln.

Was muss ich beachten, wenn ich ein Lernposter erstelle?

- Sammle und notiere alle Informationen zum Thema, die du auf dem Poster darstellen willst.
- Überlege, wie du das, was du dir merken willst, am besten darstellen kannst. Du kannst z.B. Kästen oder Tabellen verwenden, aber auch kleine Zeichnungen.

- Finde einen guten Titel für dein Plakat.
- Gestalte dein Plakat. Schreibe groß und gut leserlich.
- Hebe wichtige Punkte hervor, z.B. durch Unterstreichen oder durch unterschiedliche Farben. Verwende aber nicht zu viele verschiedene Farben, denn sonst wird dein Lernposter unübersichtlich.
- Wenn du ein Lernposter zu einer Grammatikregel machst, kannst du auch ein paar Beispielsätze aufschreiben. Am Besten kannst du dir die Regel merken, wenn du dir zwei oder drei eigene Beispielsätze ausdenkst.
- Häng dein Poster zu Hause oder in der Schule an einer Stelle auf, an der du es häufig siehst, so dass sich dir der Inhalt ganz automatisch einprägen kann.

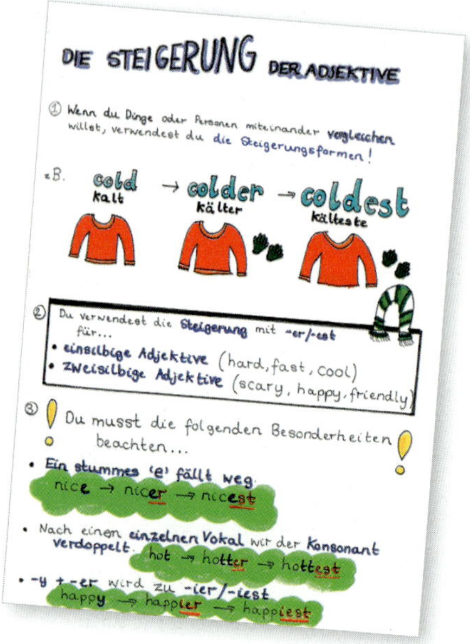

SF 3 REVISION Making notes with a crib sheet

Wozu sind Spickzettel gut?

Ein Spickzettel ermöglicht es auf sehr individuelle Weise

- den Inhalt eines Textes so zusammenzufassen, dass du ihn dir gut merken kannst
- jemandem von einem Erlebnis oder über ein Thema zu berichten
- einen kleinen Vortrag zu halten und möglichst frei vor Zuhörern zu sprechen.

Was muss ich beachten, wenn ich einen Spickzettel erstelle?

Sei kreativ! Dein Spickzettel ist eine Merkhilfe nur für dich – wichtig ist, dass **du** verstehst, was du notiert oder dargestellt hast. Diese Tipps können dir dabei helfen:

- Verwende ein möglichst kleines Blatt Papier.
- Schreibe keine ganzen Sätze, sondern nur Stichwörter oder Teilsätze.
- Verwende Symbole und kleine Zeichnungen, um Inhalte darzustellen, z.B.:
  - "+" für "and"
  - Smileys für Gefühle, Flaggen für Länder, Strichzeichnungen für Dinge und Personen, über die du schreiben oder sprechen möchtest,
  - Pfeile für Richtungen oder Ortsangaben, eine Sonne für Tag/gutes Wetter usw.
- Arrangiere alles so auf deinem Spickzettel, dass die Reihenfolge der Ereignisse oder Inhalte, die du darstellst und wiedergeben willst für dich deutlich erkennbar ist.

READING SKILLS

SF 4 REVISION Understanding new words

Das Nachschlagen unbekannter Wörter kostet Zeit und ist auch nicht immer nötig. Oft geht es auch ohne den Einsatz eines Wörterbuches.

Wie erschließe ich unbekannte Wörter?

- Viele englische Wörter werden ähnlich wie im Deutschen geschrieben oder klingen ähnlich (z.B. *brochure, statue, insect*). Manche sehen auch einem Wort aus anderen Sprachen ähnlich, z.B. *voice (French: voix; Latin: vox).*
- In manchen Wörtern stecken bekannte Teile, z.B. *bottle opener, snowshoe.*
- Bilder zum Text zeigen oft Dinge, die du im Text vielleicht nicht verstehst.
- Der Kontext, also die Wörter und Sätze um das Wort herum, kann beim Verstehen helfen, z.B. *Let's hurry. The train* ***departs*** *in ten minutes.*

SF 5 Working with an English–German dictionary

➜ p. 32

Wenn du unbekannte Wörter nicht selbst erschließen kannst, nutze ein englisch-deutsches Wörterbuch, entweder in Buchform oder im Internet.

Wie benutze ich ein englisch-deutsches Wörterbuch?

Die Leitwörter *(running heads)* oben auf der Seite helfen dir, schnell zu finden, was du suchst. Auf der linken Seite steht das erste Stichwort, auf der rechten Seite das letzte Stichwort der Doppelseite.

- *resign* ist das **Stichwort** *(headword)*. Stichwörter sind alphabetisch geordnet: *r* vor *s*, *ra* vor *re*, *rhe* vor *rhi* usw.
- Die ***kursiv*** **gedruckten** Hinweise helfen dir, die für deinen Text passende Bedeutung zu finden.
- Die **Ziffern 1, 2** usw. zeigen, dass ein Stichwort unterschiedliche Bedeutungen haben oder unterschiedlichen Wortarten angehören kann (z.B. Adjektiv, Nomen, Verb).
- **Beispielsätze und Redewendungen** sind dem Stichwort zugeordnet.
- **Unregelmäßige Verbformen, besondere Pluralformen**, die **Steigerungsformen der Adjektive** und ähnliche Hinweise stehen oft in Klammern oder sind kursiv gedruckt.
- Die **Lautschrift** gibt Auskunft darüber, wie das Wort ausgesprochen und betont wird.

resort

resign /rɪˈzaɪn/
1 BERUF • *als Vorsitzender usw* zurücktreten: *He* ***resigned from*** *the company.* Er verließ das Unternehmen
2 (*job, post*) aufgeben (*Stelle, Posten*)
3 **resign oneself to something** sich mit etwas abfinden
resignation /ˌrezɪɡˈneɪʃn/
1 BERUF • *bei Unternehmen* Kündigung; *von Minister usw* Rücktritt
2 **hand in one's resignation** *von Angestelltem* kündigen; *von Minister usw* sein Amt niederlegen
3 *Gemütszustand* Resignation
resigned /rɪˈzaɪnd/ (*look, sigh*) resigniert

resit[1] /ˌriːˈsɪt/ *Verb* (→ *sit*) *BE* (*exam*) wiederholen (*Prüfung*)
resit[2] /ˈriːsɪt/ *Substantiv* • *BE* Wiederholungsprüfung
resolution /ˌrezəˈluːʃn/
1 POLITIK Beschluss, Resolution
2 *bei Problem, Streit* Lösung
3 ≈ *Entschiedenheit* Entschlossenheit

TIPP

Wenn du ein Online-Wörterbuch verwenden möchtest, erkundige dich vorher bei deinem Lehrer/deiner Lehrerin, welche zu empfehlen sind, denn nicht alle sind gleich gut. Fast alle funktionieren aber nach den gleichen Prinzipien wie gedruckte Wörterbücher, sodass du sie problemlos ebenso verwenden kannst.

SF 6 Using a German–English dictionary

➔ p. 92

Wann brauche ich ein deutsch-englisches Wörterbuch?

Stell dir vor, du sollst einen Text über deine Lieblingsband/deinen Lieblingsverein schreiben und du möchtest sagen, wie schwer die Band/der Verein kämpfen musste, um Erfolg zu haben. Aber was heißt in diesem Fall „schwer"? In diesem Fall hilft dir ein deutsch-englisches Wörterbuch.

Wie benutze ich ein deutsch-englisches Wörterbuch?

Vieles kennst du von der Arbeit mit einem englisch-deutschen Wörterbuch:

- **Leitwörter** *(running heads)* oben auf den Seiten helfen dir, das gesuchte Wort zu finden.
- Die **Stichwörter** *(headwords)* sind alphabetisch geordnet. Beispielsätze und Redewendungen sind den Stichwörtern zugeordnet.
- Die ***kursiv*** gedruckten Hinweise helfen dir, die für deinen Text passende Bedeutung zu finden.
- Die **Ziffern 1, 2** usw. zeigen, dass ein Stichwort unterschiedlichen Wortarten angehören kann (z.B. Adjektiv, Nomen, Verb).
- Bei **schwierig auszusprechenden Wörtern** stehen auch Hinweise zu Aussprache und Betonung.
- Bei Wörtern mit vielen Bedeutungen gibt es oft weitere Hilfen und Hinweise.

Schwede

schwer
1 ↔ *leicht* • *im Gewicht* heavy /ˈhevi/
2 *(Essen, Parfüm etc)* heavy /ˈhevi/ *(meal, scent etc)*
3 ≈ *mühevoll* hard /hɑːd/: ***Sie muss schwer arbeiten.*** She has to work hard.
4 ≈ *schwierig* difficult /ˈdɪfɪkəlt/, hard /hɑːd/
5 es jemandem schwer machen make* it difficult for someone
6 sich mit etwas schwer tun find* something difficult, have* difficulty with something
7 ≈ *hart* difficult /ˈdɪfɪkəlt/: ***Sie hatte eine schwere Kindheit.*** She had a difficult childhood.
8 ≈ *schlimm, heftig* serious /ˈsɪəriəs/: ***ein schwer kranker Patient*** a seriously ill patient
9 schwer verletzt sein be* seriously injured

schwer
Das deutsche *schwer* hat zwei Hauptbedeutungen:
– *schwer* in Bezug auf das Gewicht: *heavy*, im übertragenen Sinn auch *serious, bad*:
ein schwerer Koffer *a heavy suitcase*

TIPP
Nimm nicht einfach die erste Übersetzung, die dir angeboten wird! Lies immer erst den gesamten Wörterbucheintrag, bevor du dich für eine bestimmte Übersetzung entscheidest.

SF 7 REVISION Scanning

Wozu ist Scanning gut?

Wenn du in einem Text nach Informationen oder Antworten auf eine Frage suchen sollst, reicht es oft, wenn du den Text nach Schlüsselwörtern *(keywords)* absuchst und nur dort genauer liest, wo du sie findest.

Wie scanne ich einen Text?

- Bevor du auf den Text schaust, überlege dir mögliche *keywords*, nach denen du suchen könntest. Es kann helfen, wenn du sie aufschreibst.
- Stell dir dann die *keywords* gut vor und geh mit deinen Augen sehr schnell durch den Text. Die gesuchten Wörter werden dir sofort „ins Auge springen".
- Du kannst auch mit dem Finger in breiten Bewegungen wie bei einem „S" von oben bis unten durch den Text gehen. Wenn du deine *keywords* gefunden hast, lies dort weiter, um Näheres zu erfahren.

SF 8 REVISION Taking notes

Worum geht es beim Notizen machen?

Wenn du beim Lesen oder Zuhören Notizen machst, kannst du dich später besser daran erinnern, wenn du etwas vortragen, nacherzählen oder einen Bericht schreiben sollst.

Wie mache ich Notizen?

In Texten oder Gesprächen gibt es immer wichtige und weniger wichtige Wörter. Die wichtigen Wörter sind sogenannte Schlüsselwörter *(keywords)*, und nur die solltest du notieren. Meist sind das Substantive und Verben, manchmal auch Adjektive oder Zahlen.

Folgende Punkte können dir auch helfen:

- Verwende Ziffern (z.B. „7" statt „seven").
- Verwende Symbole und Abkürzungen, z.B. ✓ („yes") und + („and"). Am besten erfindest du eigene Symbole.
- Bei Verneinungen verwende „not" oder streiche Wörter durch.

SF 9 REVISION Marking up a text

Wann sollte ich einen Text markieren?

Manchmal sollst du einen Sachtext lesen und Wichtiges zusammenfassen oder Fragen dazu beantworten. Dann kann es dir helfen, wichtige Informationen für deine Aufgabenstellung im Text zu markieren.

Wie gehe ich am besten vor?

- Lies dir die Aufgabe genau durch.
- Lies den Text und markiere nur Informationen, die für deine Aufgabe wichtig sind. Nicht jeder Satz enthält Wichtiges, und oft reicht es aus, nur ein oder zwei Wörter in einem Satz zu markieren.
- Hebe wichtige Informationen hervor, z.B. durch
  - Unterstreichen
  - Einkreisen
  - oder Markieren mit einem Textmarker.

Wichtig: Markiere nur auf Fotokopien von Texten oder in deinen eigenen Büchern.

The Beatles' success story started in 1960, when the young musicians played in clubs in Liverpool and Hamburg. They made their first record, *Love Me Do*, in London in 1962.

The Beatles' success story started in 1960, when the young musicians played in clubs in Liverpool and Hamburg. They made their first record, *Love Me Do*, in London in 1962.

The Beatles' success story started in 1960, when the young musicians played in clubs in Liverpool and Hamburg. They made their first record, *Love Me Do*, in London in 1962.

WRITING SKILLS

SF 10 Good sentences

➔ p. 16

Gute Texte bestehen aus guten Sätzen. Gute Sätze machen deinen Text interessanter und anschaulicher. Um gute Sätze zu schreiben, solltest du folgenden Dinge beachten.

Wie kann ich meine Texte lebendiger und besser gestalten?

Die folgenden Techniken helfen dir, dich gut auszudrücken und damit den Stil deiner Texte zu verbessern.

Verwende …

- ***Adjektive***, wenn du Dinge, Orte und Menschen näher beschreiben möchtest:
  - a bright face
  - a fantastic trip
- aber die Adjektive good, bad and nice nicht zu häufig in deinem Text. Ersetze sie durch andere Adjektive mit einer ähnlichen bzw. genaueren Bedeutung:
  - a nice teacher: a friendly teacher, a helpful teacher, …
  - a good book: an interesting book, a funny book, …
- ***Adverbien***, um Handlungen näher zu beschreiben:
  - They walked home slowly.
  - She talked quietly.
- Ausdrücke wie really, very, a bit etc., um Aussagen zu verdeutlichen oder zu verstärken:
  - It was a really sad story.
  - The houses are very high.
- adverbiale Bestimmungen der Zeit ***(time markers)***, um zeitliche Abfolgen oder Zeitpunkte zu verdeutlichen:
  - I am going to London next month.
  - He came home yesterday at 5 o'clock.

  (➔ *SF 13: Using time markers in a story, S. 146*)
- ***Konjunktionen*** wie and, but oder because, um deine Sätze zu verbinden und ihnen eine klare, gut nachvollziehbare Struktur zu geben:
  - We went to the London Eye, but it was very expensive.
- ***Relativsätze***, um Sätze zu verbinden oder eine Sache oder eine Person näher zu erklären:
  - This is the shop which sells the best ice cream in Berlin.

SF 11 Structuring a text

➜ p. 51

Welche Struktur braucht mein Text?

Ein guter Text besteht in der Regel aus den folgenden drei Teilen:

- eine ***Einleitung*** (introduction): hier sagst du, worum es in dem gesamten Text geht. Manchmal formulierst du hier auch ein Problem, das in dem Text erörtert werden soll.
- einen ***Haupt- oder Mittelteil*** (body): dieser Teil ist in mehrere Absätze gegliedert und präsentiert die Details zu deinem Thema.
- einen ***Schluss*** (conclusion): hier gibst du deinem Text ein passendes, interessantes Ende.

My Trip to Wales

Last summer I wanted to go to Wales because I like the mountains.

First I had to find some information on Wales. So I went to the library and looked for books about Wales. I found a book with some interesting information on hiking tours and I also found a camping guide for Wales. I went home with three books under my arm.

At home I started to plan for my trip. I read all the books and took notes on hiking trails, the weather and the equipment I would need for camping and hiking. After a few days I knew where I wanted to go and what I wanted to do there.

I did not want to go to Wales alone, so I had to find someone to go with me. I called most of my friends and told them about my plan. Some of them did not want to go hiking and others had no money for the trip. But my friend Judith agreed to go with me. We decided to go in late August.

Judith and I spent two lovely weeks in Wales. We went to Snowdonia and enjoyed the fantastic mountains. We stayed in a lovely bed and breakfast and met lots of really nice people. Before we went home we spent two very interesting days in Cardiff.

This was one of the best summer holidays I ever had. Go to Wales – it's fantastic!

SF 12 Paragraphs and topic sentences

➜ p. 38

Wozu brauche ich Absätze?

Ein Leser kann einen längeren Text einfacher lesen und schneller verstehen, wenn dieser in Absätze eingeteilt ist.

Was sollte ich bei Absätzen beachten?

- Beginne mit einem interessanten *topic sentence*.
- Fang für jeden neuen Aspekt einen neuen Absatz an.
- Beende deinen Text im letzten Absatz/in den letzten Absätzen mit einer Zusammenfassung oder etwas Persönlichem.

Was sind topic sentences?

Jeder Absatz sollte mit einem Einleitungssatz beginnen. Dieser *topic sentence* beschreibt, worum es in dem Absatz geht.

Wichtige Dinge, die du in einem *topic sentence* ansprechen kannst, sind z.B.

- ***Orte:*** *My trip to Berlin was exciting.*
- ***Personen:*** *The Beatles are one of the most famous bands in the world.*
- ***Aktivitäten:*** *Lots of people ride their bike every day.*

SF 13 Using time markers in a story

➜ p. 77

Zeitangaben ***(time marker)*** helfen dem Leser, sich in einem Text oder einer Geschichte zeitlich zurechtzufinden. Dazu machen sie einen Text anschaulicher.

Welche Zeitangaben sollte ich machen?

Verwende ***time markers***, um …

- die ***Reihenfolge von Ereignissen*** zu verdeutlichen:
  at first, next, finally, …
- zu zeigen, ***wie viel Zeit*** zwischen einzelnen Ereignissen ***vergeht***:
  for half an hour, just three minutes later, I counted thirty seconds, …
- zu verdeutlichen, ***wie langsam oder schnell*** etwas passiert:
  immediately, it took hours, faster than I could look, …
- zu sagen, wenn etwas ***zeitgleich*** passiert:
  while I was waiting, during the lesson, as we came round the corner, …
- die ***Ereignisse eines Textes/einer Geschichte*** zeitlich einzuordnen:
  two summers ago, last Halloween, on my way home from school yesterday, …

SF 14 Giving feedback – writing

➜ p. 17

Warum ist Feedback zu Texten wichtig?

Wenn du einen Text geschrieben hast, ist es oft schwierig, deine Fehler und Schwächen des Textes zu entdecken. Deshalb kann es sehr hilfreich sein, eine Rückmeldung von einem Mitschüler zu bekommen.

Was muss ich bei Feedback zu Texten beachten?

Wenn du jemandem eine Rückmeldung zu einem Text geben sollst, gelten dafür grundsätzlich die gleichen Regeln wie bei jeder anderen Art von Feedback auch. (➜ *SF 24: Peer feedback (Revision), S. 153*)

Folgende Schritte helfen, wenn du eine Rückmeldung geben sollst:

1. Lies den Text sorgfältig durch, um dir einen ersten, allgemeinen Eindruck zu verschaffen.
2. Beim zweiten Lesen achte besonders auf die Punkte, zu denen du eine Rückmeldung geben sollst. Bei geschriebenen Texten gehören dazu in der Regel
   - Inhalt,
   - Struktur,
   - Wortwahl und abwechslungsreiche Sätze,
   - Grammatik und Rechtschreibung.
3. Streiche Fehler oder weniger gelungene Teile im Text an und mache dir Notizen zu wichtigen Punkten. Wenn du einen Feedbackbogen hast, benutze ihn und trage dort dein Feedback ein.

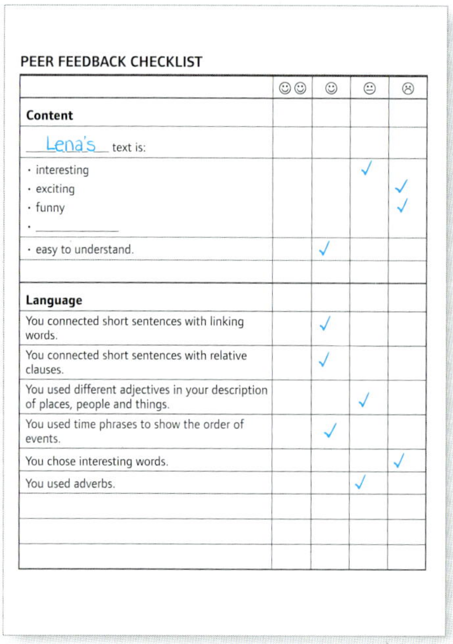

PEER FEEDBACK CHECKLIST

	☺☺	☺	😐	☹
Content				
Lena's text is:				
· interesting			✓	
· exciting				✓
· funny				✓
· ________				
· easy to understand.		✓		
Language				
You connected short sentences with linking words.		✓		
You connected short sentences with relative clauses.		✓		
You used different adjectives in your description of places, people and things.			✓	
You used time phrases to show the order of events.		✓		
You chose interesting words.				✓
You used adverbs.			✓	

4. Beginne deine Rückmeldung mit einer Aufzählung der gelungenen Teile/ Aspekte des Textes. Es ist immer gut, positiv anzufangen.

5. Erläutere deine kritischen Anmerkungen und mache Verbesserungsvorschläge. Gib Hinweise, wie dein Partner/deine Partnerin bei der Überarbeitung des Textes vorgehen könnte.

SF 15 Revising your text

➔ p. 38

Egal, ob du eine Rückmeldung von einem Partner/einer Partnerin bekommen hast oder nicht – einen Text solltest du auf jeden Fall noch einmal gut prüfen, bevor du ihn z.B. abgibst.

Worauf muss ich achten?

1. **Stimmt die *Gliederung*?**
   Jeder Text braucht
   - eine Einleitung, die in das Thema einführt,
   - einen Hauptteil, der das Thema ausführt,
   - einen Schluss, der alles auf den Punkt bringt.

   (➔ *SF 11: Structuring a text, S. 145)*

2. **Stimmt der *Aufbau* der Absätze?**
   Jeder Absatz
   - befasst sich mit einem zusammenhängenden Gedanken,
   - beginnt mit einem ***topic sentence***, der diesen Gedanken einführt.

   (➔ *SF 12: Paragraphs and topic sentences, S. 145)*

3. **Stimmen die *Verknüpfungen*?**
   Gute *linking words*
   - schaffen Verbindungen zwischen Sätzen oder Satzteilen,
   - helfen, Zusammenhänge besser darzustellen und verständlich zu machen.

   (➔ *SF 10: Good sentences, S. 144)*

4. **Sind die *Zeitangaben* richtig gesetzt?**
   Time markers
   - helfen, sich z.B. in einer Geschichte zurechtzufinden,
   - machen das Geschehen anschaulicher.

   (➔ *SF 13: Using time markers in a story, S. 146)*

5. **Enthält der Text *Adjektive* und *Adverbien*?**
   Adjektive und Adverbien
   - erlauben nähere Beschreibungen von Personen und Dingen
   - machen Texte anschaulicher.

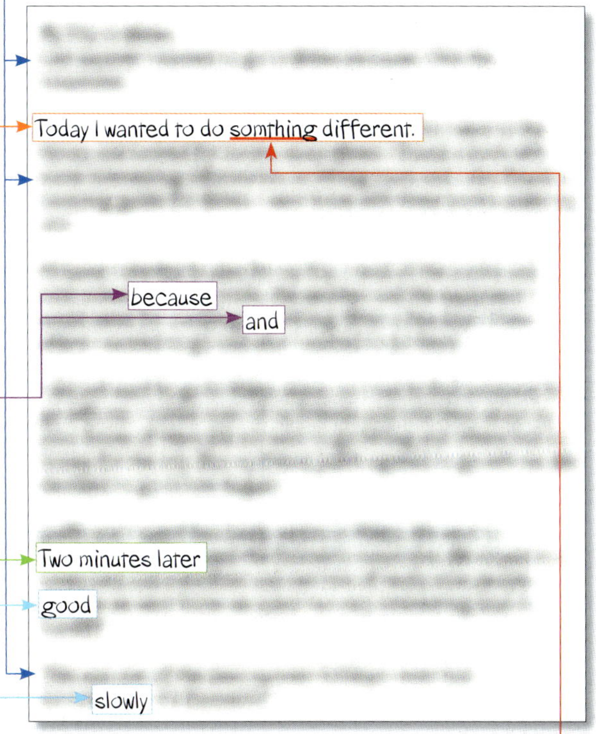

6. **Hat der Text sprachliche/grammatikalische *Fehler*?**
   Überprüfe deinen Text
   - auf Rechtschreibung,
   - grammatischen Formen, z.B. die Verbformen,
   - Satzbau *(word order)* usw.

LANGUAGE SKILLS

SF 16 REVISION Mediation

Manchmal musst du zwischen zwei Sprachen vermitteln. Das nennt man ***mediation***.

Wann brauche ich Mediation?

Hier sind einige Situationen, in denen es sein kann, dass du zwischen Deutsch und Englisch vermitteln musst:

- Du gibst englische Informationen auf deutsch wieder:
  Du fährst z.B. mit deiner Familie nach Großbritannien und deine Großeltern, Eltern oder Geschwister wollen wissen, was jemand gesagt hat oder was auf einer Informationstafel steht.
- Du gibst deutsche Informationen auf englisch wieder:
  Wenn du eine/n Austauschschüler/in aus England (oder einem anderen Land) bei dir zu Hause zu Gast hast, kann es sein, dass er/sie wenig Deutsch spricht und deine Hilfe braucht.
- In schriftlichen Prüfungen musst du manchmal in einem englischen Text gezielt nach Informationen suchen und diese auf Deutsch wiedergeben. Oder du sollst Informationen aus einem deutschen Text auf Englisch wiedergeben.

Worauf muss ich bei Mediation achten?

Übersetze nicht alles wörtlich, sondern gib nur das für die gegebene Situation Wesentliche wieder. Du kannst Unwichtiges weglassen und Sätze umformulieren.

Was kann ich tun, wenn ich ein bestimmtes Wort nicht kenne?

Vielleicht findest du es manchmal schwer, mündliche Aussagen oder schriftliche Textvorlagen in die andere Sprache zu übertragen, z. B. weil

- dein Wortschatz nicht ausreicht
- dir bekannte Wörter „im Stress" nicht einfallen
- spezielle Fachbegriffe auftauchen.

Viele Wörter kannst du umschreiben, z. B. mithilfe von Relativsätzen wie:

It's somebody/a person who …
It's something that you use to …
It's an animal that …
It's a place that/where …

SF 17 REVISION Listening

Manchmal kann es schwer sein, einem Hörtext zu folgen, weil du die Sprecher nicht sehen kannst und du dich auch noch auf die Aufgaben zum Hörtext konzentrieren musst. Die folgenden Tipps können dir beim Hörverstehen helfen.

Was kann ich vor dem Hören tun?

- Sieh dir die Aufgabenstellung genau an. Was sollst du heraushören?
- Schau nach Überschriften und Bildern zum Text. Sie können oft schon einige Fragen beantworten helfen: Wer spricht mit wem, wo sind sie, worüber reden sie?
- Überlege, was du selbst zum Thema schon weißt und welche englischen Begriffe daher im Gespräch fallen könnten.

Worauf kann ich während des Hörens achten?

- Lass dich nicht verwirren, wenn es mehrere Sprecher gibt. Versuche, die unterschiedlichen Stimmen Personen zuzuordnen. Das macht es einfacher, dem Gespräch zu folgen.
- Wenn es um generelles Hörverstehen geht, höre gezielt auf die Hintergrundgeräusche. So kannst du herausfinden, ob das Gespräch z.B. am Strand, auf der Straße oder in der Schule stattfindet.
- Sicher wirst du einiges nicht verstehen. Das ist nicht schlimm – versuche aus dem was du alles verstanden hast das Fehlende zu erschließen.

Worauf kann ich beim Hören achten, wenn es um Details geht?

- Gerate nicht in Panik, wenn du denkst, du hättest etwas Wichtiges verpasst. Konzentriere dich auf die nächste wichtige Information.
- Ignoriere Hintergrundgeräusche. Wenn du bestimmte Details heraushören sollst, sind sie unwichtig und lenken nur ab.
- Mach nur kurze Notizen, z.B. Anfangsbuchstaben, Symbole und Stichworte (➔ *SF 8: Taking notes (Revision), S. 143)*
- Je nachdem, welche Details du heraushören sollst, können Signalwörter helfen, dem Hörtext zu folgen und dich auf die Details zu konzentrieren:
  - Aufzählungen: *and, another, too, …*
  - Gegensätze: *although, but, …*
  - Gründe, Folgen: *because, so, so that, …*
  - Vergleiche: *larger/older/… than, as … as, more, most, …*
  - Reihenfolge: *before, after, then, next, later, …*

Was kann ich nach dem Hören tun?

- Vervollständige deine Notizen sofort.
- Wenn möglich, vergleiche mit einem Partner/einer Partnerin, was ihr verstanden habt.
- Wenn dir die Beantwortung einer Frage noch Schwierigkeiten macht, versuche schlau zu kombinieren.

SF 18 REVISION Speaking

Lies die beiden Dialoge. Welche Unterschiede erkennst du?
Wodurch entstehen sie?

Jen: Hi.
Ben: Hi.
Jen: It's a great parade.
Ben: Yeah.
Jen: Do you like the bands?
Ben: No.
Jen: The food smells good.
Ben: Yeah.
Jen: Do you want some too?
Ben: All right.
Jen: Do you live in Plymouth?
Ben: No.
Jen: …

Ed: Hi there, great parade, isn't it?
Jo: Yeah, I didn't know it was this big.
Ed: Is it your first time here, then?
Jo: That's right, I'm new in Plymouth.
Ed: Okay, so did you come here for the day?
Jo: Yeah, we arrived early this morning … Wow, that food smells good.
Ed: Are you hungry? Look, my friends have this pasties stall over there. Do you want to try one?
Jo: Okay, yes please.
Ed: My name's Ed, by the way.
Jo: Hello Ed, I'm Jo.

Wie kann ich freundlich ein Gespräch führen?

Wenn du dich mit jemandem auf Englisch unterhalten willst, können dir diese Hinweise helfen:

1. Eröffne das Gespräch mit einer freundlichen Anrede oder Frage.
2. Antworte nicht nur mit einem Wort, wenn dich dein Gesprächspartner/deine Gesprächspartnerin etwas fragt.
3. Zeige Interesse an deinem Gesprächspartner/deiner Gesprächspartnerin, indem du auch ein paar Fragen stellst.
4. Erzähle auch etwas von dir, um das Gespräch am Laufen zu halten.
5. Verabschiede dich am Ende freundlich.

1 *Hi, can I sit here?*
Hello, how are you?
Hi there, are you from Plymouth?

2 *Fine, thanks. / Yeah, sure.*
Yes, I am. / No, not really.

3 *What about you?*
I'm Nick and you are …?
Do you like …?
So what do you think …?

4 *I'm new here in …*
I'm with my friends over there.
I love these …
And I really like …

5 *Bye then.*
See you.
Have a good time!

PROJECT AND PRESENTATION SKILLS

SF 19 Teamwork

➔ p. 69

Bei Projekten arbeitet ihr oft im Team. Dabei solltet ihr eure unterschiedlichen Fähigkeiten und Talente einbringen und bestimmte Regeln beachten.

Was ist wichtig für gutes Teamwork?

Folgende Schritte können helfen, die Arbeit zu organisieren:

1. Legt ***Regeln*** für die Arbeit in der Gruppe fest, z.B. gegenseitige Unterstützung, pünktliches und zügiges Arbeiten, einander zuhören oder verschiedene Lösungen diskutieren usw.
2. Sammelt Ideen für die Bearbeitung eures Themas (z.B. in einer Mindmap). Wählt gemeinsam Unterthemen aus und legt die ***Arbeitsschritte*** fest, die für die Bearbeitung nötig sind.
3. ***Verteilt Rollen*** und Aufgaben nach euren Interessen und Fähigkeiten. Wenn ihr euch nicht einigen könnt, hilft Auslosen oder Würfeln.
   Folgende Rollen solltet ihr auf jeden Fall verteilen:
   - coordinator
   - writer/researcher
   - picture and layout editor
   - language watchdog
4. Macht einen ***Zeitplan*** für eure Arbeiten, an den sich alle halten sollten.
5. Am Ende der Arbeit sollte ein ***Rückblick*** stehen: Besprecht, was gelungen war und wo ihr Verbesserungsmöglichkeiten seht.

SF 20 Internet research (Finding information for a presentation)

➔ p. 69

Das Internet ist voller Informationen und es ist nicht einfach, genau die Informationen zu finden, die du benötigst

Wie finde ich die Informationen, die ich brauche?

- Überlege, was die wichtigsten ***Stichwörter*** für dein Thema sind. Für das Thema "The Beatles in Hamburg" wären *Beatles* und *Hamburg* ein guter Start.
- Gib deine Stichwörter in eine ***Suchmaschine*** ein. Je mehr gute Stichwörter du eingibst, desto genauer sind die Ergebnisse. In der Infografik rechts kannst du sehen, wie du an ganz spezielle Informationen kommen kannst.
- Sieh dir mehrere ***Suchergebnisse*** an, um zu sehen, ob sie passen. Wenn du schnell ein bestimmtes Wort wie z.B. *Hamburg* finden willst, dann kannst du mit der Tastenkombination ***Strg*** + ***F*** danach suchen. Das Wort wird dann auf der Seite markiert und du kannst schnell sehen, ob die Information relevant ist.
- Achte darauf, wer die Webseite erstellt hat, um die ***Qualität*** der Suchergebnisse einzuschätzen. Sind sie eher zuverlässig (Online-Lexikon, bekannte Medien, …) oder eher persönliche Meinungen (Forum, Fan-Seite, …)?

Internet research
Tipps und Tricks

Wenn du ganz spezifische Informationen suchst, helfen diese Tricks:

Was du suchst: Artikel aus dem *Guardian* von 2000–2014 über den FC Liverpool in der Champions League.

Wie du danach suchst:

site:theguardian.com "FC Liverpool" "champions league" 2000..2014

site:	" "	..
sucht nur auf der genannten Seite	sucht den exakten Begriff	zeigt nur Ergebnisse aus diesem Zeitraum

Was du suchst: Einen englischsprachigen Bericht, am liebsten als PDF, über den Lebensraum von Füchsen.

Wie du danach suchst:

filetype:pdf intitle:habitat of *fox

filetype:	intitle:	*
sucht nur diesen Dateityp (pdf, doc, jpg usw.)	zeigt nur Ergebnisse, in denen dieses Wort im Titel auftaucht	sucht auch Worte wie Red Fox, Black Fox, Desert Fox usw.

- Kopiere nicht einfach ganze Artikel aus dem Internet. Mach dir Notizen und verwende deine eigenen Worte, um die Inhalte wiederzugeben.
- Setz dir ein Zeitlimit für deine Recherche und ordne dann dein Material. Prüfe, ob dir etwas fehlt und suche ggf. gezielt nach nur noch diesen Informationen.
- Leg alle interessanten Materialien zu deinem Thema in einem eigenen Ordner ab. Dann kannst du sie dir später genauer ansehen und auswählen, was du nutzen möchtest.

Was die Suchmaschine auch noch kann:

Definitionen: Wenn du schnell eine Definition für ein Wort suchst, kannst du das mit **define:** tun.

define:prejudice

Konvertieren: Tippe einfach die Einheit, die du schon hast und die, die du wissen möchtest.

50 kilograms in pounds

SF 21 REVISION Describing and presenting pictures

Manchmal sollst du ein Foto vor der Klasse vorstellen. Hier sind ein paar Hilfen.

Wie stelle ich ein Foto vor?

1 Stelle das Foto vor und sage, woher es kommt.

2 Beschreibe das Foto:
- Sage, was wo zu sehen ist: *at the top/bottom* · *in the foreground/background* · *in the middle* · *on the left/right*
- Diese Präpositionen sind auch hilfreich: *behind* · *between* · *in front of* · *next to* · *under* · *over*
- Geh bei der Beschreibung in einer bestimmten Reihenfolge vor, z.B. von links nach rechts oder von oben nach unten.

3 Sage, was dir an dem Foto gefällt oder nicht.

4 Wenn du mit der Vorstellung des Fotos fertig bist, bedanke dich fürs Zuhören und frage, ob noch jemand Fragen hat.

1 *I'd like to talk about this photo of … I found it on the internet/in a magazine/…*

2 *In the foreground you can see … I think the people in the photo are talking about …/having fun/celebrating/…*

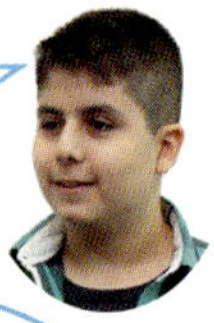

3 *I really like/don't like the photo because … It's interesting/boring/exciting/ … because …*

4 *Thank you for listening. Do you have any questions?*

SF 22 REVISION Putting a page together

Wenn du eine Bildseite gestalten sollst, z.B. einen Artikel für eine Schülerzeitung, helfen dir die folgenden Hinweise.

Wie gehe ich am besten vor?

- Sammle und sortiere die Informationen, die auf der Seite stehen sollen.
- Schreibe deinen Text und gib ihm eine klare Struktur. (➔ *SF 11: Structuring your text, S. 145*)
- Beginne einen neuen Absatz für jeden neuen Gedanken. (➔ *SF 12: Paragraphs and topic sentences, S. 145*)
- Wähle eine passende Überschrift: sie verdeutlicht, worum es in deinem Text geht und macht den Leser neugierig auf deinen Text.
- Wenn es in deinem Text um mehrere Themen geht, dann kannst Du für einzelne Abschnitte auch Zwischenüberschriften verwenden. Das gibt deinem Text eine klare Struktur und hilft dem Leser, sich schnell zu orientieren.

SF 23 REVISION Giving a presentation

➔ p. 92

Wie bereite ich eine Präsentation vor?

- Trage Informationen zu deinem Thema zusammen.
  (➔ *SF 20: Internet research (Finding information for your project), S. 151)*
- Wähle eine Form der Präsentation aus, die das Thema gut veranschaulicht (Poster, Folie, Tafel, ...).
- Schlage Wortschatz nach, den du brauchst.
  (➔ *SF 6: Using a German-English dictionary, S. 142)*
- Mach dir Notizen für deinen Vortrag, z.B. auf nummerierten Karteikarten.
- Bereite deine Medien vor (Poster, Folie, Tafelanschrieb, ...). Schreibe groß und für alle gut lesbar.
- Übe deine Präsentation zu Hause vor einem Spiegel oder vor einem kleinen Publikum (Eltern, Großeltern, Freunde). Sprich laut, deutlich und langsam.

Wie halte ich eine gute Präsentation?

- Warte, bis es ruhig ist. Schau die Zuhörer/innen an.
- Erkläre, worüber du sprechen wirst und wie deine Präsentation aufgebaut ist.
- Lies nicht von deinen Karten ab, sondern sprich möglichst frei.
- Bedanke dich fürs Zuhören und frag, ob jemand Fragen hat.

SF 24 REVISION Peer feedback

Gegenseitige Rückmeldungen sind für dich und deine Partner wichtig. Du kannst darin jemanden loben für etwas, das er/sie gut gemacht hat, Hinweise geben, wo deine Partner noch Probleme haben. Du selbst erfährst, was du schon gut kannst und was du anders machen könntest.

Was muss ich beachten?

Bei deiner Rückmeldung solltest du drei Dinge beachten:

- Halte dich an die Punkte, zu denen du Rückmeldung geben sollst, z.B. die Aussprache, Betonung und Verständlichkeit bei einem Dialog, die Rechtschreibfehler in einem Text, das Einhalten eines roten Fadens in einer Geschichte usw. Begründe deine Einschätzungen.
- Gib deine Rückmeldung mit Respekt – niemand soll sich angegriffen fühlen. Nenne zuerst Gelungenes und mache dann Verbesserungsvorschläge zu Punkten, die aus deiner Sicht noch nicht so gelungen sind.
- Wenn du eine Rückmeldung bekommst, überdenke die Vorschläge gut. Korrigiere die Fehler, die andere gefunden haben, und arbeite an den Stellen nach, wo du eventuell Probleme hattest.

What I liked	What you could do better
You chose a great photo. ☺ You spoke clearly and looked at us. ...	Next time, say what is happening in the photo. Sometimes you stood in front of the photo. ...

Grammar File – Inhalt

Seite

Das **Grammar File** (S. 154–171) fasst die in diesem Englischbuch behandelten grammatischen Themen zusammen. Hier kannst du nachsehen,

- wenn du selbstständig etwas lernen oder etwas wiederholen möchtest,
- wenn du Übungen aus dem *Practice*-Teil deines Englischbuches oder aus dem *Workbook* bearbeitest,
- wenn du dich auf einen Test vorbereiten willst.

Besonders wichtig sind die Stellen mit den **roten Ausrufezeichen** (!). Sie zeigen, was im Deutschen anders ist, und machen dich auf besondere Fehlerquellen aufmerksam.

Verweise wie ➔ *Unit 1: p. 21, exercises 1–3* zeigen dir, welche **Übungen** zum gerade behandelten grammatischen Thema gehören.

In English: The simple past

In English-Abschnitte enthalten kurze Zusammenfassungen der wichtigsten grammatischen Regeln auf Englisch.

Additional information

Mit **Additional information** sind zusätzliche Informationen gekennzeichnet, die du dir auch gut anschauen solltest.

Die **grammatischen Fachbegriffe** *(grammatical terms)* kannst du auf den Seiten 170–171 nachschlagen.

Am Ende der Abschnitte stehen kleine **Aufgaben** zur **Selbstkontrolle**. Hier kannst du überprüfen, ob du das gerade behandelte Thema verstanden hast. Auf S. 171 kannst du nachsehen, ob deine Lösungen richtig sind.

GF 1 The past Die Vergangenheit

1.1 REVISION The simple past — Die einfache Form der Vergangenheit

*Last Saturday, Mo and Luke **went** to* One New Change. *They **didn't want** to go shopping there, they **wanted** to go up on the roof.*

*On the roof, they **saw** lots of tourists and **heard** lots of different languages. Later, they **talked** to a girl called Emily and her parents. Mo **told** them about the Shard … and about his blog.*

Wenn du über **Vergangenes** berichtest – z.B., wenn du eine Geschichte erzählst –, benutzt du überwiegend das ***simple past***.
Das *simple past* drückt aus, dass etwas **zu einem bestimmten Zeitpunkt** oder **in einem bestimmten Zeitraum** in der Vergangenheit stattfand.

Das *simple past* steht häufig mit Zeitangaben wie ***last Saturday, yesterday, two years ago, in 2010***.

want* → *wanted ***arrive* → *arrived***
stop* → *stopped ***try* → *tried***

◀ Bei **regelmäßigen** Verben hängst du ***-ed*** an den Infinitiv, um das *simple past* zu bilden.

go* → *went ***meet* → *met***
hear* → *heard ***tell* → *told***

◀ **Unregelmäßige** Verben haben eine eigene Form für das *simple past*, die du einzeln lernen musst.

➜ *Liste der unregelmäßigen Verben, S. 246–247*

*Mo and Luke **didn't meet** their friends at the shopping centre.*
*– Who **did** they **meet**? **Did** they **meet** their parents?*
*No, they **didn't**. They met Emily.*

◀ **Verneinte Aussagesätze** im *simple past* werden mit ***didn't*** gebildet, **Fragen** mit ***did***.

(**Ausnahme**: Verneinungen und Fragen mit dem Verb ***be*** werden nicht mit ***did*** gebildet:
Was it expensive? – No, it wasn't.)

➜ *Unit 1: p. 12, exercise 2*

Die einfache Form der Vergangenheit

Bejahte Aussagen	Verneinte Aussagen	Fragen
I/You/He/She/It talk**ed** …	I/You/He/She/It **didn't** talk …	**Did** I/you/he/she/it talk …?
We/They talk**ed** …	We/They **didn't** talk …	**Did** we/they talk …?

In English: The simple past

You use the **simple past**

- when you want to say or ask when something happened
- when you talk about things in the past (e.g. when you tell a story).

1.2 REVISION The present perfect

Das *present perfect*

*Luke **has been** at the shopping centre before.*
*But he**'s** never **been** up on the roof.*
Luke ist schon einmal im Einkaufszentrum gewesen.
Aber er war noch nie auf dem Dach.

Auch das ***present perfect*** wird verwendet, um über etwas zu sprechen, das in der Vergangenheit geschehen ist. Aber es ist nicht wichtig oder gar nicht bekannt, wann das war – ein genauer Zeitpunkt wird nicht genannt.

*Mo **hasn't been** up the Shard yet. It's too expensive.*
***Have** you ever **visited** the Shard?*

Das *present perfect* steht oft mit Adverbien der unbestimmten Zeit wie ***just, already, often, never, not … yet, before***.

*Emily **has given** Mo her number. Now he can text her.*

◄ Das ***present perfect*** wird oft verwendet, wenn man betonen will, dass ein vergangenes Geschehen wichtig für die Gegenwart oder die Zukunft ist: Emily hat Mo ihre Nummer gegeben; jetzt kann Mo ihr Mails schicken.

Das ***present perfect*** wird mit ***have/has*** **+ 3. Form des Verbs** (Partizip Perfekt; englisch: *past participle*) gebildet.

visit* → *visited ***phone* → *phoned***
plan* → *planned ***copy* → *copied***

◄ Bei **regelmäßigen** Verben hängst du ***-ed*** an den Infinitiv, um das *past participle* zu bilden (wie bei der Bildung der *simple past*-Form).

be* → *been ***take* → *taken***
give* → *given ***see* → *seen***

◄ **Unregelmäßige** Verben haben eigene *past participle*-Formen, die du einzeln lernen musst.

➜ *Liste der unregelmäßigen Verben, S. 246–247*

➜ *Unit 1: p. 12, exercise 3*

Das *present perfect*

Bejahte Aussagen	Verneinte Aussagen	Fragen
I've visited …	I haven't visited …	Have I/you/we/they visited …?
You've visited …	You haven't visited …	
He**'s**/She**'s**/It**'s** visited … (= He/She/It **has** visited …)	He/She/It hasn't visited …	Has he/she/it visited …
We've/They've visited …	We/They haven't visited …	

In English: The present perfect
You use the **present perfect**
- to say that something has happened (not when it happened).

1.3 REVISION Present perfect or simple past?

Present perfect oder *simple past*?

Mo: ***Have** you **been** here before?*

Luke: *Yeah, I **came** with Dad **a few months ago**.*
*We **bought** mum's birthday present here.*

Mo: *So, **have** you **been** up on the roof too?*

*"We only **arrived** **yesterday evening**, so we **haven't seen** much yet."*

➜ *Unit 1: p. 13, exercise 4*

- ***Present perfect:***
  - wenn du sagen willst, **dass etwas (irgendwann) geschehen ist**
  - wenn du fragen willst, **ob etwas geschehen ist**

  Ein Zeitpunkt wird nicht genannt (er ist nicht wichtig oder nicht bekannt).
- ***Simple past:***
  - wenn du sagen oder fragen willst, **wann etwas geschehen ist**

  In *simple past*-Sätzen stehen oft genaue Zeitangaben wie *yesterday, last year, an hour ago, in 2012*.

Alles verstanden? Dann vervollständige jetzt diese beiden kurzen Dialoge. Wo muss es *simple past* sein, wo *present perfect*? (Auf S. 171 kannst du nachschauen, ob deine Lösungen richtig sind.)

1 Katie: *Hannah and I … (decide) to go to that rock concert in Bath. Do you want to come with us?*
Daniel: *No, thanks. I … (see) both bands on TV last month, and I … (not like) them.*

2 Thomas: *Hi Jessica. … (you/just arrive)?*
Jessica: *Yes, I'm a bit late. … (the meeting/start yet)?*
Thomas: *I think so. Mr Carter … (go in) a few minutes ago.*

1.4 The present perfect progressive

Die Verlaufsform des *present perfect*

*You**'ve been watching** TV for hours.*
Du siehst (schon) seit Stunden fern.

***Have** you **been waiting** long?*
Wartest du schon lange?

*How long **has** she **been going** to this school?*
Wie lange/Seit wann geht sie (schon) auf diese Schule?

Mit dem ***present perfect progressive*** kannst du ausdrücken, dass etwas in der Vergangenheit begonnen hat und bis jetzt andauert.

! Im **Deutschen** benutzen wir meist das Präsens:
*Ich **warte** hier seit fünf Minuten.*
Im **Englischen** steht das *present perfect progressive*:
*I**'ve been waiting** here for five minutes.*

Das *present perfect progressive*

I've been waiting …
You've been waiting …
He's/She's/It's been waiting …
(= He/She/It **has** been waiting …)
We've/They've been waiting …

Have you been waiting long?
Has he/she/it been waiting long?
How long have they been waiting?
How long has he/she/it been waiting?

Das ***present perfect progressive*** wird mit ***have/has been*** + ***ing*-Form** gebildet.

! Im **Deutschen** verwenden wir **„seit"**, um zu sagen, seit wann oder wie lange etwas schon andauert. Im **Englischen** wird zwischen ***since*** und ***for*** unterschieden:

1 *I**'ve been watching** TV **since** 10 o'clock.*
Ich sehe seit 10 Uhr fern.

*England **has been playing** better **since** the break.*
England spielt besser seit der Halbzeitpause.

◄ 1 Mit ***since*** gibt man einen **Zeitpunkt** an:
since 10 o'clock; since 2012; since Monday morning; since I was born
since* + *Zeitpunkt drückt aus, **seit wann** etwas bereits andauert.

2 *I**'ve been waiting** here **for** five minutes, boys.*
Ich warte hier (schon) seit fünf Minuten, Jungs.

*We**'ve been living** here **for** 14 years now.*
Wir wohnen jetzt (schon) seit 14 Jahren hier.

◄ 2 Mit ***for*** gibt man einen **Zeitraum** an:
for hours; for 14 years; for five minutes; for a long time.
for* + *Zeitraum drückt aus, **wie lange** etwas bereits andauert.

***since* + Zeitpunkt – *for* + Zeitraum**

It's **4 o'clock**. Hannah and Declan are in the kitchen.

They've been working in the kitchen …
… **since 3:30**. — seit 15 Uhr 30
… **for half an hour**. — seit einer halben Stunde

➜ *Unit 1: p. 21, exercises 1–3*

In English: The present perfect progressive

You use the **present perfect progressive**

- to say that something began in the past and is still going on now.

Sieh dir die Bilder an und schreib die dazu passenden Sätze in dein Heft.

1 

They – wait – a long time

2 

She – read – lunchtime

3 

He – play – an hour

Additional information

*They**'ve been** in London since last month.*
Sie sind seit letztem Monat in London.

*We**'ve had** our dog for more than three years now.*
Wir haben unseren Hund jetzt seit mehr als drei Jahren.

*How long **have** you **known** your boyfriend?*
Wie lange kennst du deinen Freund (schon)?

Would you like to visit me in Sydney?
*– I'd love to. I**'ve** always **wanted** to go to Australia.*
… Ich wollte schon immer nach Australien reisen

! Verben, die nicht Tätigkeiten, sondern **Zustände** beschreiben, werden in der Regel **nicht in der Verlaufsform** verwendet (siehe die Beispiele links).

Wichtige Zustandsverben sind

- ***be*** („sein"), ***have*** („haben, besitzen"), ***own*** („besitzen")
- ***believe*** („glauben"), ***know*** („wissen, kennen"), ***think*** („meinen, glauben")
- ***like*** („mögen"), ***love*** („lieben"), ***want*** („wollen, haben wollen")

1.5 The past perfect

Das *past perfect*

*Aunt Mary **woke up** when we **arrived**. The owner's daughter **showed** us our cottage.*
Tante Mary wachte auf, als wir ankamen. Die Tochter der Besitzerin zeigte uns unser Cottage.

◄ Wie du weißt, gebraucht man überwiegend das *simple past*, wenn man über Vergangenes redet.

*When the guests arrived, Mum **had** already **gone** to bed.*
Als die Gäste ankamen, war Mutter schon ins Bett gegangen.

*I **had planned** to ride down to the beach, so we had a big argument.*
Ich hatte geplant, hinunter zum Strand zu reiten, …

◄ Wenn du sagen willst, dass etwas **noch vor etwas anderem in der Vergangenheit** stattgefunden hatte, verwendest du das ***past perfect*** (deutsch: Vorvergangenheit, Plusquamperfekt).

Handlung 1 *(past perfect)* geschah vor **Handlung 2**:

*When I **had shown** (1) them their cottage, I **said** (2) good night.*

*My mother **went** to bed when the guests arrived.*
Meine Mutter ging ins Bett, als die Gäste ankamen.
(die Gäste kamen, und sie ging ins Bett)

*My mother **had gone** to bed when the guests arrived.*
Meine Mutter war ins Bett gegangen, als die Gäste ankamen.
(sie war schon im Bett, als die Gäste ankamen)

! Beachte die Bedeutungsunterschiede, je nachdem, ob du das ***simple past*** oder das ***past perfect*** verwendest.

Das *past perfect*

Bejahte Aussagen	**Verneinte Aussagen**	**Fragen**
I had visited …	I hadn't seen …	Had I closed …?
You had visited …	You hadn't seen …	Had you closed …?
He/She/It had visited …	He/She/It hadn't seen …	Had he/she/it closed …?
We/They had visited …	We/They hadn't seen …	Had we/they closed …?

Das ***past perfect*** wird mit ***had*** (Kurzform: ***'d***) und der **3. Form des Verbs** (Partizip Perfekt; englisch: *past participle*) gebildet.

*I was sure I **had seen** this before.*
Ich war sicher, dass ich dies schon einmal **gesehen hatte**.

*I was sure I **had been** here before.*
Ich war sicher, dass ich schon einmal hier **gewesen war**.

! Das ***past perfect*** wird immer mit ***had*** gebildet, egal ob im Deutschen „**hatte**" oder „**war**" steht.

➔ *Unit 4: p. 76, exercises 5–6*

In English: The past perfect
You use the **past perfect**
- for actions that finished before a time in the past.

Sieh dir die Bilder genau an und vervollständige die Sätze.
Wo muss es *simple past* sein, wo *past perfect*?

Holly didn't go to the cinema because …

1 *she … (leave) her money at home.*
2 *the queue … (be) too long.*

Matthew bought lots of apples because …

3 *they … (be) very cheap.*
4 *his mother … (ask) him to get some fruit.*

GF 2 The future Die Zukunft

2.1 REVISION The *will*-future — Das Futur mit *will*

*When **will** Mum **be** back? – She **won't be** back till tomorrow.*

Mit ***will/won't* + Infinitiv** sagst du, was in der Zukunft geschehen wird.

*I'm sure you**'ll** soon **speak** Welsh as well as the others.*

◂ Wenn **Vermutungen** geäußert werden, steht häufig *I (don't) think, I'm (not) sure, maybe* oder *probably*.

*Wales **will get** a lot of rain tomorrow, and it **will be** very windy in Scotland.*

◂ Oft geht es um Dinge, die man nicht beeinflussen kann, z.B. **Vorhersagen** über das Wetter.

*Laugh with the others, then you**'ll feel** better.*
Lach mit den anderen, dann **fühlst** du dich besser.

! Im Deutschen benutzen wir oft das Präsens, wenn wir Vermutungen äußern oder Vorhersagen machen. Im Englischen steht das *will-future*.

➔ *Unit 2: p. 31, exercise 2*

2.2 REVISION The *going to*-future

The Evans family ***is going to move*** *to Wales.*
Mrs Evans is happy that they ***are going to live*** *in the country.*

Das Futur mit *going to*

Wenn es um **Vorhaben, Pläne, Absichten** für die Zukunft geht, verwendet man ***am/are/is going to*** **+ Infinitiv**.

! ***going to*** hat hier nichts mit „gehen" zu tun. ***I'm going to*** … bedeutet so viel wie „Ich werde …", „Ich habe vor …".

2.3 REVISION The present progressive: future meaning

Emily and her new class ***are climbing*** *Mt Snowdon next weekend.*

What ***are*** *you* ***doing*** *on Sunday?* ***Are*** *you* ***going*** *skiing again?*

Das *present progressive*: futurische Bedeutung

Wenn etwas für die Zukunft **fest verabredet** ist, kannst du auch das ***present progressive*** benutzen. Es muss aber deutlich sein, dass es sich um etwas Zukünftiges handelt, z.B. durch eine Zeitangabe *(next weekend, tomorrow, on Sunday)* oder aus dem Zusammenhang.

(Man nennt diese Verwendung des *present progressive* manchmal *diary future*, weil es dabei oft um Verabredungen geht, die schon im Terminkalender eingetragen sind.)

Additional information

2.4 The simple present: future meaning

The next train to Cardiff ***leaves*** *at 8:25.*

Our French classes ***start*** *on Monday.*

Das *simple present*: futurische Bedeutung

Auch das ***simple present*** kann futurische Bedeutung haben. Es wird verwendet, wenn ein zukünftiges Geschehen durch einen **Fahrplan**, ein **Programm** oder Ähnliches genau festgelegt ist. Verben wie ***arrive, leave, go, open, close, start, stop*** werden häufig so verwendet.

(Diese Verwendung des *simple present* wird als *timetable future* bezeichnet.)

In English: Talking about the future

You often use the **will-future** to talk about the future.
But …

- you use the **going to-future** for intentions and plans for the future
- you can use the **present progressive** to talk about what you have arranged to do in the future
- you can use the **simple present** for future events that are listed in a timetable or programme.

Schreibe die Sätze mit der passenden Futurform in dein Heft.

1 *Do you think it … tomorrow?* *(will rain / is raining)*
2 *Have you got any plans for this summer? – Yes, we … to Spain.* *('ll fly / 're going to fly)*
3 *Do you like your new flat? – Well, it's too small, really. We … out again. We've already started looking.* *('ll move / 're going to move)*
4 *Are you free next Friday? – No, I … Julian.* *('ll meet / 'm meeting)*

GF 3 Conditional sentences Bedingungssätze

3.1 REVISION Conditional sentences, type 1

Bedingungssätze, Typ 1

Emily: ***If** I **hear** one more word of Welsh, **I'll scream**!*
Wenn ich noch ein walisisches Wort höre, dann schreie ich!

Dad: *You**'ll** soon **speak** Welsh as well as the others **if** you **don't give up**.*
Du wirst bald genauso gut Walisisch sprechen wie die anderen, wenn du nicht aufgibst.

Dad: ***If** you **laugh** with the others, you **won't feel** so bad.*
Wenn du mit den anderen lachst, fühlst du dich nicht so schlecht.

Emily: *I **can't laugh** at their jokes if I don't understand them, Dad.*

Dad: *If they speak too fast, **ask** them to slow down.*

➜ *Unit 2: p. 31, exercise 3*

Bedingungssätze vom Typ 1 sind „**Was ist, wenn …**"-Sätze: Sie beschreiben, was unter bestimmten Bedingungen geschieht oder nicht geschieht.

Die Bedingung steht im *if*-Satz. Der Hauptsatz sagt aus, was passiert, wenn die Bedingung erfüllt wird:

Bedingung	Folge für die Zukunft
***If** it **rains**,*	*we**'ll stay** at home.*
simple present	***will-future***

Im *if*-Satz steht das *simple present*. Im Hauptsatz steht meist das *will-future*.

◄ Im Hauptsatz können auch *can, must, could, should* + Infinitiv oder ein Imperativ stehen.

3.2 Conditional sentences, type 2

Bedingungssätze, Typ 2

Dylan: ***If** you **gave** me a pound for every trip, I **would be** rich.*
Wenn du mir für jeden Ausflug ein Pfund geben würdest, dann wäre ich reich.

! Kein *would* im *if*-Satz! Nicht: *If you ~~would give~~ me …*

Dylan: ***If** I **had** a kayak, **I'd paddle** right down from the top to this pool.*
Wenn ich ein Kajak hätte, würde ich geradewegs … hinunterpaddeln.

*Emily **wouldn't feel** so bad **if** her Welsh **was** better.*
Emily würde sich nicht so schlecht fühlen, wenn ihr Walisisch besser wäre.

*If Philip read the message, he **could get** the wrong idea.*
… könnte er das missverstehen.

➜ *Unit 2: pp. 36–37, exercises 1–4*

Bedingungssätze vom Typ 2 sind „**Was wäre, wenn …**"-Sätze: Sie drücken aus, dass etwas nicht sehr wahrscheinlich oder sogar unmöglich ist:

1 ***If** we **met** Emily in Wales, we **would go** climbing together.*

2 *"**If** I **were** you, **I'd go** down the waterfall inside a beach ball", said Philip.*

Es ist unwahrscheinlich, dass wir Emily in Wales treffen (Satz 1), und Philip ist nun einmal nicht Dylan (Satz 2). Die Sprecher/innen drücken nur aus, was geschehen würde oder der Fall wäre, wenn …

Bedingung	Folge für die Zukunft
***If** you **did** that,*	*you **would die**.*
simple past	***would + infinitive***

Im *if*-Satz steht das *simple past*. Im Hauptsatz steht meist *would* + Infinitiv (Kurzform: *'d*).

◄ Im Hauptsatz kann auch *could* („könnte") + Infinitiv stehen.

! Beachte, dass nach ***I*** im *if*-Satz oft ***were*** statt ***was*** steht:
If I were a cat …
(*If I was* … ist aber ebenfalls möglich.)

In English: Conditional sentences

- **Type 1:**

  simple present — will-future or can/must/should + infinitive

  *If she **wins** the competition, she **will be** the star of the whole school.*

  The speaker thinks there is a good chance that she will win the competition.

- **Type 2:**

  simple past — would + infinitive or could + infinitive

  *If she **won** the competition, she **would be** the star of the whole school.*

  The speaker thinks it is less probable that she will win the competition.

Vervollständige die Sätze in deinem Heft. Achte auf die richtige Form der Verben.

1 *If the weather **is** nice, we … (have) a picnic in the park.*
2 ***Would** you **change** anything if you … (be) the head teacher at your school?*
3 *What **would** you **do** if your classmates … (make) fun of you?*
4 *If we really **go** to Wales this summer, I … (try) to climb Mount Snowdon.*
5 *If I **had** more money, I … (travel) all over Europe in the summer.*
6 *If you … (not hurry up) now, you'**ll be** late for school.*

GF 4 Relative clauses Relativsätze

4.1 REVISION Relative pronouns Relativpronomen

Mit **Relativsätzen** beschreibt man genauer, über wen oder was man spricht.

*These shops are for **tourists** who like the Beatles.*
Diese Läden sind für Touristen, die die Beatles mögen.

◂ Das Relativpronomen ***who*** steht in Relativsätzen, die **Personen** beschreiben:
*The **girl/boy/student/tourists** who …*

*It's a **market** which sells food and clothes.*

◂ Das Relativpronomen ***which*** steht in Relativsätzen, die **Dinge** (und Tiere) beschreiben:
*The **market/bag/dogs/places** which …*

*John Lennon is **the Beatle** that Gareth likes best.*

*Mathew Street is the **street** that's full of tourist shops.*

◂ Das Relativpronomen ***that*** wird für Personen und Dinge verwendet.

! Beachte

– die unterschiedliche **Wortstellung** in englischen und deutschen Relativsätzen

*… for tourists **who** like **the Beatles**.*
… für Touristen, **die die Beatles** mögen.

– die **Stellung der Präposition** in englischen Relativsätzen.

*What was the name of the market **that we went** to?*
Wie hieß der Markt, zu **dem wir gegangen sind**?

➔ *Unit 3: p. 48 , exercises 2–3*

In English: Relative Pronouns

You use
- **who** for people
- **which** for things
- **that** for people and things.

4.2 Contact clauses

Relativsätze ohne Relativpronomen

	subject
Gareth is the boy	***who likes** the Beatles.*
... der Junge,	**der** die Beatles mag.
Where are the shops	***which sell** Beatles souvenirs?*
... die Läden,	**die** Beatles-Souvenirs verkaufen?

Das Relativpronomen kann **Subjekt** oder **Objekt** sein.

◂ Hier sind die Relativpronomen **Subjekt des Relativsatzes**. Sie stehen **direkt vor dem Verb**.

	object	subject	
John is the Beatle	*who*	*Gareth*	***likes** best.*
... der Beatle,	den	Gareth	am liebsten mag.
Remember the plan	*that*	*we*	***made**, Gareth?*
... an den Plan,	den	wir	gemacht haben, ...?

◂ Hier sind die Relativpronomen **Objekt des Relativsatzes**. Auf das Relativpronomen folgt das Subjekt des Relativsatzes, und dann das Verb.

John is the Beatle		*Gareth*	***likes** best.*
Remember the plan		*we*	***made**, Gareth?*

Wenn das Relativpronomen **Objekt** ist, wird es oft **weggelassen**. (Das ist im Deutschen nicht möglich.) Relativsätze ohne Relativpronomen werden ***contact clauses*** genannt.

*Where's the shop **that sells** plantains?*

! Vorsicht:
Wenn das **Relativpronomen direkt vor dem Verb** steht, dann ist es **Subjekt** und **darf nicht weggelassen werden**.

➔ *Unit 3: p. 49, exercises 4–5*

In English: Contact clauses

- The relative pronoun can be the subject or the object of the relative clause.
- When the relative pronoun is the object of the relative clause, you can leave it out.
- A relative clause without a relative pronoun is called a **contact clause**.

In welchen Sätzen kannst du das **Relativpronomen** weglassen?
Schreibe die Sätze als ***contact clauses*** in dein Heft.

1 *It is Gareth **who** thinks that plantains are green bananas.*
2 *Look, that's the cathedral **that** the choir went to for the concert.*
3 *Chinatown Arch is the gate **that** Gwen saw in the guidebook.*
4 *Gwen is the girl **who** wanted to go to Greaty.*
5 *It was Morgan's plan **that** made everybody happy.*
6 *Birkenhead is the town **which** you can see across the Mersey.*

GF 5 The passive Das Passiv

5.1 Active and passive — Aktiv und Passiv

subject	**verb (active)**	
Young men	***wear***	*masks with animal faces.*

Junge Männer tragen Masken mit Tiergesichtern.

◄ Mit einem **Aktivsatz** drückst du aus, **wer oder was etwas tut**. Das Subjekt des Aktivsatzes führt die Handlung aus. Der Beispielsatz sagt etwas über junge Männer aus – nämlich, dass sie Masken tragen.

subject	**verb (passive)**	
Animal masks	***are worn***	*in Nigeria today.*

Tiermasken werden heute in Nigeria getragen.

◄ **Passivsätze** drücken aus, **mit wem oder was etwas geschieht**.
Der Beispielsatz sagt etwas über Tiermasken aus – nämlich, dass sie in Nigeria getragen werden.

The slavery museum ***was founded*** *to tell the story of slavery.*
Das Sklaverei-Museum wurde gegründet, um die Geschichte der Sklaverei zu erzählen.

Two computers ***were stolen*** *from the museum's office last night.*

The car crashed into a wall, but the driver ***wasn't hurt****.*

Were *many people* ***killed*** *in the plane crash?*

Mit einem **Passivsatz** kannst du Handlungen beschreiben, ohne zu sagen, wer die Handlung ausführt. Oft ist gar nicht bekannt oder nicht wichtig, wer die Handlung ausführt.

Daher wird das Passiv oft in Nachrichten und Zeitungsberichten (z.B. über Unfälle oder Verbrechen), in technischen Beschreibungen und auf Schildern verwendet, wenn man den „Täter" oder „Verursacher" nicht nennen kann oder nicht nennen will.

◄ Im Deutschen verwenden wir oft einen Aktivsatz mit „man" in Situationen, in denen im Englischen ein Passivsatz steht.

5.2 The passive: form — Das Passiv: Form

First, the mud for the houses ***is made****.*
Then the floors and walls ***are built*** *with the mud.*

The goat face mask ***was made*** *in West Africa.*
Udus ***were used*** *to carry water.*

➔ *Unit 3: pp. 54–55, exercises 1–3, 5*

Das **Passiv** bildest du mit einer **Form von *be*** und der **3. Form des Verbs** (Partizip Perfekt; *past participle*).

Simple present: ***am/are/is*** **+ *past participle***
The mud ***is made*** *…*
The walls ***are built*** *…*

Simple past: ***was/were*** **+ *past participle***
The mask ***was made*** *…*
Udus ***were used*** *…*

➔ *Liste der unregelmäßigen Verben, S. 246–247*

5.3 Passive sentences with *by* — Passivsätze mit *by*

Udus ***are played by*** *women.*
Udus werden von Frauen gespielt.

Over 30 houses ***were destroyed by a storm****.*
Über 30 Häuser wurden durch ein Unwetter zerstört.

➔ *Unit 3: p. 55, exercise 4*

Wenn man in einem Passivsatz den „Täter" oder „Verursacher" nennen will, verwendet man die Präposition ***by*** („von", „durch").

In English: The passive

- An **active** sentence describes what somebody (or something) does:
  The Hills sell *fruit and vegetables.*
  (You are talking about what the Hills do.)
- A **passive** sentence describes what is done or what happens to people or things; often we do not say who does the action:
  Fruit and vegetables are sold *at lots of markets.*
  (You are talking about where people can buy fruit and vegetables.)
- **Passive** sentences are made with a form of ***be*** + **past participle**.
- You can use ***by*** in a passive sentence if you want to say who does the action:
  The song 'Imagine' is sung ***by John Lennon.***

Vervollständige die Passivsätze in deinem Heft mit den Verben aus den Kästchen.
Achte auf die richtige Zeitform (*simple present* oder *simple past*).

build · call · open · play · speak · write

1 *The djembe* ***is*** *… with bare hands, not with sticks.*
2 *The street market in Great Homer Street … 'Greaty'.*
3 *The new Beatles museum … by the mayor last Saturday.*
4 *The Beatles Platz in Hamburg … as a monument to the famous band's time in Germany.*
5 *German … in Germany, Switzerland and Austria.*
6 *The song 'We will rock you' … by* Queen.

GF 6 Modals and their substitutes Modale Hilfsverben und ihre Ersatzverben

6.1 REVISION Modal auxiliaries Modale Hilfsverben

Can, may, must, should usw. sind **modale Hilfsverben** (*modal auxiliaries* oder kurz: *modals*). Sie drücken aus, was jemand tun **kann, darf, muss, soll** usw.

1 *I* ***can clear*** *the table.*
Can you ***wash*** *the dishes?*

2 *Yes, I* ***can****. / No, I* ***can't****.*

3 *I* ***must help*** *Dad in the garden now.*
We ***should visit*** *Grandma tomorrow.*

1 Modale Hilfsverben werden zusammen mit dem Infinitiv eines Vollverbs verwendet. Frage und Verneinung werden ohne *do/does/did* gebildet.
2 Nur in Kurzantworten können modale Hilfsverben allein stehen.
3 Modale Hilfsverben beziehen sich in der Regel auf die Gegenwart oder die Zukunft.

! Vorsicht bei ***must***, ***mustn't*** und ***needn't***:

You ***must feed*** *the cats. They're hungry.*

- Mit ***must*** drückt man aus, dass jemand etwas **tun muss**.

You ***needn't feed*** *the dogs. Mum has fed them already.*

- Mit ***needn't*** drückt man aus, dass jemand etwas **nicht tun muss**.

You ***mustn't feed*** *the birds. Bread is bad for them.*

- Mit ***mustn't*** drückt man aus, dass jemand etwas **nicht tun darf**.

➔ *Unit 4: p. 68, exercise 2*

6.2 *(to) be able to – (to) be allowed to – (to) have to*

(to) be able to – (to) be allowed to – (to) have to

Wenn es um „können", „dürfen", „müssen" in der **Vergangenheit** oder der **Zukunft** geht, werden meist **Ersatzverben** verwendet:

*I forgot my key, but I **was able to get** in through the window.*
*Tomorrow is Saturday, so we'**ll be able to sleep** a bit longer.*

◂ **„können"**: *(to)* ***be able to***
– jemand konnte etwas tun (Vergangenheit): *was/were able to …*
– jemand wird etwas tun können (Zukunft): *will be able to …*

***Were** you **allowed to take** photos at the concert?*
– Yes, we were.
*You'**ll be allowed to go** to discos when you're a bit older.*

◂ **„dürfen"**: *(to)* ***be allowed to***
– jemand durfte etwas tun (Vergangenheit): *was/were allowed to …*
– jemand wird etwas tun dürfen (Zukunft): *will be allowed to …*

*I felt so ill that I **had to stay** in bed.*

*If it doesn't work the first time, you'**ll have to try** again.*

◂ **„müssen"**: *(to)* ***have to***
– jemand musste etwas tun (Vergangenheit): *had to …*
– jemand wird etwas tun müssen (Zukunft): *will have to …*

! Beachte die folgenden Hinweise:

1 *I'**m not allowed to go** to parties.*
*Have you got a minute? I **have to talk** to you.*

1 Alle Ersatzverben können auch im *simple present* verwendet werden.

2 *I looked everywhere, but I **couldn't find** my key.*
*I **could hear** music, but I **couldn't see** anybody.*

2 Zu *can* gibt es auch die Vergangenheitsform *could*, die überwiegend in verneinten Sätzen vorkommt. Die bejahte Form *could* wird häufig mit Verben der Wahrnehmung *(see, hear, …)* verwendet.

3 ***Did** you **have to wait** long?*
*You **don't have to show** your passport when you cross the border.*

3 Das Ersatzverb *(to) have to* bildet Fragen und Verneinungen im *simple present* und *simple past* mit *do/does/did*.

➜ *Unit 4: p. 72, exercises 1–3*

In English: Modals and their substitutes

- **Modal auxiliaries** like *can, may, must, should*, etc.
  – are followed by an infinitive (without *to*): *You should feed the cats now.*
  – never have *do/does/did* in questions and negatives: *Sorry, I can't help you.*
  – are usually used to talk about the present or the future: *Could I have a glass of water, please?* (present) *Can we go to the zoo tomorrow?* (future)

- **Substitutes** are used to form other tenses:

can („können")	– *(to) be able to*:	*The driver was able to stop the car.* *I'll be able to buy a new car with this money.*
can, may („dürfen")	– *(to) be allowed to*:	*We weren't allowed to use a dictionary.* *I'll be allowed to drive next year.*
must („müssen")	– *(to) have to*:	*We didn't have to wait long.* *We'll have to work very hard next month.*

Vervollständige das Gespräch mit Formen von *have to* (2x), *be able to*, *be allowed to* und *not be allowed to*:

1 Katie: *My mother is so strict. Yesterday I wanted to go out, but I … stay in and clean my room.*
2 Hannah: *My parents are strict too. I'm sure I … go to Jessica's party on Friday.*
3 Daniel: *Well, I think I … go, but I … be home by ten again, as usual.*
4 Holly: *I'm going to a music festival on Friday, so I … go to the party.*

GF 7 Reflexive pronouns Reflexivpronomen

7.1 *myself, yourself, himself, herself, itself, ourselves, yourselves, themselves*

*You have to **look after** **yourself** at sea.*
Auf dem Meer muss man auf **sich** **aufpassen**.

*Dolphins can't **protect** **themselves** from fishing boats.*
Delfine können **sich** nicht vor Fischerbooten **schützen**.

Reflexive pronouns

Singular		Plural	
myself	(ich) mir/mich	**ourselves**	(wir) uns
yourself	(du) dir/dich	**yourselves**	(ihr) euch
himself	(er) sich	**themselves**	(sie) sich
herself	(sie) sich		
itself	(er/sie/es) sich		

*When I was little, I always **felt** scared in the dark. When my parents were out, I often tried to **hide** in a cupboard. But that all **changed** when I got older, and now I don't **worry** any more.*

➜ *Unit 5: p. 85, exercise 2*

Morph is enjoying himself by the sea.

myself, yourself, himself, herself, itself, ourselves, yourselves, themselves

Reflexivpronomen bezeichnen dieselbe Person oder Sache wie das Subjekt des Satzes:

***John** went home and made **himself** a cup of tea.*
***John** ging heim und machte **sich** eine Tasse Tee.*

Das Reflexivpronomen ***himself*** bezieht sich zurück auf das Subjekt ***John***.

Die Betonung liegt auf der zweiten Silbe:
myself [maɪˈself] *usw.*
ourselves [aʊəˈselvz] *usw.*

! Es gibt eine Reihe von Verben, die im Deutschen **mit „sich"** gebraucht werden, im Englischen aber **ohne Reflexivpronomen**. Beispiele:

(to) **change**	*sich ändern*
(to) **feel**	*sich fühlen*
(to) **hide**	*sich verstecken*
(to) **imagine**	*sich (etwas) vorstellen*
(to) **meet**	*sich treffen*
(to) **move**	*sich bewegen*
(to) **relax**	*sich entspannen*
(to) **remember**	*sich erinnern*
(to) **sit down**	*sich hinsetzen*
(to) **wonder**	*sich fragen*
(to) **worry**	*sich Sorgen machen*

Merke dir auch diese Wendungen:

*Enjoy **yourself**.*	*Viel Spaß! / Amüsier dich gut!*
*Help **yourself**.*	*Greif zu! / Bedien dich!*

In English: Reflexive pronouns
A **reflexive pronoun** (e.g. *myself, themselves*) refers back to the subject of the sentence (e.g. *I, my sisters*).
I *cut* ***myself*** *with a breadknife.* ***My sisters*** *can look after* ***themselves****.*

7.2 *themselves* or *each other?*

themselves oder *each other?*

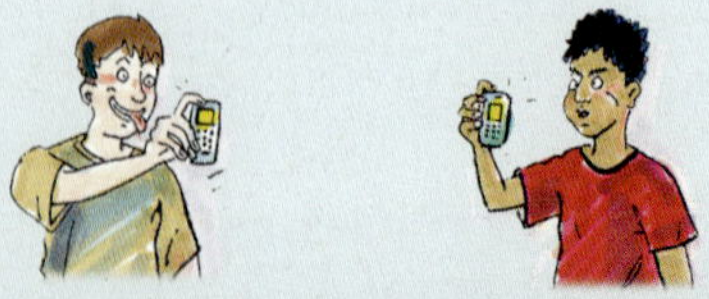

Finn and Asif are taking photos of ***themselves****.*
Finn und Asif machen Fotos von **sich (selbst)**.

Das Reflexivpronomen ***themselves*** steht für „**sich**" im Sinne von „**sich selbst**".

Now they are taking photos of ***each other****.*
Jetzt fotografieren sie **sich gegenseitig**.

Wenn „**sich gegenseitig**", „**einander**" gemeint ist, verwendest du ***each other***.

➔ *Unit 5: p.85, exercise 3*

Sieh dir die Bilder an und vervollständige die Sätze. Brauchst du *themselves* oder *each other?*

1 *They're laughing at …*
2 *They might hurt …*
3 *They're teaching … German.*
4 *They're talking to … on the phone.*

1

2

3

4

GF 8 Indirect speech Die indirekte Rede

8.1 Direct and indirect speech

Direkte und indirekte Rede

Direct speech *Skye says,* ***"It's too noisy."***
Skye sagt: **„Es ist zu laut."**

◀ In der **direkten Rede** *(direct speech)* gibt man **wörtlich** wieder, was jemand sagt oder schreibt (oder gesagt oder geschrieben hat).
Direkte Rede steht gewöhnlich in Anführungszeichen.

Indirect speech *Skye* ***says (that) it's too noisy.***
Skye **sagt, dass es zu laut ist.**

◀ In der **indirekten Rede** *(indirect speech* oder *reported speech)* **berichtet** man, was jemand sagt oder schreibt (oder gesagt oder geschrieben hat).
Die indirekte Rede wird mit Verben wie *say, tell sb., add, answer, explain, write* eingeleitet.

! Im Englischen steht vor der indirekten Rede **kein Komma**, und das Wort *that* („dass") wird oft weggelassen.

8.2 Indirect speech: tense changes

Indirekte Rede: Veränderungen der Zeitform

*I'**m** tired of it.*
*I **don't want** to be in this play any more!*

*Skye **told** Lewis that she **was** tired of it.*
*She **said** she **didn't want** to be in the play any more.*
Skye erzählte Lewis, dass sie es satt habe.
Sie sagte, dass sie bei dem Stück nicht mehr mitmachen wollte.

Wenn das einleitende Verb im ***simple past*** steht (*she **said**, she **told** me* usw.), werden in der indirekten Rede meist andere Zeitformen verwendet als in der direkten Rede: Die Zeitformen der direkten Rede werden um eine Zeitstufe in die Vergangenheit „zurückverschoben" (auf Englisch nennt man das *backshift of tenses*).

◄ So wird z.B. das *simple present* der direkten Rede in der indirekten Rede „zurückverschoben" zum *simple past*:
*"I'**m** …" → she **was** …*
*"I **don't want** …" → she **didn't want** …*

Tense changes

	Direct speech	Indirect speech
present → past	"We **need** you."	Lewis **told** Skye that they **needed** her.
	"No one **is missing** their cues."	Sandra **said** no one **was missing** their cues.
***will*-future → *would* + infinitive**	"We**'ll** never **get** it right."	Sandra **said** they **would** never **get** it right.
can* → *could	"I **can't hear** the cue."	Skye **said** she **couldn't hear** the cue.
past → past perfect[1]	"Skye **started** to cry."	Lewis **said** that Skye **had started** to cry.

[1] *Past tense*-Formen der direkten Rede werden in der indirekten Rede oft beibehalten, also nicht ins *past perfect* verändert: Lewis **said** that Skye **started** to cry.

Ella (zu Lucy): *"**I**'ll call **you** when **we**'re back."*

(Lucy berichtet ihrer Schwester:)
*Ella told me that **she** would call **me** when **they** were back.*

(Ella berichtet ihrem Vater:)
*I told Lucy that **I** would call **her** when **we** were back.*

◄ Wie im Deutschen werden in der indirekten Rede die Pronomen verändert, je nachdem, wer wem berichtet.

➜ *Unit 5: pp. 90–91, exercises 1–3*

In English: Indirect speech

- In **direct speech**, we repeat word for word what someone has said or written. We usually use quotation marks: *"I'm tired," she said.* In **indirect speech**, we report what someone has said or written: *She said/told me that she was tired.*
- If the **reporting verb** is in the **past** (*said, told,* etc.), there is usually a change of tenses – the verb forms move back a step into the past ("backshift of tenses"): **present → past, *will* → *would*, *can* → *could*.**

Berichte, was Iain gesagt hat. Schreib die Sätze in der indirekten Rede in dein Heft. Achte darauf, die richtigen Pronomen zu verwenden.

1 *"I love helping to make dolphin sightings."* — *Iain said he …*
2 *"Identifying dolphins isn't easy."* — *He explained that identifying dolphins …*
3 *"We're all looking forward to our next trip."* — *He told me they …*
4 *"We'll go out in our kayaks tomorrow."* — *He said that …*
5 *"You have to look after yourself at sea."* — *He also said you …*
6 *"You can't go out alone."* — *He added that …*

Grammatical terms (Grammatische Fachbegriffe)

active ['æktɪv]	Aktiv	*A heavy storm* ***destroyed*** *twelve houses.*
adjective ['ædʒɪktɪv]	Adjektiv (Eigenschaftswort)	*good, new, green, interesting, …*
adverb ['ædvɜːb]	Adverb	*today, there, outside, very, …*
adverb of frequency ['friːkwənsi]	Häufigkeitsadverb	*always, usually, often, sometimes, never*
adverb of indefinite time [ɪn'defɪnət]	Adverb der unbestimmten Zeit	*already, ever, just, never, before, yet, …*
adverb of manner ['mænə]	Adverb der Art und Weise	*nicely, happily, quietly, slowly, well, fast, …*
article ['ɑːtɪkl]	Artikel	*the, a, an*
backshift of tenses ['bækʃɪft]	Rückverschiebung der Zeitformen	*"I'm tired."* → *She said (that) she* ***was*** *tired.*
comparative [kəm'pærətɪv]	Komparativ (1. Steigerungsform)	*older; more expensive*
comparison [kəm'pærɪsn]	Steigerung	*old – older – oldest;* *expensive – more expensive – most expensive*
compound ['kɒmpaʊnd]	Zusammensetzung	*somebody, anyone, something, …*
conditional sentence [kən'dɪʃənl]	Bedingungssatz	*If I see Sam, I'll tell him.*
conjunction [kən'dʒʌŋkʃn]	Konjunktion	*and, but, …; because, when, …*
direct speech [ˌdaɪrekt 'spiːtʃ]	direkte Rede	***"I'm tired."***
contact clause ['kɒntækt klɔːz]	Relativsatz ohne Relativpronomen	*Here's the report* ***I've written****.*
***going to*-future** ['fjuːtʃə]	Futur mit *going to*	***I'm going to watch*** *TV tonight.*
imperative [ɪm'perətɪv]	Imperativ (Befehlsform)	*Open your books. Don't talk.*
indirect speech [ˌɪndərekt 'spiːtʃ]	indirekte Rede	*She said (that)* ***she was tired****.*
infinitive [ɪn'fɪnətɪv]	Infinitiv (Grundform des Verbs)	*(to) open, (to) go, …*
irregular verb [ɪ'regjələ]	unregelmäßiges Verb	*(to) go – went – gone,* *(to) see – saw – seen, …*
modal auxiliary [ˌməʊdl‿ɔːg'zɪliəri]	modales Hilfsverb, Modalverb	*can, may, might, needn't, should, must, …*
negative statement ['negətɪv]	verneinter Aussagesatz	*I don't like oranges.*
noun [naʊn]	Nomen, Substantiv	*Justin, girl, man, time, name, …*
object ['ɒbdʒɪkt]	Objekt	*Justin has* ***a new camera****.*
object question	Objektfrage, Frage nach dem Objekt	***Who did*** *Mrs Pascoe* ***invite*** *to tea?*
passive ['pæsɪv]	Passiv	*Twelve houses* ***were destroyed*** *by a storm.*
past participle [ˌpɑːst 'pɑːtɪsɪpl]	Partizip Perfekt	*checked, phoned, tried, gone, eaten, …*
past perfect [ˌpɑːst 'pɜːfɪkt]	*past perfect* (Vorvergangenheit, Plusquamperfekt)	*I* ***had*** *already* ***gone*** *to bed when they arrived.*
past progressive [ˌpɑːst prə'gresɪv]	Verlaufsform der Vergangenheit	*Olivia* ***was playing*** *cards.*
personal pronoun [ˌpɜːsənl 'prəʊnaʊn]	Personalpronomen (persönliches Fürwort)	*I, you, he, she, it, we, they;* *me, you, him, her, it, us, them*
plural ['plʊərəl]	Plural, Mehrzahl	
positive statement ['pɒzətɪv]	bejahter Aussagesatz	*I like oranges.*
possessive determiner [pəˌzesɪv dɪ'tɜːmɪnə]	Possessivbegleiter (besitzanzeigender Begleiter)	*my, your, his, her, its, our, their*
possessive form [pəˌzesɪv 'fɔːm]	s-Genitiv	*Sam's sister, the Blackwells' house, …*
preposition [ˌprepə'zɪʃn]	Präposition	*after, at, in, into, near, next to, …*
present perfect [ˌpreznt 'pɜːfɪkt]	*present perfect*	*We****'ve made*** *some scones for you.*
present perfect progressive [ˌpreznt ˌpɜːfɪkt prə'gresɪv]	Verlaufsform des *present perfect*	*He****'s been watching*** *TV for hours.*
present progressive [ˌpreznt prə'gresɪv]	Verlaufsform der Gegenwart	*Olivia* ***is playing*** *cards.*
pronoun ['prəʊnaʊn]	Pronomen (Fürwort)	
question tag ['kwestʃn tæg]	Frageanhängsel	*isn't he?, are you?, can't we?, …*
question word ['kwestʃn wɜːd]	Fragewort	*who?, what?, when?, where?, how?, …*
reflexive pronoun [rɪˌfleksɪv 'prəʊnaʊn]	Reflexivpronomen	*myself, yourself, themselves, …*
regular verb ['regjələ]	regelmäßiges Verb	*(to) help – helped, (to) look – looked, …*
relative clause [ˌrelətɪv 'klɔːz]	Relativsatz	*I like teachers* ***who laugh a lot****.*
relative pronoun [ˌrelətɪv 'prəʊnaʊn]	Relativpronomen	*who – which – that*
short answer [ˌʃɔːt‿'ɑːnsə]	Kurzantwort	*Yes, I am. / No, we don't. / …*
simple past [ˌsɪmpl 'pɑːst]	einfache Form der Vergangenheit	*Olivia* ***played*** *cards last Friday.*
simple present [ˌsɪmpl 'preznt]	einfache Form der Gegenwart	*Olivia* ***plays*** *cards every Friday evening.*

singular ['sɪŋgjələ]	Singular, Einzahl	
statement ['steɪtmənt]	Aussage(satz)	
sub-clause ['sʌbklɔːz]	Nebensatz	*I like Plymouth* ***because I like the sea****.*
subject ['sʌbdʒɪkt]	Subjekt	***Justin/He*** *has a new camera.*
subject question	Subjektfrage, Frage nach dem Subjekt	***Who invited*** *the Coopers to tea?*
substitute ['sʌbstɪtjuːt]	Ersatzverb (eines Modalverbs)	*be able to, be allowed to, have to*
superlative [su'pɜːlətɪv]	Superlativ (2. Steigerungsform)	*(the) oldest; (the) most expensive*
verb [vɜːb]	**1.** Verb; **2.** Prädikat	*go, help, look, see, …* *Reading* ***can be*** *fun.*
***will*-future** ['fjuːtʃə]	Futur mit *will*	*I'm sure you****'ll like*** *the new maths teacher.*
yes/no question	Entscheidungsfrage	*Are you 14? Do you like oranges?*

Lösungen der Grammar-File-Aufgaben

p. 157
1 Katie: *Hannah and I* ***have decided*** *to go to that rock concert in Bath. Do you want to come with us?*
Daniel: *No, thanks. I* ***saw*** *both bands on TV last month, and I* ***didn't like*** *them.*
2 Thomas: *Hi Jessica.* ***Have*** *you* ***just arrived****?*
Jessica: *Yes, I'm a bit late.* ***Has*** *the meeting* ***started yet****?*
Thomas: *I think so. Mr Carter* ***went in*** *a few minutes ago.*

p. 158
1 *They****'ve been waiting for*** *a long time.*
2 *She****'s been reading since*** *lunchtime.*
3 *He****'s been playing for*** *an hour.*

p. 159
1 *Holly didn't go to the cinema because she* ***had left*** *her money at home.*
2 *Holly didn't go to the cinema because the queue* ***was*** *too long.*
3 *Matthew bought lots of apples because they* ***were*** *very cheap.*
4 *Matthew bought lots of apples because his mother* ***had asked*** *him to get some fruit.*

p. 160
1 *Do you think it* ***will rain*** *tomorrow?*
2 *Have you got any plans for this summer? – Yes, we****'re going to fly*** *to Spain.*
3 *Do you like your new flat? – Well, it's too small really. We****'re going to move*** *out again. We've already started looking.*
4 *Are you free next Friday? – No, I****'m meeting*** *Julian.*

p. 162
1 *If the weather* ***is*** *nice, we****'ll have*** *a picnic in the park.*
2 ***Would*** *you* ***change*** *anything if you* ***were*** *the headteacher at your school?*
3 *What* ***would*** *you* ***do*** *if your classmates* ***made*** *fun of you?*
4 *If we really* ***go*** *to Wales this summer, I****'ll try*** *to climb Mount Snowdon.*
5 *If I* ***had*** *more money, I* ***would travel*** *(I****'d travel****) all over Europe in the summer.*
6 *If you* ***don't hurry up*** *now, you****'ll be*** *late for school.*

p. 163
Sätze 2, 3, 6:
2 *Look, that's the cathedral the choir went to for the concert.*
3 *Chinatown Arch is the gate Gwen saw in the guidebook.*
6 *Birkenhead is the town you can see across the Mersey.*

p. 165
1 *The djembe* ***is played*** *with bare hands, not with sticks.*
2 *The street market in Great Homer Street* ***is called*** *'Greaty'.*
3 *The new Beatles museum* ***was opened*** *by the mayor last Saturday.*
4 *The Beatles Platz in Hamburg* ***was built*** *as a monument to the famous band's time in Germany.*
5 *German* ***is spoken*** *in Germany, Switzerland and Austria.*
6 *The song 'We will rock you'* ***was written*** *by Queen.*

p. 167
1 Katie: *My mother is so strict. Yesterday I wanted to go out, but I* ***had to*** *stay in and clean my room.*
2 Hannah: *My parents are strict too. I'm sure I* ***won't be allowed to*** *go to Jessica's party on Friday.*
3 Daniel: *Well, I think I****'ll be allowed to*** *go, but I****'ll have to*** *be home by ten again, as usual.*
4 Holly: *I'm going to a music festival on Friday, so I* ***won't be able to*** *go to the party.*

p. 168
1 *They're laughing at each other.*
2 *They might hurt themselves.*
3 *They're teaching themselves German.*
4 *They're talking to each other on the phone.*

p. 169
1 *Iain said he loved helping to make dolphin sightings.*
2 *He explained that identifying dolphins wasn't easy.*
3 *He told me they were all looking forward to their next trip.*
4 *He said that they would go out in their kayaks tomorrow.*
5 *He said you had to look after yourself at sea.*
6 *He added that you couldn't go out alone.*

Vocabulary

Das **Vocabulary** (S. 172 – 197) enthält alle Wörter und Wendungen deines Englischbuches, die du lernen musst. Sie stehen in der Reihenfolge, in der sie im Buch zum ersten Mal vorkommen.

Hier siehst du, wie das **Vocabulary** aufgebaut ist:

Diese Zahl gibt die **Seite** an, auf der die Wörter zum ersten Mal vorkommen. p. 11 = Seite 11

Die **Lautschrift** zeigt dir, wie ein Wort ausgesprochen wird. Eine Übersicht über alle **Lautschriftzeichen** findest du auf S. 242. Die Lautschriftzeichen stehen auch unten auf den **Vocabulary**-Seiten.

p. 11	**south** [saʊθ]	Süden; nach Süden; südlich	**north** [nɔːθ] · **north-west** [nɔːθˈwest] · **north-east** [nɔːθˈiːst] · **west** [west] · **east** [iːst] · **south-west** [saʊθˈwest] · **south-east** [saʊθˈiːst] · **south** [saʊθ]
	darkness [ˈdɑːknəs]	Dunkelheit, Finsternis	
	false [fɔːls]	falsch	**true** ◄► **false** — (L) falsus, -a, -um
p. 14	**in fact** [ɪn ˈfækt]	eigentlich, in Wirklichkeit	I thought he was ... Wales.
	fact [fækt]	Tatsache, Fakt	Here are some interesting **facts** about London. (L) factum, -i n
			The **figures** aren't correct. Please check them again. ! stress: **figure** [ˈfɪɡə]
			! Schreibung: **parliament** — (F) le parlement

Eingerückte Wörter lernst du am besten zusammen mit dem vorausgehenden Wort, weil die beiden zusammengehören.

Dies ist das „Gegenteil"-Zeichen: **true** ist das Gegenteil von **false**.

Diese **Kästen** solltest du dir immer besonders gut ansehen: Hier sind Vokabeln zu einem bestimmten Thema zusammengestellt. Oder du erfährst mehr über ein Wort und wie es verwendet wird.

Das **rote Ausrufezeichen** bedeutet: Vorsicht, hier macht man leicht Fehler!

German "während"

- vor einem Nomen: **during** — Jack phoned **during** the football match. Jack rief **während** des Fußballspiels an.
- vor einem Nebensatz: **while** — Jack phoned **while** we were watching the football match. Jack rief an, **während** wir das Fußballspiel schauten.

(to) **guard** [ɡɑːd]	bewachen	

Im **Vocabulary** werden folgende **Abkürzungen** verwendet:

p. = page (Seite) pp. = pages (Seiten)
sth. = something (etwas) sb. = somebody (jemand)
jn. = jemanden jm. = jemandem
pl = *plural* (Mehrzahl)
infml = *informal* (umgangssprachlich)
(F) = *verwandtes Wort im Französischen*
(L) = *verwandtes Wort im Lateinischen*

Wenn du **nachschlagen** möchtest, was ein englisches Wort bedeutet oder wie man es ausspricht, dann verwende das **English – German Dictionary** auf den Seiten 198 – 220. Und wenn du vergessen hast, wie etwas auf Englisch heißt, dann kann dir das **German – English Dictionary** auf den Seiten 221 – 242 eine erste Hilfe sein.

[iː] green · [i] happy · [ɪ] big · [e] red · [æ] cat · [ɑː] class · [ɒ] song · [ɔː] door · [uː] blue · [ʊ] book · [ʌ] mum · [ɜː] girl · [ə] a partner

Unit 1 This is London

pp. 8/9	**the best thing about …**	das Beste an …	**The best thing about** the film was the music.

Part A

p. 10	**huge** [hjuːdʒ]	riesig, sehr groß	Little Andrew got a **huge** teddy bear for his birthday.
	as soon as [əz ˈsuːn‿əz]	sobald, sowie	I'll call you **as soon as** I'm home.
	cathedral [kəˈθiːdrəl]	Kathedrale, Dom	! Betonung: **ca<u>the</u>dral** [kəˈθiːdrəl] (F) la cathédrale
	palace [ˈpæləs]	Palast, Schloss	! Betonung: **<u>pa</u>lace** [ˈpæləs] (F) le palais
	Welsh [welʃ]	Walisisch; walisisch	Some people in Wales speak English and **Welsh**.
	(to) **reply (to)** [rɪˈplaɪ]	antworten (auf); erwidern, entgegnen	Why didn't you **reply to** my email? "That isn't London Bridge," he **replied**. "It's Tower Bridge."
	Europe [ˈjʊərəp]	Europa	
	western [ˈwestən]	westlich, West-	Spain is one of the biggest countries in **western** Europe.
	I see.	Aha! / Verstehe.	
	lift [lɪft]	Fahrstuhl, Aufzug	
	amazing [əˈmeɪzɪŋ]	erstaunlich, unglaublich	
	How do you know …?	Woher weißt/kennst du …?	**How do you know** so much about cows? – My grandparents have a farm.
	post [pəʊst]	Posting *(auf Blog)*, Blog-Eintrag	
	carnival [ˈkɑːnɪvl]	Karneval, Fasching	**Carnival** is a big event in German cities like Cologne and Mainz, but people in Britain don't celebrate it. ! In Großbritannien wird mit **carnival** jegliche Art von Straßenumzügen mit Musik- und Tanzgruppen, Festwagen u.Ä. bezeichnet.
	test [test]	Test	
	(to) **be into** sth. *(infml)*	etwas mögen, auf etwas stehen	My sister **is into** reggae at the moment.
	(to) **enjoy** [ɪnˈdʒɔɪ]	genießen	The film was fantastic. I really **enjoyed** it.
	by the way [ˌbaɪ ðə ˈweɪ]	übrigens	Oh, **by the way,** Grandma called this morning.
p. 11	**south** [saʊθ]	Süden; nach Süden; südlich	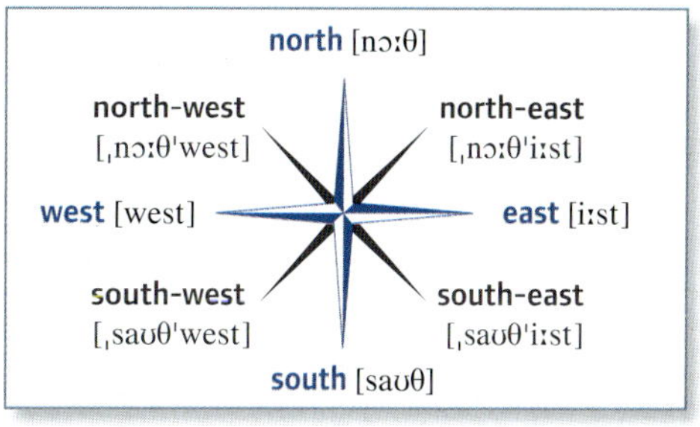
	darkness [ˈdɑːknəs]	Dunkelheit, Finsternis	
	clue [kluː]	(Lösungs-)Hinweis; Anhaltspunkt	Nobody knows who killed the man. The police are still looking for **clues** in his house.
	skyline [ˈskaɪlaɪn]	Skyline; Horizont	
	false [fɔːls]	falsch	**true** ◄► **false** (L) falsus, -a, -um

[eɪ] name · [aɪ] time · [ɔɪ] boy · [əʊ] old ·
[aʊ] town · [ɪə] here · [eə] where · [ʊə] tour

p. 12	(to) **go together**	zusammenpassen, zueinander passen	I don't think pink and orange **go together**.
	the Tube [tjuːb] *(no pl)*	die U-Bahn *(in London)*	*English:* **on the Tube** *German:* **in der U-Bahn**
	the underground [ˈʌndəgraʊnd] *(no pl)*	die U-Bahn	In London, **the underground** is called "the Tube".
	(to) **stay (at/with)** [steɪ]	*(vorübergehend)* wohnen, übernachten (in/bei)	Did you **stay at** a hotel? – No, we didn't. We **stayed with** my grandma.
	timetable [ˈtaɪmteɪbl]	Fahrplan	! **timetable** = **1.** Stundenplan; **2.** Fahrplan
	gallery [ˈgæləri]	Galerie	! Betonung: **gallery** [ˈgæləri] (F) la galerie
	restaurant [ˈrestrɒnt]	Restaurant	(F) le restaurant
p. 13	**stress** [stres]	Betonung	Where's the **stress** in "gallery"? – On the first syllable.
	stress mark [ˈstres mɑːk]	Betonungszeichen	
	small talk	Smalltalk *(spontan geführtes Gespräch in umgangssprachlichem Ton)*	
	culture [ˈkʌltʃə]	Kultur	! stress: **culture** [ˈkʌltʃə] (F) la culture (L) cultura, -ae *f*
	(to) **expect** sth. [ɪkˈspekt]	etwas erwarten	(L) exspectare

Part B

p. 14	**attraction** [əˈtrækʃn]	Attraktion; Anziehungspunkt	The British Museum is one of London's biggest tourist **attractions**. (F) l'attraction *(f)* (L) trahere *(ziehen)*
	natural history [ˌnætʃrəl ˈhɪstri]	Naturkunde	
	entry [ˈentri]	Eintritt, Zutritt	**Entry** into museums is usually free in Britain. (F) l'entrée *(f)*
	in fact [ɪn ˈfækt]	eigentlich, in Wirklichkeit	I thought he was English, but **in fact** he was from Wales.
	fact [fækt]	Tatsache, Fakt	Here are some interesting **facts** about London. (L) factum, -i *n*
	the UK (the United Kingdom) [ˌjuː ˈkeɪ], [juˌnaɪtɪd ˈkɪŋdəm]	das Vereinigte Königreich	**the UK** = Great Britain (England, Scotland, Wales) and Northern Ireland
	(to) **reserve** [rɪˈzɜːv]	reservieren, buchen	We'll have to **reserve** a table if we want to eat there. (F) réserver
	step [step]	Stufe	! **step** = **1.** Stufe; **2.** Schritt
	chance [tʃɑːns]	Gelegenheit, Möglichkeit, Chance	If you have the **chance**, you should go to the British Museum. (F) la chance
p. 15	**figure** [ˈfɪgə]	Zahl, Ziffer	The **figures** aren't correct. Please check them again. ! stress: **figure** [ˈfɪgə]
	less (than) [les]	weniger (als)	I have **less** money than you. = You have more money than me.
	tortoise [ˈtɔːtəs]	(Land-)Schildkröte	a **tortoise**

steps

a tortoise

[b] boat · [p] pool · [d] dad · [t] ten · [g] good · [k] cat · [m] mum · [n] no · [ŋ] song · [l] hello · [r] red · [w] we · [j] you

	on top of each other	übereinander, aufeinander	Can you put all those plates **on top of each other**, please?
	parliament ['pɑːləmənt]	Parlament	! Schreibung: **parliament** Ⓕ le parlement
	at one time	zur selben Zeit, gleichzeitig	It's hard to understand if everyone talks **at one time**.
	Christmas ['krɪsməs]	Weihnachten	! Der 1. Weihnachtsfeiertag heißt **Christmas Day**.
	ticket office ['tɪkɪt_ˌɒfɪs]	Fahrkartenschalter; Kasse *(für den Verkauf von Eintrittskarten)*	
	detail ['diːteɪl]	Detail, Einzelheit	! stress: **detail** ['diːteɪl] Ⓕ le détail
	adult ['ædʌlt]	Erwachsene(r)	Free entry for children. **Adults** pay £1.50. Ⓕ l'adulte *(m/f)*
	a family of four	eine vierköpfige Familie	
	during ['djʊərɪŋ]	während	

German "während"

- vor einem Nomen: **during** — Jack phoned **during** the football match. Jack rief **während** des Fußballspiels an.
- vor einem Nebensatz: **while** — Jack phoned **while** we were watching the football match. Jack rief an, **während** wir das Fußballspiel schauten.

	(to) **guard** [gɑːd]	bewachen	
	raven ['reɪvn]	Rabe	a **raven** 
	blood [blʌd]	Blut	
	(to) **be home to** sth.	Heimat sein für etwas; etwas beheimaten	The Amazon area **is home to** the world's largest rainforest.
	jewels *(pl)* ['dʒuːəlz]	Juwelen	! stress: **jewels** ['dʒuːəlz]
	education [ˌedʒu'keɪʃn]	(Schul-, Aus-)Bildung; Erziehung	You need a good **education** if you want to get a good job. Ⓕ l'éducation *(f)* Ⓛ educere *(großziehen)*
p. 16	**instead of** [ɪn'sted_əv]	anstelle von, statt	! • **instead of** = anstelle von – I'd like chips **instead of** rice, please. • **instead** = stattdessen – I don't like rice. Can I have chips **instead**?
	exact [ɪg'zækt]	genau	What's the **exact** size of London? Do you know?
	linking word ['lɪŋkɪŋ wɜːd]	Bindewort	
	(to) **link** [lɪŋk]	verbinden, verknüpfen	You can **link** two sentences with "and", for example.
	queue [kjuː]	Schlange, Reihe *(wartender Menschen)*	 a **queue** They're queuing in front of the cinema.
	worth [wɜːθ]	wert	The correct answer is **worth** five points.
	(to) **roar** [rɔː]	brüllen	
	crowded ['kraʊdɪd]	voller Menschen; überfüllt	The old city centre is often **crowded** with tourists.

[f] father · [v] river · [s] sister · [z] please · [ʃ] shop · [ʒ] television · [tʃ] teacher · [dʒ] Germany · [θ] thanks · [ð] this · [h] here

p. 17	**feedback** ['fi:dbæk]	Rückmeldung, Feedback	The hotel wants to get some **feedback** from the people who have stayed there.
	(to) **improve** [ɪm'pru:v]	verbessern; sich verbessern	This book helps you to **improve** your English. Your English will **improve** if you watch English films.
	(to) **react (to)** [ri'ækt]	reagieren (auf)	I called him but he didn't **react**. (F) réagir
	content ['kɒntent]	Inhalt	(F) le contenu
	(to) **connect** [kə'nekt]	verbinden, verknüpfen	= (to) link
	(to) **point** sth. **out (to** sb.**)** [ˌpɔɪnt‿'aʊt]	(jn.) auf etwas hinweisen	"Be careful!" he said, and **pointed out** a snake in the grass.
	spelling ['spelɪŋ]	Rechtschreibung; Schreibweise	
p. 18	**line** [laɪn]	(U-Bahn-)Linie	(F) la ligne (L) linea, -ae *f*
	northbound ['nɔ:θbaʊnd]	Richtung Norden	
	(to) **change** [tʃeɪndʒ]	umsteigen	Take the Bakerloo Line southbound and **change** to the Central Line westbound at Oxford Circus. (F) changer
p. 19	(to) **be slow**	nachgehen *(Uhr)*	It's twenty past eight. – No, it isn't. It's half past eight. Your watch **is slow**. (to) **be slow** ◄► (to) **be fast**
	(to) **work**	funktionieren	I need your help. My computer doesn't **work**.
	(to) **head for** sth. [hed]	auf etwas zusteuern/zugehen/zufahren	As soon as we arrived at the coast, we **headed for** the beach.
	announcement [ə'naʊnsmənt]	Durchsage, Ansage	We'll have to wait for the **announcement** to find out where our train leaves. (F) l'annonce *(f)*
	message ['mesɪdʒ]	Botschaft, Aussage	**!** **message** = (F) le message **1.** Nachricht – John left a **message** for you. **2.** Botschaft – I think the poem has an interesting **message**.
	platform ['plætfɔ:m]	Bahnsteig, Gleis	

Part C

p. 20	(to) **be on**	eingeschaltet sein, an sein *(Radio, Licht usw.)*; laufen, übertragen werden *(Programm, Sendung)*	The lights **are on**, so they must be at home. (to) **be on** ◄► (to) **be off** Can we watch TV, Mum? The football **is on**.
	No way! [ˌnəʊ 'weɪ]	Auf keinen Fall! / Kommt nicht in Frage!	Dad, can you give me £120 for a new pair of jeans? – £120? **No way!** You can have £70.
	for hours/weeks/...	seit Stunden/Wochen/...	"You've been watching TV **for hours**." –
	since 10 o'clock/last week/... [sɪns]	seit 10 Uhr/letzter Woche/...	"No, I haven't. I've been watching TV **since 10**."
	And anyway, ... ['eniweɪ]	Und überhaupt, ...	I don't have time to go. **And anyway**, it's too expensive.
	try [traɪ]	Versuch	verb: (to) **try** – noun: **try**

[i:] green · [i] happy · [ɪ] big · [e] red · [æ] cat · [ɑ:] class · [ɒ] song ·
[ɔ:] door · [u:] blue · [ʊ] book · [ʌ] mum · [ɜ:] girl · [ə] a partner

	remote control [rɪˌməʊt kən'trəʊl] (*kurz auch:* **remote**)	Fernbedienung	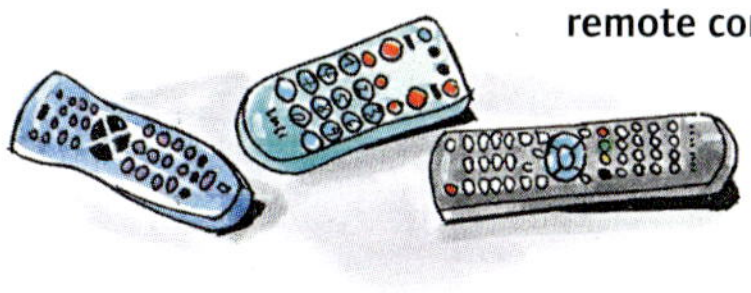 **remote controls**
	(to) **turn** sth. **up/down** [tɜːn]	etwas lauter/leiser stellen	Can you **turn up** the radio? I want to hear the news.

(to) turn

1. The London Eye **turns** very slowly. — **sich drehen**
2. The woman **turned** (*auch:* **turned round / turned around**) and looked at me. — **sich umdrehen**
3. The boy **turned to** his father and smiled. — **sich jm. zuwenden**
4. Please **turn on** the TV. And **turn up** the sound. — **einschalten … lauter stellen**
5. First you **turn left**. Then you **turn right**. — **(nach) links/rechts abbiegen**

	each other [iːtʃ‿'ʌðə]	sich (gegenseitig), einander	Luke looked at Mo and Mo looked at Luke. = Luke and Mo looked at **each other**.
	pub [pʌb]	Kneipe, Lokal	
	a while [waɪl]	eine Weile, einige Zeit	First we watched the monkeys **for a while**. (… eine Weile, eine Zeit lang)
	tap [tæp]	*(leichtes)* Klopfen	In the middle of night, we heard a **tap** on the door.
	Off you go now. [ɒf]	Ab mit euch jetzt! / Los mit euch jetzt!	

off

1. **weg, los** — The thieves took our bag and ran **off**. She turned around and walked **off**.
2. **von … herunter** — He fell **off** his bike and broke his leg. She jumped **off** the wall and ran away.

- (to) **get off the bus/boat/plane** — aus dem Bus/Boot/Flugzeug aussteigen
- (to) **take sth. off** — etwas ausziehen *(Kleidung)*; etwas absetzen *(Hut, Helm)*
- (to) **turn sth. off** — etwas ausschalten *(Radio, Fernsehen, Licht)*

	towards the station/Mr Bell [tə'wɔːdz]	auf den Bahnhof/Mr Bell zu, in Richtung Bahnhof/Mr Bell	When the fire started, everyone ran **towards** the door.
p. 21	**tense** [tens]	(grammatische) Zeit, Tempus	the **past tense**, the **present tense**, the **future tense** (L) tempus, -oris *n*
	(to) **go on**	im Gang sein; andauern	The film was so boring, and it **went on** for hours.
	situation [ˌsɪtʃu'eɪʃn]	Situation	! stress: **situation** [ˌsɪtʃu'eɪʃn] (F) la situation
p. 22	**route** [ruːt]	Strecke, Route	(F) la route
	speed [spiːd]	Geschwindigkeit	
	It was a pity that … ['pɪti]	Es war schade, dass …	**It's a pity that** Jake can't come to our party.

The Notting Hill Carnival Parade

p. 24	(to) **hold onto** sth. [həʊld], **held, held** [held]	sich an etwas festhalten	She **held onto** the table and tried to stand up.
	(to) **scan** sth. **(for** sth.**)** [skæn]	etwas (nach etwas) absuchen	I **scanned** the crowd/the garden for my sister but couldn't see her.
	(to) **fill** [fɪl]	füllen	
	pavement ['peɪvmənt]	Gehweg, Bürgersteig	

	available [ə'veɪləbl]	erhältlich, verfügbar; erreichbar *(am Telefon)*	Tickets for the concert will be **available** soon.
	all around her	überall um sie herum	Suddenly there was darkness **all around** her.
	whistle ['wɪsl]	(Triller-)Pfeife	a **whistle**
	(to) **blow the whistle** [bləʊ], **blew** [bluː], **blown** [bləʊn]	pfeifen *(auf der Trillerpfeife)*	
	(to) **panic** ['pænɪk]	in Panik geraten	! spelling: -ing form: **panicking**; simple past: **panicked** (F) paniquer
	exactly [ɪg'zæktli]	genau	! • adjective: **exact** – What's the **exact** size of Spain? • adverb: **exactly** – Sue and Jack are **exactly** the same size. (F) exactement
	(to) **bend down** [bend], **bent**, **bent** [bent]	sich hinunterbeugen, sich bücken	She saw a coin on the ground and **bent down** to pick it up.
	rope [rəʊp]	Seil	
	wing [wɪŋ]	Flügel	**wing**
	rainbow ['reɪnbəʊ]	Regenbogen	
	dizzy ['dɪzi]	schwindlig	All the noise and the lights made her feel **dizzy**.
	hip [hɪp]	Hüfte	
	you	man	How do **you** say that in English? (Wie sagt man …?) That's not how **you** do it! (So macht man das nicht!)
	rhythm ['rɪðəm]	Rhythmus	(F) le rythme
p. 25	(to) **scare** sb. [skeə]	jn. erschrecken; jm. Angst machen	verb: (to) **scare** – adjectives: **scared** (verängstigt), **scary** (unheimlich)
	loudspeaker [ˌlaʊd'spiːkə]	Lautsprecher; Megaphon	
	(to) **mind** [maɪnd]	etwas dagegen haben	

(to) mind

He **won't mind** if we sit down here for a while.	Es wird ihm nichts ausmachen. … / Er wird nichts dagegen haben, …
I'd like to ask you a question, **if you don't mind**.	…, wenn Sie nichts dagegen haben.
Do you mind if I open the window?	Stört es Sie, …? / Haben Sie etwas dagegen, …?

(to) **rest** [rest]	ruhen, sich ausruhen	They sat down in the park to **rest** for a moment.
no sign of … [saɪn]	keine Spur von …	We scanned the crowd, but there was **no sign of** my sister.
…, he said **under his breath**. [breθ]	…, sagte er flüsternd / murmelte er.	

Unit 2 Welcome to Snowdonia

Part A

p. 30	**empty** ['empti]	leer	**full** ◄► **empty**
	scientist ['saɪəntɪst]	Naturwissenschaftler/in	someone who has studied science (L) scientia, -ae *f (Wissen)*
	(to) **study** ['stʌdi]	studieren; untersuchen, beobachten; lernen	She **studied** English in Dublin in the 1980s. His dream was to **study** seals on the Welsh coast. There's a test on Monday so I have to **study** at the weekend. (L) studere

[b] **boat** · [p] **pool** · [d] **dad** · [t] **ten** · [g] **good** · [k] **cat** · [m] **mum** · [n] **no** · [ŋ] **song** · [l] **hello** · [r] **red** · [w] **we** · [j] **you**

	workshop ['wɜːkʃɒp]	Werkstatt	! **workshop** = **1.** Werkstatt; **2.** Lehrgang, Workshop
	carpenter ['kɑːpəntə]	Tischler/in, Zimmerer/Zimmerin	someone who works with wood to make things like tables, chairs, etc.
	furniture ['fɜːnɪtʃə] *(no pl)*	Möbel	! **furniture** hat keinen Plural: The **furniture is** new. Die **Möbel sind** neu. **ein Möbel(stück)** = **a piece of furniture**
	oil [ɔɪl]	Öl	 
	a piece of … [piːs]	ein Stück …	**a piece of wood** **a piece of paper**
	hammer ['hæmə]	Hammer	
	(to) **come over (to)**	herüberkommen (zu/nach), vorbeikommen (bei)	Why don't you **come over to** our place on Friday evening?
	probably ['prɒbəbli]	wahrscheinlich	! • adverb: **probably** („wahrscheinlich") – Jake is late. He's **probably** missed the bus again. • adjective: **probable** („wahrscheinlich") – How **probable** is a white Christmas this year?
	(to) **make fun of** sb./sth.	sich über jn./etwas lustig machen	Don't **make fun of** me or I'll tell Mum!
	(to) **give up**	aufgeben	
	tonight [tə'naɪt]	heute Nacht, heute Abend	
p. 31	**architect** ['ɑːkɪtekt]	Architekt/in	! stress: **architect** ['ɑːkɪtekt] (F) l'architecte *(m/f)* (L) architectus, -i *m*
	astronaut ['æstrənɔːt]	Astronaut/in	! stress: **astronaut** ['æstrənɔːt] (F) l'astronaute *(m/f)* (L) nauta, -ae *m (Seemann)*
	hairdresser ['heədresə]	Friseur/in	
	musician [mju'zɪʃn]	Musiker/in	someone who plays an instrument (F) le musicien, la musicienne
	painter ['peɪntə]	Maler/in	(F) le/la peintre
	natural ['nætʃrəl]	natürlich	the **natural** world = die Welt der Natur, die Natur (L) natura, ae *f (Geburt; Wesen)*
p. 32	**headword** ['hedwɜːd]	Stichwort *(im Wörterbuch)*	
	part of speech [ˌpɑːt‿əv 'spiːtʃ]	Wortart	Nouns, verbs, adjectives, etc. are all **parts of speech**.
	translation [træns'leɪʃn]	Übersetzung	verb: (to) **translate** – noun: **translation** (L) transferre *(hinübertragen)*
	coal [kəʊl]	Kohle	
	underground [ˌʌndə'graʊnd]	unterirdisch, unter der Erde	Some animals – like rabbits – live **underground**.
	(to) **ground** sb. [graʊnd]	jm. Hausarrest/Ausgehverbot erteilen	If you come home so late again, I'll **ground** you for two weeks.
	official [ə'fɪʃl] *(adj)*	amtlich, Amts-	! stress: **official** [ə'fɪʃl] (F) officiel, le
	official [ə'fɪʃl] *(n)*	Beamte(r), Beamtin	(L) officium, -i *n (Dienst)*
	police *(pl)* [pə'liːs]	Polizei	! **police** ist ein Pluralwort! *English:* The **police are** on **their** way. *German:* Die **Polizei ist** auf dem Weg.

[f] father · [v] river · [s] sister · [z] please · [ʃ] shop · [ʒ] television · [tʃ] teacher · [dʒ] Germany · [θ] thanks · [ð] this · [h] here

(to) look after/around/for/…

• (to) **look after** sb.	I often have to **look after** my little brother.	**aufpassen auf; sich kümmern um**
• (to) **look around**	I like your new flat. Can I **look around**?	**sich umsehen**
• (to) **look for** sb./sth.	I'm **looking for** my keys. Have you seen them?	**suchen**
• (to) **look forward to** sth.	We're all **looking forward to** the summer holidays.	**sich freuen auf**
• (to) **look into** sth.	The officials are going to **look into** the problem.	**untersuchen, prüfen**
• (to) **look up**	She heard a noise and **looked up** from her book.	**hochsehen, aufschauen**
• (to) **look** sth. **up**	I don't understand this word. I'll have to **look** it **up**.	**nachschlagen** *(Wörter, Informationen)*

(to) come across/down/over/…

• (to) **come across** sb./sth.	Later we **came across** a beautiful village.	**stoßen auf,** *(zufällig)* **treffen**
• (to) **come down with** sth.	Jack can't take part. He's **come down with** a cold.	**bekommen** *(Krankheit)*, **erkranken an**
• (to) **come over**	John **came over** to watch the football with us.	**herüberkommen, vorbeikommen**
• (to) **come up with** sth.	Then my sister **came up with** a brilliant idea.	**haben, kommen auf** *(Idee, Vorschlag)*

Part B

p. 34 **national** ['næʃnəl]	national, National-	! stress: **na**tional ['næʃnəl] (F) national, e (L) natio, -onis *f*
altogether [ˌɔːltə'geðə]	insgesamt, alles in allem	We've raised a lot of money for charity – £400 **altogether**.
hostel ['hɒstl]	Herberge, Wohnheim	
(to) **wonder** ['wʌndə]	sich fragen, gern wissen wollen	Have you ever **wondered** why we have Christmas trees?
(to) **pretend** [prɪ'tend]	so tun, als ob	He **pretended** to be ill so that he could miss school. The boys shouted after her, but she **pretended** not to hear them.
Me neither. ['naɪðə], ['niːðə]	Ich auch nicht.	"I don't know the answer." – "**Me neither.**" **Me too.** ◄► **Me neither.**
(to) **go by**	vergehen, vorübergehen *(Zeit)*	Time always **goes by** too quickly in the holidays.
stupid ['stjuːpɪd]	dumm, blöd	**stupid** ◄► **clever** (F) stupide
downstream [ˌdaʊn'striːm]	flussabwärts	
edge [edʒ]	Rand, Kante	 The ball rolled down the hill and dropped off the **edge** of the cliff.
(to) **reach** [riːtʃ]	erreichen	If we leave now, we'll **reach** Wales before dinner.
stick [stɪk]	Stock	
(to) **grab** [græb]	schnappen, packen	I was late, so I **grabbed** my school bag and ran to the bus stop.
p. 35 **steep** [stiːp]	steil	You can't ride your bike up that hill. It's too **steep**. 
(to) **sing along (with** sb.**)**	(mit jm.) mitsingen	
(to) **join in** (sth.)	(bei etwas) mitmachen	

[iː] green · [i] happy · [ɪ] big · [e] red · [æ] cat · [ɑː] class · [ɒ] song · [ɔː] door · [uː] blue · [ʊ] book · [ʌ] mum · [ɜː] girl · [ə] a partner

	before long	schon bald	The afternoon passed quickly and **before long** it was time to say goodbye.
	(to) **tell** sb. **(not) to do** sth.	jn. auffordern, etwas (nicht) zu tun; jm. sagen, dass er/sie etwas (nicht) tun soll	The teacher **told** the students **to** be quiet. How often do I have to **tell** you **not to** hit your brother?
p. 36	**warning** ['wɔːnɪŋ]	Warnung	
	movie ['muːvi]	Film	
p. 37	**head teacher** [ˌhed 'tiːtʃə]	Schulleiter/in	
	(to) **allow** [ə'laʊ]	erlauben, zulassen	**!** • (to) **allow** = <u>erlauben, zulassen</u> – **Does** your school **allow** you to use mobiles? • (to) **be allowed to do** sth. = <u>etwas tun dürfen</u> – **Are** you **allowed to use** mobiles at school?
p. 38	**topic sentence** [ˌtɒpɪk 'sentəns]	*Satz, der in das Thema eines Absatzes einführt*	
	(to) **be connected** [kə'nektɪd]	verbunden sein	

Numbers

- *English:* **3.5** = three **point** five
  German: **3,5** = drei **Komma** fünf
  Im Englischen steht ein **Punkt**, im Deutschen ein **Komma**.
- *English:* **1,500** = one thousand five hundred
  German: **1.500** = eintausendfünfhundert
  Im Englischen steht oft ein **Komma** in Zahlen, die größer als 1 000 sind. Im Deutschen steht dort manchmal ein **Punkt**.

	climb [klaɪm]	Aufstieg, Anstieg	verb: (to) **climb** – noun: **climb**
	summit ['sʌmɪt]	Gipfel	**summit**  (F) le sommet (L) summus, -a, -um *(höchster)*
	(to) **manage** sth. ['mænɪdʒ]	etwas schaffen; etwas zustande bringen	We wanted to be back home at 6, but we didn't **manage** it. I didn't **manage** to visit the Tower while I was in London.
	(to) **continue** sth. [kən'tɪnjuː]	etwas fortsetzen	We went inside and **continued** our conversation.
	downhill [ˌdaʊn'hɪl]	bergab	**downhill** ◄► **uphill** (bergauf) **downstream** ◄► **upstream** (flussaufwärts)
	energy ['enədʒi]	Energie, Kraft	**!** stress: <u>**en**</u>**ergy** ['enədʒi] (F) l'énergie *(f)*
	a total of … ['təʊtl]	eine Gesamtsumme von …; insgesamt	We raised **a total of** £ 400 for charity.
	bar [bɑː]	Riegel *(Schokolade, Müsli)*, Tafel *(Schokolade)*	
	hero ['hɪərəʊ], *pl* **heroes**	Held/in	(F) le héros, la héroïne
	(to) **revise** [rɪ'vaɪz]	überarbeiten; *(Lernstoff)* wiederholen	He had to **revise** his work because there were too many mistakes. I have a test tomorrow, so I must **revise** tonight. (F) réviser
	(to) **organize** ['ɔːgənaɪz]	organisieren; ordnen	**!** stress: <u>**or**</u>**ganize** ['ɔːgənaɪz] (F) organiser
	(to) **add (to)** [æd]	hinzufügen, addieren (zu)	(L) addere
p. 39	**difficult** ['dɪfɪkəlt]	schwierig, schwer	**easy** ◄► **difficult**
	carrot ['kærət]	Möhre, Karotte	**!** stress: <u>**car**</u>**rot** ['kærət]

Snowdonia at night

p. 40 (to) **press** [pres]	drücken	
finally ['faɪnəli]	endlich, schließlich	He tried again and again to open the door, and **finally** he managed it. (F) finalement (L) finis, -is *m (Ende, Ziel)*
(to) **be able to do** sth. ['eɪbl]	etwas tun können; fähig sein / in der Lage sein, etwas zu tun	Finally the rain stopped and we **were able to** go home.
meal [miːl]	Mahlzeit, Essen	Me and my sister always prepare the evening **meal** on Fridays.
(to) **keep doing** sth. [kiːp], **kept, kept** [kept]	etwas immer wieder / immer weiter tun; etwas ständig tun	I tried to speak, but he **kept interrupting** me. **Keep smiling** – and never give up.
silently ['saɪləntli]	lautlos; schweigend	adverb: **silently** – adjective: **silent** (still, leise) (L) silentium, -i *n (Schweigen)*
corridor ['kɒrɪdɔː]	Gang, Korridor	a **corridor** 
star [stɑː]	Stern	
magical ['mædʒɪkl]	zauberhaft, wundervoll; magisch	The first time I was on stage with my band was one of the most **magical** moments in my life.
(to) **lie down** [ˌlaɪ 'daʊn], **lay** [leɪ], **lain** [leɪn]	sich hinlegen	I'm so tired. I think I'll **lie down** for half an hour. (to) **lie down** ◄► (to) **get up**
busy ['bɪzi]	belebt, geschäftig, hektisch	It was too **busy** in the dining room, so we went upstairs. (*etwa:* Im Esszimmer war zu viel los, …) The week before Christmas is a **busy** time for most shops.
(to) **clear** [klɪə]	räumen; abräumen	(to) **clear** the table / the dishes / your desk / the road
breeze [briːz]	Brise	
(to) **have a look (at** sth.**)**	nachschauen; einen Blick auf etwas werfen	What was that noise in the garden? – I don't know. Let's go and **have a look**.
(to) **sit up**	sich aufsetzen	The sound of a bell woke her. She **sat up** and opened her eyes.
wooden ['wʊdn]	hölzern; Holz-	a **wooden** puppet 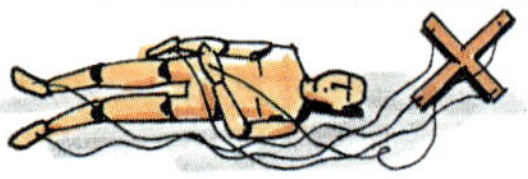
wide [waɪd]	weit; breit	"Open your mouth **wide**, please," said the dentist. I don't think the Elbe is as **wide** as the Mississippi.
figure ['fɪgə]	Figur, Gestalt	! **figure** = **1.** Figur, Gestalt; **2.** Zahl, Ziffer stress: **figure** ['fɪgə] (L) figura, -ae *f*
p. 41 **note** [nəʊt]	Note *(Musik)*	! **note** = **1.** Notiz, Mitteilung; **2.** Note
such a … [sʌtʃ]	so ein/e …; solch ein/e …	**such a** thing/person = a thing/person like that

such a + noun	**so + adjective**
Olivia is **such a** nice **person**. … **so** ein netter Mensch	Olivia is **so nice**. … **so** nett
It was **such a** good **film** that I watched it twice. … **so** ein guter Film	The film was **so good** that I watched it twice. … **so** gut

[b] **boat** · [p] **pool** · [d] **dad** · [t] **ten** · [g] **good** · [k] **cat** · [m] **mum** · [n] **no** · [ŋ] **song** · [l] **hello** · [r] **red** · [w] **we** · [j] **you**

	(to) **make** sth. **up**	sich etwas ausdenken	Today we had to **make up** a story and tell it to our classmates.
	(to) **argue** [ˈɑːɡjuː]	streiten; sich streiten	My brother and sister **argue** from morning till night. "But, Mum …," he said. "**Don't argue**," she replied. („Widersprich mir nicht" …)
	bite [baɪt]	Biss, Bissen	
	director [dəˈrektə]	Leiter/in	(F) le directeur, la directrice
	office [ˈɒfɪs]	Büro	(L) officium, -i *n* *(Dienst)*
p. 42	**how to do** sth.	wie man etwas macht / machen kann / machen soll	I don't know **how to do** this exercise. Can you help me?

Question word + to-infinitive: how to … / what to … / who to … / where to …

Can you tell me **how to get** to the station?	Können Sie mir sagen, wie ich zum Bahnhof komme/kommen kann?
I don't know **what to do**.	Ich weiß nicht, was ich tun soll.
I need help, but I don't know **who to ask**.	Ich brauche Hilfe, aber ich weiß nicht, wen ich fragen kann/soll.
We had no idea **where to go**.	Wir hatten keine Ahnung, wohin wir gehen sollten.

(to) **behave** [bɪˈheɪv]	sich verhalten, sich benehmen	If you **behave** like that again, I'll ground you for a month.
mop [mɒp]	Wischmopp	noun: **mop** – verb: (to) **mop** (wischen *(Fußboden)*)

He's **mopping** the floor.

(to) **splash** sb. [splæʃ]	jn. nass spritzen	
punishment [ˈpʌnɪʃmənt]	Bestrafung, Strafe	
point of view [ˌpɔɪnt‿əv ˈvjuː]	Standpunkt	*English:* from my **point of view** *German:* von meinem **Standpunkt** aus gesehen; aus meiner **Sicht** (F) le point de vue

Unit 3 A weekend in Liverpool

p. 45	(to) **explore** [ɪkˈsplɔː]	erkunden, erforschen	It's exciting to **explore** new places. (F) explorer (L) explorare
	cruise [kruːz]	Kreuzfahrt, Schiffsreise, Bootsfahrt	

They're going on a **cruise**.

international [ˌɪntəˈnæʃnəl]	international	**national** ◄► **international** (F) international, e (L) inter nationes *(zwischen den Völkern)*
slavery [ˈsleɪvəri]	Sklaverei	
slave [sleɪv]	Sklave, Sklavin	(F) l'esclave *(m/f)*

Part A

p. 46	**stuff** [stʌf] *(infml)*	Zeug, Kram	What's the red **stuff** on your shirt? Ketchup?	
	after that	danach	First I feed my cats. **After that** I have breakfast. **after that** ◄► **before that** (davor)	
	normal ['nɔːməl]	normal	! stress: **normal** ['nɔːməl]	(F) normal, e
	(to) **protest** [prə'test]	protestieren		(F) protester
	protest ['prəʊtest]	Protest	! verb: (to) **protest** [prə'test] – noun: **protest** ['prəʊtest]	
p. 47	**guidebook** ['gaɪdbʊk]	Reiseführer		
	quite [kwaɪt]	ziemlich; völlig, ganz	It's **quite** cold. You should take a coat. You're **quite** right. It was my mistake.	
	banana [bə'nɑːnə]	Banane		(F) la banane
	actually ['æktʃuəli]	eigentlich; übrigens; tatsächlich		

actually

Das Wort **actually** kann im Deutschen – je nach Situation – mit **eigentlich, übrigens, tatsächlich** wiedergegeben werden. Manchmal hat es auch überhaupt keine Entsprechung.

Man verwendet **actually**,

• wenn man jemanden höflich darauf hinweisen möchte, dass er/sie etwas Falsches gesagt hat	I'm not English, **actually**: I'm Welsh. **Actually**, London is bigger than Paris.
• wenn man ausdrücken möchte, dass etwas in Wirklichkeit anders ist oder war, als man erwartet hat	I didn't think I would enjoy the party, but it was **actually** fun.
• als entschuldigende Einleitung, wenn man etwas Unangenehmes mitzuteilen hat.	When are you going to give me my MP3 player back? – **Actually**, I can't. I've lost it.

	(to) **cook** [kʊk]	kochen; zubereiten		
p. 48	**well-known** [ˌwel'nəʊn], ['welˌnəʊn]	bekannt, wohlbekannt	! spelling: Lady Gaga is **well known** all over the world. She's a **well-known** singer.	
	engineer [ˌendʒɪ'nɪə]	Ingenieur/in		(F) l'ingénieur (L) ingenium, -i *n* *(Begabung)*
	sportsperson ['spɔːtspɜːsn]	Sportler/in		
	soldier ['səʊldʒə]	Soldat/in		(F) le soldat, la soldate
	(to) **design** [dɪ'zaɪn]	entwerfen, konstruieren, entwickeln	What's your uncle's job? – He **designs** cars.	(L) signum, -i *n* *(Zeichen, Bild)*
	design [dɪ'zaɪn]	Design; Gestaltung; Konstruktion		
	(to) **found** [faʊnd]	gründen	! (to) **found** – **founded** – **founded** (gründen) (to) **find** – **found** – **found** (finden)	
	(to) **invent** [ɪn'vent]	erfinden		(F) inventer (L) invenire
	crossword ['krɒswɜːd]	Kreuzworträtsel		
p. 49	**member** ['membə]	Mitglied		(F) le membre (L) membrum, -i *n*
p. 51	**introduction** [ˌɪntrə'dʌkʃn]	Einleitung, Einführung		(F) l'introduction *(f)*
	body ['bɒdi]	Hauptteil *(eines Textes)*		
	conclusion [kən'kluːʒn]	Schluss(folgerung)		(F) la conclusion
	several ['sevrəl]	mehrere, verschiedene	**Several** shops here sell John Lennon sunglasses.	

[iː] green · [i] happy · [ɪ] big · [e] red · [æ] cat · [ɑː] class · [ɒ] song · [ɔː] door · [uː] blue · [ʊ] book · [ʌ] mum · [ɜː] girl · [ə] a partner

opinion [ə'pɪnjən]	Meinung	*English:* **In my opinion …** *German:* **Meiner Meinung nach …** (F) l'opinion *(f)* (L) opinio, -onis *f*
(to) **end** [end]	enden; beenden	(to) **start** ◄► (to) **end**
schedule ['ʃedjuːl]	(Zeit-)Plan, Programm	The starting time could change, so check the **schedule** before you come.
(to) **get/have a day off** [ɒf]	einen Tag frei bekommen/haben	When Mum and Dad **have a day off**, we often go surfing or sailing.
(to) **earn** [ɜːn]	verdienen *(Geld)*	
experience [ɪk'spɪəriəns] *(no pl)*	Erfahrung(en)	We'd love to hear about your **experience** during your trip to Liverpool. (F) l'expérience *(f)* (L) peritus, -a, -um *(erfahren)*
As John Lennon said ...	Wie John Lennon (einmal) sagte …	**As** you know, Liverpool is the home of the Beatles.
(to) **be born** [bɔːn]	geboren sein/werden	*English:* I **was born** in 1998. (*not:* I ~~am born~~ in …) *German:* Ich **bin** 1998 **geboren**.
(to) **grow up** [ˌgrəʊ‿'ʌp], **grew up** [ˌgruː‿'ʌp], **grown up** [ˌgrəʊn‿'ʌp]	erwachsen werden; aufwachsen	When I **grow up**, I want to be an artist. When my grandparents were **growing up**, there was no internet.
modern ['mɒdən]	modern	! stress: **mo**dern ['mɒdən] (F) moderne
success [sək'ses]	Erfolg	(F) le succès
(to) **perform** [pə'fɔːm]	auftreten *(Künstler/in)*	The Beatles first **performed** in the USA in 1964.
popular (with) ['pɒpjələ]	populär, beliebt (bei)	*English:* Beatles songs are very **popular with** people who were born in the 1950s and 1960s. *German:* … beliebt **bei** … (F) populaire (L) populus, -i *m* *(Volk)*
monument (to) ['mɒnjumənt]	Denkmal, Monument (für/zum Gedenken an)	(F) le monument (L) monumentum, -i *n*
a **one-hour** concert	ein einstündiges Konzert	*English:* a **one-hour** concert • a **three-week** holiday • a **30-minute** ride *German:* ein **einstündiges** Konzert • ein **drei-wöchiger** Urlaub • eine **30-minütige** Fahrt
(to) **remember** sth.	an etwas denken; sich etwas merken	**Remember**: The simple past of *do* is *did*. I can never **remember** your phone number. ! (to) **remember** sth. = **1.** sich an etwas erinnern; **2.** an etwas denken *(etwas nicht vergessen)*; **3.** sich etwas merken
if	ob	! **if** = **1.** ob – I don't know **if** I can come to your party. **2.** wenn, falls – I'll come to your party **if** I can.
way [weɪ]	Art und Weise	

way ("Art und Weise")

Try to introduce your topic **in an interesting way**.	auf eine interessante Art und Weise
In this way, you will make sure that everyone enjoys your talk.	auf diese Weise
I like **the way** Oliver ended his talk.	die Art und Weise, wie …
John is like his father **in some/many ways**.	in mancher/vielerlei Hinsicht

[eɪ] **name** · [aɪ] **time** · [ɔɪ] **boy** · [əʊ] **old** ·
[aʊ] **town** · [ɪə] **here** · [eə] **where** · [ʊə] **tour**

Part B

p. 52	(to) **lead** [liːd], **led, led** [led]	führen, leiten	This road **leads** to the next village.
	leader ['liːdə]	Leiter/in	Our Maths teacher is also **leader** of our school choir.
	trade [treɪd]	Handel	the activity of buying and selling
	mask [mɑːsk]	Maske	
	horn [hɔːn]	Horn	
	people ['piːpl]	Volk	(L) populus, -i *m*
	clay [kleɪ]	Ton, Lehm	
	shape [ʃeɪp]	Form, Gestalt	*English:* Those glasses **are** an interesting **shape**. *German:* Die Brille **hat** eine interessante **Form**.
	pot [pɒt]	Gefäß; Topf	**several pots** 
	(to) **carry** ['kæri]	tragen; befördern	! He's **carrying** a heavy box. (Er trägt eine schwere Kiste.) He's **wearing** jeans and a red T-shirt. (Er trägt Jeans und ein rotes T-Shirt.)   This ferry doesn't **carry** more than two cars.
	bare [beə]	nackt, bloß *(Hände, Arme, Füße)*	
	respect [rɪ'spekt]	Respekt, Achtung	
	ancestor ['ænsestə]	Vorfahr/in	Our **ancestors** lived shorter lives than we do. (F) l'ancêtre *(m)*
p. 53	**captive** ['kæptɪv]	Gefangene(r)	(L) captivus, -i *m*
	plantation [plɑːn'teɪʃn]	Plantage	
	cruel ['kruːl]	grausam	I don't like zoos. I think it's **cruel** to put animals in cages. (F) cruel, le (L) crudelis, -e
	(to) **survive** [sə'vaɪv]	überleben	(F) survivre (L) vivere *(leben)*
	conditions *(pl)* [kən'dɪʃnz]	Verhältnisse, Bedingungen	It's too cold and too noisy in this office. I can't work in these **conditions**. (F) les conditions *(f)* (L) condicio, -onis *f*
	triangle ['traɪæŋgl]	Dreieck	(F) le triangle
p. 54	**room** [ruːm]	Platz	There's not enough **room** for all of us in the car.
	material [mə'tɪəriəl]	Material, Stoff	(F) le matériel
	(to) **cover** ['kʌvə]	bedecken, zudecken	It was cold so she **covered** her baby with her jacket. His desk is always **covered** with books and articles.
p. 55	**contest** ['kɒntest]	Wettbewerb	
	goal net ['gəʊl net]	Tornetz	
	airport ['eəpɔːt]	Flughafen	(F) l'aéroport *(m)* (L) portus, -us *m* *(Hafen)*

[b] boat · [p] pool · [d] dad · [t] ten · [g] good · [k] cat ·
[m] mum · [n] no · [ŋ] song · [l] hello · [r] red · [w] we · [j] you

	community [kə'mju:nəti]	Gemeinde; Gemeinschaft	Bayern Munich has a big **community** of fans all over Germany. (L) communis, -e *(gemeinsam)*
	mosque [mɒsk]	Moschee	

Part C

p. 56	**score** [skɔ:]	Spielstand; Punktestand	*English:* What's the **score**? *German:* Wie steht es?
	final ['faɪnl]	letzte(r, s), End-	The **final** score was 2 : 0. (*you say:* two nil)
p. 57	**sunshine** ['sʌnʃaɪn]	Sonnenschein	
p. 58	**referee** [ˌrefə'ri:]	Schiedsrichter/in	
	goalkeeper ['gəʊlki:pə]	Torwart, Torfrau	

	(to) **order** ['ɔ:də]	ordnen	! (to) **order** = **1.** ordnen; **2.** bestellen the right **order** = die richtige Reihenfolge
	(to) **structure** ['strʌktʃə]	strukturieren, gliedern	(F) structurer
	equipment [ɪ'kwɪpmənt] *(no pl)*	Ausrüstung	(F) l'équipement *(m)*
	stadium ['steɪdiəm]	Stadion	(F) le stade
	pitch [pɪtʃ]	(Sport-)Platz, Spielfeld	
	manager ['mænɪdʒə]	Trainer/in *(von Sportmannschaften)*	
	scarf [skɑ:f], *pl* **scarves** [skɑ:vz]	Schal	
	free kick [ˌfri: 'kɪk]	Freistoß	
p. 59	**bully** ['bʊli]	(Schul-)Tyrann	
	(to) **solve** [sɒlv]	lösen	We had a lot of problems at first, but in the end we **solved** them all. (L) solvere
	slow motion [ˌsləʊ 'məʊʃn]	Zeitlupe	

A Liverpool hero

p. 60	it was **no** different	es war nicht anders	The weather in June was **no** better than in May.
	canal [kə'næl]	Kanal	(F) le canal
	(to) **shine** [ʃaɪn], **shone, shone** [ʃɒn]	scheinen *(Sonne)*	
	laughter ['lɑ:ftə]	Gelächter	verb: (to) **laugh** – noun: **laughter**
	surface ['sɜ:fɪs]	Oberfläche	(F) la surface
	(to) **seem (to be/do)** [si:m]	(zu sein/zu tun) scheinen	He **seems (to be)** very sad. What's wrong?
	(to) **burn** [bɜ:n]	brennen; verbrennen	The lights in the flat are **burning**. They must be in. Don't **burn** the magazines. I haven't read them yet.
	(to) **drown** [draʊn]	ertrinken	She jumped into the river to save the boy from **drowning**.

[f] father · [v] river · [s] sister · [z] please · [ʃ] shop · [ʒ] television · [tʃ] teacher · [dʒ] Germany · [θ] thanks · [ð] this · [h] here

	nowhere ['nəʊweə]	nirgendwo; nirgendwohin	*English:* **out of nowhere** *German:* (wie) aus dem Nichts
	(to) **dive in** [daɪv‿'ɪn]	hineinspringen	
p. 61	(to) **marry** sb. ['mæri]	jn. heiraten	verb: (to) **marry** – adjective: **married**
	career [kə'rɪə]	Karriere	Choosing a **career** as a police officer is one way to help your community. (F) la carrière
	sailor ['seɪlə]	Seemann, Matrose, Matrosin	
	body ['bɒdi]	Leiche	
	local ['ləʊkl]	örtlich, Lokal-; am/vom Ort	We like to buy food from **local** farmers. (F) local, e (L) locus, -i *m (Ort)*
	(to) **spread, spread, spread** [spred]	(sich) ausbreiten, verbreiten	The fire quickly **spread** to other parts of the building.
	funeral ['fjuːnərəl]	Trauerfeier	
	(to) **take place** [teɪk 'pleɪs]	stattfinden	Our next school trip will **take place** in October.
	(to) **name** [neɪm]	(be)nennen	**Name** three pop bands that you like.

Unit 4 My trip to Ireland

p. 64	**impression** [ɪm'preʃn]	Eindruck	(F) l'impression *(f)*
p. 65	**brochure** ['brəʊʃə]	Broschüre, Prospekt	! stress: **<u>bro</u>chure** ['brəʊʃə] (F) la brochure
	practical ['præktɪkl]	praktisch	Your ideas are good, but can you give me some **practical** help, too? (F) pratique

Part A

p. 66	**northern** ['nɔːðən]	nördlich, Nord-	**northern** ['nɔːðən] **western** ['westən]  **eastern** ['iːstən] **southern** ['sʌðən] ! Aussprache: **south** [saʊθ] – **southern** ['sʌðən]
	coffee ['kɒfi]	Kaffee	(F) le café
	giant ['dʒaɪənt]	Riese	(F) le géant
	it **might** be the other side [maɪt]	es könnte die andere Seite sein	You **might** see the Queen if you wait outside Buckingham Palace. (= Maybe you'll see the Queen if you wait …)

möglich – wahrscheinlich – sicherlich

My parents	**may** **might** **could** **should** **must**	be at home now.	Meine Eltern	sind jetzt **vielleicht** zu Hause. **könnten** jetzt **(vielleicht)** zu Hause sein. **könnten** jetzt zu Hause sein. **sollten/müssten eigentlich** jetzt zu Hause sein. **müssen** jetzt zu Hause sein.

as well [əz 'wel]	auch, ebenso	We don't only sell books, we sell magazines **as well**. You might **as well** stay here tonight. (Du könntest heute Nacht ebenso gut hier bleiben.)

[iː] green · [i] happy · [ɪ] big · [e] red · [æ] cat · [ɑː] class · [ɒ] song · [ɔː] door · [uː] blue · [ʊ] book · [ʌ] mum · [ɜː] girl · [ə] a partner

column ['kɒləm]	Säule	(F) la colonne
(to) **rise up** [ˌraɪz‿'ʌp], **rose** [rəʊz], **risen** ['rɪzn]	aufragen, emporragen *(Berge, Säulen, Türme, …)*	
nearly ['nɪəli]	fast, beinahe	= almost
(to) **form** [fɔːm]	bilden, formen	(L) forma, -ae *f (Form, Gestalt)*
proud (of) [praʊd]	stolz (auf)	She's a very good student. We're **proud of** her.
challenge ['tʃælɪndʒ]	Herausforderung	My first day at *Gymnasium* was a **challenge** for me.
(to) **challenge** sb. **(to** sth.**)** ['tʃælɪndʒ]	jn. herausfordern (zu etwas)	We **challenged** them **to** a game of basketball. Maths doesn't really **challenge** me at the moment.
(to) **be left** [left]	übrig sein	There **aren't** any biscuits **left**. I've eaten them all.
Shall I …? [ʃæl]	Soll ich …?	It's hot in here. **Shall I** open the window?
advert ['ædvɜːt]	Werbespot, Werbung; Anzeige, Inserat	We bought our dog after we saw an **advert** in the local paper.
curious ['kjʊəriəs]	wissbegierig, neugierig	My brother is very **curious** and always wants to learn everything about everything. (F) curieux, se (L) cura, -ae *f (Sorge, Neugier)*
polite [pə'laɪt]	höflich	(F) poli, e
impolite [ˌɪmpə'laɪt]	unhöflich	**polite ◄► impolite** (F) impoli, e
p. 68 **border** ['bɔːdə]	Grenze	Spain only has a **border** with Portugal and France.
(to) **change** [tʃeɪndʒ]	wechseln, umtauschen *(Geld)*	Don't forget to **change** money if you want to travel to Britain. (F) changer
currency ['kʌrənsi]	Währung	Until 2001, Germany's **currency** was the *Deutsche Mark*.
the EU [ˌiː 'juː] **(the European Union** [ˌjʊərəpiːən 'juːniən]**)**	die Europäische Union	
euro (€) ['jʊərəʊ]	Euro	

Pounds and euros

In **Britain**, you pay with **pounds** and **pence**.

You say:	*You write:*
fifty p [piː] / **fifty pence** [pens]	**50 p**
one pound / a pound	**£ 1**
two pounds fifty	**£ 2.50**

In **Germany**, you pay with **euros** and **cents**.

You say:	*You write:*
fifty cents [sents]	**€ 0.50**
one euro / a euro	**€ 1**
two euros fifty	**€ 2.50**

ID card [ˌaɪ 'diː kɑːd]	Personalausweis	
nation ['neɪʃn]	Nation, Volk	(F) la nation (L) natio, -onis *f*
passport ['pɑːspɔːt]	(Reise-)Pass	(F) le passeport
peace [piːs]	Friede, Frieden	**peace ◄► war** (F) la paix (L) pax, pacis *f*
police station [pə'liːs steɪʃn]	Polizeiwache, -revier	
population [ˌpɒpju'leɪʃn]	Bevölkerung, Einwohner(zahl)	(F) la population (L) populus, -i *m*
president ['prezɪdənt]	Präsident/in	! stress: **<u>pre</u>sident** ['prezɪdənt] (F) le président, la présidente
republic [rɪ'pʌblɪk]	Republik	! stress: **re<u>pub</u>lic** [rɪ'pʌblɪk] (L) res publica *f*
state [steɪt]	Staat	(F) l'état *(m)* (L) status, -us *m (Zustand)*

[eɪ] name · [aɪ] time · [ɔɪ] boy · [əʊ] old · [aʊ] town · [ɪə] here · [eə] where · [ʊə] tour

	visa ['viːzə]	Visum	Germans need a **visa** if they travel to India.
	pet [pet]	Haustier	
	(to) **steal** [stiːl], **stole** [stəʊl], **stolen** ['stəʊlən]	stehlen	Where is your bike? – Somebody has **stolen** it.
	bank [bæŋk]	Bank	(F) la banque
p. 69	**coordinator** [kəʊ'ɔːdɪneɪtə]	Koordinator/in	
	layout ['leɪaʊt]	Layout, Gestaltung	
	editor ['edɪtə]	Redakteur/in; Herausgeber/in	(F) l'éditeur *(m)*, l'éditrice *(f)* (L) edere *(bekanntmachen)*
	research *(no pl)* ['riːsɜːtʃ]	Recherche, Forschung(en)	I have to do some **research** on Ireland for homework.
	result [rɪ'zʌlt]	Ergebnis, Resultat	Have you heard the football **results**? Did we win? (F) le résultat
	(to) **suggest** sth. **(to** sb.**)** [sə'dʒest]	(jm.) etwas vorschlagen	*English:* Dad **suggested that we go** to the cinema. *German:* Dad **schlug vor**, ins Kino **zu gehen**. ! (*not:* Dad suggested ~~to go~~ …)
	discussion [dɪ'skʌʃn]	Diskussion	(F) la discussion
	decision [dɪ'sɪʒn]	Entscheidung	verb: (to) **decide** – noun: **decision** (F) la décision

Part B

p. 70	**angel** ['eɪndʒl]	Engel	(F) l'ange *(m)*
	heaven ['hevn]	Himmel *(im religiösen Sinn)*	! clouds in the **sky** angels in **heaven**
	service ['sɜːvɪs]	Gottesdienst	(L) servire *(dienen)*
	(to) **check** sth. **out** [ˌtʃek_'aʊt] *(infml)*	sich etwas anschauen, anhören; etwas ausprobieren	Our new CD is called "No sky in heaven". **Check it out**!
	He was like: "Stop …" *(infml)*	Und er so: „Stop …"	
	motorbike ['məʊtəbaɪk]	Motorrad	
p. 71	**suit** [suːt]	Anzug	
	(to) **smoke** [sməʊk]	rauchen	
	pipe [paɪp]	(Tabaks-)Pfeife	

He's **smoking** a **pipe**.

	like *(infml)*	als ob	What's he doing? – He looks **like** he's crying. ! Diese umgangssprachliche Verwendung von **like** wird von manchen als falsches Englisch empfunden. Besonders im Schriftlichen solltest du **as if** für das deutsche „als ob" benutzen: He looks **as if** he's crying.
p. 72	**hell** [hel]	Hölle	**heaven ◄► hell**
	by 8 pm [baɪ]	bis (spätestens) 20 Uhr	You must be here **by** 8 pm. (= not later than 8 pm)
	(to) **have a shower** ['ʃaʊə]	(sich) duschen	*English:* First I make tea, then I **have a shower**. *German:* …, dann dusche ich (mich).
	electronic [ɪˌlek'trɒnɪk]	elektronisch	(F) électronique

[b] **boat** · [p] **pool** · [d] **dad** · [t] **ten** · [g] **good** · [k] **cat** · [m] **mum** · [n] **no** · [ŋ] **song** · [l] **hello** · [r] **red** · [w] **we** · [j] **you**

	the Atlantic (Ocean) [ət'læntɪk]	der Atlantik, der Atlantische Ozean	
p. 73	**beginning** [bɪ'gɪnɪŋ]	Anfang, Beginn	verb: (to) **begin** – noun: **beginning**
	guest [gest]	Gast	
	facial expression [ˌfeɪʃl_ɪk'spreʃn]	Gesichtsausdruck, Mimik	
	interaction [ˌɪntər'ækʃn]	Interaktion, Umgang	(L) agere *(tun, handeln)*

Part C

p. 74	**arrival** [ə'raɪvl]	Ankunft	verb: (to) **arrive** – noun: **arrival** (F) l'arrivée *(f)*
	weird [wɪəd]	seltsam, komisch	I have a **weird** feeling that something is wrong.
	ride [raɪd]	Ritt, Ausritt	
	(to) **be alive** [ə'laɪv]	leben, am Leben sein	(to) **be alive** ◄► (to) **be dead**
	argument ['ɑːgjumənt]	Streit, Auseinandersetzung	! stress: **argument** ['ɑːgjumənt]
	(to) **miss** [mɪs]	vermissen	I enjoyed my trip to France, but I **missed** my friends. ! (to) **miss** = **1.** verpassen; **2.** vermissen
	round here [ˌraʊnd 'hɪə]	hier in der Gegend	**Round here**, we're all United fans.
	(to) **stare (at** sb./sth.) [steə]	(jn./etwas an)starren	You shouldn't **stare at** people. It's impolite.
	(to) **care about** sth. [keə]	etwas wichtig nehmen	(L) curare *(sorgen für)*

(to) care

1. I **don't care** about money.	Geld ist mir egal.
2. In the city, people **wouldn't care** what I looked like.	In der Großstadt wäre es den Leuten egal, wie ich aussehe / würde sich niemand darum kümmern, wie ich aussehe.
3. I really **care** about animals.	Tiere liegen mir sehr am Herzen. / Tiere sind mir sehr wichtig.
4. Her parents are really rich. – Who **cares**?	Ihre Eltern sind richtig reich. – Na und? / Wen interessiert das?

	(to) **be starving** ['stɑːvɪŋ]	einen Riesenhunger haben	
	(to) **unpack** [ˌʌn'pæk]	auspacken	(to) **pack** (packen, einpacken) ◄► (to) **unpack**
	God [gɒd]	Gott	
	(to) **dislike** [dɪs'laɪk]	nicht mögen, nicht leiden können	(to) **like** ◄► (to) **dislike**
p. 75	**bang** [bæŋ]	Knall	
	regional ['riːdʒənl]	regional	local – **regional** – national – international (F) régional, e
	accent ['æksənt]	Akzent	! stress: **accent** ['æksənt] (F) l'accent *(m)*
	standard ['stændəd]	Standard; Standard-	(F) le standard
p. 76	**boyfriend** ['bɔɪfrend]	Freund	
	girlfriend ['gɜːlfrend]	Freundin	
	(to) **welcome** sb. **(to)** ['welkəm]	jn. begrüßen (in), jn. willkommen heißen (in)	I'll make tea. Can you **welcome** the guests?
p. 77	(to) **pass** [pɑːs]	vergehen, vorübergehen *(Zeit)*	The lesson was so interesting that the time **passed** really quickly. (F) passer
	next [nekst]	als Nächstes	That was nice. What are we going to do **next**?
	Easter ['iːstə]	Ostern	

[f] **f**ather · [v] **r**iver · [s] **s**ister · [z] plea**s**e · [ʃ] **sh**op · [ʒ] televi**s**ion ·
[tʃ] **t**eacher · [dʒ] **G**ermany · [θ] **th**anks · [ð] **th**is · [h] **h**ere

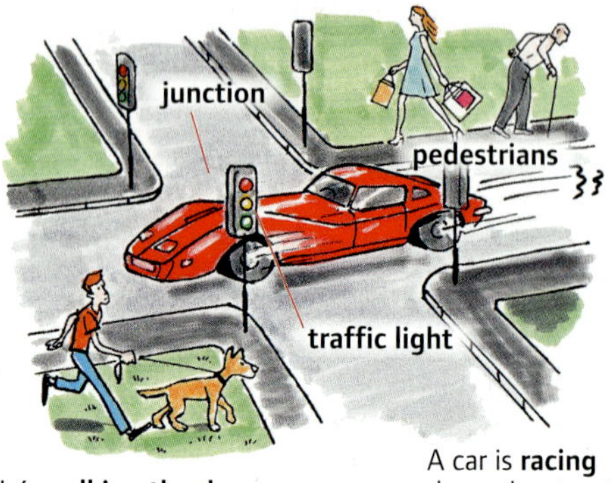

junction ['dʒʌŋkʃn]	(Straßen-)Kreuzung	
pedestrian [pə'destriən]	Fußgänger/in	
(to) **walk the dog**	mit dem Hund rausgehen, den Hund ausführen	
(to) **kick** [kɪk]	treten	
(to) **race** [reɪs]	rasen	
traffic light ['træfɪk laɪt] (*oft auch:* **traffic lights** *(pl)*)	(Verkehrs-)Ampel	
traffic ['træfɪk]	Verkehr	He's **walking the dog.** / A car is **racing** down the street.
(to) **turn** red/brown/cold/… [tɜːn]	rot/braun/kalt/… werden	! **turn** = „werden" wird hauptsächlich für Farbveränderungen und Wetterwechsel verwendet.
van [væn]	Transporter, Lieferwagen	
(to) **spin around** [ˌspɪn‿ə'raʊnd]**, spun, spun** [spʌn]	sich (im Kreis) drehen; herumwirbeln	The girl **spun around** until she fell to the ground.
(to) **park** [pɑːk]	parken	
immediately [ɪ'miːdiətli]	sofort	My dog comes **immediately** when I call her. (F) immédiatement
siren ['saɪrən]	Sirene	! stress: **<u>si</u>ren** ['saɪrən]
(to) **be gone** [gɒn]	weg sein, nicht (mehr) da sein	I don't know where Steve is. He was here two minutes ago and now he**'s gone**.

The horse ride

p. 78	**none (of …)** [nʌn]	keine(r, s) (von …)	He had 11 cousins but **none of** them lived near him.
	a couple ['kʌpl]	ein Paar; ein paar	 **a young couple**  **a couple of sandwiches**
	folk *(pl)* [fəʊk] *(infml)*	Leute	The **folk** round here are very friendly to tourists.
	line [laɪn]	Reihe	! **line** = **1.** Linie; **2.** Zeile; **3.** Reihe
	What's up?	Was gibt's? / Was ist los?	Can you come and help me? – Why, **what's up?**
	trail [treɪl]	Weg, Pfad	There are lots of good riding **trails** in the hills behind our house.
	(to) **sigh** [saɪ]	seufzen	
	Now that …	Jetzt, wo … / Nun, da …	**Now that** the school year is nearly over, we can make plans for the holidays.
	slippery ['slɪpəri]	rutschig, glatt	
	ditch [dɪtʃ]	Graben	
p. 79	**in the old days**	früher (einmal)	**In the old days**, there were no cars. People walked or rode horses.
	gravestone ['greɪvstəʊn]	Grabstein	a **gravestone** 
	(to) **bury** ['beri]	begraben, beerdigen	He died on holiday in Spain and was **buried** there.

famine ['fæmɪn]	Hungersnot	(L) fames, -is *f* *(Hunger)*
disease [dɪ'ziːz]	*(ansteckende)* Krankheit	! • **disease** wird für ansteckende oder sehr ernsthafte Erkrankungen verwendet: She has a blood **disease**. Thousands of trees died from **disease**. • Das allgemeinere Wort für „Krankheit" ist **illness**: After a week of **illness**, she went back to school.
(to) **emigrate** ['emɪgreɪt]	auswandern, emigrieren	(F) émigrer
government ['gʌvənmənt]	Regierung	(F) le gouvernement
export ['ekspɔːt]	Export, Ausfuhr	(F) l'export *(m)*
stream [striːm]	Bach	She stopped at the **stream** and drank some water. 
ashes *(pl)* ['æʃɪz]	Asche *(sterbliche Überreste)*	! • **ash** („Asche") wird verwendet für das, was übrig bleibt, wenn Holz, Papier, Kohle, Tabak verbrennt. • **ashes** *(pl)* („Asche") wird verwendet, – für die sterblichen Überreste nach der Einäscherung eines Verstorbenen; – für die Überreste nach einem Brand (z.B. eines Hauses).
glad [glæd]	froh, dankbar	
death [deθ]	Tod	
especially [ɪ'speʃli]	besonders, vor allem	I love chocolate, **especially** chocolate from Belgium.
thought [θɔːt]	Gedanke	verb: (to) **think, thought, thought** – noun: **thought**

Unit 5 Extraordinary Scotland

p. 82 **extraordinary** [ɪk'strɔːdnri]	außergewöhnlich	(F) extraordinaire (L) extra *(außerhalb von)*; ordo, inis *f* *(Reihe)*
(to) **promote** sth. [prə'məʊt]	Werbung machen für etwas	Shakira is on tour. She's **promoting** her new album.
bagpipes *(pl)* ['bægpaɪps]	Dudelsack	
Look out!	Achtung! / Aufgepasst!	**Look out**, a car's coming!
p. 83 (to) **compete in** sth. [kəm'piːt]	an etwas teilnehmen *(Wettkampf)*	
sheepdog ['ʃiːpdɒg]	Hütehund	! Mit **sheepdog** werden in Großbritannien oft Border Collies bezeichnet, da Schäfer meist diese Hunderasse als Hütehund einsetzen.
trials *(pl)* ['traɪəlz]	Turnier, Wettkampf	
the Highlands *(pl)* ['haɪləndz]	das schottische Hochland	
on board [bɔːd]	an Bord	*English:* **on board** the ship/ferry *German:* **an Bord** des Schiffes/der Fähre
yacht [jɒt]	Jacht	! pronunciation: **yacht** [jɒt]
wee [wiː] *(bes. Scottish English, infml)*	klein	I live in a **wee** house in the Highlands. (= little, small)
isle [aɪl]	*(kleine)* Insel, Eiland	! Das Wort **isle** wird vor allem in dichterischer Sprache und in Eigennamen verwendet. (F) l'île *(f)* (L) insula, -ae *f*

[eɪ] name · [aɪ] time · [ɔɪ] boy · [əʊ] old ·
[aʊ] town · [ɪə] here · [eə] where · [ʊə] tour

(to) **identify** sb./sth. **(by** sth.**)** [aɪ'dentɪfaɪ]	jn./etwas identifizieren (anhand von etwas)	She **identified** the thief **by** his very big nose. (F) identifier
dolphin ['dɒlfɪn]	Delfin	! stress: **dolphin** ['dɒlfɪn]
social media *(pl)* [ˌsəʊʃl 'miːdiə]	soziale Medien	
unusual [ʌn'juːʒuəl]	ungewöhnlich	Snow is very **unusual** in June.
usual ['juːʒuəl]	gewöhnlich, üblich	adjective: **usual** – Dad came home earlier than **usual**. adverb: **usually** – He **usually** comes home later.

Part A

p. 84	**volunteer** [ˌvɒlən'tɪə]	Freiwillige(r), Ehrenamtliche(r)	(F) le/la volontaire
	sighting ['saɪtɪŋ]	Sichtung	The first **sighting** of the Loch Ness monster was in 1933.
	(to) **put your hand up**	sich melden	**Put your hand up** if you know the answer.
	(to) **photograph** ['fəʊtəgrɑːf]	fotografieren	
	pollution [pə'luːʃn]	(Umwelt-)Verschmutzung	(F) la pollution
	(to) **spend time/money (on)** [spend]**, spent, spent** [spent]	Zeit verbringen (mit); Geld ausgeben (für)	Mum says I **spend** too much time in front of my computer. My brother **spends** a lot of money **on** DVDs.
	(to) **protect** sb./sth. **(from** sb./sth.**)** [prə'tekt]	jn./etwas (be)schützen (vor jm./etwas)	Wear a hat to **protect** your head **from** the sun. Animals might get dangerous if they're trying to **protect** their young. (F) protéger
	(to) **teach** [tiːtʃ]**, taught, taught** [tɔːt]	unterrichten, lehren	Mr Schwarz is a teacher. He **teaches** English. My sister is **teaching** me to play the guitar. (= … bringt mir das Gitarrespielen bei.)
	dorsal fin [ˌdɔːsl 'fɪn]	Rückenflosse	
	(to) **record** [rɪ'kɔːd]	aufzeichnen *(Musik, Daten)*; dokumentieren *(Daten)*	The Beatles **recorded** their albums in London. I **recorded** every little detail in my little black book.
	location [ləʊ'keɪʃn]	Position, Standort	(L) locus, -i *m* *(Ort)*
	(to) **monitor** ['mɒnɪtə]	nachverfolgen; überwachen	Almost everything we do on the internet can be **monitored** by somebody.
	movement ['muːvmənt]	Bewegung	verb: (to) **move** – noun: **movement** (F) le mouvement (L) movere *(bewegen)*
	rough [rʌf]	stürmisch, rau *(See)*	The sea was so **rough** that we stayed in the harbour.
	calm [kɑːm]	ruhig	My mum has a very **calm** voice. (F) calme
	seasick ['siːsɪk]	seekrank	I always get **seasick** on a boat when the sea is rough.
p. 85	(to) **keep** [kiːp]**, kept, kept** [kept]	aufheben, aufsparen; aufbewahren	Don't spend all your money now. **Keep** some for later. You should always **keep** milk in a cool place.
	(to) **relax** [rɪ'læks]	sich entspannen, sich ausruhen	
p. 87	(to) **escape** [ɪ'skeɪp]	fliehen	His grandfather **escaped** from Germany in 1940.
	escape [ɪ'skeɪp]	Flucht	

[b] boat · [p] pool · [d] dad · [t] ten · [g] good · [k] cat ·
[m] mum · [n] no · [ŋ] song · [l] hello · [r] red · [w] we · [j] you

split screen [splɪt 'skriːn]	geteilter Bildschirm; Bildschirm(auf)teilung	

Part B

p. 88	**cue** [kjuː]	Stichwort, Signal *(Theater)*	He says "Where is she?" and that's your **cue** to enter.
	fault [fɔːlt]	Schuld, Fehler	Why didn't you wake me up this morning? It's your **fault** that I'll be late for school.
	backstage [ˌbæk'steɪdʒ]	hinter der Bühne	another word for "behind the stage"
	rehearsal [rɪ'hɜːsl]	Probe *(Theater)*	
	no one else [els]	niemand anders; niemand sonst	**No one else** has to help at home as much as I do.

... else

Oh Dad, why can't I go to Henry's party? **Everybody else** is allowed to go.	**alle anderen; sonst jeder**
I'm so tired. **Someone else** will have to wash the dishes.	**jemand anders**
Do you need **anything else** from the shops?	**sonst noch etwas**
What else can you tell us about Scotland?	**was (sonst) noch**
Who else wants to go to the festival in Edinburgh?	**wer (sonst) noch**

	(to) **concentrate (on** sth.**)** ['kɒnsntreɪt]	sich konzentrieren (auf etwas)	Please be quiet. I can't **concentrate** on my work. ! stress: **con**centrate ['kɒnsntreɪt] (F) se concentrer
	(to) **pick on** sb. [pɪk] *(infml)*	auf jm. herumhacken	It's not nice to **pick on** people if they're fat.
	(to) **be tired of** sth. ['taɪəd]	genug von etwas haben; etwas satt haben	**I'm tired of** this book. It's too long and very boring.
	position [pə'zɪʃn]	Platz, Position	! stress: po**si**tion [pə'zɪʃn] (F) la position (L) ponere *(stellen)*
p. 89	**tough** [tʌf]	(knall)hart, schwierig	Starting at a new school is a **tough** thing for most students.
	(to) **tread on** sb.'s **toes** [tred], **trod** [trɒd], **trodden** ['trɒdn] *(infml)*	jm. auf die Füße/Zehen treten *(auch im übertragenen Sinne)*	Hey, look out – you just **trod on** my **toes**! Maybe **I'm treading on** some people's **toes** here, but I think I could do the job better than everybody else.
	(to) **give** sb. **a hard time** *(infml)*	jn. fertig machen, jm. einheizen; jm. das Leben schwer machen	
	(to) **calm down** [ˌkɑːm 'daʊn]	sich beruhigen	*English:* (to) **calm down** | (to) **calm sb. down** *German:* **sich beruhigen** | **jn. beruhigen**
	description [dɪ'skrɪpʃn]	Beschreibung	verb: (to) **describe** – noun: **description** (F) la description (L) scribere *(schreiben)*
p. 90	**direct** [də'rekt], [daɪ'rekt]	direkt	**direct** ◄► **indirect** [ˌɪndə'rekt], [ˌɪndaɪ'rekt] (F) direct, e / indirect, e
p. 91	**whenever** [ˌwen'evə]	wann (auch) immer; egal, wann	

whenever, wherever, whatever, whoever

At my school, we're allowed to use dictionaries **whenever** we want.	... **wann immer wir wollen**
I'll find you, **wherever** you are.	... **wo immer du (auch) bist / egal, wo du bist**
We will help you, **whatever** happens.	... **was immer auch geschieht / egal, was geschieht**
Whoever told you that was wrong.	**Wer immer dir das auch erzählt hat,** ...

platform ['plætfɔːm]	Plattform	! **platform** = **1.** Plattform; **2.** Bahnsteig, Gleis
comedian [kə'miːdiən]	Komiker/in, Komödiant/in	(F) le comédien, la comédienne

[f] **f**ather · [v] ri**v**er · [s] **s**ister · [z] plea**s**e · [ʃ] **sh**op · [ʒ] televi**s**ion · [tʃ] tea**ch**er · [dʒ] **G**ermany · [θ] **th**anks · [ð] **th**is · [h] **h**ere

	entertainment [ˌentəˈteɪnmənt]	Unterhaltung	There's usually lots of **entertainment** on a cruise ship: films, shows, concerts, competitions, etc.
	(to) **interest** sb. [ˈɪntrəst]	jn. interessieren	! • He**'s interested in** films. Er interessiert sich für … • Films **interest** him. Filme interessieren ihn.
p. 92	**handout** [ˈhændaʊt]	Handout, Handzettel	
	transparency [trænsˈpærənsi]	Folie	
	lynx [lɪŋks], *pl* **lynx** *or* **lynxes**	Luchs	
	habitat [ˈhæbɪtæt]	Lebensraum	The natural **habitat** of the panda is China. (L) habitare *(wohnen)*
	coat [kəʊt]	Fell	
	predator [ˈpredətə]	Raubtier	! pronunciation: **predator** [ˈpredətə] (L) praeda, -ae *f (Beute)*
	mammal [ˈmæml]	Säugetier	
	territory [ˈterətri]	Revier, Territorium	(F) le territoire (L) terra, -ae *f (Erde, Land)*
p. 93	**element** [ˈelɪmənt]	Element	
	necessary [ˈnesəsəri]	notwendig, nötig	You can phone me on my mobile if **necessary**. (F) nécessaire (L) necesse est *(es ist notwendig)*

Missing

p. 94	**missing** [ˈmɪsɪŋ]	verschollen, vermisst	
	heather [ˈheðə]	Heide(kraut)	
	below [bɪˈləʊ]	unten, darunter; unter, unterhalb (von)	From the plane, the buildings **below** were so small. Your mouth is **below** your nose.
	above [əˈbʌv]	oben, darüber; über, oberhalb (von)	The buildings looked very small from **above**. Your eyes are **above** your nose.
	tension [ˈtenʃn]	Spannung, Anspannung	(F) la tension
	whistle [ˈwɪsl]	Pfiff	! **whistle** = **1.** pfeifen; **2.** Pfiff; **3.** (Triller-)Pfeife
	in horror [ˈhɒrə]	entsetzt	We watched **in horror** as Messi scored his fifth goal.
	noise [nɔɪz]	Geräusch; Lärm	noun: **noise** – adjective: **noisy**
	(to) **reach over** [ˌriːtʃ_ˈəʊvə]	die Hand ausstrecken	He **reached over** and quietly stole a biscuit.
	dry [draɪ]	trocken	**dry** ◄► **wet**
	(to) **beat** [biːt], **beat** [biːt], **beaten** [ˈbiːtn]	schlagen; besiegen	I **beat** my father at tennis last Sunday.
	(to) **read** sb.'s **mind** [maɪnd]	jemandes Gedanken lesen	Sometimes I wish I could **read your mind**.
	shepherd [ˈʃepəd]	Schäfer/in, Schafhirte/-hirtin	

[iː] green · [i] happy · [ɪ] big · [e] red · [æ] cat · [ɑː] class · [ɒ] song · [ɔː] door · [uː] blue · [ʊ] book · [ʌ] mum · [ɜː] girl · [ə] a partner

	jealous (of) ['dʒeləs]	neidisch (auf); eifersüchtig (auf)	You get so much pocket money! I'm really **jealous**. She was **jealous of** her baby brother. She thought her parents loved him more.
	(to) **hate** [heɪt]	hassen	(to) **love** ◄► (to) **hate**
p. 95	(to) **burst into tears, burst, burst** [bɜːst]	in Tränen ausbrechen	When I saw that the dog was dead, I immediately **burst into tears**.
	gently ['dʒentli]	behutsam, sanft	
	awake [ə'weɪk]	wach	**awake** ◄► **asleep**
	(to) **knock (on** sth.**)** [nɒk]	(an)klopfen (an etwas)	I **knocked** and went in.
	memorial [mə'mɔːriəl]	Denkmal; Gedenk-	There's a war **memorial** by the church in our village. (L) memoria, -ae *f* *(Erinnerung)*
p. 96	**in second place**	auf dem zweiten Platz; an zweiter Stelle	(L) secundus, -a, -um *(zweiter)*

5

Text File

Text 8

The Off-side Trap by Mary Colson

Setting	Schauplatz
Football club disco.	Disco im Fußballclub.
Maxine really fancies Paul and he quite likes her. They're thirteen years old. He's hugely into football – she knows nothing about it but has to pretend she does in order to make conversation. While their thoughts are being spoken, Maxine and Paul are experiencing awkward silences, looking ill at ease and searching for something to say. There is a prevailing embarrassed awkwardness throughout their dialogue.	Maxine findet Paul echt toll und er mag sie auch irgendwie. Sie sind 13. Er steht voll auf Fußball – sie hat keine Ahnung davon, muss aber so tun als ob, um sich mit ihm zu unterhalten. Während Maxines und Pauls Gedanken gesprochen werden, ertragen die beiden eine peinliche Stille, in der sie sich nicht wohl fühlen und überlegen, was sie sagen könnten. Das ganze Gespräch hindurch wirken sie verlegen und unbeholfen.

Dictionary

Das **Dictionary** besteht aus **zwei alphabetischen Wörterlisten**:
English – German (S. 198 – 220) und **German – English** (S. 221 – 242)

Im **English – German Dictionary** kannst du nachschlagen, wenn du wissen möchtest, was ein englisches Wort bedeutet, wie man es ausspricht oder wie es geschrieben wird.

Im **Dictionary** werden folgende **Abkürzungen und Symbole** verwendet:

sth. = something (etwas) sb. = somebody (jemand) jn. = jemanden jm. = jemandem
pl = *plural* (Mehrzahl) *infml* = *informal* (umgangssprachlich)
° Mit diesem Kringel sind Wörter markiert, die nicht zum Lernwortschatz gehören.

▶ Der Pfeil weist auf Kästen im **Vocabulary** (S. 172 – 197) hin, in denen du weitere Informationen zu diesem Wort findest.

Die **Fundstellenangaben** zeigen, wo ein Wort zum ersten Mal vorkommt.
I = Band 1; II = Band 2; III 1 (15) = Band 3, Unit 1, Seite 15

Tipps zur Arbeit mit einem Wörterbuch findest du im Skills File auf Seite 141.

A

a [ə]:
1. ein, eine I
2. once a week einmal pro Woche II

°**abbey** ['æbi] Abtei, Kloster

abbreviation [əˌbriːvi'eɪʃn] Abkürzung II

able ['eɪbl]: **be able to do sth.** etwas tun können; fähig sein / in der Lage sein, etwas zu tun III 2 (40)

about [ə'baʊt]:
1. about you/… über dich/… I **about yourself** über dich selbst I **It's about …** Es geht um … / Es handelt von … **know about sth.** sich mit etwas auskennen; über etwas Bescheid wissen II **the best thing about …** das Beste an … III 1 (8) **What about you?** Und du? / Und was ist mit dir?; Und ihr? / Und was ist mit euch? I **What is the story about?** Wovon handelt die Geschichte? / Worum geht es in der Geschichte? I
2. about 300 ungefähr 300 II

above [ə'bʌv] oben, darüber; über, oberhalb (von) III 5 (94)

accent ['æksənt] Akzent III 4 (75)

access ['ækses] Zugang, Zutritt I

°**accompany** [ə'kʌmpəni] begleiten

across [ə'krɒs]: **across the street** (quer) über die Straße II

act [ækt] schauspielern II

°**Act of Union** [ækt] Vereinigungsgesetz

act out [ˌækt‿'aʊt] vorspielen I

action ['ækʃn] Action; Handlung, Tat I

°**active** ['æktɪv] aktiv

activity [æk'tɪvəti] Aktivität I **free-time activities** Freizeitaktivitäten I

actor ['æktə] Schauspieler/in I

actually ['æktʃuəli] eigentlich; übrigens; tatsächlich III 3 (47)
▶ S. 184 actually

add (to) [æd] hinzufügen, ergänzen, addieren (zu) III 2 (38)

adder ['ædə] Kreuzotter II

address [ə'dres] Adresse, Anschrift I

adjective ['ædʒɪktɪv] Adjektiv II

°**admire** [əd'maɪə] bewundern

adopted [ə'dɒptɪd] adoptiert, Adoptiv- II

adult ['ædʌlt] Erwachsene(r) III 1 (15)

°**advantage** [əd'vɑːntɪdʒ] Vorteil

adventure [əd'ventʃə] Abenteuer II

adverb ['ædvɜːb] Adverb II

advert ['ædvɜːt] Werbespot, Werbung III 4 (66)

°**advice** [əd'vaɪs] Rat(schlag)

°**afraid** [ə'freɪd]: **be afraid** Angst haben

after ['ɑːftə]:
1. after breakfast nach dem Frühstück I **right after you** gleich nach dir II **after that** danach III 3 (46)
2. nachdem II **just after …** gleich nachdem …; kurz nachdem … II
3. run after sb. hinter jm. herrennen I

afternoon [ˌɑːftə'nuːn] Nachmittag I **in the afternoon** nachmittags, am Nachmittag I **on Saturday afternoon** am Samstagnachmittag I **this afternoon** heute Nachmittag II

again [ə'gen] wieder; noch einmal I **again and again** immer wieder II

against [ə'genst] gegen I

age [eɪdʒ] Alter I **… is your age …** ist in deinem Alter; … ist so alt wie du II

ago [ə'gəʊ]: **two days ago** vor zwei Tagen II

agree [ə'griː]: **agree with sb.** jm. zustimmen I **agree on sth.** sich auf etwas einigen I

°**agreement** [ə'griːmənt] Abkommen

air [eə] Luft II

airport ['eəpɔːt] Flughafen III 3 (55)

°**album** ['ælbəm] Album

alive [ə'laɪv]: **be alive** leben, am Leben sein III 4 (74)

all [ɔːl] alles; alle I **all around her** überall um sie herum III 1 (24) **all of Plymouth** ganz Plymouth, das ganze Plymouth I **all alone** ganz allein II **all day** den ganzen Tag II °**all over this land** im ganzen Land **all the time** die ganze Zeit II **one all** eins zu eins; eins beide III 3 (56)

allow [ə'laʊ] erlauben, zulassen III 2 (37) **be allowed to do sth.** etwas tun dürfen II

all right [ɔːl 'raɪt] okay; in Ordnung I

almost ['ɔːlməʊst] fast, beinahe I

alone [ə'ləʊn] allein II **all alone** ganz allein II

along [ə'lɒŋ]: **along the street / …** die Straße / … entlang I **sing along (with sb.)** (mit jm.) mitsingen III 2 (35)

aloud [ə'laʊd]: **read aloud** laut (vor)lesen II

already [ɔːl'redi] schon, bereits II

also ['ɔːlsəʊ] auch I

altogether [ˌɔːltə'geðə] insgesamt, alles in allem III 2 (34)

always ['ɔːlweɪz] immer I

am: 4 am [ˌeɪ‿'em] 4 Uhr morgens I

amazing [ə'meɪzɪŋ] erstaunlich, unglaublich III 1 (10)

an [æn], [ən] ein, eine I

ancestor ['ænsestə] Vorfahr/in III 3 (52)

and [ænd], [ənd] und I

angel ['eɪndʒl] Engel III 4 (70)

°**Anglican** ['æŋglɪkən] anglikanisch

angry ['æŋgri] wütend I **angry with sb.** wütend, böse auf jn. II

animal ['ænɪml] Tier I **my favourite animal** mein Lieblingstier I

announcement [ə'naʊnsmənt] Durchsage, Ansage III 1 (19)

another [ə'nʌðə]:
1. ein(e) andere(r, s) I
2. noch ein(e) I

answer ['ɑːnsə]:
1. antworten; beantworten I **answer**

the phone ans Telefon gehen II
2. Antwort I
ant [ænt] Ameise I
any ['eni]: **Are there any ...?** Gibt es (irgendwelche) ...? I **not ... any more** nicht mehr II **There aren't any ...** Es gibt keine / Es sind keine ... I
anybody ['enibɒdi]: anybody? (irgend)jemand? II **not ... anybody** niemand II
anyone ['eniwʌn]: anyone? (irgend)jemand? II **not ... anyone** niemand II
anything ['eniθɪŋ]: anything? (irgend)etwas? II **not ... anything** nichts II
Anyway, ... ['eniweɪ] Jedenfalls, ... / Aber egal, ... II **And anyway, ...** Und überhaupt, ... III 1 (20)
apartment [ə'pɑːtmənt] Wohnung II
appear [ə'pɪə] erscheinen, auftauchen II
apple ['æpl] Apfel II
appointment [ə'pɔɪntmənt] Verabredung, Termin I
April ['eɪprəl] April I
aquarium [ə'kweəriəm] Aquarium; Aquarienhaus I
°**arc** [ɑːk] Bogen
°**arch** [ɑːtʃ] Bogen
architect ['ɑːkɪtekt] Architekt/in III 2 (31)
°**architecture** ['ɑːkɪtektʃə] Architektur
°**archive** ['ɑːkaɪv] Archiv
are [ɑː] bist; sind; seid I **Are you ...?** Bist du ...? I **The DVDs are ...** Die DVDs kosten ... I
area ['eəriə] Bereich; Gebiet, Gegend I
aren't [ɑːnt]: **you aren't ...** du bist nicht ...; du bist kein/e ...; ihr seid nicht ...; ihr seid kein/e ... I
argue ['ɑːgjuː] streiten; sich streiten III 2 (41)
argument ['ɑːgjumənt]:
1. Streit, Auseinandersetzung III 4 (74)
°**2.** Argument
arm [ɑːm] Arm II **take sb. by the arm** jn. am Arm nehmen II
armchair ['ɑːmtʃeə] Sessel I
around [ə'raʊnd]:
1. around the library / ... in der Bücherei / ... umher I **all around her** überall um sie herum III 1 (24) **look around (the farm)** sich (auf der Farm) umsehen II
► S. 180 (to) look ...
walk/run/... around herumlaufen, umherspazieren / herumrennen, umherrennen II
2. um ... herum II **around 6 pm** um 18 Uhr herum, gegen 18 Uhr II
arrange [ə'reɪndʒ] anordnen I
arrival [ə'raɪvl] Ankunft III 4 (74)
arrive [ə'raɪv] ankommen, eintreffen I
art [ɑːt] Kunst I
article ['ɑːtɪkl] Artikel II

artist ['ɑːtɪst] Künstler/in II **street artist** Straßenkünstler/in II
as [æz], [əz]:
1. als, während II
2. (not) as big as (nicht) so groß wie II
3. as a child als Kind II **She works as a teacher.** Sie arbeitet als Lehrerin. II
4. as he said ... Wie er (einmal) sagte ... III 3 (51)
5. as soon as sobald, sowie III 1 (10)
6. as if als ob III 4 (71)
ash [æʃ] Asche III 4 (79) **ashes** *(pl)* Asche *(sterbliche Überreste)* III 4 (79)
ask [ɑːsk] fragen I **ask a question** eine Frage stellen I **ask for sth.** um etwas bitten II **ask sb. the way** jn. nach dem Weg fragen II **ask sb. to do sth.** jemanden bitten, etwas zu tun I
asleep [ə'sliːp]: **be asleep** schlafen II **fall asleep** einschlafen I
°**assess** [ə'ses] einschätzen
assistant [ə'sɪstənt] *(auch* **shop assistant***)* Verkäufer/in II
astronaut ['æstrənɔːt] Astronaut/in III 2 (31)
as well [əz 'wel] auch, ebenso III 4 (66)
at [æt], [ət] an, bei, in I **at 14 Dean Street** in der Deanstraße 14 I **at first** zuerst, anfangs, am Anfang II **at Grandma's (house/flat)** bei Oma II **at home** daheim, zu Hause I **at last** endlich, schließlich I **at least** zumindest, wenigstens II **at lunchtime** mittags I **at night** nachts, in der Nacht I **at school** in der Schule I **at the moment** gerade, im Moment I **at the top (of)** oben, am oberen Ende, an der Spitze (von) II **at the weekend** am Wochenende I
ate [et], [eɪt] *siehe* **eat**
Atlantic [ət'læntɪk]: **the Atlantic (Ocean)** der Atlantik, der Atlantische Ozean III 4 (72)
attack [ə'tæk] angreifen II
attic ['ætɪk] Dachboden I **in the attic** auf dem Dachboden I
°**attract** [ə'trækt] anziehen, anlocken
attraction [ə'trækʃn] Attraktion; Anziehungspunkt III 1 (14)
audience ['ɔːdiəns] Publikum, Zuschauer/innen, Zuhörer/innen II
audition [ɔː'dɪʃn] Vorsprechen, Vorsingen, Vorspielen II
August ['ɔːgəst] August I
aunt [ɑːnt] Tante I
author ['ɔːθə] Autor/in I
autumn ['ɔːtəm] Herbst I
available [ə'veɪləbl] erhältlich, verfügbar; erreichbar *(Telefon)* III 1 (24)
awake [ə'weɪk] wach III 5 (95)
away [ə'weɪ] weg, fort I
awful ['ɔːfl] schrecklich, fürchterlich II
°**aye** [aɪ] ja *(bes. schottisch, nordenglisch)*

B

back [bæk]:
1. zurück I
2. Rücken II
3. from the back of the bus aus dem hinteren Teil des Busses II
background ['bækgraʊnd] Hintergrund II **background file** *Hintergrundinformation(en)* I
backstage [ˌbæk'steɪdʒ] hinter der Bühne III 5 (88)
bacon ['beɪkən] Schinkenspeck II
bad [bæd] schlecht, schlimm I **go bad** *(fish, cheese, eggs)* schlecht werden II
bag [bæg] Tasche, Beutel, Tüte I **school bag** Schultasche I
bagpipes *(pl)* ['bægpaɪps] Dudelsack III 5 (82)
ball [bɔːl] Ball I
banana [bə'nɑːnə] Banane III 3 (47)
band [bænd] Band, (Musik-)Gruppe II
bang [bæŋ] Knall III 4 (75)
bank [bæŋk] Bank III 4 (68)
bar [bɑː] Riegel *(Schokolade, Müsli)*, Tafel *(Schokolade)* III 2 (38)
bare [beə] nackt, bloß *(Hände, Arme, Füße)* III 3 (52)
bark [bɑːk]:
1. bellen I
2. Bellen III 5 (95)
barman ['bɑːmən], *pl* **barmen** ['bɑːmən] Barkeeper III 1 (20)
barn [bɑːn] Scheune II
basket ['bɑːskɪt] Korb I
basketball ['bɑːskɪtbɔːl] Basketball I
°**bass** [beɪs] Bassgitarre
bath [bɑːθ] Bad II
bathroom ['bɑːθruːm] Badezimmer I
battle ['bætl] Schlacht; Kampf II
be [bi], **was/were, been:** sein I
beach [biːtʃ] Strand I
bear [beə] Bär I
beard [bɪəd] Bart II
beautiful ['bjuːtɪfl] schön II
beat [biːt], **beat, beaten** schlagen; besiegen III 5 (94)
beaten ['biːtn] *siehe* **beat**
became [bɪ'keɪm] *siehe* **become**
because [bɪ'kɒz] weil I °**because of** wegen
become [bɪ'kʌm], **became, become** werden II
bed [bed] Bett I **bed and breakfast** Frühstückspension; Zimmer mit Frühstück III 1 (12)
bedroom ['bedruːm] Schlafzimmer I
beef [biːf]: **roast beef** Rinderbraten I
°**Beefeater** ['biːfiːtə] *Torwächter des Towers von London*
been [biːn]:
1. *siehe* **be**
2. Have you ever been to ...? ... Bist du schon in ... gewesen? II

beep [biːp] piepen II
before [bɪ'fɔː]:
1. bevor I
2. vor I **before school/lessons** vor der Schule *(vor Schulbeginn)* / vorm Unterricht I **before long** schon bald III 2 (35) **before that** davor III 3 (46)
3. (vorher) schon mal II **not/never before** (vorher) noch nie II
began [bɪ'gæn] *siehe* **begin**
begin [bɪ'gɪn], **began, begun** beginnen, anfangen II
beginning [bɪ'gɪnɪŋ] Anfang, Beginn III 4 (73) **in the beginning** anfangs, zuerst III 4 (73)
begun [bɪ'gʌn] *siehe* **begun**
behave [bɪ'heɪv] sich verhalten, sich benehmen III 2 (42)
behind [bɪ'haɪnd] hinter I **from behind** von hinten II **right behind you** direkt hinter dir, genau hinter dir II
believe [bɪ'liːv] glauben II
bell [bel] Klingel, Glocke I
below [bɪ'ləʊ] unten, darunter; unter, unterhalb (von) III 5 (94)
bend down [bend], **bent, bent** sich hinunterbeugen, sich bücken III 1 (24)
bent [bent] *siehe* **bend**
best [best]: **the best** der/die/das beste; die besten; am besten I **the best thing about ...** das Beste an ... III 1 (8)
better ['betə] besser I **better than ever** besser als je zuvor II
between [bɪ'twiːn] zwischen I
big [bɪg] groß I **big wheel** Riesenrad I **the biggest** der/die/das größte; am größten I
bike [baɪk] Fahrrad I **ride a bike** Fahrrad fahren I
°**bilingual** [ˌbaɪ'lɪŋgwəl] zweisprachig
bird [bɜːd] Vogel I
birthday ['bɜːθdeɪ] Geburtstag I **My birthday is in May.** Ich habe im Mai Geburtstag. I **My birthday is on 5th May.** Ich habe am 5. May Geburtstag. I **When's your birthday?** Wann hast du Geburtstag? I
biscuit ['bɪskɪt] Keks, Plätzchen I
bit [bɪt]:
1. *siehe* **bite**
2. **a bit** ein bisschen, etwas II
bite [baɪt]:
1. **(bit, bitten)** beißen I
2. Biss, Bissen III 2 (41)
bitten ['bɪtn] *siehe* **bite**
black [blæk] schwarz I
blew [bluː] *siehe* **blow**
blog [blɒg] Blog *(Weblog, digitales Tagebuch)* II
blogger ['blɒgə] Blogger/in III 1 (11)
blond *(bei Frauen oft:* **blonde**) [blɒnd] blond I
blood [blʌd] Blut III 1 (15)
blow [bləʊ], **blew, blown: blow sth. out** etwas auspusten, ausblasen II
blow (a whistle) pfeifen *(auf der Trillerpfeife)* III 1 (24)
blown [bləʊn] *siehe* **blow**
blue [bluː] blau I
board [bɔːd]:
1. (Wand-)Tafel I
2. **on board** an Bord III 5 (83) **on board the ship** an Bord des Schiffes III 5 (83)
boarding school ['bɔːdɪŋ skuːl] Internat II
boat [bəʊt] Boot, Schiff I
body ['bɒdi]:
1. Körper I **part of the body** Körperteil II
2. Leiche III 3 (61)
3. Hauptteil *(eines Textes)* III 3 (51)
book [bʊk] Buch I
bookshop ['bʊkʃɒp] Buchladen, Buchhandlung I
°**boom** [buːm] Aufschwung
boot [buːt] Stiefel II
border ['bɔːdə] Grenze III 4 (68)
bored [bɔːd]: **be/feel bored** gelangweilt sein, sich langweilen II
boring ['bɔːrɪŋ] langweilig I
born [bɔːn]: **be born** geboren sein/werden III 3 (51) **I was born in 1998.** Ich bin 1998 geboren. III 3 (51)
both [bəʊθ] beide II
bottle ['bɒtl] Flasche I
bottom ['bɒtəm]: **at the bottom** unten, am unteren Ende (von) II
bought [bɔːt] *siehe* **buy**
bow [baʊ] sich verneigen, sich verbeugen II
bowl [bəʊl] Schüssel II
box [bɒks] Kasten, Kiste, Kästchen I **telephone box** Telefonzelle III 1 (15)
boy [bɔɪ] Junge I
boyfriend ['bɔɪfrend] Freund III 4 (76)
°**Boy Scouts** [ˌbɔɪ‿'skaʊts] Pfadfinder
°**bracket** ['brækɪt] Klammer *(in Texten)*
bread [bred] Brot I
break [breɪk]:
1. Pause I
2. **(broke, broken)** zerbrechen, kaputt machen I; brechen, kaputt gehen I
breakfast ['brekfəst] Frühstück I **have breakfast** frühstücken I **bed and breakfast** Frühstückspension; Zimmer mit Frühstück III 1 (12)
°**breakthrough** ['breɪkθruː] Durchbruch
breath [breθ] Atem, Atemzug II **he said ... under his breath** ..., sagte er flüsternd / murmelte er. III 1 (25)
breeze [briːz] Brise III 2 (40)
bridge [brɪdʒ] Brücke II
bright [braɪt] strahlend, leuchtend, hell I
brilliant ['brɪliənt] glänzend, großartig, genial II
bring [brɪŋ], **brought, brought** (mit-, her)bringen II **bring in** *(hay)* einbringen *(Heu)* II
British ['brɪtɪʃ] britisch I
brochure ['brəʊʃə] Broschüre, Prospekt III 4 (65)
broke [brəʊk] *siehe* **break**
broken [brəʊkən]:
1. *siehe* **break**
2. zerbrochen, kaputt; gebrochen II
°**broomstick** ['bruːmstɪk] Besenstiel
brother ['brʌðə] Bruder I
brought [brɔːt] *siehe* **bring**
brown [braʊn] braun I
°**brutal** ['bruːtl] brutal
°**bubble** ['bʌbl]: **speech bubble** Sprechblase
bucket ['bʌkɪt] Eimer II
build [bɪld], **built, built** bauen II
building ['bɪldɪŋ] Gebäude II
built [bɪlt] *siehe* **build**
bully ['bʊli] (Schul-)Tyrann III 3 (59)
burger ['bɜːgə] Hamburger II
burn [bɜːn] brennen; verbrennen III 3 (60)
burst [bɜːst], **burst, burst: burst into tears** in Tränen ausbrechen III 5 (95)
bury ['beri] begraben, beerdigen III 4 (79)
bus [bʌs] Bus I **go by bus** mit dem Bus fahren I **get on a bus** (in einen Bus) einsteigen II
busy ['bɪzi] belebt, geschäftig, hektisch III 2 (40) **be busy** beschäftigt sein; viel zu tun haben I
but [bʌt], [bət] aber I
butterfly ['bʌtəflaɪ] Schmetterling I
buy [baɪ], **bought, bought** kaufen I
by [baɪ]:
1. **by the sea** am Meer I **take sb. by the arm** jn. am Arm nehmen II
2. **go by car/bus/...** mit dem Auto/Bus/... fahren I
3. **by ...** von ... II
4. **by 8 pm** bis (spätestens) 20 Uhr III 4 (72)
5. **by the way** [ˌbaɪ ðə 'weɪ] übrigens III 1 (10)
°6. **by yourself** allein, auf eigene Faust
Bye. [baɪ] Tschüs. I

C

café ['kæfeɪ] Café I
cage [keɪdʒ] Käfig I
cake [keɪk] Kuchen I
call [kɔːl]:
1. rufen; anrufen; nennen I **call out the names** die Namen aufrufen II
2. *(auch:* **phone call**) Anruf, Telefonat II
called [kɔːld]: **be called** heißen, genannt werden I
caller ['kɔːlə] Anrufer/in II
calm [kɑːm]:
1. ruhig III 5 (84)
2. **calm down** sich beruhigen III 5 (89) **calm sb. down** jn. beruhigen III 5 (89)
came [keɪm] *siehe* **come**

camera ['kæmərə] Kamera, Fotoapparat I
cameraman ['kæmrəmæn], *pl* **cameramen** ['kæmrəmen] Kameramann I
camping ['kæmpɪŋ] Camping, Zelten II **go camping** zelten gehen II
campsite ['kæmpsaɪt] Zeltplatz II
can [kæn], [kən] können I **we cannot** ['kænɒt], **we can't** [kɑːnt] ... wir können nicht ... I
canal [kə'næl] Kanal III 3 (60)
candle ['kændl] Kerze II
canteen [kæn'tiːn] Kantine, (Schul-)Mensa I
cap [kæp] Mütze, Kappe II
°**capital** ['kæpɪtl] Hauptstadt
captain ['kæptɪn] Kapitän/in I
caption ['kæpʃn] Bildunterschrift I
captive ['kæptɪv] Gefangene(r) III 3 (53)
car [kɑː] Auto I **go by car** mit dem Auto fahren I **get in(to) a car** (in ein Auto) einsteigen II
caravan ['kærəvæn] Wohnwagen II
card (to) [kɑːd] Karte (an) I
care [keə]: **care about sth.** etwas wichtig nehmen III 4 (74) **I don't care about money.** Geld ist mir egal. III 4 (74) **I really care about animals.** Tiere liegen mir sehr am Herzen. / Tiere sind mir sehr wichtig. III 4 (74) **Who cares?** Na und? / Wen interessiert das? III 4 (74)
► S. 191 (to) care
career [kə'rɪə] Karriere III 3 (61)
careful ['keəfl] vorsichtig I
°**Caribbean** [ˌkærɪ'biːən] karibisch
carnival ['kɑːnɪvl] Karneval, Fasching III 1 (10)
carpenter ['kɑːpəntə] Tischler/in, Zimmerer/Zimmerin III 2 (30)
°**carriage** ['kærɪdʒ] Kutsche
carrot ['kærət] Möhre, Karotte III 2 (39)
carry ['kæri] tragen; befördern III 3 (52)
cart [kɑːt] Karren I
°**cartoon** [kɑː'tuːn] Cartoon
cash desk ['kæʃ desk] Kasse *(in Geschäften)* II
cast [kɑːst] Besetzung; Mitwirkende *(Theaterstück, Film)* II
castle ['kɑːsl] Burg, Schloss I
cat [kæt] Katze I **big cat** Großkatze III 5 (92)
catch [kætʃ], **caught, caught** fangen I
cathedral [kə'θiːdrəl] Kathedrale, Dom III 1 (10)
caught [kɔːt] *siehe* **catch**
°**causeway** ['kɔːzweɪ] Damm
cave [keɪv] Höhle II
°**céilidh** ['keɪli] Tanz- und Musikveranstaltung *(bes. in Schottland und Irland)*
celebrate ['selɪbreɪt] feiern II
celebration [ˌselɪ'breɪʃn] Feier II
°**Celtic** ['seltɪk] keltisch
cent [sent] Cent III 4 (68)
► S. 189 Pounds and euros

centre ['sentə] Zentrum; Mitte I **shopping centre** Einkaufszentrum II
century ['sentʃəri] Jahrhundert I
chain [tʃeɪn] Kette I
°**chain game** ['tʃeɪn geɪm] Kettenspiel
chair [tʃeə] Stuhl I
challenge ['tʃælɪndʒ] Herausforderung III 4 (66)
challenge sb. (to sth.) ['tʃælɪndʒ] jn. herausfordern (zu etwas) III 4 (66)
champion ['tʃæmpiən] Meister/in, Champion II
chance [tʃɑːns] Gelegenheit, Möglichkeit, Chance III 1 (14)
change [tʃeɪndʒ]:
1. (ver)ändern; sich (ver)ändern II
2. wechseln, umtauschen *(Geld)* III 4 (68)
3. umsteigen III 1 (18)
4. Wechselgeld II
°5. Änderung
chaos ['keɪɒs] Chaos I
character ['kærəktə]:
1. Figur, Person *(in Roman, Film, Theaterstück)* I
°2. Charakter, Wesen
charity ['tʃærəti] Wohlfahrtsorganisation; Wohltätigkeit, wohltätige Zwecke II
chat [tʃæt]:
1. chatten III 4 (74); plaudern III 4 (78)
2. Chat III 5 (89)
cheap [tʃiːp] billig, preiswert I
check [tʃek]:
1. Überprüfung, Kontrolle I
2. (über)prüfen, kontrollieren I **check sth. out** [ˌtʃek‿'aʊt] *(infml)* sich etwas anschauen, anhören; etwas ausprobieren III 4 (70)
checklist ['tʃeklɪst] Checkliste III 1 (17)
cheer [tʃɪə] jubeln II
cheese [tʃiːz] Käse I
chess [tʃes] Schach I
chest [tʃest] Brust, Brustkorb II
child [tʃaɪld], *pl* **children** ['tʃɪldrən] Kind I
chips *(pl)* [tʃɪps] Pommes frites II
chocolate ['tʃɒklət]:
1. Schokolade I
2. Praline II
choir ['kwaɪə] Chor II °**choir leader** Chorleiter/in
choose [tʃuːz], **chose, chosen** aussuchen, (aus)wählen; sich aussuchen I
chorus ['kɔːrəs] Refrain II
chose [tʃəʊz] *siehe* **choose**
chosen [tʃəʊzn] *siehe* **choose**
Christmas ['krɪsməs] Weihnachten III 1 (15) **Christmas Day** 1. Weihnachtstag *(25. Dezember)* III 1 (15)
church [tʃɜːtʃ] Kirche II
cinema ['sɪnəmə] Kino I
circle ['sɜːkl] Kreis II
city ['sɪti] Stadt, Großstadt II
°**clan** [klæn] Sippe
clap [klæp] (Beifall) klatschen II **Clap your hands.** Klatscht in die Hände. II

class [klɑːs] (Schul-)Klasse I °**in class** im Unterricht
classmate ['klɑːsmeɪt] Mitschüler/in, Klassenkamerad/in I
classroom ['klɑːsruːm] Klassenzimmer I
clause [klɔːz]: **main clause** Hauptsatz III 2 (36)
clay [kleɪ] Ton, Lehm III 3 (52)
clean [kliːn]:
1. sauber machen, putzen I
2. sauber II
clear [klɪə]:
1. klar, deutlich II
2. räumen; abräumen III 2 (40)
clever ['klevə] klug, schlau I
cliff [klɪf] Klippe II
climb [klaɪm]:
1. klettern; hinaufklettern (auf) II
2. Aufstieg, Anstieg III 2 (38)
clock [klɒk] (Wand-, Stand-, Turm-)Uhr I °**clock face** Zifferblatt °**clock wheel** Zahnrad (Uhr)
close [kləʊz] schließen II
°**close** [kləʊs] eng
closely ['kləʊsli]: **look closely** genau hinschauen II
clothes *(pl)* [kləʊðz] Kleidung, Kleidungsstücke I
°**clothing** ['kləʊðɪŋ] Kleidung
cloud [klaʊd] Wolke II
cloudy ['klaʊdi] bewölkt II
clown [klaʊn] Clown II
club [klʌb] Klub I **join a club** in einen Klub eintreten; sich einem Klub anschließen I
clue [kluː] (Lösungs-)Hinweis; Anhaltspunkt III 1 (11)
coal [kəʊl] Kohle III 2 (32) **coal mine** Kohlebergwerk III 2 (32)
coast [kəʊst] Küste I
coat [kəʊt]:
1. Mantel II
2. Fell III 5 (92)
cocoa ['kəʊkəʊ] Kakao II
coffee ['kɒfi] Kaffee III 4 (66)
coin [kɔɪn] Münze I
cola ['kəʊlə] Cola I
cold [kəʊld]:
1. kalt I **be cold** frieren I
2. **have a cold** eine Erkältung haben, erkältet sein II
collect [kə'lekt] sammeln I
colon ['kəʊlən] Doppelpunkt II
colour ['kʌlə] Farbe I
column ['kɒləm]:
1. Säule III 4 (66)
°2. Spalte
°**combination** [ˌkɒmbɪ'neɪʃn] Verbindung, Kombination
°**combine** [kəm'baɪn] kombinieren
come [kʌm], **came, come** kommen I **come across sth.** stoßen auf etwas, etwas *(zufällig)* treffen III 2 (32) **come down with sth.** etwas bekommen *(Krankheit)*, erkranken an etwas III 2 (32) **come in** hereinkommen I **Come on,**

Dad. Na los, Dad! / Komm, Dad! I
come over herüberkommen (zu/nach), vorbeikommen (bei) III 2 (30) **come up with sth.** etwas haben, kommen auf etwas (Idee, Vorschlag) III 2 (32)
▶ S. 180 (to) come …
comedian [kə'mi:diən] Komiker/in, Komödiant/in III 5 (91)
comedy ['kɒmədi] Comedyshow, Komödie II
comma ['kɒmə] Komma II
°**comment** ['kɒment] Kommentar °**make a comment** einen Kommentar abgeben
°**commentator** ['kɒmənteɪtə] (Radio-, Fernseh-)Kommentator/in
community [kə'mju:nəti] Gemeinde; Gemeinschaft III 3 (55)
°**company** ['kʌmpəni] Firma
°**compare** [kəm'peə] vergleichen
compete [kəm'pi:t]: **compete in sth.** an etwas teilnehmen *(Wettkampf)* III 5 (83)
competition [ˌkɒmpə'tɪʃn] Wettbewerb II
°**complete** [kəm'pli:t] vervollständigen
°**completely** [kəm'pli:tli] vollständig
computer [kəm'pju:tə] Computer I
concentrate ['kɒnsntreɪt]: **concentrate (on sth.)** sich konzentrieren (auf etwas) III 5 (88)
concert ['kɒnsət] Konzert II **a one-hour concert** ein einstündiges Konzert III 3 (51)
conclusion [kən'klu:ʒn] Schluss(folgerung) III 3 (51)
conditions *(pl)* [kən'dɪʃnz] Verhältnisse, Bedingungen III 3 (53)
°**conflict** ['kɒnflɪkt] Konflikt
connect [kə'nekt] verbinden, verknüpfen III 1 (17) **be connected** verbunden sein III 2 (38)
°**conservation** [ˌkɒnsə'veɪʃn] (Umwelt-)Schutz, Erhaltung
consonant ['kɒnsənənt] Konsonant, Mitlaut II
content ['kɒntent] Inhalt III 1 (17)
contest ['kɒntest] Wettbewerb III 3 (55)
context ['kɒntekst] (Satz-, Text-)Zusammenhang, Kontext II
continue [kən'tɪnju:]:
1. **continue sth.** etwas fortsetzen III 2 (38)
2. sich fortsetzen, weitergehen III 4 (77)
conversation [ˌkɒnvə'seɪʃn] Gespräch, Unterhaltung II
cook [kʊk] kochen; zubereiten III 3 (47)
cool [ku:l]:
1. cool I
2. kühl II
3. **cool off** sich abkühlen III 3 (60)
coordinator [kəʊ'ɔ:dɪneɪtə] Koordinator/in III 4 (69)
copy ['kɒpi]:
1. kopieren, abschreiben I
2. Kopie; Exemplar II
corner ['kɔ:nə] Ecke I **corner shop** Laden an der Ecke; Tante-Emma-Laden I **on the corner of Church Road and London Road** Church Road, Ecke London Road II
cornflakes ['kɔ:nfleɪks] Cornflakes I
correct [kə'rekt]:
1. richtig, korrekt II
2. korrigieren, verbessern II
°**correction** [kə'rekʃn] Korrektur, Berichtigung
corridor ['kɒrɪdɔ:] Gang, Korridor III 2 (40)
cost [kɒst], **cost, cost** kosten II
costume ['kɒstju:m] Kostüm, Verkleidung II
cottage ['kɒtɪdʒ] Häuschen, Cottage II
cough [kɒf]: **have a cough** Husten haben II
could [kʊd], [kəd]:
1. **he could …** er konnte … I **we couldn't …** ['kʊdnt] wir konnten nicht … I
2. **What could be better?** Was könnte besser sein? II
▶ S. 188 möglich – wahrscheinlich – sicherlich
count [kaʊnt] zählen I **count to ten** bis zehn zählen
°**countess** ['kaʊntəs], ['kaʊntes] Gräfin
country ['kʌntri] Land *(Staat)* II
countryside ['kʌntrisaɪd] Landschaft, *(ländliche)* Gegend II
county ['kaʊnti] Grafschaft *(in Großbritannien)* I
couple ['kʌpl]: **a couple** ein Paar; ein paar III 4 (78)
course [kɔ:s] Kurs, Lehrgang I
courtyard ['kɔ:tjɑ:d] Innenhof II
cousin ['kʌzn] Cousin, Cousine I
cover ['kʌvə]:
1. bedecken, zudecken III 3 (54)
°2. abdecken
°3. **inside cover** Umschlaginnenseite
cow [kaʊ] Kuh II
crab [kræb] Krebs I
crash [kræʃ] crashen II
cream [kri:m] Sahne I
°**create** [kri'eɪt] (er)schaffen, hervorbringen
crib sheet ['krɪb ʃi:t] *(infml)* Spickzettel, Merkzettel II
cricket ['krɪkɪt] Cricket I
°**criterion** [kraɪ'tɪəriən], *pl* **criteria** Kriterium
cross [krɒs] überqueren; sich kreuzen II
°**cross out** [ˌkrɒs‿'aʊt] durchstreichen
crossword ['krɒswɜ:d] Kreuzworträtsel III 3 (48)
crowd [kraʊd] (Menschen-)Menge II
crowded ['kraʊdɪd] voller Menschen; überfüllt III 1 (16)
crown [kraʊn] Krone II
cruel ['kru:l] grausam III 3 (53)
cruise [kru:z] Kreuzfahrt, Schiffsreise, Bootsfahrt III 3 (45)
cry [kraɪ] schreien; weinen II
cue [kju:] Stichwort, Signal *(Theater)* III 5 (88)
culture ['kʌltʃə] Kultur III 1 (13)
cup [kʌp]: **a cup of tea** eine Tasse Tee I **World Cup** Weltmeisterschaft III 3 (55)
cupboard ['kʌbəd] Schrank I
curious ['kjʊəriəs] wissbegierig, neugierig III 4 (66)
currency ['kʌrənsi] Währung III 4 (68)
curry ['kʌri] Curry(gericht) III 1 (16)
cut [kʌt], **cut, cut** schneiden II **Cut!** Schnitt! *(beim Filmen)* II

D

dad [dæd] Papa, Vati I
dance [dɑ:ns]:
1. tanzen I
2. Tanz II
dance floor ['dɑ:ns flɔ:] Tanzfläche II
dancer ['dɑ:nsə] Tänzer/in II
danger ['deɪndʒə] Gefahr II
dangerous ['deɪndʒərəs] gefährlich I
dark [dɑ:k]:
1. dunkel I
2. Dunkelheit III 2 (40)
darkness ['dɑ:knəs] Dunkelheit, Finsternis III 1 (11)
darling ['dɑ:lɪŋ] Schatz, Liebling III 3 (61)
daughter ['dɔ:tə] Tochter II
day [deɪ] Tag I **all day** den ganzen Tag II **day of the week** Wochentag I **get/have a day off** einen Tag frei bekommen/haben III 3 (51) **go on day trips** Tagesausflüge machen II
dead [ded] tot I
dear [dɪə]:
1. **Oh dear!** Oje! II
2. **dear** liebe(r, s) II
death [deθ] Tod III 4 (79)
December [dɪ'sembə] Dezember I
decide [dɪ'saɪd] beschließen, sich entscheiden II
decision [dɪ'sɪʒn] Entscheidung III 4 (69)
deck [dek] Deck, Terrasse I
°**decline** [dɪ'klaɪn] zurückgehen
deep [di:p] tief II
deer [dɪə], *pl* **deer** Reh, Hirsch II
°**defeat** [dɪ'fi:t] besiegen
defend [dɪ'fend]: **defend sb./sth. (against sb./sth.)** jn./etwas verteidigen (gegen jn./etwas) II
°**defender** [dɪ'fendə] Verteidiger/in
delicious [dɪ'lɪʃəs] köstlich, lecker II
demonstration [ˌdemən'streɪʃn] Demonstration, Vorführung II
dentist ['dentɪst] Zahnarzt/-ärztin II
describe sth. (to sb.) [dɪ'skraɪb] (jm.) etwas beschreiben II
description [dɪ'skrɪpʃn] Beschreibung III 5 (89)
°**deserted** [dɪ'zɜ:tɪd] verlassen
design [dɪ'zaɪn]:
1. entwerfen, konstruieren, entwickeln

III 3 (48)
2. Design; Gestaltung; Konstruktion III 3 (48) **design and technology** Design und Technik I
designer [dɪ'zaɪnə] Designer/in II
desk [desk] Schreibtisch I
dessert [dɪ'zɜːt] Nachtisch, Nachspeise I
destroy [dɪ'strɔɪ] zerstören II
detail ['diːteɪl] Detail, Einzelheit III 1 (15)
dialogue ['daɪəlɒg] Dialog II
diary ['daɪəri] Tagebuch; Kalender I
dictionary ['dɪkʃənri] alphabetisches Wörterverzeichnis, Wörterbuch I
did [dɪd] *siehe* **do**
die [daɪ] sterben I
different ['dɪfrənt] verschieden; anders I **it was no different** es war nicht anders III 3 (60)
difficult ['dɪfɪkəlt] schwierig, schwer III 2 (39)
dining room ['daɪnɪŋ ruːm] Esszimmer I
dinner ['dɪnə] Abendessen, Abendbrot I **have dinner** zu Abend essen I
°**dinosaur** ['daɪnəsɔː] Dinosaurier
direct [də'rekt], [daɪ'rekt] direkt III 5 (90)
°**directions** *(pl)* [də'rekʃənz]: **stage directions** Regieanweisungen
director [də'rektə]:
1. Leiter/in III 2 (41)
2. Regisseur/in II
dirty ['dɜːti] schmutzig II
disappear [ˌdɪsə'pɪə] verschwinden II
disco ['dɪskəʊ] Disko II
°**discuss sth.** [dɪ'skʌs] über etwas diskutieren, etwas besprechen
discussion [dɪ'skʌʃn] Diskussion III 4 (69)
disease [dɪ'ziːz] *(ansteckende)* Krankheit III 4 (79)
dishes *(pl)* ['dɪʃɪz]: **clear the dishes** das Geschirr abräumen III 2 (40) **wash the dishes** das Geschirr abwaschen, spülen II
dislike [dɪs'laɪk] nicht mögen, nicht leiden können III 4 (74)
dislikes [dɪs'laɪks]: **likes and dislikes** *(pl)* Vorlieben und Abneigungen I
°**distance** ['dɪstəns] Entfernung
ditch [dɪtʃ] Graben III 4 (78)
dive in [daɪv_'ɪn] (mit dem Kopf voran) hineinspringen III 3 (60)
divorced [dɪ'vɔːst] geschieden I
dizzy ['dɪzi] schwindlig III 1 (24)
do [duː], **did, done** machen, tun I **do sport** Sport treiben I °**Does it now?** Tatsächlich? / Ist das so? **Don't go.** [dəʊnt] Geh nicht. I **he doesn't have time** er hat keine Zeit I
°**dock** [dɒk] Hafen
°**dockland(s)** ['dɒklænd] Hafenviertel
doctor ['dɒktə] Arzt/Ärztin, Doktor II
dog [dɒg] Hund I **walk the dog** mit dem Hund rausgehen, den Hund ausführen III 4 (77)
dolphin ['dɒlfɪn] Delfin III 5 (83)
done [dʌn] *siehe* **do**
door [dɔː] Tür I
doorbell ['dɔːbel] Türklingel II
dorsal fin [ˌdɔːsl 'fɪn] Rückenflosse III 5 (84)
double ['dʌbl] Doppel- I
down [daʊn] hinunter, herunter; nach unten I **down there** dort unten II **up and down** auf und ab; rauf und runter I
downhill [ˌdaʊn'hɪl] bergab III 2 (38)
downstairs [ˌdaʊn'steəz] unten; nach unten *(im Haus)* I
downstream [ˌdaʊn'striːm] flussabwärts III 2 (34)
draft [drɑːft] Entwurf II
drama ['drɑːmə] Schauspiel; darstellende Kunst II
drank [dræŋk] *siehe* **drink**
draw [drɔː], **drew, drawn** zeichnen I
drawing ['drɔːɪŋ] Zeichnung I
drawn [drɔːn] *siehe* **draw**
°**dreadlocks** *(pl)* ['dredlɒks] Dreadlocks, Rastalocken
dream [driːm] Traum I
dress [dres] Kleid I
dress up [ˌdres_'ʌp]:
1. sich verkleiden II
2. sich schick anziehen II
drew [druː] *siehe* **draw**
drink [drɪŋk]:
1. **(drank, drunk)** trinken I
2. Getränk I
drive [draɪv], **drove, driven** *(mit dem Auto)* fahren II
driven ['drɪvn] *siehe* **drive**
drop [drɒp] fallen III 2 (34) **drop sth.** etwas fallen lassen II
drove [drəʊv] *siehe* **drive**
drown [draʊn] ertrinken III 3 (60)
drum [drʌm] Trommel I **drums** *(pl)* Schlagzeug I **play the drums** Schlagzeug spielen I
drummer ['drʌmə] Trommler/in; Schlagzeuger/in III 1 (24)
drunk [drʌŋk] *siehe* **drink**
dry [draɪ] trocken III 5 (94)
during ['djʊərɪŋ] während III 1 (15)
▶ S. 175 German "während"
DVD [ˌdiːviː'diː] DVD I

E

each [iːtʃ] jeder, jede, jedes (einzelne) II
each other [iːtʃ_'ʌðə] sich (gegenseitig), einander III 1 (20)
ear [ɪə] Ohr I
early ['ɜːli] früh I
earn [ɜːn] verdienen *(Geld)* III 3 (51)
earphones *(pl)* ['ɪəfəʊnz] Ohrhörer, Kopfhörer II
earth [ɜːθ] Erde *(der Planet)* II **on earth** auf der Erde II
east [iːst] Osten; nach Osten; östlich III 1 (11) **eastbound** ['iːstbaʊnd] Richtung Osten III 1 (18)
Easter ['iːstə] Ostern III 4 (77)
eastern ['iːstən] östlich, Ost- III 4 (66)
easy ['iːzi] leicht, einfach I
eat [iːt], **ate, eaten** essen I
eaten ['iːtn] *siehe* **eat**
edge [edʒ] Rand, Kante III 2 (34)
edit ['edɪt] bearbeiten; schneiden *(Film, Video)* I
editor ['edɪtə] Redakteur/in; Herausgeber/in III 4 (69)
education [ˌedʒu'keɪʃn] (Schul-, Aus-) Bildung; Erziehung III 1 (15)
°**EEC** [ˌiː iː'siː] EWG (Europäische Wirtschaftsgemeinschaft)
°**effect** [ɪ'fekt] Wirkung
e.g. [ˌiː 'dʒiː] z.B. (zum Beispiel) II
egg [eg] Ei II
°**Egyptian** [i'dʒɪpʃn] ägyptisch, Ägypter/in
eight [eɪt] acht I
either ['aɪðə], ['iːðə]: **not … either** auch nicht II
electronic [ɪˌlek'trɒnɪk] elektronisch III 4 (72)
element ['elɪmənt] Element III 5 (93)
elephant ['elɪfənt] Elefant I
eleven [ɪ'levn] elf I
else [els]: **anything else** sonst noch etwas III 5 (88) **everybody else** alle anderen; sonst jeder III 5 (88) **no one else** niemand anders; niemand sonst III 5 (88) **someone else** jemand anders III 5 (88) **what else?** was (sonst) noch? III 5 (88) **who else?** wer (sonst) noch? III 5 (88)
▶ S. 195 else
email ['iːmeɪl] E-Mail I
emigrate ['emɪgreɪt] auswandern, emigrieren III 4 (79)
empty ['empti] leer III 2 (30)
encore ['ɒŋkɔː] Zugabe II
end [end]:
1. Ende, Schluss I
2. enden; beenden III 3 (51)
ending ['endɪŋ] Ende, (Ab-)Schluss II
enemy ['enəmi] Feind/in II
energy ['enədʒi] Energie, Kraft III 2 (38)
engineer [ˌendʒɪ'nɪə] Ingenieur/in III 3 (48)
English ['ɪŋglɪʃ] Englisch; englisch I **in English** auf Englisch I
enjoy [ɪn'dʒɔɪ] genießen III 1 (10) **Enjoy yourself.** Viel Spaß! / Amüsiere dich gut! III 5 (GF/167)
enough [ɪ'nʌf] genug I
enter ['entə]:
1. betreten, hineingehen in II
°**2.** eintragen
entertainment [ˌentə'teɪnmənt] Unterhaltung III 5 (91)
entry ['entri]:
1. Eintrag, Eintragung *(im Tagebuch, Wörterbuch)* II
2. Eintritt, Zutritt III 1 (14)
equipment *(no pl)* [ɪ'kwɪpmənt] Ausrüstung III 3 (58)
°**escalator** ['eskəleɪtə] Rolltreppe

escape [ɪ'skeɪp]:
1. fliehen III 5 (87)
2. Flucht III 5 (87)
especially [ɪ'speʃli] besonders, vor allem III 4 (79)
etc. (et cetera) [et'setərə] usw. (und so weiter) II
EU, the [ˌiː 'juː] die Europäische Union III 4 (68)
°**Eurasian** [ju'reɪʒn] eurasisch
euro ['jʊərəʊ] Euro III 4 (68)
▶ S. 189 Pounds and euros
Europe ['jʊərəp] Europa III 1 (10)
European Union, the [ˌjʊərəpiːən 'juːniən] die Europäische Union III 4 (68)
eurozone ['jʊərəʊzəʊn] Eurozone III 4 (71)
even ['iːvn] sogar II **not even** (noch) nicht einmal II
even if ['iːvn‿ɪf] selbst wenn II
evening ['iːvnɪŋ] Abend I **in the evening** abends, am Abend I **this evening** heute Abend II
event [ɪ'vent] Ereignis II
ever ['evə] jemals II **better than ever** besser als je zuvor II **for ever** (für) immer; ewig II
every day/colour/boat ['evri] jeder Tag / jede Farbe / jedes Boot I
everybody ['evribɒdi] jeder; alle I
everyday ['evrideɪ] Alltags- I
everyone ['evriwʌn] jeder; alle I
everything ['evriθɪŋ] alles II
everywhere ['evriweə] überall II
exact [ɪg'zækt] genau III 1 (16)
exactly [ɪg'zæktli] genau III 1 (24)
example [ɪg'zɑːmpl] Beispiel II
except [ɪk'sept] außer, bis auf II
excited [ɪk'saɪtɪd] aufgeregt, gespannt I
exciting [ɪk'saɪtɪŋ] aufregend, spannend I
exclamation mark [ˌeksklə'meɪʃn mɑːk] Ausrufezeichen II
Excuse me, … [ɪk'skjuːz miː] Entschuldigung, … / Entschuldigen Sie, … II
exercise ['eksəsaɪz] Aufgabe, Übung I
exercise book ['eksəsaɪz bʊk] Schulheft, Übungsheft I
°**exhibit** [ɪg'zɪbɪt] Ausstellungsstück
expect [ɪk'spekt] erwarten III 1 (13)
°**expenses** *(pl)* [ɪk'spensɪz]: **travel expenses** Reisekosten
expensive [ɪk'spensɪv] teuer I
experience [ɪk'spɪəriəns]:
1. Erfahrung(en) III 3 (51)
°**2.** Erlebnis
°**experiment** [ɪk'sperɪmənt] experimentieren
explain sth. to sb. [ɪk'spleɪn] jm. etwas erklären, erläutern I
°**explanation** [ˌeksplə'neɪʃn] Erklärung
explore [ɪk'splɔː] erkunden, erforschen III 3 (45)
export ['ekspɔːt] Export, Ausfuhr III 4 (79)
°**export** [ɪk'spɔːt] ausführen, exportieren

expression [ɪk'spreʃn] Ausdruck III 4 (73)
extraordinary [ɪk'strɔːdnri] außergewöhnlich III 5 (82)
eye [aɪ] Auge I °**in your eyes** aus deiner Sicht; deiner Meinung nach

F

°**fab: the Fab Four** [fæb] die fabelhaften Vier *(Bezeichnung für die Beatles)*
°**fabulous** ['fæbjələs] fabelhaft
face [feɪs] Gesicht I
facial expression [ˌfeɪʃl‿ɪk'spreʃn] Gesichtsausdruck, Mimik III 4 (73)
fact [fækt] Tatsache, Fakt III 1 (14) **in fact** eigentlich, in Wirklichkeit III 1 (14) °**fact sheet** Info-Blatt
fair [feə] fair, gerecht I
°**fairy** ['feəri] Fee
fall [fɔːl], **fell, fallen** fallen, stürzen; hinfallen I **fall asleep** einschlafen I
fallen ['fɔːlən] *siehe* **fall**
false [fɔːls] falsch III 1 (11)
family ['fæməli] Familie I **a family of four** eine vierköpfige Familie III 1 (15) **the Bell family** (die) Familie Bell I °**family name** Familienname, Nachname **family tree** (Familien-)Stammbaum I **host family** Gastfamilie II
famine ['fæmɪn] Hungersnot III 4 (79)
famous (for) ['feɪməs] berühmt (für, wegen) II
fan [fæn] Fan, Anhänger/in I
fantastic [fæn'tæstɪk] fantastisch I
far [fɑː] weit (entfernt) I **so far** bis jetzt; bis hierher II
farm [fɑːm] Bauernhof, Farm I
farmer ['fɑːmə] Bauer/Bäuerin, Landwirt/in I
farmhouse ['fɑːmhaʊs] Bauernhaus III 5 (95)
fashion ['fæʃn] Mode II
fast [fɑːst] schnell I **be fast** vorgehen *(Uhr)* III 1 (19)
fat [fæt] dick, fett I
father ['fɑːðə] Vater I
fault [fɔːlt] Schuld, Fehler III 5 (88)
favourite ['feɪvərɪt]: **my favourite animal** mein Lieblingstier I
February ['februəri] Februar I
fed [fed] *siehe* **feed**
feed [fiːd], **fed, fed** füttern I **feeding time** Fütterungszeit I
feedback *(no pl)* ['fiːdbæk] Rückmeldung, Feedback III 1 (17)
feel [fiːl], **felt, felt** fühlen; sich fühlen I; sich anfühlen III 2 (30) **I feel sick.** Mir ist schlecht. II **I don't feel well** Ich fühle mich nicht gut. / Mir geht's nicht gut. II
feeling ['fiːlɪŋ] Gefühl I
feet [fiːt] *Plural von* **foot** II
fell [fel] *siehe* **fall**
felt [felt] *siehe* **feel**

felt pen [felt 'pen] Filzstift II
fence [fens] Zaun II
ferry ['feri] Fähre I
festival ['festɪvl] Fest, Festival II
few [fjuː]: **a few** ein paar, einige II
field [fiːld] Feld, Acker, Weide II
°**fiercely** ['fɪəsli]: **fight fiercely** heftig, erbittert kämpfen
fight [faɪt]:
1. (fought, fought) kämpfen I **fight sb.** jn. bekämpfen II
2. Kampf, Schlägerei III 4 (66)
fighter ['faɪtə] Kämpfer/in II
figure ['fɪgə]:
1. Zahl, Ziffer III 1 (15)
2. Figur, Gestalt III 2 (40)
file [faɪl]: **background file** *Hintergrundinformation(en)* I **grammar file** *Zusammenfassung der Grammatik jeder Unit* I **skills file** *Übersicht über Lern- und Arbeitstechniken* I
fill [fɪl] füllen III 1 (24)
film [fɪlm]:
1. filmen I
2. Film I °**film-maker** Filmemacher/in
fin [fɪn] Flosse III 5 (84) **dorsal fin** Rückenflosse III 5 (84)
final ['faɪnl]:
1. Finale, Endspiel I
2. letzte(r, s), End- III 3 (56)
finally ['faɪnəli] endlich, schließlich III 2 (40)
find [faɪnd], **found, found** finden I **Find someone who …** Finde jemanden, der … I **find sth. out** etwas herausfinden II °**find out about sth.** sich über etwas informieren
fine [faɪn] fein II **Fine, thanks.** Gut, danke. I
finger ['fɪŋgə] Finger II
finish ['fɪnɪʃ]:
1. enden I
2. finish sth. etwas beenden; mit etwas fertig werden/sein I
°**3. finish sth**. etwas vervollständigen; etwas abschließen
finished ['fɪnɪʃt]: **We're finished.** Wir sind fertig. I
fire ['faɪə] Feuer II
fireplace ['faɪəpleɪs] Kamin II
firework ['faɪəwɜːk] Feuerwerkskörper II
fireworks *(pl)* ['faɪəwɜːks] Feuerwerk II
first [fɜːst] zuerst, als Erstes I **at first** zuerst, anfangs, am Anfang II **the first day** der erste Tag I
°**first-aid kit** [fɜːst‿'eɪd ˌkɪt] Erste-Hilfe-Kasten
fish [fɪʃ]:
1. *pl* **fish** Fisch I
2. fish sth. out etwas herausfischen III 2 (34)
fishing ['fɪʃɪŋ] Fischerei III 5 (84)
five [faɪv] fünf I
flag [flæg] Fahne, Flagge II

flash [flæʃ] Lichtblitz II **a flash of lightning** ein Blitz II
flat [flæt] Wohnung I
flew [fluː] *siehe* **fly**
floor [flɔː]:
1. Fußboden I
2. Stock(werk) II
flower ['flaʊə] Blume; Blüte II
flown [fləʊn] *siehe* **fly**
fly [flaɪ], **flew, flown** fliegen II
folk [fəʊk] *(pl, infml)* Leute III 4 (78)
follow ['fɒləʊ] folgen I **Follow me.** Folg(t) mir. I °**the following ...** die folgenden ...
food [fuːd] Essen; Lebensmittel; Futter I
foot [fʊt], *pl* **feet** [fiːt] Fuß II
football ['fʊtbɔːl] Fußball I
°**footpath** ['fʊtpɑːθ] Fußweg, Pfad
footprint ['fʊtprɪnt] Fußabdruck II
for [fɔː], [fə] für I **for ever** (für) immer; ewig II **for example** zum Beispiel II **for hours/weeks/...** seit Stunden/Wochen/... III 1 (20) **for miles** meilenweit II **for the first time** zum ersten Mal III 1 (14) **What's for lunch?** Was gibt es zum Mittagessen? I **What's for homework?** Was haben wir als Hausaufgabe auf? I
foreground ['fɔːgraʊnd] Vordergrund II
forest ['fɒrɪst] Wald II
forget [fə'get], **forgot, forgotten** vergessen I
forgot [fə'gɒt] *siehe* **forget**
forgotten [fə'gɒtn] *siehe* **forget**
fork [fɔːk] Gabel II
form [fɔːm]:
1. Form I
2. bilden, formen III 4 (66)
forward ['fɔːwəd]: **look forward to sth.** sich auf etwas freuen II
▶ S. 180 (to) look ...
fought [fɔːt] *siehe* **fight**
foul [faʊl] Foul III 3 (58)
found [faʊnd]:
1. *siehe* **find**
2. gründen III 3 (48)
°**fountain** ['faʊntən] Brunnen
four [fɔː] vier I **a family of four** eine vierköpfige Familie III 1 (15)
free [friː]:
1. frei I **free time** Freizeit, freie Zeit I **free-time activities** Freizeitaktivitäten I **free kick** Freistoß III 3 (58)
2. kostenlos II °**for free** umsonst
°**freedom** ['friːdəm] Freiheit
°**freeze frame** ['friːz freɪm] Standbild
French [frentʃ] Französisch I
fresh [freʃ] frisch II
Friday ['fraɪdeɪ], ['fraɪdi] Freitag I
friend ['frend] Freund/in I
friendly ['frendli] freundlich I
fries *(pl)* [fraɪz] Pommes frites II
°**fringe** [frɪndʒ] Rand *(das Fringe-Festival findet am Rande des offiziellen Edinburger Festivals statt)*
frog [frɒg] Frosch I
from [frɒm], [frəm] aus, von I **from ... to ...** von ... bis ... I
front [frʌnt] Vorderseite I **in front of** vor *(räumlich)* **to the front** nach vorne II °**front inside cover** vordere Umschlaginnenseite
frown [fraʊn] die Stirn runzeln II
fruit [fruːt] Obst, Früchte; Frucht I **fruit salad** Obstsalat I
full (of) [fʊl] voll II **full sentence** ganzer Satz II
full stop [ˌfʊl 'stɒp] Punkt II
fun [fʌn] Spaß I **have fun** Spaß haben, sich amüsieren I **make fun of sb./sth.** sich über jn./etwas lustig machen III 2 (30) **That sounds fun.** Das klingt nach Spaß. I **Was it fun?** Hat es Spaß gemacht? I
funeral ['fjuːnərəl] Trauerfeier III 3 (61)
funny ['fʌni] witzig, komisch I
fun park ['fʌn pɑːk] Vergnügungspark II
furniture *(no pl)* ['fɜːnɪtʃə] Möbel III 2 (30) **The furniture is new.** Die Möbel sind neu. III 2 (30) **a piece of furniture** ein Möbel(stück) III 2 (30)
further ['fɜːðə] weiter II
furthest ['fɜːðɪst] am weitesten II
future ['fjuːtʃə]:
1. Zukunft II
2. zukünftige(r, s) II

G

°**Gaelic** ['geɪlɪk] Gälisch *(die irische Sprache)*
gallery ['gæləri] Galerie III 1 (12)
game [geɪm] Spiel I
°**gap** [gæp] Lücke **Mind the gap!** *etwa:* Vorsicht, Lücke!
garage ['gærɑːʒ], ['gærɪdʒ] Garage I
garden ['gɑːdn] Garten I
gardening ['gɑːdnɪŋ] Gärtnern, Gartenarbeit I
gate [geɪt] Tor, Pforte, Gatter II
gave [geɪv] *siehe* **give**
gel [dʒel] Gel II
°**general** ['dʒenrəl] allgemeine(r, s)
°**generation** [ˌdʒenə'reɪʃn] Generation
gently ['dʒentli] behutsam, sanft III 5 (95)
geography [dʒi'ɒgrəfi] Geografie I
German ['dʒɜːmən] Deutsch; deutsch I **in German** auf Deutsch I
get [get], **got, got**:
1. bekommen I **Did you get it?** *(infml)* Hast du es mitbekommen/verstanden? I **get paid** Geld bekommen III 4 (70) **get sth.** (sich) etwas besorgen, (sich) etwas holen II
2. gelangen, (hin)kommen I **get in touch (with sb.)** (mit jm.) Kontakt aufnehmen; sich (mit jm.) in Verbindung setzen II **get in(to) a car/taxi** in ein Auto/Taxi) einsteigen II **get into trouble** in Schwierigkeiten geraten, Ärger kriegen III 2 (40) **get on a bus/train/plane** in einen Bus/Zug, in ein Flugzeug einsteigen II **get off a bus/boat** aus einem Bus/Boot aussteigen I **get out of a car** aus einem Auto aussteigen II
▶ S. 177 off
3. get on vorankommen, zurechtkommen II
4. get up aufstehen I
5. get angry/cold/... wütend/kalt/... werden I **get ready (for)** sich fertig machen (für), sich vorbereiten (auf) II
ghost [gəʊst] Geist, Gespenst I
giant ['dʒaɪənt] Riese III 4 (66)
giraffe [dʒə'rɑːf] Giraffe I
girl [gɜːl] Mädchen I
girlfriend ['gɜːlfrend] Freundin III 4 (76)
give [gɪv], **gave, given:** geben I **give a talk (about)** einen Vortrag / eine Rede halten (über) I **give sb. a lift** jn. mitnehmen II **give sb. a hug** jn. umarmen II **give up** aufgeben III 2 (30) **give sb. a hard time** jn. fertig machen, jm. einheizen III 5 (89)
given ['gɪvn] *siehe* **give**
glad [glæd] froh, dankbar III 4 (79)
glass [glɑːs] Glas II **a glass of water** ein Glas Wasser II
glasses *(pl)* ['glɑːsɪz] (eine) Brille II
°**glen** [glen] Tal *(bes. schottisch)*
glove [glʌv] Handschuh II
glue [gluː] Klebstoff I
glue stick ['gluː stɪk] Klebestift I
go [gəʊ], **went, gone:**
1. gehen; fahren I **go by** *(time)* vergehen, vorübergehen *(Zeit)* III 2 (34) **go down** untergehen *(Sonne)* I **go for a walk** spazieren gehen, einen Spaziergang machen I **go green/hard/...** grün/hart/... werden II °**go hungry** hungern **go in** hineingehen II **go on 1.** weiterreden, fortfahren; weitermachen I **2.** im Gang sein; andauern III 1 (21) **go on day trips** Tagesausflüge machen II **go red** rot werden, erröten II **go together** zusammenpassen, zueinander passen III 1 (12) **go with sth.** zu etwas gehören, zu etwas passen I **Here we go.** Los geht's. / Jetzt geht's los. I **I'm going to sing a song.** Ich werde ein Lied singen. / Ich habe vor ein Lied zu singen. II
2. Have a go. Versuch's mal. I
goal [gəʊl] Tor *(Sport)* III 3 (55) **goal net** Tornetz III 3 (55)
goalkeeper ['gəʊlkiːpə] Torwart, Torfrau III 3 (58)
goat [gəʊt] Ziege II
God [gɒd] Gott III 4 (74)
go-kart ['gəʊ kɑːt] Gokart II
gold [gəʊld]:
1. Gold I
2. golden, Gold- II
°**golden** ['gəʊldn] golden

gone [gɒn] *siehe* **go** **be gone** weg sein, nicht (mehr) da sein III 4 (77)
good [gʊd]:
1. gut I **be good at kung fu** gut sein in Kung-Fu; gut Kung-Fu können I **Good luck!** Viel Glück! I **Good morning.** Guten Morgen. I
2. brav II
Goodbye. [ˌgʊd'baɪ] Auf Wiedersehen. I
good-looking [ˌgʊd'lʊkɪŋ] gutaussehend II
goods *(pl)* [gʊdz] Waren, Güter I
got [gɒt]:
1. *siehe* **get**
2. **Have you got ...?** Haben Sie ...? / Hast du ...? / Habt ihr ...? II
government ['gʌvənmənt] Regierung III 4 (79)
grab [græb] schnappen, packen III 2 (34)
gram (g) [græm] Gramm II
grammar file ['græmə ˌfaɪl] *Zusammenfassung der Grammatik* I
grandfather ['grænfɑːðə] Großvater I
grandma ['grænmɑː] Oma I **at Grandma's (house/flat)** bei Oma II
grandmother ['grænmʌðə] Großmutter I
grandpa ['grænpɑː] Opa I
grandparents *(pl)* ['grænpeərənts] Großeltern I
grass [grɑːs] Gras; Rasen II
grave [greɪv] Grab II
gravestone ['greɪvstəʊn] Grabstein III 4 (79)
great [greɪt] großartig I
green [griːn] grün I
grew [gruː] *siehe* **grow**
grey [greɪ] grau I
groan [grəʊn]:
1. Stöhnen II
2. stöhnen II
ground [graʊnd]:
1. (Erd-)Boden II °**rugby/football ground** Rugby-/Fußballplatz
2. **ground sb.** jm. Hausarrest/Ausgehverbot erteilen III 2 (32)
group (of) [gruːp] Gruppe I
grow [grəʊ], **grew, grown**:
1. anbauen, anpflanzen I
2. wachsen II
3. **grow up** [ˌgrəʊ‿'ʌp] erwachsen werden; aufwachsen III 3 (51)
grown [grəʊn] *siehe* **grow**
guard [gɑːd]:
1. Wachposten, Wache II
2. bewachen III 1 (15)
guess [ges] raten, erraten, schätzen I **Guess what, Dad ...** Stell dir vor, Papa .../Weißt du was, Papa ... I
guest [gest] Gast III 4 (73)
guide [gaɪd] Fremdenführer/in; Reiseleiter/in II
guidebook ['gaɪdbʊk] Reiseführer III 3 (47)
guinea pig ['gɪni pɪg] Meerschweinchen I

guitar [gɪ'tɑː] Gitarre I **play the guitar** Gitarre spielen I
gym [dʒɪm] Turnhalle I
gymnastics [dʒɪm'næstɪks] Gymnastik, Turnen I

H

habitat ['hæbɪtæt] Lebensraum III 5 (92)
had [hæd] *siehe* **have**
hair [heə] Haar, Haare I
hairdresser ['heədresə] Friseur/in III 2 (31)
half [hɑːf], *pl* **halves** [hɑːvz] Halbzeit I **half past ten** halb elf (10.30 / 22.30) I **at half-time** zur Halbzeit III 3 (56) °**half the population** die Hälfte der Bevölkerung
hall [hɔːl]: **town hall** Rathaus II
hamburger ['hæmbɜːgə] Hamburger II
hammer ['hæmə]:
1. Hammer III 2 (30)
2. hämmern III 2 (35)
hamster ['hæmstə] Hamster II
hand [hænd]:
1. Hand I **Clap your hands.** Klatscht in die Hände. II **put your hand up** sich melden III 5 (84)
2. **hand sth. in** etwas abgeben; etwas einreichen II
handout ['hændaʊt] Handout, Handzettel III 5 (92)
hang [hæŋ], **hung, hung**: hängen II °**hang up** aufhängen
happen (to) ['hæpən] geschehen, passieren (mit) II
happy ['hæpi] glücklich, froh I
harbour ['hɑːbə] Hafen I
hard [hɑːd] schwer, schwierig; hart I **give sb. a hard time** jn. fertig machen, jm. einheizen; III 5 (89) **go hard** *(bread)* hart werden II
°**harmonica** [hɑː'mɒnɪkə] Mundharmonika
has [hæz]: **he/she has** er/sie hat I
hat [hæt] Hut II
hate [heɪt] hassen III 5 (94)
have [hæv], [həv], **had, had** haben I **Have a go.** Versuch's mal. I **have breakfast** frühstücken I **have lunch/dinner** zu Mittag/Abend essen I **have fun** Spaß haben, sich amüsieren I **have to do** tun müssen I **I'll have a tea/...** Ich nehme einen Tee/... *(beim Essen, im Restaurant)* II **May I have a word with you?** Kann ich Sie kurz sprechen? II
have got [hæv 'gɒt], [həv 'gɒt], **had, had** haben II **Have you got ...?** Haben Sie ...? / Hast du ...? / Habt ihr ...? II
hay [heɪ] Heu II
he [hiː] er I

head [hed]
1. Kopf I
2. **head for sth.** auf etwas zusteuern/zugehen/zufahren III 1 (19)
headache ['hedeɪk]: **have a headache** Kopfschmerzen haben II
°**heading** ['hedɪŋ] Überschrift
°**headquarters** [ˌhed'kwɔːtəz] Zentrale, Hauptsitz
head teacher [ˌhed 'tiːtʃə] Schulleiter/in III 2 (37)
headword ['hedwɜːd] Stichwort *(im Wörterbuch)* III 2 (32)
°**health service** ['helθ ˌsɜːvɪs] Gesundheitswesen
hear [hɪə], **heard, heard** hören I
heard [hɜːd] *siehe* **hear**
heart [hɑːt] Herz II
°**heath** [hiːθ] Heide
heather ['heðə] Heide(kraut) III 5 (94)
heaven ['hevn] Himmel *(im religiösen Sinn)* III 4 (70)
heavy ['hevi] schwer *(von Gewicht)* II **heavy rain** starker Regen, heftiger Regen II
held [held] *siehe* **hold**
hell [hel] Hölle III 4 (72)
Hello. [hə'ləʊ] Hallo. / Guten Tag. I
help [help]:
1. Hilfe I
2. helfen I **Help yourself.** Greif zu! / Bedien dich! III 5 (GF/167)
helper ['helpə] Helfer/in II
her [hɜː], [hə]:
1. ihr, ihre I **her best friend** ihr bester Freund / ihre beste Freundin I
2. sie; ihr I
here [hɪə] hier; hierher I **Here we go.** Los geht's. / Jetzt geht's los. I **Here you are.** Bitte sehr. / Hier bitte. II **near here** (hier) in der Nähe I **over here** hier herüber II **up here** hier oben; nach hier oben II
°**heritage** ['herɪtɪdʒ]: **World Heritage Site** Welterbestätte
hero ['hɪərəʊ], *pl* **heroes** Held/in III 2 (38)
hers [hɜːz] ihrer, ihre, ihrs II
herself [hɜː'self] sich III 5 (85)
hid [hɪd] *siehe* **hide**
hidden ['hɪdn] *siehe* **hide**
hide [haɪd], **hid, hidden** sich verstecken, etwas verstecken I
°**hieroglyphics** *(pl)* [ˌhaɪərə'glɪfɪks] Hieroglyphen(schrift)
high [haɪ] hoch I
highland ['haɪlənd]: **the Highlands** *(pl)* das schottische Hochland III 5 (83)
highlight ['haɪlaɪt] hervorheben, markieren *(mit Textmarker)* II
°**high-tech company** [ˌhaɪ'tek] High-tech-Firma
hill [hɪl] Hügel I
him [hɪm] ihn; ihm I
himself [hɪm'self] sich III 5 (85)
hip [hɪp] Hüfte III 1 (24)

his [hɪz]:
1. his friend sein Freund / seine Freundin I
2. seiner, seine, seins II
hiss [hɪs] zischen II
°**historical** [hɪ'stɒrɪkl] historisch
history ['hɪstri] Geschichte I **natural history** Naturkunde III 1 (14)
hit [hɪt], **hit, hit:**
1. prallen, stoßen gegen I
2. schlagen II
3. treffen II
hobby ['hɒbi] Hobby I
hold [həʊld], **held, held** halten I **Hold on a minute.** Bleib / Bleiben Sie am Apparat. *(am Telefon)* II **hold onto sth.** sich an etwas festhalten III 1 (24) °**hold sth. up** etwas aufhalten, etwas hochhalten
hole [həʊl] Loch II
holiday ['hɒlədeɪ] Urlaub II **be on holiday** in Urlaub sein II **go on holiday** in Urlaub fahren II
holidays *(pl)* ['hɒlədeɪz] Ferien I
home [həʊm] Heim, Zuhause I **at home** daheim, zu Hause I **be home to …** Heimat sein für etwas; etwas beheimaten III 1 (15) **come/go home** nach Hause kommen/gehen I
hometown [,həʊm'taʊn] Heimatstadt I
homework ['həʊmwɜːk] Hausaufgabe(n) I **Do your homework.** Mach deine Hausaufgaben. I **What's for homework?** Was haben wir als Hausaufgabe auf? I
honour ['ɒnə] Ehre II
hope [həʊp] hoffen I
horn [hɔːn] Horn III 3 (52)
horror ['hɒrə]: **in horror** entsetzt III 5 (94)
horse [hɔːs] Pferd I °**on horseback** ['hɔːsbæk] zu Pferd
hospital ['hɒspɪtl] Krankenhaus II
host family ['həʊst fæməli] Gastfamilie II
hostel ['hɒstl] Herberge, Wohnheim III 2 (34)
hot [hɒt] heiß I
hotel [həʊ'tel] Hotel II
hour ['aʊə] Stunde I **an hour** pro Stunde III 1 (15) **a one-hour concert** ein einstündiges Konzert III 3 (51) °**ring out the hour** durch den (Glocken-)Schlag die Uhrzeit bekanntgeben
house [haʊs] Haus I
how [haʊ] wie I **How are you?** Wie geht's? / Wie geht es dir/euch? I **How do you know (about …)?** Woher weißt/kennst du …? III 1 (10) **How do you like it?** Wie findest du es (sie/ihn)? / Wie gefällt es (sie/er) dir? I **How many?** Wie viele? I **How much?** Wie viel? I **How much are …?** Was kosten …? I **How much is …?** Was kostet …? I **How old are you?** Wie alt bist du? I **how to do sth.** wie man etwas macht / machen kann / machen soll III 2 (42)
▶ S. 183 Question words + to-infinitive
°**however** [haʊ'evə] jedoch
hug [hʌg]:
1. jn. umarmen II
2. give sb. a hug jn. umarmen II
huge [hjuːdʒ] riesig, sehr groß III 1 (10)
hundred [hʌndrəd]: **a/one hundred** einhundert I
hung [hʌŋ] *siehe* **hang**
hungry ['hʌŋgri]: **be hungry** hungrig sein, Hunger haben I °**go hungry** hungern
hurry ['hʌri] eilen; sich beeilen II **hurry up** sich beeilen I
hurt [hɜːt], **hurt, hurt:** schmerzen, wehtun; verletzen II
hyphen ['haɪfən] Bindestrich II

I

I [aɪ] ich I **I'm from Plymouth.** Ich bin/komme aus Plymouth. I **I'm two years old.** Ich bin zwei Jahre alt. I
ice [aɪs] Eis II
ice cream [,aɪs 'kriːm] (Speise-)Eis I
iced tea [,aɪst 'tiː] Eistee II
ICT [,aɪ siː 'tiː] Informations- und Kommunikationstechnologie I
ID card [,aɪ 'diː kɑːd] Personalausweis III 4 (68)
idea [aɪ'dɪə] Idee; Vorstellung I
identify [aɪ'dentɪfaɪ]: **identify sb./sth. (by sth.)** jn./etwas identifizieren (anhand von etwas) III 5 (83)
if [ɪf]:
1. wenn, falls II **even if** selbst wenn II **if-clause** Nebensatz mit *if* III 2 (36)
2. ob III 3 (51)
3. as if als ob III 4 (71)
ill [ɪl] krank II
illness ['ɪlnəs] Krankheit III 4 (79)
imagine sth. [ɪ'mædʒɪn] sich etwas vorstellen I
immediately [ɪ'miːdiətli] sofort III 4 (77)
impolite [,ɪmpə'laɪt] unhöflich III 4 (66)
important [ɪm'pɔːtnt] wichtig I
impossible [ɪm'pɒsəbl] unmöglich II
impression [ɪm'preʃn] Eindruck III 4 (64)
improve [ɪm'pruːv] verbessern; sich verbessern III 1 (17)
in [ɪn] in I **be in** zu Hause sein II **come in** hereinkommen I **in 1580** im Jahr 1580 I **in a loud voice** mit lauter Stimme II °**in class** im Unterricht **in front of** vor *(räumlich)* I **in German** auf Deutsch I **in the afternoon** nachmittags, am Nachmittag I **in the attic** auf dem Dachboden I **in the evening** abends, am Abend I **in the morning** morgens, vormittags, am Morgen/Vormittag I **in the photo** auf dem Foto I **in the world** auf der Welt II
°**independent** [,ɪndɪ'pendənt] unabhängig
Indian ['ɪndiən] Inder/in; indisch II
indirect [,ɪndə'rekt], [,ɪndaɪ'rekt] III 5 (90)
°**industry** ['ɪndəstri] verarbeitende Industrie; Fertigungsindustrie
infinitive [ɪn'fɪnətɪv] Infinitiv III 2 (36)
°**influence** ['ɪnfluəns] beeinflussen
information (about/on) *(no pl)* [,ɪnfə'meɪʃn] Information(en) (über) I **Information and Communications Technology** Informations- und Kommunikationstechnologie I
inside [,ɪn'saɪd]:
1. drinnen; nach drinnen I
2. die Innenseite; das Innere III 1 (14)
3. inside sth. innerhalb von etwas II
°**4. inside cover** Umschlaginnenseite
instead [ɪn'sted] stattdessen II
instead of [ɪn'sted‿əv] anstelle von, statt III 1 (16)
instrument ['ɪnstrəmənt] Instrument I
°**insurance** [ɪn'ʃʊərəns] Versicherung
interaction [,ɪntər'ækʃn] Interaktion, Umgang III 4 (73)
interest ['ɪntrəst] interessieren III 5 (91)
interested ['ɪntrəstɪd]: **be interested (in)** sich interessieren (für), interessiert sein (an) II
interesting ['ɪntrəstɪŋ] interessant I
international [,ɪntə'næʃnəl] international III 3 (45)
interrupt [,ɪntə'rʌpt] unterbrechen II
interview ['ɪntəvjuː]:
1. Interview II
2. interviewen, befragen I
into ['ɪntʊ]:
1. into the kitchen in die Küche (hinein) I
2. be into sth. *(infml)* etwas mögen, auf etwas stehen III 1 (10)
introduce sth./sb. (to sb.) [,ɪntrə'djuːs] etwas/jn. (jm.) vorstellen II
introduction [,ɪntrə'dʌkʃn] Einleitung, Einführung III 3 (51)
invade (a country) [ɪn'veɪd] (in ein Land) einmarschieren II
invent [ɪn'vent] erfinden III 3 (48)
invitation (to) [,ɪnvɪ'teɪʃn] Einladung (zu, nach) I
invite sb. (to) [ɪn'vaɪt] jn. einladen (zu) II
irregular [ɪ'regjələ] unregelmäßig II
is [ɪz]: **Is it Monday?** Ist es Montag? I **Is that you?** Bist du's? / Bist du das? I **The book is …** Das Buch kostet … I
island ['aɪlənd] Insel I
isle [aɪl] (kleine) Insel, Eiland III 5 (83)
isn't ['ɪznt]: **he/she/it isn't (= is not)** er/sie/es ist nicht … I
°**IT** [,aɪ 'tiː] Informationstechnologie

it [ɪt] er, sie, es I
it's … (= it is) [ɪts] er/sie/es ist … I
itself [ɪt'self] sich III 5 (85)
its name [ɪts] sein Name / ihr Name I

J

jacket ['dʒækɪt] Jacke II
jam [dʒæm] Marmelade I
January ['dʒænjuəri] Januar I
jealous ['dʒeləs] neidisch (auf); eifersüchtig (auf) III 5 (94)
jeans *(pl)* [dʒiːnz] Jeans I
jeep [dʒiːp] Jeep III 4 (75)
jewels *(pl)* ['dʒuːəlz] Juwelen III 1 (15)
jigsaw ['dʒɪgsɔː] Puzzle II
job [dʒɒb]:
1. Job, (Arbeits-)Stelle I
2. Aufgabe II
join [dʒɔɪn]:
1. **join a club** in einen Klub eintreten; sich einem Klub anschließen I
2. **join in (sth.)** (bei etwas) mitmachen III 2 (35)
joke [dʒəʊk] Witz I
journey ['dʒɜːni] Reise, Fahrt II
judo ['dʒuːdəʊ] Judo I
juggle sth. ['dʒʌgl] mit etwas jonglieren II
juggler ['dʒʌglə] Jongleur/in II
juice [dʒuːs] Saft II
July [dʒu'laɪ] Juli I
jump [dʒʌmp]:
1. springen I **jump up** aufspringen, hochspringen II
2. Sprung I
junction ['dʒʌŋkʃn] (Straßen-)Kreuzung III 4 (77)
June [dʒuːn] Juni I
just [dʒʌst]:
1. (einfach) nur, bloß I
2. gerade (eben), soeben II **just after …** gleich nachdem …; kurz nachdem … II **just then** genau in dem Moment; gerade dann II
3. **just like** genau wie … II

K

°**kaleidoscope** [kə'laɪdəskəʊp] Kaleidoskop
kayak ['kaɪæk] Kajak III 5 (84)
keep [kiːp], **kept, kept**:
1. aufheben; aufsparen; aufbewahren III 5 (85)
2. **keep doing sth.** etwas immer wieder / immer weiter tun; etwas ständig tun III 2 (40)
°3. **keep fit** gesund/fit bleiben
°4. **keep to a plan** einen Plan einhalten
kept [kept] *siehe* **keep**
key [kiː]:
1. Schlüssel II
2. Schlüssel- II
keyword ['kiːwɜːd] Schlüsselwort I
kick [kɪk]:
1. treten III 4 (77)
2. **free kick** Freistoß III 3 (58)
kid [kɪd] Kind I
kill [kɪl] töten II
kilogram, kilo (kg) ['kɪləgræm], ['kiːləʊ] Kilogramm, Kilo I
kilometre (km) ['kɪləmiːtə], [kɪ'lɒmɪtə] Kilometer I **square kilometre** Quadratkilometer II
°**kilt** [kɪlt] Schottenrock
kind [kaɪnd]:
1. **a kind of …** eine Art (von) … I
2. freundlich, nett II
king [kɪŋ] König II
kingdom ['kɪŋdəm] Königreich III 1 (14)
kiss [kɪs] küssen; sich küssen II
kit [kɪt] Ausrüstung I °**first-aid kit** Erste-Hilfe-Kasten
kitchen ['kɪtʃɪn] Küche I
knee [niː] Knie II
kneel [niːl], **knelt, knelt** knien II
knelt [nelt] *siehe* **kneel**
knew [njuː] *siehe* **know**
knife [naɪf], *pl* **knives** [naɪvz] Messer II
knight [naɪt] Ritter II
knock (on sth.) [nɒk] (an)klopfen (an etwas) III 5 (95)
know [nəʊ], **knew, known** wissen; kennen I **I don't know.** Ich weiß (es) nicht. I **know about sth.** sich mit etwas auskennen; über etwas Bescheid wissen II **…, you know.** …, weißt du. / …, wissen Sie. I
known [nəʊn] *siehe* **know**
kung fu [ˌkʌŋ 'fuː] Kung Fu I

L

label ['leɪbl]:
1. beschriften; etikettieren II
2. Beschriftung; Schild, Etikett II
lain [leɪn] *siehe* **lie**
lake [leɪk] (Binnen-)See I
lamb [læm] Lamm II
lamp [læmp] Lampe I °**lamp post** Laternenpfahl
land [lænd]:
1. landen, an Land gehen II
2. Land II
language ['læŋgwɪdʒ] Sprache I
laptop ['læptɒp] Laptop III 4 (68)
large [lɑːdʒ] groß II
°**lark** [lɑːk] Lerche
°**lass** [læs] Mädel, Mädchen *(bes. schottisch, nordenglisch)*
last [lɑːst]:
1. **last Friday** letzten Freitag I **last year's …** das … vom letzten Jahr II
2. **at last** endlich, schließlich I
late [leɪt] spät I **You're late.** Du bist spät dran. / Du bist zu spät. I **stay up late** lang aufbleiben II
later ['leɪtə] später I
°**Latin** ['lætɪn] Latein; lateinisch
laugh [lɑːf] lachen I **laugh at sb./sth.** über jn./etwas lachen; jn. auslachen III 2 (30)
laughter ['lɑːftə] Gelächter III 3 (60)
lay [leɪ] *siehe* **lie**
layout ['leɪaʊt] Layout, Gestaltung III 4 (69)
lead [liːd], **led, led** führen, leiten III 3 (52)
leader ['liːdə] Leiter/in III 3 (52)
learn [lɜːn] lernen I
least ['liːst]: **at least** zumindest, wenigstens II
leave [liːv], **left, left**:
1. verlassen; zurücklassen I
2. lassen II **leave a message** eine Nachricht hinterlassen II **leave sth.** etwas übrig lassen II °**leave sth. out** etwas auslassen
3. (weg)gehen; abfahren II
led [led] *siehe* **lead**
left [left]:
1. *siehe* **leave**
2. linke(r, s); (nach) links II **on the left** links/auf der linken Seite II
3. **be left** übrig sein III 4 (66)
leg [leg] Bein I
legend ['ledʒənd] Legende, Sage II
°**leprechaun** ['leprəkɔːn] Leprechaun, Kobold *(Wesen der irischen Mythologie)*
less (than) [les] weniger (als) III 1 (15)
lesson ['lesn] (Unterrichts-)Stunde I **before lessons** vorm Unterricht I
let [let], **let, let** lassen I **Let me show you …** Lass mich dir … zeigen. I **Let's …** Lass(t) uns … I **Let's go to England.** Lass(t) uns nach England gehen/fahren. I
letter ['letə]:
1. Brief I
2. Buchstabe I
library ['laɪbrəri] Bibliothek, Bücherei I
lie [laɪ], **lay, lain** liegen II **lie down** sich hinlegen III 2 (40)
life [laɪf], *pl* **lives** [laɪvz] Leben I
life jacket ['laɪf dʒækɪt] Schwimmweste I
°**lifetime** ['laɪftaɪm] Leben(szeit)
lift [lɪft]:
1. Mitfahrgelegenheit II **give sb. a lift** jn. mitnehmen II
2. Fahrstuhl, Aufzug III 1 (10)
light [laɪt]:
1. Licht I **traffic light** (Verkehrs-)Ampel *(oft auch:* **traffic lights** *(pl))* III 4 (77)
2. **(lit, lit)** anzünden II **light sth. up** etwas erhellen *(aufleuchten lassen)* II
lightning *(no pl)* ['laɪtnɪŋ] Blitz II **a flash of lightning** ein Blitz II

like [laɪk]:
1. mögen, gernhaben I **I like ...** Ich mag ... I **I'd like ...** Ich hätte gern .../Ich möchte ... I **I'd like to go** Ich möchte gehen/Ich würde gern gehen I
2. like boys wie Jungen I **just like** genau wie ... II **like that** so *(auf diese Weise)* I **like this** so II **What's she like?** Wie ist sie (so)? I **What was it like?** Wie war es? II
3. *(infml)* als ob III 4 (71)
4. He was like: "Stop!" *(infml)* Und er so: „Stop!" III 4 (70)
likes and dislikes *(pl)* [ˌlaɪks‿ən 'dɪslaɪks] Vorlieben und Abneigungen I
line [laɪn]:
1. Zeile I
2. (U-Bahn-)Linie III 1 (18)
3. Reihe III 4 (78)
°**4.** line the streets die Straßen säumen
link ['lɪŋk]:
1. verbinden, verknüpfen III 1 (16)
linking word Bindewort III 1 (16)
°**2.** Link, Verknüpfung, Verbindung
lion ['laɪən] Löwe I
lip [lɪp] Lippe II
list [lɪst]:
1. Liste I
2. auflisten III 4 (74)
listen ['lɪsn] zuhören, horchen I
listen to sb. jm. zuhören I **listen to sth.** sich etwas anhören I **Listen, Justin.** Hör zu, Justin. I
listener ['lɪsənə] Zuhörer/in II
lit [lɪt] *siehe* **light**
litter bin ['lɪtə bɪn] Abfalleimer II
little ['lɪtl] klein I
live [lɪv] leben; wohnen I
living room ['lɪvɪŋ ruːm] Wohnzimmer I
local ['ləʊkl] örtlich, Lokal-; am/vom Ort; einheimisch III 3 (61)
location [ləʊ'keɪʃn] Position, Standort III 5 (84)
°**loch** [lɒx], [lɒk] *(Binnen-)See in Schottland*
lonely ['ləʊnli] einsam I
long [lɒŋ] lang I **(the) longest ...** der/die/das längste ...; am längsten II
look [lʊk]:
1. schauen I **Look, ...** Sieh mal, .../Schau mal, ... I **look after sb.** auf jn. aufpassen; sich um jn. kümmern II **look at** anschauen, ansehen I **look for sth.** etwas suchen I **look forward to sth.** sich auf etwas freuen II **look happy / ...** glücklich / ... aussehen I **look into sth.** etwas untersuchen, prüfen III 2 (32) **Look out!** Achtung! Aufgepasst! III 5 (82) **look sth. up** etwas nachschlagen III 2 (32) **look up** hochsehen, aufschauen II
▶ S. 180 (to) look ...
2. have a look nachschauen **have a look at sth.** einen Blick auf etwas werfen III 2 (40)

lose [luːz], **lost, lost** verlieren II
lost [lɒst] *siehe* **lose**
lot [lɒt]: **a lot** viel I **That helped us a lot.** Das hat uns sehr geholfen. I **lots of ...** viel ..., viele ... I
loud [laʊd] laut I **in a loud voice** mit lauter Stimme II
loudspeaker [ˌlaʊd'spiːkə] Lautsprecher; Megaphon III 1 (25)
love [lʌv]:
1. lieben, sehr mögen I **I'd love to ...** Ich würde sehr gern ... II
2. Love, ... Alles Liebe, ... *(Briefschluss)* II
lovely ['lʌvli] schön, hübsch, herrlich, entzückend II
luck [lʌk]: **Good luck!** Viel Glück! I
lucky ['lʌki]: **be lucky** Glück haben II **Lucky you.** Du Glückspilz. II
lunch [lʌntʃ] Mittagessen I **have lunch** zu Mittag essen I **What's for lunch?** Was gibt es zum Mittagessen? I
lunchtime ['lʌntʃtaɪm] Mittagszeit I **at lunchtime** mittags I
lynx [lɪŋks], *pl* **lynx** *or* **lynxes** Luchs III 5 (92)

M

°**m** *Abkürzung für* **million** *und* **metre**
mad [mæd] verrückt I **go mad** verrückt werden
made [meɪd]:
1. *siehe* **make**
2. be made of sth. aus etwas (gemacht) sein II
magazine [ˌmægə'ziːn] Zeitschrift I
magic ['mædʒɪk] magisch, Zauber- II
magical ['mædʒɪkl] zauberhaft, wundervoll; magisch III 2 (40)
mail [meɪl] E-Mail II
main [meɪn] Haupt- II **main clause** Hauptsatz III 2 (36)
°**majestic** [mə'dʒestɪk] majestätisch
make [meɪk], **made, made:**
1. machen; herstellen I °**make a comment** einen Kommentar abgeben **make a wish** sich etwas wünschen I **make friends** Freunde finden I **make fun of sb./sth.** sich über jn./etwas lustig machen III 2 (30) **make sb. sth.** jn. zu etwas machen II **make sth. up** sich etwas ausdenken III 2 (41) **make sure that ...** sich vergewissern, dass ...; darauf achten, dass ...; dafür sorgen, dass ... II
°**2.** bilden
make-up ['meɪk‿ʌp] Make-up II
malaria [mə'leəriə] Malaria III 2 (32)
mall [mɔːl] (großes) Einkaufszentrum I
mammal ['mæml] Säugetier III 5 (92)
man [mæn], *pl* **men** [men] Mann I
manage sth. ['mænɪdʒ] etwas schaffen; etwas zustande bringen III 2 (38)

manager ['mænɪdʒə] Trainer/in *(von Sportmannschaften)* III 3 (58)
°**manufacturing** [ˌmænju'fæktʃərɪŋ]: **manufacturing industry** verarbeitende Industrie
many ['meni] viele I **How many?** Wie viele? I
map [mæp] Landkarte; Stadtplan I **on the map** auf der Landkarte; auf dem Stadtplan I
March [mɑːtʃ] März I
mark [mɑːk]:
1. markieren II **mark sth. up** etwas markieren, kennzeichnen II
2. stress mark Betonungszeichen III 1 (13)
°**marker** ['mɑːkə] Kennzeichnung, Markierung
market ['mɑːkɪt] Markt I
married (to) ['mærɪd] verheiratet (mit) I
marry sb. ['mæri] jn. heiraten III 3 (61)
mask [mɑːsk] Maske III 3 (52)
master ['mɑːstə] Meister/in I
match [mætʃ]:
1. Spiel, Wettkampf, Match I
°**2. match sth. (to sth.)** etwas (zu etwas) zuordnen
material [mə'tɪəriəl] Material, Stoff III 3 (54)
maths [mæθs] Mathematik I
matter: What's the matter? ['mætə] Was ist denn?/Was ist los? I
°**maximum** ['mæksɪməm] Höchstbetrag
May [meɪ] Mai I
may [meɪ] dürfen II **May I have a word with you?** Kann ich Sie kurz sprechen? II **they may be ...** sie sind vielleicht ... III 4 (66)
▶ S. 188 möglich – wahrscheinlich – sicherlich
maybe ['meɪbi] vielleicht I
mayor [meə] Bürgermeister/in II
me [miː] mich; mir I **Me too.** Ich auch. I
meal [miːl] Mahlzeit, Essen III 2 (40)
mean [miːn], **meant, meant:**
1. bedeuten II
2. meinen II
meaning ['miːnɪŋ] Bedeutung II
meant [ment] *siehe* **mean**
meat [miːt] Fleisch I
°**mediate** ['miːdieɪt] vermitteln *(auch sprachlich)*
media ['miːdiə]: **social media** *(pl)* soziale Medien III 5 (83)
mediation [ˌmiːdi'eɪʃn] Sprachmittlung, Mediation I
meet [miːt], **met, met:**
1. treffen; kennenlernen I **Nice to meet you.** Freut mich, dich/euch/Sie kennenzulernen. I
2. sich treffen I
°**meeting** ['miːtɪŋ] Begegnung
melt [melt] schmelzen II
member ['membə] Mitglied III 3 (49)
°**membership** ['membəʃɪp] Mitgliedschaft

memorial [mə'mɔːriəl] Denkmal; Gedenk- III 5 (95)
memory ['meməri] Erinnerung II
men [men] *Plural von* **man** I
message ['mesɪdʒ]:
1. Nachricht II **text message** SMS II
2. Botschaft, Aussage III 1 (19)
met [met] *siehe* **meet**
metre ['miːtə] Meter I
middle ['mɪdl] Mitte I **in the middle** in der Mitte I
°**midfielder** [ˌmɪd'fiːldə] Mittelfeldspieler/in
midnight ['mɪdnaɪt] Mitternacht I
might [maɪt]: **it might be the other side** es könnte die andere Seite sein III 4 (66) °**I might have been born in ...** Es mag zwar so sein, dass ich in ... geboren bin.
▶ S. 188 möglich – wahrscheinlich – sicherlich
mile [maɪl] Meile *(ca. 1,6 km)* II **for miles** meilenweit II
milk [mɪlk] Milch I
°**Milky Way** [ˌmɪlki 'weɪ] Milchstraße
million ['mɪljən] Million II
mind [maɪnd]:
1. **read sb.'s mind** jemandes Gedanken lesen III 5 (94)
2. etwas dagegen haben III 1 (25)
▶ S. 178 (to) mind
°3. **Mind the gap!** *etwa:* Vorsicht, Lücke!
°**mind map** ['maɪnd mæp] Mindmap
mine [maɪn]:
1. meiner, meine, meins II
2. Bergwerk, Mine III 2 (32) **coal mine** Kohlebergwerk III 2 (32)
3. Mine III 2 (32)
4. abbauen III 2 (32)
minibus ['mɪnibʌs] Kleinbus I
minute ['mɪnɪt] Minute I **wait a minute** Warte einen Moment. / Moment mal. I **a 30-minute ride** eine 30-minütige Fahrt III 3 (51)
mirror ['mɪrə] Spiegel II
miss [mɪs]:
1. verpassen I
2. vermissen III 4 (74)
Miss [mɪs]: **Miss Bell** Frau Bell *(übliche Anrede von Lehrerinnen)* I
missing ['mɪsɪŋ] verschollen, vermisst III 5 (94) **the missing words** die fehlenden Wörter I **be missing** fehlen II
mist [mɪst] (leichter) Nebel, Dunst(schleier) II
mistake [mɪ'steɪk] Fehler II **make a mistake** einen Fehler machen II
°**misunderstanding** [ˌmɪsʌndə'stændɪŋ] Missverständnis
°**mix** [mɪks]:
1. mischen
2. Mischung
mobile (phone) [ˌməʊbaɪl 'fəʊn] Mobiltelefon, Handy I

model ['mɒdl]:
1. Model II
2. Modell III 1 (16)
modern ['mɒdən] modern III 3 (51)
moment ['məʊmənt] Moment I **at the moment** gerade, im Moment I
Monday ['mʌndeɪ], ['mʌndi] Montag I **on Monday** am Montag I
money ['mʌni] Geld I
monitor ['mɒnɪtə] nachverfolgen; überwachen III 5 (84)
monkey ['mʌŋki] Affe I
monster ['mɒnstə] Monster I
month [mʌnθ] Monat I
monument (to) ['mɒnjumənt] Denkmal, Monument (für / zum Gedenken an) III 3 (51)
moon [muːn] Mond I **at full moon** bei Vollmond II
moonlight ['muːnlaɪt] Mondlicht III 2 (40)
moor [mɔː], [mʊə] Hochmoor II
mop [mɒp]:
1. Wischmopp III 2 (42)
2. wischen *(Fußboden)* III 2 (42)
more [mɔː] mehr I **more beautiful (than)** schöner (als) II **one more photo** noch ein Foto; ein weiteres Foto II
morning ['mɔːnɪŋ] Morgen, Vormittag I **Good morning.** Guten Morgen. I **in the morning** morgens, vormittags, am Morgen/Vormittag I **tomorrow morning** morgen früh, morgen Vormittag II
°**moron** ['mɔːrɒn] *(infml)* Trottel
mosque [mɒsk] Moschee III 3 (55)
most [məʊst]: **most people** die meisten Menschen II **most of them** die meisten von ihnen II **(the) most beautiful** der/die/das schönste ...; am schönsten II
mother ['mʌðə] Mutter I
motion ['məʊʃn] **slow motion** Zeitlupe III 3 (59)
motorbike ['məʊtəbaɪk] Motorrad III 4 (70)
mountain ['maʊntən] Berg II
mouth [maʊθ] Mund; Maul I
move [muːv]:
1. bewegen; sich bewegen I
2. **move (to)** umziehen (nach) II **move in** einziehen II **move into a house** einziehen in ein Haus... II
movement ['muːvmənt] Bewegung III 5 (84)
movie ['muːvi] Film III 2 (36)
MP3 player [ˌem piː 'θriː ˌpleɪə] MP3-Spieler I
Mr Schwarz ['mɪstə] Herr Schwarz I
Mrs Schwarz ['mɪsɪz] Frau Schwarz I
much [mʌtʃ] viel I **How much ...?** Wie viel ...? I **How much are ...?** Was kosten ...? I **How much is ...?** Was kostet ...? I
mud [mʌd] Schlamm, Matsch II
mug [mʌg]: **a mug (of)** ein Becher II

mum [mʌm] Mama, Mutti I
°**murder** ['mɜːdə] ermorden
museum [mju'ziːəm] Museum I
music ['mjuːzɪk] Musik I
musical ['mjuːzɪkl]:
1. Musical II
°2. musikalisch
musician [mju'zɪʃn] Musiker/in III 2 (31)
must [mʌst] müssen II **you mustn't do it** ['mʌsnt] du darfst es nicht tun II
▶ S. 188 möglich – wahrscheinlich – sicherlich
my [maɪ] mein/e I **My birthday is in May.** Ich habe im Mai Geburtstag. I **My birthday is on 5th August.** Ich habe am 5. August Geburtstag. I **My name is ...** Ich heiße ... I
myself [maɪ'self] mich, mir III 5 (84)

N

name [neɪm]:
1. Name I **My name is ...** Ich heiße ... I **What's your name?** Wie heißt du? / Wie heißt ihr? I
2. (be)nennen III 3 (61)
narrow ['nærəʊ] schmal, eng II
nation ['neɪʃn] Nation, Volk III 4 (68)
national ['næʃnəl] national, National- III 2 (34)
natural ['nætʃrəl] natürlich III 2 (31) **natural history** Naturkunde III 1 (14) **natural world** (Welt der) Natur III 2 (31)
navy ['neɪvi] Marine I
near [nɪə] in der Nähe von, nahe (bei) I **near here** (hier) in der Nähe I
nearby ['nɪəbaɪ]: **a nearby town** eine nahegelegene Stadt II
nearly ['nɪəli] fast, beinahe III 4 (66)
necessary ['nesəsəri] notwendig III 5 (93)
neck [nek] Hals II
need [niːd] brauchen, benötigen I **need to do sth.** etwas tun müssen II **you needn't do it** ['niːdnt] du musst es nicht tun II
°**negative** ['negətɪv] negativ
neighbour ['neɪbə] Nachbar/in II
neither ['naɪðə], ['niːðə]: **me neither** Ich auch nicht. III 2 (34)
nervous ['nɜːvəs] nervös, aufgeregt II
net [net] Netz III 5 (84) **goal net** Tornetz III 3 (55)
never ['nevə] nie, niemals I
new [njuː] neu I
news *(no pl)* [njuːz]:
1. Nachrichten I
2. Neuigkeiten II
New Year's Eve [ˌnjuː jɪəz‿'iːv] Silvester II
next [nekst]:
1. **next year's ...** das ... vom nächsten Jahr II **the next question** die nächste Frage I
2. als Nächstes III 4 (77)
3. **next to** ['nekst tʊ] neben II

nice [naɪs] nett, schön I **Nice to meet you.** Freut mich, dich/euch/Sie kennenzulernen. I

night [naɪt] Nacht I **at night** nachts, in der Nacht I

nil [nɪl] null, Null III 3 (56)

nine [naɪn] neun I

no [nəʊ]:
1. nein I **No, that's wrong.** Nein, das ist falsch. / Nein, das stimmt nicht. I
2. kein, keine I **it was no different** es war nicht anders III 3 (60) **No way!** Auf keinen Fall! / Kommt nicht in Frage! III 1 (20)

nobody ['nəʊbədi] niemand I

nod [nɒd] nicken II

noise [nɔɪz] Geräusch; Lärm III 5 (94)

noisy ['nɔɪzi] laut, lärmend, voller Lärm II

none (of) [nʌn] keine(r, s) (von ...) III 4 (78)

no one ['nəʊ wʌn] niemand I

normal ['nɔːməl] normal III 3 (46)

north [nɔːθ] Norden; nach Norden; nördlich III 1 (11) **northbound** ['nɔːθbaʊnd] Richtung Norden III 1 (18) **north-east** [ˌnɔːθ‿'iːst] Nordosten; nach Nordosten; nordöstlich III 1 (11) **northern** ['nɔːðən] nördlich, Nord- III 4 (66) **north-west** [ˌnɔːθ'west] Nordwesten; nach Nordwesten; nordwestlich III 1 (11)

nose [nəʊz] Nase I

not [nɒt] nicht I **he/she/it is not** er/sie/es ist nicht ... I **not till three** erst um drei, nicht vor drei II **not ... yet** noch nicht I

note [nəʊt]:
1. Notiz, Mitteilung I **make notes (on/about sth.)** (sich) Notizen machen (über/zu etwas) *(zur Vorbereitung)* II **take notes (on/about sth.)** (sich) Notizen machen (über/zu etwas) *(beim Lesen oder Zuhören)* II
2. Note *(Musik)* III 2 (41)

nothing ['nʌθɪŋ] (gar) nichts I

noun [naʊn] Nomen, Substantiv III 1 (12)

November [nəʊ'vembə] November I

now [naʊ] nun, jetzt I °**Does it now?** Tatsächlich? / Ist das so? **Now that ...** Jetzt, wo ... / Nun, da ... III 4 (78) **right now** jetzt gerade II

nowhere ['nəʊweə] nirgendwo; nirgendwohin III 3 (60) **out of nowhere** (wie) aus dem Nichts III 3 (60)

number ['nʌmbə] Zahl, Nummer, Ziffer I Anzahl III 2 (39)

O

o [əʊ] Null *(in Telefonnummern)* I

object ['ɒbdʒɪkt], ['ɒbdʒekt] Objekt II

ocean ['əʊʃn] Ozean I

°**Och** [ɒx] Ach *(bes. schottisch)*

o'clock [ə'klɒk]: **at 1 o'clock** um 1 Uhr / um 13 Uhr I

October [ɒk'təʊbə] Oktober I

of [ɒv], [əv] von I

of course [əv 'kɔːs] natürlich, selbstverständlich I

off [ɒf]: **Off you go now.** Ab mit euch jetzt! / Los mit euch jetzt! III 1 (20) **be off** aus(geschaltet) sein *(Radio, Licht usw.)* III 1 (20) **fall off a bike** vom Fahrrad herunterfallen III 1 (20) **get/have a day off** einen Tag frei bekommen/haben III 3 (51) **run off** wegrennen III 1 (20)
► S. 177 off

offer ['ɒfə] anbieten II

office ['ɒfɪs] Büro III 2 (41) **ticket office** Fahrkartenschalter; Kasse *(für den Verkauf von Eintrittskarten)* III 1 (15)

official [ə'fɪʃl]
1. amtlich, Amts- III 2 (32)
2. Beamte(r), Beamtin III 2 (32)

often ['ɒfn], ['ɒftən] oft I

oh [əʊ]: **Oh, it's you.** Ach, du bist es. I

oil [ɔɪl] Öl III 2 (30)

old [əʊld] alt I **in the old days** früher (einmal) III 4 (79)

°**Olympics, the** [ə'lɪmpɪks] Olympiade

on [ɒn] auf I **be on** eingeschaltet sein, an sein *(Radio, Licht usw.)*; laufen, übertragen werden *(Programm, Sendung)* III 1 (20) **on earth** auf der Erde II **on Monday** am Montag I **on Monday afternoon** am Montagnachmittag I **on the phone** am Telefon II **on the plane** im Flugzeug II **on the radio** im Radio I **on top of each other** übereinander, aufeinander III 1 (15) **on TV** im Fernsehen III 1 (20) **walk/run/... on** weitergehen/-laufen/... II

once [wʌns]:
1. einmal II °**at once** auf einmal **once a week/year** einmal pro Woche/Jahr II
°2. einst

one [wʌn] eins I **a one-hour concert** ein einstündiges Konzert III 3 (51) **one all** eins zu eins; eins beide III 3 (56) **one by one** einzeln; einer nach dem anderen II **one night/day** eines Nachts/Tages II **one-syllable** einsilbige(r, s) II **a white one** ein weißer / eine weiße / ein weißes II **this one** diese(r, s) II **two black ones** zwei schwarze II **Which one?** Welche(r, s)? II

online [ˌɒn'laɪn] online II

only ['əʊnli]:
1. nur, bloß I **the only ...** der/die/das einzige ...; die einzigen... II
2. erst I

onto ['ɒntʊ] auf (... hinauf) I

open ['əʊpən]:
1. öffnen, aufmachen I; sich öffnen I **opening times** *(pl)* Öffnungszeiten III 1 (15)
2. geöffnet, offen I

opinion [ə'pɪnjən] Meinung III 3 (51) **in my opinion** meiner Meinung nach III 3 (51)

°**opponent** [ə'pəʊnənt] Gegner/in

opposite ['ɒpəzɪt] gegenüber (von) II

or [ɔː] oder I

orange ['ɒrɪndʒ]:
1. orange I
2. Orange, Apfelsine I

order ['ɔːdə]:
1. Reihenfolge I
2. bestellen II
3. ordnen III 3 (58)

organize ['ɔːgənaɪz] organisieren; ordnen III 2 (38)

°**original** [ə'rɪdʒənl] original, ursprünglich

other ['ʌðə] andere(r, s) I

otter ['ɒtə] Otter II

our ['aʊə] unser/e I

ours ['aʊəz] unserer, unsere, unseres II

ourselves [ɑː'selvz], [aʊə'selvz] uns III 5 (85)

out ['aʊt]:
1. heraus, hinaus, nach draußen II **out and about** unterwegs II
2. **be out** nicht zu Hause sein, nicht da sein II
3. **out of ...** ['aʊt‿əv] aus ... (heraus/hinaus) I

outdoor ['aʊtdɔː] Außen-, im Freien II

outside [ˌaʊt'saɪd]:
1. draußen; nach draußen I **outside the house** vor dem Haus, außerhalb vom Haus II
2. die Außenseite; das Äußere III 1 (14)

over ['əʊvə]:
1. über I **run over (to)** hinüberrennen (zu/nach) II **over to ...** hinüber zu/nach ... I **over here** hier herüber II **over there** da drüben, dort drüben II
2. **over 4 years** über 4 Jahre; mehr als 4 Jahre I
3. **be over** vorbei / zu Ende sein I

own [əʊn]:
1. besitzen II
2. **my own room/...** mein eigenes Zimmer/... II
3. **on my/your/their/... own** allein II

P

p [piː] *Abkürzung für „pence", „penny"* I

pack [pæk] packen III 4 (74)

packet ['pækɪt] Packung, Päckchen II

°**paddle** ['pædl] paddeln

page [peɪdʒ] Seite I **What page are we on?** Auf welcher Seite sind wir? I

paid [peɪd]:
1. *siehe* **pay**
2. **get paid** Geld bekommen III 4 (70)

paint [peɪnt] (an)streichen; (an)malen II

painted ['peɪntɪd] bemalt, angemalt II

painter ['peɪntə] Maler/in III 2 (31)

pair [peə]: **a pair (of)** ein Paar II

palace ['pæləs] Palast, Schloss III 1 (10)
pancake ['pænkeɪk] Pfannkuchen II
panic ['pænɪk], **panicked, panicked** in Panik geraten III 1 (24)
paper ['peɪpə]:
1. Zeitung I
2. Papier I
parade [pə'reɪd] Parade, Umzug II
paragraph ['pærəgrɑːf] Absatz *(in einem Text)* I
parents *(pl)* ['peərənts] Eltern I
park [pɑːk]:
1. Park I
2. parken III 4 (77)
parliament ['pɑːləmənt] Parlament III 1 (15)
part [pɑːt] Teil I **part of speech** Wortart III 2 (32) **part of the body** Körperteil II **take part in sth.** an etwas teilnehmen II
partner ['pɑːtnə] Partner/in I
party ['pɑːti] Party I
pass [pɑːs]:
1. vergehen, vorübergehen *(Zeit)* III 4 (77)
2. **pass sth./sb.** an etwas/jm. vorbeigehen/vorbeifahren II
3. **pass sth. around** etwas herumgeben, herumreichen II
°**passenger** ['pæsɪndʒə] Passagier/in
passport ['pɑːspɔːt] (Reise-)Pass III 4 (68)
past [pɑːst]:
1. Vergangenheit I
2. **half past ten** halb elf (10.30 / 22.30) I **quarter past ten** Viertel nach zehn (10.15 / 22.15) I
3. vorbei (an), vorüber (an) II
path [pɑːθ] Pfad, Weg II
°**pattern** ['pætn] Muster
pause [pɔːz] innehalten, pausieren; eine Pause einlegen II
pavement ['peɪvmənt] Gehweg, Bürgersteig III 1 (24)
paw [pɔː] Pfote, Tatze II
pay (for sth.) [peɪ], **paid, paid** (etwas) bezahlen II **get paid** Geld bekommen III 4 (70)
PE [ˌpiː‿'iː] Sportunterricht, Turnen I
peace [piːs] Friede, Frieden III 4 (68)
peaceful ['piːsfl] friedlich; friedfertig II
pedestrian [pə'destriən] Fußgänger/in III 4 (77) **pedestrian zone** Fußgängerzone II
pen [pen] Kugelschreiber, Stift, Füller I
°**penalty** ['penəlti] Elfmeter **penalty area** Strafraum
pence [pens] Pence *(Plural von* **penny***)* I
▶ S. 189 Pounds and euros
pencil ['pensl] Bleistift I
pencil case ['pensl keɪs] Federmäppchen I
people ['piːpl]:
1. *(Singular)* Volk III 3 (52)
2. *(Plural)* Leute, Menschen I
pepper ['pepə] Pfeffer I
°**per cent** [pə 'sent] Prozent

perfect ['pɜːfɪkt] perfekt, ideal I
perform [pə'fɔːm] auftreten *(Künstler/in)* III 3 (51)
performer [pə'fɔːmə] Künstler/in III 5 (88)
person ['pɜːsn] Person I
pet [pet] Haustier III 4 (68)
phone [fəʊn]:
1. Telefon I **answer the phone** ans Telefon gehen II **on the phone** am Telefon II
2. **phone sb.** jn. anrufen II
phone call ['fəʊn kɔːl] *(kurz auch:* **call***)* Anruf; Telefongespräch II
photo ['fəʊtəʊ] Foto I **in the photo** auf dem Foto I **take photos** fotografieren, Fotos machen I
photograph ['fəʊtəgrɑːf] fotografieren III 5 (84)
phrase [freɪz] Ausdruck, (Rede-)Wendung I
Physical Education [ˌfɪzɪkl‿ˌedʒu'keɪʃn] Sportunterricht, Turnen I
piano [pi'ænəʊ] Klavier, Piano I **play the piano** Klavier spielen I
pick [pɪk]: **pick on sb.** auf jm. herumhacken III 5 (88) **pick sb. up** jn. abholen II **pick sth. up** etwas aufheben *(vom Boden)*, etwas hochheben II
picnic ['pɪknɪk] Picknick I
picture ['pɪktʃə] Bild I **in the picture** auf dem Bild I
piece (of) [piːs] ein Stück … III 2 (30)
pig [pɪg] Schwein I
pink [pɪŋk] pink, rosa I
pipe [paɪp] Pfeife III 4 (71)
°**piper** ['paɪpə] Dudelsackspieler/in
pitch [pɪtʃ] (Sport-)Platz, Spielfeld III 3 (58)
pity ['pɪti]: **It was a pity that …** Es war schade, dass … III 1 (22)
pizza ['piːtsə] Pizza I
place [pleɪs] Ort, Platz, Stelle I **in second place** auf dem zweiten Platz; an zweiter Stelle III 5 (96) **take place** stattfinden III 3 (61)
plan [plæn]:
1. Plan I
2. planen II
plane [pleɪn] Flugzeug II **get on a plane** in ein Flugzeug einsteigen II **on the plane** im Flugzeug II
planet ['plænɪt] Planet I
plant [plɑːnt]:
1. Pflanze II
2. pflanzen II
°**plantain** ['plæntеɪn] Kochbanane
plantation [plɑːn'teɪʃn] Plantage III 3 (53)
plaster ['plɑːstə] (Heft-)Pflaster II
plastic ['plæstɪk] Plastik, Kunststoff II
plate [pleɪt] **a plate of …** ein Teller … I

platform ['plætfɔːm]:
1. Plattform III 5 (91)
2. Bahnsteig, Gleis III 1 (19)
play [pleɪ]:
1. spielen I **play the drums / the guitar / the piano** Schlagzeug/Gitarre/Klavier spielen I
2. abspielen *(CD, DVD)* I
3. Theaterstück I
player ['pleɪə] Spieler/in I
please [pliːz] bitte I
pm: 4 pm [ˌpiː‿'em] 4 Uhr nachmittags / 16 Uhr I
pocket ['pɒkɪt] Tasche *(Manteltasche, Hosentasche usw.)* II
poem ['pəʊɪm] Gedicht II
point [pɔɪnt]:
1. Punkt I **point: 1.6 (one point six)** 1,6 (eins Komma sechs) III 2 (38) **point of view (on sth.)** Standpunkt (in/über/zu etwas) III 2 (42) **from my point of view** aus meiner Sicht III 2 (42)
▶ S. 181 Numbers
2. **point to sth.** auf etwas zeigen, deuten I
3. **point sth. at sb.** etwas auf jn. richten I
4. **point sth. out (to sb.)** (jn.) auf etwas hinweisen III 1 (17)
police *(pl)* [pə'liːs] Polizei III 2 (32) **police officer** Polizist/in I **police station** Polizeiwache, -revier III 4 (68) **The police are on their way.** Die Polizei ist auf dem Weg. III 2 (32)
policeman [pə'liːsmən] Polizist I
policewoman [pə'liːswʊmən] Polizistin III 5 (95)
polite [pə'laɪt] höflich III 4 (66)
pollution [pə'luːʃn] (Umwelt-)Verschmutzung III 5 (84)
pony ['pəʊni] Pony II
pool [puːl] Schwimmbad, Schwimmbecken I
poor [pɔː], [pʊə] arm I
°**pop (music)** [pɒp] Popmusik
popular (with) ['pɒpjələ] populär, beliebt (bei) III 3 (51)
population [ˌpɒpju'leɪʃn] Bevölkerung, Einwohner(zahl) III 4 (68)
position [pə'zɪʃn] Platz, Position III 5 (88)
post [pəʊst]:
1. Posting *(auf Blog)*, Blog-Eintrag III 1 (10)
°2. **lamp post** Laternenpfahl
postcard ['pəʊstkɑːd] Postkarte II
poster ['pəʊstə] Poster I
post office ['pəʊst‿ɒfɪs] Postamt II
pot [pɒt] Gefäß; Topf III 3 (52)
potato [pə'teɪtəʊ], *pl* **potatoes** Kartoffel I
pound [paʊnd] Pfund *(britische Währung)* I
▶ S. 189 Pounds and euros
pour [pɔː] gießen II
practical ['præktɪkl] praktisch III 4 (65)

practice ['præktɪs] Übung I
practise ['præktɪs] üben, trainieren I
predator ['predətə] Raubtier III 5 (92)
°**Premier League** [ˌpremiə 'liːg] *höchste englische Spielklasse (Fußball)*
prepare sth. [prɪ'peə] etwas vorbereiten I
present ['preznt]:
1. Geschenk I
2. Gegenwart II
°3. vorhanden, anwesend
present sth. (to sb.) [prɪ'zent] (jm.) etwas präsentieren, vorstellen II
presentation [ˌprezn'teɪʃn] Präsentation, Vorstellung II
president ['prezɪdənt] Präsident/in III 4 (68)
press [pres] drücken III 2 (40)
pretend [prɪ'tend] so tun, als ob III 2 (34)
pretty ['prɪti] hübsch II
price [praɪs] (Kauf-)Preis I
prince [prɪns] Prinz II
princess [ˌprɪn'ses], ['prɪnses] Prinzessin II
prison ['prɪzn] Gefängnis I
prize [praɪz] Preis, Gewinn II
probable ['prɒbəbl] wahrscheinlich III 2 (30)
probably ['prɒbəbli] wahrscheinlich II
problem ['prɒbləm] Problem I
°**product** ['prɒdʌkt] Produkt, Ware
profile ['prəʊfaɪl] Profil; Beschreibung, Porträt I
programme ['prəʊgræm] Programm *(auch im Theater usw.)*; (Radio-, Fernseh-)Sendung I
°**prohibit** [prə'hɪbɪt] verbieten
project ['prɒdʒekt] Projekt II
promise ['prɒmɪs] versprechen II
promote sth. [prə'məʊt]:
1. Werbung machen für etwas III 5 (82)
°2. etwas fördern
pronunciation [prəˌnʌnsi'eɪʃn] Aussprache I
protect sb./sth. (from sb./sth.) [prə'tekt] jn./etwas (be)schützen (vor jm./etwas) III 5 (84)
°**protection** [prə'tekʃn] Schutz
protest [prə'test] protestieren III 3 (46)
protest ['prəʊtest] Protest III 3 (46)
proud (of) [praʊd] stolz (auf) III 4 (66)
°**provide** [prə'vaɪd] bereitstellen
pub [pʌb] Kneipe, Lokal III 1 (20)
pull [pʊl] ziehen I **pull sth. out** etwas herausziehen II
pullover ['pʊləʊvə] Pullover II
punctuation [ˌpʌŋktʃu'eɪʃn] Zeichensetzung II
punishment ['pʌnɪʃmənt] Bestrafung, Strafe III 2 (42)
puppet ['pʌpɪt] Marionette, Handpuppe II
purple ['pɜːpl] violett, lila I
push [pʊʃ] drücken, schieben, stoßen I
put [pʊt], **put, put** legen, stellen, *(etwas wohin)* tun I **put sth. down** etwas hinlegen III 2 (30) **put sth. on** etwas anziehen *(Kleidung)*; etwas aufsetzen *(Hut, Helm)* II °**put sth. together** etwas zusammenstellen **put your hand up** sich melden III 5 (84)

Q

quarter ['kwɔːtə]: **quarter past ten** Viertel nach zehn (10.15 / 22.15) I
quarter to eleven Viertel vor elf (10.45 / 22.45) I
queen [kwiːn] Königin II
question ['kwestʃən] Frage I
question mark Fragezeichen II
queue [kjuː]:
1. Schlange stehen, sich anstellen II
2. Schlange, Reihe *(wartender Menschen)* III 1 (16)
quick [kwɪk] schnell II
quiet ['kwaɪət] ruhig, still, leise I
quite [kwaɪt] ziemlich; völlig, ganz III 3 (47)
quiz [kwɪz] Quiz, Ratespiel I

R

rabbit ['ræbɪt] Kaninchen I
race [reɪs]:
1. Rennen, (Wett-)Lauf II
2. rasen III 4 (77)
radio ['reɪdiəʊ] Radio I **on the radio** im Radio I
rain [reɪn]:
1. Regen II **heavy rain** starker Regen, heftiger Regen II
2. regnen II
rainbow ['reɪnbəʊ] Regenbogen III 1 (24)
raincoat ['reɪnkəʊt] Regenmantel II
rainforest ['reɪnfɒrɪst] Regenwald II
rainy ['reɪni] regnerisch II
raise money (for sth.) [reɪz] Geld sammeln (für etwas) II
rally ['ræli] Rallye II
ran [ræn] *siehe* **run**
rang [ræŋ] *siehe* **ring**
rat [ræt] Ratte I
raven ['reɪvn] Rabe III 1 (15)
reach [riːtʃ] erreichen III 2 (34) **reach over** die Hand ausstrecken III 5 (94)
react (to) [ri'kt] reagieren (auf) III 1 (17)
read [riːd], **read** [red], **read** [red] lesen I **read sb.'s mind** jemandes Gedanken lesen III 5 (94)
reader ['riːdə] Leser/in II
ready ['redi] bereit, fertig I
real ['riːəl] echt, wirklich II
really ['rɪəli] echt, wirklich I
reason ['riːzn] Grund, Begründung II
°**rebel** ['rebl] sich auflehnen, rebellieren
recipe ['resəpi] (Koch-)Rezept II
°**recognize** ['rekəgnaɪz] erkennen
record [rɪ'kɔːd] aufzeichnen *(Musik, Daten)*; dokumentieren *(Daten)* III 5 (84)
°**record** ['rekɔːd] Schallplatte
recorder [rɪ'kɔːdə] Blockflöte II
red [red] rot I **go red** rot werden, erröten II
referee [ˌrefə'riː] Schiedsrichter/in III 3 (58)
°**referendum** [ˌrefə'rendəm] Volksentscheid, Referendum
°**refreshment** [rɪ'freʃmənt] Imbiss, Erfrischung
°**region** ['riːdʒən] Region
regional ['riːdʒənl] regional III 4 (75)
regular ['regjələ] regelmäßig II
rehearsal [rɪ'hɜːsl] Probe *(Theater)* III 5 (88)
°**rehearse** [rɪ'hɜːs] proben
°**relationship** [rɪ'leɪʃnʃɪp] Verhältnis
relax [rɪ'læks] sich entspannen, sich ausruhen III 5 (85)
religion [rɪ'lɪdʒən] Religion I
remember sth. [rɪ'membə]:
1. sich an etwas erinnern I
2. an etwas denken; sich etwas merken III 3 (51)
remote (control) [rɪˌməʊt kən'trəʊl] Fernbedienung III 1 (20)
repeat [rɪ'piːt] wiederholen II
reply (to) [rɪ'plaɪ] antworten (auf); erwidern, entgegnen III 1 (10)
report [rɪ'pɔːt]:
1. Bericht, Reportage II
°2. berichten
°**reporter** [rɪ'pɔːtə] Reporter/in
republic [rɪ'pʌblɪk] Republik III 4 (68)
rescue ['reskjuː] retten II
research ['riːsɜːtʃ] Recherche, Forschung(en) III 4 (69)
reserve [rɪ'zɜːv] reservieren, buchen III 1 (14)
respect [rɪ'spekt] Respekt, Achtung III 3 (52)
responsible [rɪ'spɒnsəbl] verantwortlich II
rest [rest]:
1. ruhen, sich ausruhen III 1 (25)
2. Rest III 2 (42)
restaurant ['restrɒnt] Restaurant III 1 (12)
result [rɪ'zʌlt] Ergebnis, Resultat III 4 (69)
revise [rɪ'vaɪz] überarbeiten; *(Lernstoff)* wiederholen III 2 (38)
revision [rɪ'vɪʒn] Wiederholung *(des Lernstoffs)* II
°**revolution** [ˌrevə'luːʃn] Revolution
rhyme [raɪm] Reim; Vers I
rhythm ['rɪðəm] Rhythmus III 1 (24)
rich [rɪtʃ] reich I
ridden ['rɪdn] *siehe* **ride**
ride [raɪd]:
1. Fahrt I; Ritt, Ausritt III 4 (74)
2. **(rode, ridden)** reiten; (Rad) fahren II **ride a bike** Fahrrad fahren I
riding ['raɪdɪŋ] Reiten I

right [raɪt]:
1. richtig I **sb. is right** jemand hat Recht I **Yes, that's right.** Ja, das ist richtig. / Ja, das stimmt. I
2. rechte(r, s); (nach) rechts II **on the right** rechts/auf der rechten Seite II
3. right now jetzt gerade II
4. ..., right? ..., nicht wahr? II
5. right behind you direkt hinter dir, genau hinter dir II **right after you** gleich nach dir II
ring [rɪŋ]:
1. (rang, rung) klingeln, läuten II °**ring out the hour** durch den (Glocken-)Schlag die Uhrzeit bekanntgeben
2. Ring II
rise up [ˌraɪz_ˈʌp], **rose, risen** aufragen, emporragen *(Berge, Säulen, Türme, ...)* III 4 (66)
risen [ˈrɪzn] *siehe* **rise**
°**risk assessment** [ˈrɪsk_əˌsesmənt] Risikoeinschätzung
°**rival** [ˈraɪvl] Rivale, Rivalin
river [ˈrɪvə] Fluss I
road [rəʊd] Straße I **at 8 Beach Road** in der Beach Road 8 I **in Beach Road** in der Beach Road I
roar [rɔː] brüllen III 1 (16)
roast beef [ˌrəʊst ˈbiːf] Rinderbraten I
roast potatoes *(pl)* [ˌrəʊst pəˈteɪtəʊz] *im Backofen in Fett gebackene Kartoffeln* I
rock [rɒk]:
1. Fels, Felsen I
2. rock (music) Rockmusik II
rocky [ˈrɒki] felsig, steinig II
rode [rəʊd] *siehe* **ride**
role [rəʊl] Rolle *(in einem Theaterstück, Film)* II
roll [rəʊl] rollen II
roof [ruːf] Dach II
room [ruːm]:
1. Zimmer, Raum I
2. Platz III 3 (54)
rope [rəʊp] Seil III 1 (24)
rose [rəʊz] *siehe* **rise**
rough [rʌf] stürmisch, rau (See) III 5 (84)
round [raʊnd] **round the world** um die Welt II **round here** hier in der Gegend III 4 (74)
roundabout [ˈraʊndəbaʊt] Kreisverkehr II
route [ruːt] Strecke, Route III 1 (22)
royal [ˈrɔɪəl] königlich II
rubber [ˈrʌbə] Radiergummi I
rubbish [ˈrʌbɪʃ] Müll, Abfall II
rucksack [ˈrʌksæk] Rucksack I
°**rugby** [ˈrʌgbi] Rugby
ruin [ˈruːɪn] Ruine II
rule [ruːl] Regel, Vorschrift II
ruler [ˈruːlə] Lineal I
run [rʌn], **ran, run** rennen, laufen I **run after sb.** hinter jm. herrennen I **run around** herumrennen, umherrennen II **run off** wegrennen III 1 (20) **run on** weiterlaufen II **run over (to)** (zu/nach ...) hinüberrennen II ► S. 177 off
rung [rʌŋ] *siehe* **ring** II
runner [ˈrʌnə] Läufer/in II

S

sad [sæd] traurig I
said [sed] *siehe* **say**
sail [seɪl]:
1. segeln II **go sailing** segeln; segeln gehen I **sailing boat** Segelboot I
°**2.** fahren *(Schiff)*, auslaufen, in See stechen
sailor [ˈseɪlə] Seemann, Matrose, Matrosin III 3 (61)
salad [ˈsæləd] Salat *(als Gericht oder Beilage)* I **fruit salad** Obstsalat I
samba [ˈsæmbə] Samba I
same [seɪm]: **the same as ...** der-/die-/dasselbe wie ... I
sand [sænd] Sand I
sandwich [ˈsænwɪtʃ], [ˈsænwɪdʒ] Sandwich, (zusammengeklapptes) belegtes Brot I
sang [sæŋ] *siehe* **sing**
sat [sæt] *siehe* **sit**
Saturday [ˈsætədeɪ], [ˈsætədi] Samstag, Sonnabend I **on Saturday afternoon** am Samstagnachmittag I
save [seɪv] retten I
saw [sɔː] *siehe* **see**
say [seɪ], **said, said** sagen I **Say hello to ... for me.** Grüß ... von mir. II
scan sth. (for sth.) [skæn] etwas (nach etwas) absuchen III 1 (24) **scan a text** einen Text schnell nach bestimmten Wörtern/Informationen absuchen II
scare sb. [skeə] jn. erschrecken; jm. Angst machen III 1 (25)
scared [skeəd] verängstigt II
scarf [skɑːf], *pl* **scarves** [skɑːvz] Schal III 3 (58)
scary [ˈskeəri] unheimlich, gruselig I
scene [siːn] Szene I
schedule [ˈʃedjuːl], [ˈskedjuːl,] (Zeit-)Plan, Programm III 3 (51)
school [skuːl] Schule I **at school** in der Schule I **before school** vor der Schule *(vor Schulbeginn)* I **in front of the school** vor der Schule *(vor dem Schulgebäude)* I **school bag** Schultasche I
science [ˈsaɪəns] Naturwissenschaft I
scientist [ˈsaɪəntɪst] Naturwissenschaftler/in III 2 (30)
scone [skɒn], [skəʊn] *kleines rundes Milchbrötchen, leicht süß* I
°**scoop** [skuːp] schöpfen
score [skɔː]:
1. einen Treffer erzielen, ein Tor schießen I
2. Spielstand; Punktestand III 3 (56) **What's the score?** Wie steht es? III 3 (56)
scream [skriːm]:
1. schreien II
2. Schrei III 3 (60)
screen [skriːn] Bildschirm II
sea [siː] Meer I
seagull [ˈsiːgʌl] Möwe I
seal [siːl] Robbe I
seasick [ˈsiːsɪk] seekrank III 5 (84)
seat [siːt] Sitz, Platz II
second [ˈsekənd]:
1. zweite(r, s) I **second biggest** zweitgrößte(r, s) II
2. Sekunde II
see [siː], **saw, seen** sehen; besuchen I; *(Arzt)* aufsuchen II **I see.** Aha! / Verstehe. III 1 (10) **See you.** Bis gleich. / Bis bald. I **..., you see.** ..., weißt du. II
seem (to be/do) [siːm] (zu sein/zu tun) scheinen III 3 (60)
seen [siːn] *siehe* **see**
sell [sel], **sold, sold** verkaufen I
send [send], **sent, sent** schicken, senden I
sent [sent] *siehe* **send**
sentence [ˈsentəns] Satz I **full sentence** ganzer Satz II **topic sentence** Satz, der in das Thema eines Absatzes einführt III 2 (38)
September [sepˈtembə] September I
service [ˈsɜːvɪs] Gottesdienst III 4 (70)
set [set] Satz, Set II
seven [ˈsevn] sieben I
several [ˈsevrəl] mehrere, verschiedene III 3 (51)
shadow [ˈʃædəʊ] Schatten II
shake [ʃeɪk], **shook, shaken** schütteln II
shaken [ʃeɪkn] *siehe* **shake**
shall [ʃæl]: **Shall I ...?** Soll ich ...? III 4 (66)
shape [ʃeɪp] Form, Gestalt III 3 (52) **Those glasses are an interesting shape.** Die Brille hat eine interessante Form. III 3 (52)
°**shard** [ʃɑːd] Scherbe
shark [ʃɑːk] Hai I
sharpener [ˈʃɑːpnə] Anspitzer I
she [ʃiː] sie I
sheep [ʃiːp], *pl* **sheep** Schaf II
sheepdog [ˈʃiːpdɒg] Hütehund III 5 (83)
shelf [ʃelf], *pl* **shelves** [ʃelvz] Regal I
shepherd [ˈʃepəd] Schäfer/in, Schafhirte/-hirtin III 5 (94)
°**shimmer** [ˈʃɪmə] schimmern
°**shin guard** [ˈʃɪn gɑːd] Schienbeinschützer
shine [ʃaɪn], **shone, shone** scheinen *(Sonne)* III 3 (60)
ship [ʃɪp] Schiff I
°**shipbuilding** [ˈʃɪpbɪldɪŋ] Schiffbau
°**shipyard** [ˈʃɪpjɑːd] (Schiffs-)Werft
shirt [ʃɜːt] Hemd II; Trikot III 3 (58)
°**shock** [ʃɒk] schockieren, entsetzen

shocked [ʃɒkt] schockiert, entsetzt II

shoe [ʃuː] Schuh I

shone [ʃɒn] *siehe* **shine**

shook [ʃʊk] *siehe* **shake**

°**shooting star** [ˌʃuːtɪŋ ˈstɑː] Sternschnuppe

shop [ʃɒp]:
1. Laden I **corner shop** Laden an der Ecke; Tante-Emma-Laden I **shop assistant** Verkäufer/in II
2. einkaufen II

shopper [ˈʃɒpə] (Ein-)Käufer/in II

shopping [ˈʃɒpɪŋ]: **do the/some shopping** einkaufen gehen; Einkäufe erledigen II **go shopping** einkaufen gehen I **shopping centre** Einkaufszentrum II **shopping mall** (großes) Einkaufszentrum I

shore [ʃɔː] Ufer, Strand II

short [ʃɔːt] kurz I

shorts *(pl)* [ʃɔːts] Shorts, kurze Hose I

should [ʃʊd], [ʃəd]: **You should …** Du solltest … / Ihr solltet … / Sie sollten … II
▶ S. 188 möglich – wahrscheinlich – sicherlich

shoulder [ˈʃəʊldə] Schulter II

shout [ʃaʊt] schreien, rufen I

show [ʃəʊ]:
1. **(showed, shown)** zeigen I
2. Show, Vorstellung II

shower [ˈʃaʊə] Dusche III 4 (72) **have a shower** (sich) duschen III 4 (72)

shown [ʃəʊn] *siehe* **show**

shy [ʃaɪ] schüchtern, scheu II

sick [sɪk] krank I **be sick** sich übergeben II **I feel sick.** Mir ist schlecht. II **I'm going to be sick.** Ich muss mich übergeben. II

side [saɪd] Seite II

sigh [saɪ] seufzen III 4 (78)

sights *(pl)* [saɪts] Sehenswürdigkeiten I

sighting [ˈsaɪtɪŋ] Sichtung III 5 (84)

sign [saɪn] Schild; Zeichen I **no sign of …** keine Spur von … III 1 (25)

silent [ˈsaɪlənt] still, leise III 2 (40)

silently [ˈsaɪləntli] lautlos; schweigend III 2 (40)

silky [ˈsɪlki] seidig I

silly [ˈsɪli]:
1. albern; blöd I
2. Dummerchen I

°**silver** [ˈsɪlvə] silbern

similar (to sth./sb.) [ˈsɪmələ] (etwas/jm.) ähnlich II

since [sɪns]: **since 10 o'clock / last week** seit 10 Uhr / letzter Woche III 1 (20)

sing [sɪŋ], **sang, sung** singen I **sing along (with sb.)** (mit jm.) mitsingen III 2 (35)

singer [ˈsɪŋə] Sänger/in II

single [ˈsɪŋgl] ledig, alleinstehend I

°**singles** *(pl)* [ˈsɪŋgəlz] Einzelturnier

°**sir** [sɜː] Sir *(höfliche Anrede, z. B. für Kunden, Vorgesetzte oder Lehrer)*

siren [ˈsaɪrən] Sirene III 4 (77)

sister [ˈsɪstə] Schwester I

sit [sɪt], **sat, sat** sitzen; sich setzen I **sit down** sich hinsetzen I **sit up** sich aufsetzen III 2 (40)

°**site** [saɪt]: **social networking site** *eine Website zur Bildung und Unterhaltung sozialer Netzwerke* **work site** Arbeitsort **World Heritage Site** Welterbestätte

situation [ˌsɪtʃuˈeɪʃn] Situation III 1 (21)

six [sɪks] sechs I

size [saɪz] Größe II **What size tea would you like?** Wie groß soll der/dein Tee sein? II

skates [skeɪts] Inlineskates I

skating [ˈskeɪtɪŋ] Inlineskaten, Rollschuhlaufen I

skill [skɪl] Fertigkeit II **skills file** *Übersicht über Lern- und Arbeitstechniken* I **study skills** *Lern- und Arbeitstechniken* I

skirt [skɜːt] Rock II

sky [skaɪ] Himmel II

skyline [ˈskaɪlaɪn] Skyline, Horizont III 1 (11)

°**skype** [skaɪp] per Skype telefonieren

slave [sleɪv] Sklave, Sklavin III 3 (45)

slavery [ˈsleɪvəri] Sklaverei III 3 (45)

sleep [sliːp]:
1. **(slept, slept)** schlafen I
2. Schlaf III 2 (31)

sleepover [ˈsliːpəʊvə] Schlafparty I

slept [slept] *siehe* **sleep**

slippery [ˈslɪpəri] rutschig, glatt III 4 (78)

slow [sləʊ] langsam I **be slow** nachgehen *(Uhr)* III 1 (19) **slow motion** Zeitlupe III 3 (59)

small [smɔːl] klein I **small talk** Smalltalk *(spontan geführtes Gespräch in umgangssprachlichem Ton)* III 1 (13)

smell [smel] riechen I **smell sth.** an etwas riechen I **smell good** gut riechen II

smile [smaɪl]:
1. lächeln I **smile at sb.** jn. anlächeln I
2. Lächeln III 4 (78)

smiley [ˈsmaɪli] Smiley I

smoke [sməʊk] rauchen III 4 (71)

smuggle [ˈsmʌgl] schmuggeln I

smuggler [ˈsmʌglə] Schmuggler/in I

smuggling [ˈsmʌglɪŋ] der Schmuggel, das Schmuggeln I

snack [snæk] Snack, Imbiss I

snake [sneɪk] Schlange I

sneeze [sniːz] niesen I

snow [snəʊ] Schnee II

°**snowy** [ˈsnəʊi] verschneit

so [səʊ]:
1. also; deshalb, daher I
2. **so cool/nice** so cool/nett I **so far** bis jetzt; bis hierher II
▶ S. 182 such/so
3. **So?** Und? / Na und? I
4. **so that / so** sodass, damit II

social [ˈsəʊʃl]: **social media** *(pl)* soziale Medien III 5 (83) °**social services** *(pl)* Sozialwesen

sock [sɒk] Socke II

sofa [ˈsəʊfə] Sofa I

soft [sɒft] weich I **in a soft voice** sanft II

softly [ˈsɒftli] sanft III 5 (94) **she sang softly** sie sang leise II

sold [səʊld] *siehe* **sell**

soldier [ˈsəʊldʒə] Soldat/in III 3 (48)

solo [ˈsəʊləʊ] Solo- II

solve [sɒlv] lösen III 3 (59)

some [sʌm] einige, ein paar; etwas I

somebody [ˈsʌmbədi] jemand I

someone [ˈsʌmwʌn] jemand I

something [ˈsʌmθɪŋ] etwas I

sometimes [ˈsʌmtaɪmz] manchmal I

son [sʌn] Sohn II

song [sɒŋ] Lied, Song I

soon [suːn] bald I

sore [sɔː] wund II **have a sore throat** Halsschmerzen haben II

sorry [ˈsɒri]: **(I'm) sorry.** Tut mir leid. / Entschuldigung. I **I'm sorry about …** Es tut mir leid wegen … I

°**soul** [səʊl] Seele

sound [saʊnd]:
1. klingen, sich anhören I
2. Geräusch; Klang I
°3. Ton

soup [suːp] Suppe I

south [saʊθ] Süden; nach Süden; südlich III 1 (11) **southbound** [ˈsaʊθbaʊnd] Richtung Süden III 1 (18) **south-east** [ˌsaʊθ‿ˈiːst] Südosten; nach Südosten; südöstlich III 1 (11) **southern** [ˈsʌðən] südlich, Süd- III 4 (66)

south-west [ˌsaʊθˈwest] Südwesten; nach Südwesten; südwestlich III 1 (11)

souvenir [ˌsuːvəˈnɪə] Andenken, Souvenir II

spaghetti [spəˈgeti] Spagetti I

Spanish [ˈspænɪʃ] spanisch II

speak [spiːk], **spoke, spoken** sprechen I; reden II **speak to sb.** mit jm. sprechen II

speaker [ˈspiːkə] Sprecher/in I; Redner/in II

special [ˈspeʃl] besondere(r, s) II

speech [spiːtʃ]:
1. *(offizielle)* Rede II
2. **part of speech** Wortart III 2 (32)

°**speech bubble** [ˈspiːtʃ bʌbl] Sprechblase

speed [spiːd] Geschwindigkeit III 1 (22)

°**speed sth. up** [ˌspiːd‿ˈʌp] etwas beschleunigen

spell [spel] buchstabieren I

spelling [ˈspelɪŋ] Rechtschreibung; Schreibweise III 1 (17)

spend [spend], **spent, spent**: **spend time (on)** Zeit verbringen (mit) **spend money (on)** Geld ausgeben (für) III 5 (84)

spent [spent] *siehe* **spend**
spin around [ˌspɪn‿ə'raʊnd], **spun, spun** sich (im Kreis) drehen; herumwirbeln III 4 (77)
°**spirit** ['spɪrɪt] Geist, Seele
splash sb. [splæʃ] jn. nass spritzen III 2 (42)
split screen [splɪt 'skriːn] geteilter Bildschirm; Bildschirm(auf)teilung III 5 (87)
spoke [spəʊk] *siehe* **speak**
spoken [spəʊkn] *siehe* **speak**
spoon [spuːn] Löffel II °**a spoonful of sth.** ['spuːnfʊl] ein Esslöffel (voll) etwas
sport [spɔːt] Sport; Sportart I **do sport** Sport treiben I
sportsperson ['spɔːtspɜːsn] Sportler/in III 3 (48)
spot [spɒt] Fleck, Punkt I
spread [spred], **spread, spread** (sich) ausbreiten, verbreiten III 3 (61)
spring [sprɪŋ] Frühling I
spun [spʌn] *siehe* **spin**
square kilometre, sq km [skweə] Quadratkilometer II
stadium ['steɪdiəm] Stadion III 3 (58)
stage [steɪdʒ] Bühne II °**stage directions** *(pl)* Regieanweisungen
stairs *(pl)* [steəz] Treppe; Treppenstufen II
stall [stɔːl] (Markt-)Stand II
stamp [stæmp] Stempel II
stand [stænd], **stood, stood** stehen; sich (hin)stellen II **stand up** aufstehen III 2 (40)
standard ['stændəd] Standard; Standard- III 4 (75)
star [stɑː]:
1. (Film-, Pop-)Star I
2. Stern III 2 (40) °**shooting star** Sternschnuppe
stare (at sb./sth.) [steə] (jn./etwas an) starren III 4 (74)
°**starfleet** ['stɑːfliːt] Sternenflotte
start [stɑːt] anfangen, beginnen I
starving ['stɑːvɪŋ]: **be starving** einen Riesenhunger haben III 4 (74)
state [steɪt] Staat III 4 (68)
°**statement** ['steɪtmənt] Aussage
station ['steɪʃn] Bahnhof II
stay [steɪ] bleiben I; *(vorübergehend)* wohnen, übernachten III 1 (12) **stay in touch (with sb.)** (mit jm.) Kontakt halten; (mit jm.) in Verbindung bleiben II **stay up late** lang aufbleiben II
steal [stiːl], **stole, stolen** stehlen III 4 (68)
°**steel** [stiːl] Stahl
steep [stiːp] steil III 2 (35)
steer [stɪə] steuern, lenken I
step [step]:
1. Schritt I
2. Stufe III 1 (14)
stick [stɪk]:
1. Stock III 2 (34)
2. **(stuck, stuck) stick sth. into sth.** etwas in etwas stechen, stecken II
sticky ['stɪki] klebrig II
still [stɪl]:
1. (immer) noch I
2. trotzdem, dennoch II
°3. Standbild
stole [stəʊl] *siehe* **steal**
stolen [stəʊln] *siehe* **steal**
stomach ['stʌmək] Magen II
stone [stəʊn] Stein II
stood [stʊd] *siehe* **stand**
stop [stɒp]:
1. anhalten, stoppen I **Stop it!** *(infml)* Hör auf (damit)! / Lass das! II
2. Halt; Station, Haltestelle II
storm [stɔːm] Sturm, Unwetter, Gewitter II °**take the world by storm** die Welt im Sturm erobern
story ['stɔːri] Geschichte, Erzählung I
°**stowaway** ['stəʊəweɪ] blinde(r) Passagier/in
straight on [streɪt‿'ɒn] geradeaus weiter II
strange [streɪndʒ] seltsam, komisch I
strawberry ['strɔːbəri] Erdbeere II
stream [striːm] Bach III 4 (79)
street [striːt] Straße I **at 14 Dean Street** in der Deanstraße 14 **in Dean Street** in der Dean Street I °**line the streets** die Straßen säumen **street artist** Straßenkünstler/in II
stress [stres]:
1. Betonung III 1 (13) **stress mark** Betonungszeichen III 1 (13)
°2. betonen
°**striker** ['straɪkə] Angreifer/in, Stürmer/in
strong [strɒŋ] stark, kräftig II
structure ['strʌktʃə]:
1. strukturieren, gliedern III 3 (58)
°2. Struktur, Gliederung
stuck [stʌk] *siehe* **stick**
student ['stjuːdənt] Schüler/in; Student/in I
studio ['stjuːdiəʊ] Studio I
study ['stʌdi] studieren; untersuchen, beobachten; lernen III 2 (30) **study skills** *Lern- und Arbeitstechniken* I **study poster** Lernposter II
stuff [stʌf] Zeug, Kram III 3 (46)
°**stunning** ['stʌnɪŋ] fantastisch, atemberaubend
stupid ['stjuːpɪd] dumm, blöd III 2 (34)
°**style** [staɪl] Stil
sub-clause ['sʌbklɔːz] Nebensatz I
subject ['sʌbdʒɪkt], ['sʌbdʒekt]:
1. Schulfach I
2. Subjekt II
°**substitute** ['sʌbstɪtjuːt] Ersatzspieler/in
subtitle ['sʌbtaɪtl] Untertitel I
success [sək'ses] Erfolg III 3 (51)
°**successful** [sək'sesfl] erfolgreich
such [sʌtʃ]: **such a** so ein/e …; solch ein/e … III 2 (41)
▶ S. 182 such/so
suddenly ['sʌdnli] plötzlich, auf einmal I
°**sugar** ['ʃʊgə] Zucker
suggest sth. (to sb.) [sə'dʒest] (jm.) etwas vorschlagen III 4 (69) **Dad suggested that we go to the cinema.** Papa schlug vor, ins Kino zu gehen.
°**suggestion** [sə'dʒestʃən] Vorschlag
suit [suːt] Anzug III 4 (71)
°**sum sth. up** [ˌsʌm‿'ʌp] etwas zusammenfassen
summer ['sʌmə] Sommer I
summit ['sʌmɪt] Gipfel III 2 (38)
sun [sʌn] Sonne I
Sunday ['sʌndeɪ], ['sʌndi] Sonntag I
°**sunflower** ['sʌnflaʊə] Sonnenblume
sung [sʌŋ] *siehe* **sing**
sunglasses *(pl)* ['sʌnglɑːsɪz] (eine) Sonnenbrille II
sunny ['sʌni] sonnig II
sunshine ['sʌnʃaɪn] Sonnenschein III 3 (57)
°**supporter** [sə'pɔːtə] Befürworter/in
sure [ʃʊə], [ʃɔː] sicher II **make sure that …** sich vergewissern, dass …; darauf achten, dass …; dafür sorgen, dass … II
surface ['sɜːfɪs] Oberfläche III 3 (60)
surprise [sə'praɪz]:
1. Überraschung II
°2. überraschen
surprised [sə'praɪzd] überrascht I
survive [sə'vaɪv] überleben III 3 (53)
swam [swæm] *siehe* **swim**
°**swap** [swɒp] tauschen
sweet [swiːt] süß II
sweets *(pl)* [swiːts] Süßigkeiten II
swim [swɪm], **swam, swum** schwimmen I
swimmer ['swɪmə] Schwimmer/in I
swimming pool ['swɪmɪŋ puːl] Schwimmbad, Schwimmbecken I
sword [sɔːd] Schwert I
swum [swʌm] *siehe* **swim**
syllable ['sɪləbl] Silbe II **one-/two-syllable** ein-/zweisilbig II
symbol ['sɪmbl] Symbol II

T

table ['teɪbl]:
1. Tisch I **table tennis** Tischtennis II
2. Tabelle I
take [teɪk], **took, taken** nehmen, mitnehmen; (weg-, hin)bringen I; *(Zeit)* brauchen; dauern II **take notes (on/about sth.)** (sich) Notizen machen (über/zu etwas) *(beim Lesen oder Zuhören)* II **take part in sth.** an etwas teilnehmen II **take photos** fotografieren, Fotos machen I **take place** stattfinden III 3 (61) **take sb. by the arm** jn. am

Arm nehmen II **take sth. off** etwas ausziehen *(Kleidung)*; etwas absetzen *(Hut, Helm)* II **take sth. out** etwas herausnehmen II **°take the world by storm** die Welt im Sturm erobern **°take turns (to do sth.)** sich abwechseln (etwas zu tun)
► S. 177 off

takeaway ['teɪkəweɪ] *Restaurant/Imbissgeschäft, das auch Essen zum Mitnehmen verkauft; Essen zum Mitnehmen* II

taken ['teɪkən] *siehe* **take**

talented ['tæləntɪd] begabt, talentiert II

talk [tɔːk]:
1. Vortrag, Referat, Rede I **give a talk (about)** einen Vortrag / eine Rede halten (über) I
2. talk (to) reden (mit), sich unterhalten (mit) I

tall [tɔːl] groß *(Person)*; hoch *(Gebäude, Baum)* II

tap [tæp]:
1. tippen, *(vorsichtig)* klopfen II **°she taps her foot** sie wippt mit dem Fuß
2. *(leichtes)* Klopfen III 1 (20)

°tartan ['tɑːtn] Schottenkaro, -stoff

task [tɑːsk] Aufgabe I

taste [teɪst] schmecken I

tasty ['teɪsti] lecker II

taught [tɔːt] *siehe* **teach**

taxi ['tæksi] Taxi II

tea [tiː] Tee I; *leichte Nachmittags- oder Abendmahlzeit* II

teach [tiːtʃ], **taught, taught** unterrichten, lehren III 5 (84) **teach sb. to do sth.** jm. etwas beibringen, etwas zu tun III 5 (84)

teacher ['tiːtʃə] Lehrer/in I

team [tiːm] Team, Mannschaft I

tear [tɪə] Träne II

teaspoon ['tiːspuːn] Teelöffel II

teeth [tiːθ] *Plural von* **tooth**

telephone ['telɪfəʊn] Telefon I **telephone box** Telefonzelle III 1 (15)

tell [tel], **told, told**: **tell sb. about sth.** jm. von etwas erzählen; jm. über etwas berichten I **tell sb. the way (to …)** jm. den Weg (nach …) beschreiben II **tell sb. (not) to do sth.** jn. auffordern, etwas (nicht) zu tun; jm. sagen, dass er/sie etwas (nicht) tun soll III 2 (35)

temperature ['temprətʃə] Temperatur, Fieber II **have a temperature** Fieber haben II

ten [ten] zehn I

tennis ['tenɪs] Tennis I **table tennis** Tischtennis II

tense [tens] *(grammatische)* Zeit, Tempus III 1 (21)

tension ['tenʃn] Spannung, Anspannung III 5 (94)

tent [tent] Zelt II

term [tɜːm] Trimester II

°terrace ['terəs] Stehtribüne

terrible ['terəbl] schrecklich, furchtbar II

territory ['terətri] Revier, Territorium III 5 (92)

test ['test]:
1. Test, (Klassen-)Arbeit III 1 (10) **°test match** internationales Spiel *(bei Cricket und Rugby)*
2. testen, prüfen III 2 (34)

text [tekst]:
1. Text I
2. *(auch* **text message***)* SMS II
3. text sb. jm. eine SMS schicken I

than [ðæn], [ðən]: **bigger than** größer als II

thank sb. [θæŋk] jm. danken III 4 (71)

thanks ['θæŋks] Danke. I **thanks to Maya** dank Maya II

Thank you. ['θæŋk juː] Danke. I **Thank you for listening.** Danke, dass ihr zugehört habt. / Danke für eure Aufmerksamkeit. II

that [ðæt], [ðət]:
1. it shows that … es zeigt, dass … I
2. that group die Gruppe (dort), jene Gruppe I
3. that's das ist I
4. der/die/das; die *(Relativpronomen)* II
5. that's why deshalb, darum II

the [ðə] der, die, das; die I

theatre ['θɪətə] Theater II

their [ðeə] ihr I **their first day** ihr erster Tag I

theirs [ðeəz] ihrer, ihre, ihrs II

them [ðem], [ðəm] sie; ihnen I

theme [θiːm] Thema II

themselves [ðəm'selvz] sich III 5 (84)

then [ðen] dann I **just then** genau in dem Moment; gerade dann II

there [ðeə] da, dort; dahin, dorthin I **down there** dort unten II **over there** da drüben, dort drüben II **There are …** Es sind/gibt … I **There's …** Es ist/gibt … I

thermometer [θə'mɒmɪtə] Thermometer II

these [ðiːz] diese, die (hier) I

they [ðeɪ] sie *(Plural)* I **they're (= they are)** sie sind … I

thief [θiːf], *pl* **thieves** [θiːvz] Dieb/in I

thing [θɪŋ] Sache, Ding, Gegenstand I

think [θɪŋk], **thought, thought** denken, glauben I **think of sth.** sich etwas ausdenken; an etwas denken I

third [θɜːd] dritte(r, s) I **third biggest** drittgrößte(r, s) II

thirsty ['θɜːsti]: **be thirsty** durstig sein, Durst haben I

this [ðɪs]:
1. This is … Dies ist … / Das ist … I
2. this place/break/subject dieser Ort / diese Pause / dieses Fach I **this time** dieses Mal II **this afternoon/evening/…** heute Nachmittag/Abend/… II **this year's …** das diesjährige … II

those [ðəʊz] die … dort; jene … I

°though [ðəʊ] obwohl

thought [θɔːt]:
1. Gedanke III 4 (79)
2. *siehe* **think**

thousand ['θaʊznd] Tausend, tausend III 2 (38)
► S. 181 Numbers

three [θriː] drei I

threw [θruː] *siehe* **throw**

throat [θrəʊt] Hals, Kehle II **have a sore throat** Halsschmerzen haben II

through [θruː] durch I

throw [θrəʊ], **threw, thrown** werfen I

thrown [θrəʊn] *siehe* **throw**

thunder ['θʌndə] Donner II

Thursday ['θɜːzdeɪ], ['θɜːzdi] Donnerstag I

ticket ['tɪkɪt] Eintrittskarte I; Fahrkarte I **ticket office** Fahrkartenschalter; Kasse *(für den Verkauf von Eintrittskarten)* III 1 (15)

till [tɪl]: **till 1 o'clock** bis 1 Uhr I **not till three** erst um drei, nicht vor drei II

time [taɪm]:
1. Zeit; Uhrzeit I **at one time** zur selben Zeit, gleichzeitig III 1 (15) **feeding time** Fütterungszeit I **free time** Freizeit, freie Zeit I **free-time activities** Freizeitaktivitäten I **What time is it?** Wie spät ist es? I
2. Mal II **this time** dieses Mal II

timetable ['taɪmteɪbl]:
1. Stundenplan I
2. Fahrplan III 1 (12)

tin [tɪn] Dose II

°tiny ['taɪni] winzig

tip [tɪp] Tipp I

tired ['taɪəd] müde I **be tired of sth.** genug von etwas haben; etwas satt haben III 5 (88)

title ['taɪtl] Titel, Überschrift I

to [tu], [tə]:
1. zu, nach I **count to ten** bis zehn zählen **from … to …** von … bis … I **to the front** nach vorne II
2. Nice to meet you. Freut mich, dich/euch/Sie kennenzulernen. I
3. quarter to eleven Viertel vor elf (10.45 / 22.45) I
4. um zu II

toast [təʊst] Toast(brot) III 2 (41)

°tobacco [tə'bækəʊ] Tabak

today [tə'deɪ] heute I

toe [təʊ] Zeh II

together [tə'geðə] zusammen I

toilet ['tɔɪlət] Toilette I

told [təʊld] *siehe* **tell**

tomato [tə'mɑːtəʊ], *pl* **tomatoes** Tomate II

tomorrow [tə'mɒrəʊ] morgen II **tomorrow morning** morgen früh, morgen Vormittag II

tongue [tʌŋ] Zunge II

tongue-twister ['tʌŋˌtwɪstə] Zungenbrecher II

tonight [tə'naɪt] heute Nacht, heute Abend III 2 (30)

too [tuː]:
1. auch I
2. **too late/cold/big/…** zu spät/kalt/groß/… I

took [tʊk] *siehe* **take**
°**tool** [tuːl] Werkzeug
tooth [tuːθ], *pl* **teeth** [tiːθ] Zahn II
toothache ['tuːθeɪk]: **have a toothache** Zahnschmerzen haben II
top [tɒp]:
1. Spitze II **at the top (of)** oben, am oberen Ende, an der Spitze (von) II **on top of each other** übereinander, aufeinander III 1 (15)
2. Spitzen-, oberste(r, s) I
3. Top, Oberteil I

topic ['tɒpɪk] Thema, Themengebiet II **topic sentence** Satz, der in das Thema eines Absatzes einführt III 2 (38)
torch [tɔːtʃ]:
1. Taschenlampe II
2. Fackel II

tortoise ['tɔːtəs] (Land-)Schildkröte III 1 (15)
°**toss** [tɒs] schleudern
total ['təʊtl]: **a total of …** eine Gesamtsumme von …; insgesamt III 2 (38)
touch [tʌtʃ]:
1. berühren, anfassen I
2. **get in touch (with sb.)** (mit jm.) Kontakt aufnehmen; sich (mit jm.) in Verbindung setzen II **stay in touch (with sb.)** (mit jm.) Kontakt halten; (mit jm.) in Verbindung bleiben II

tough [tʌf] (knall)hart, schwierig III 5 (89)
tour ['tʊər]:
1. **tour (of)** Rundgang, Rundfahrt, Reise (durch) I
°2. auf Tournee gehen; bereisen

tourist ['tʊərɪst] Tourist/in I
towards [tə'wɔːdz]: **towards the station / John** auf den Bahnhof / John zu, in Richtung Bahnhof / John III 1 (20)
tower ['taʊə] Turm I
town [taʊn] Stadt I **town hall** Rathaus II
toy [tɔɪ] Spielzeug I
tractor ['træktə] Traktor II
trade [treɪd] Handel III 3 (52)
°**trader** ['treɪdə] Kaufmann, Händler
°**tradition** [trə'dɪʃn] Tradition
traditional [trə'dɪʃənl] traditionell II
traffic ['træfɪk] Verkehr III 4 (77) **traffic light** (Verkehrs-)Ampel *(oft auch:* **traffic lights** *(pl))* III 4 (77)
trail [treɪl] Weg, Pfad III 4 (78)
train [treɪn]:
1. Zug II **get on a train** in einen Zug einsteigen II
2. trainieren II

trainer ['treɪnə] Turnschuh I
training ['treɪnɪŋ] Training(sstunde) I
translate [træns'leɪt] übersetzen II
translation [træns'leɪʃn] Übersetzung III 2 (32)
transparency [træns'pærənsi] Folie *(für Projektor)* III 5 (92)
travel ['trævl] reisen I
traveller ['trævələ] Reisende(r) I
tread [tred], **trod, trodden**: **tread on sb.'s toes** jm. auf die Füße/Zehen treten *(auch im übertragenen Sinne)* III 5 (89)
°**treasure** ['treʒə] Schatz
tree [triː] Baum I
trials *(pl)* ['traɪəlz] Turnier, Wettkampf III 5 (83)
triangle ['traɪæŋgl] Dreieck III 3 (53)
trick [trɪk] Kunststück, Trick II
trip [trɪp] Ausflug; Reise I **go on day trips** Tagesausflüge machen II
trod [trɒd] *siehe* **tread**
trodden [trɒdn] *siehe* **tread**
trophy ['trəʊfi] Pokal; Trophäe I
trouble ['trʌbl]: **be in trouble** in Schwierigkeiten sein; Ärger kriegen I **get into trouble** in Schwierigkeiten geraten, Ärger kriegen III 2 (40)
trousers *(pl)* ['traʊzəz] Hose II
true [truː] wahr I
°**trust** [trʌst] Stiftung
truth [truːθ] Wahrheit II
try [traɪ]:
1. (aus)probieren; versuchen I
2. Versuch III 1 (20)

T-shirt ['tiːʃɜːt] T-Shirt I
tube [tjuːb]: **the Tube** die U-Bahn *(in London)* III 1 (12) **on the Tube** in der U-Bahn III 1 (12)
Tuesday ['tjuːzdeɪ], ['tjuːzdi] Dienstag I **on Tuesday** am Dienstag I
tulip ['tjuːlɪp] Tulpe II
tunnel ['tʌnl] Tunnel II
°**Turkish** ['tɜːkɪʃ] Türkisch; türkisch
turn [tɜːn]:
1. **(It's) my turn.** Ich bin dran / an der Reihe. I °**take turns** sich abwechseln *(etwas zu tun)*
2. sich umdrehen III 1 (20) **turn around** sich umdrehen; wenden, umdrehen I **turn round** sich umdrehen III 1 (20) **turn to sb.** sich jm. zuwenden; sich an jn. wenden II
3. **turn sth. down** etwas leiser stellen III 1 (20) **turn sth. off** etwas ausschalten II **turn sth. on** etwas einschalten I **turn sth. up** etwas lauter stellen III 1 (20) ▶ S. 177 off
4. **turn left/right** (nach) links/rechts abbiegen II
5. **turn red/brown/cold** rot/braun/kalt werden III 4 (77) ▶ S. 177 (to) turn

TV [ˌtiː'viː] Fernsehen, Fernsehgerät I **on TV** im Fernsehen III 1 (20)
twelve [twelv] zwölf I
twice [twaɪs] zweimal II
twins *(pl)* [twɪnz] Zwillinge I
two [tuː] zwei I **two-syllable** zweisilbig II

U

°**ugly** ['ʌgli] hässlich
UK [ˌjuː 'keɪ]: **the UK** das Vereinigte Königreich III 1 (14)
umbrella [ʌm'brelə] Regenschirm I
uncle ['ʌŋkl] Onkel I
under ['ʌndə] unter I
underground [ˌʌndə'graʊnd] unterirdisch, unter der Erde III 2 (32) **the underground** die U-Bahn III 1 (12)
underline [ˌʌndə'laɪn] unterstreichen II
understand [ˌʌndə'stænd], **understood, understood** verstehen I
understood [ˌʌndə'stʊd] *siehe* **understand**
unfair [ʌn'feə] unfair, ungerecht III 2 (42)
unhappy [ʌn'hæpi] unglücklich II
uniform ['juːnɪfɔːm] Uniform I
°**union** ['juːniən] Vereinigung, Union
unit ['juːnɪt] Kapitel, Lektion I
united [ju'naɪtɪd] vereinigt **the United Kingdom** [juˌnaɪtɪd 'kɪŋdəm] das Vereinigte Königreich III 1 (14)
°**unless …** [ən'les] es sei denn, …
unpack [ˌʌn'pæk] auspacken III 4 (74)
until [ən'tɪl] bis II **not until** erst, nicht vor III 3 (51)
unusual [ʌn'juːʒuəl] ungewöhnlich III 5 (83)
up [ʌp] hinauf, herauf; (nach) oben I **up and down** auf und ab; rauf und runter I **up here** hier oben; nach hier oben II **up to** bis (zu) II **What's up?** Was gibt's? / Was ist los? III 4 (78)
uphill [ˌʌp'hɪl] bergauf III 2 (38)
upstairs [ˌʌp'steəz] oben; nach oben *(im Haus)* I
upstream [ˌʌp'striːm] flussaufwärts III 2 (38)
us [ʌs], [əs] uns I
use [juːz] benutzen, verwenden I
usual ['juːʒuəl] gewöhnlich, üblich III 5 (83)
usually ['juːʒuəli] meistens, normalerweise, gewöhnlich I

V

valley ['væli] Tal II
°**vampire** ['væmpaɪə] Vampir/in
van [væn] Transporter, Lieferwagen III 4 (77)
vegetables *(pl)* ['vedʒtəblz] Gemüse I
vegetarian [ˌvedʒə'teəriən]:
1. Vegetarier/in II
2. vegetarisch II

verb [vɜːb] Verb III 1 (12)
verse [vɜːs] Vers, Strophe II
very ['veri] sehr I
video ['vɪdiəʊ] Video I
video camera ['vɪdiəʊ ˌkæmərə] Videokamera I

view (of) [vjuː] Aussicht, Blick (auf) II **point of view (on sth.)** Standpunkt (in/über/zu etwas) III 2 (42)
village ['vɪlɪdʒ] Dorf I
visa ['viːzə] Visum III 4 (68)
visit ['vɪzɪt]:
1. besuchen I
2. Besuch I

visitor ['vɪzɪtə] Besucher/in, Gast II
vocabulary [və'kæbjələri] Vokabelverzeichnis, Wörterverzeichnis I
voice [vɔɪs] Stimme I **in a loud voice** mit lauter Stimme II °**voice-over** Offstimme, Kommentar
volleyball ['vɒlibɔːl] Volleyball I
volunteer [ˌvɒlən'tɪə]:
1. sich freiwillig melden; freiwillig/ehrenamtlich arbeiten *(unbezahlt)* III 2 (37)
2. Freiwillige(r), Ehrenamtliche(r) III 5 (84)

°**vote** [vəʊt] stimmen; abstimmen
vowel ['vaʊəl] Vokal, Selbstlaut II

W

waist [weɪst] Taille II
wait (for) [weɪt] warten (auf) I **wait a minute** Warte einen Moment. / Moment mal. I **I can't wait to see ...** Ich kann es kaum erwarten, ... zu sehen II
wake up [ˌweɪk_'ʌp], **woke, woken:**
1. aufwachen I
2. **wake sb. up** jn. (auf)wecken II

walk [wɔːk]:
1. Spaziergang I **go for a walk** spazieren gehen, einen Spaziergang machen I
2. (zu Fuß) gehen I **walk around** herumlaufen, umherspazieren II **walk on** weitergehen II **walk the dog** mit dem Hund rausgehen, den Hund ausführen III 4 (77)

wall [wɔːl] Mauer; Wand II
wander ['wɒndə] herumlaufen; herumirren II
want [wɒnt]: **want sth.** etwas (haben) wollen I **want to do sth.** etwas tun wollen I
war [wɔː] Krieg III 4 (189) °**be at war** sich im Krieg befinden; Krieg führen
warm [wɔːm] warm I
warning ['wɔːnɪŋ] Warnung III 2 (36)
was [wɒz], [wəz]:
1. *siehe* **be**
2. **I wish I was there.** Ich wünschte, ich wäre da. II

wash [wɒʃ] waschen, wischen III 2 (42) **wash the dishes** *(pl)* das Geschirr abwaschen, spülen II
watch [wɒtʃ]:
1. Armbanduhr I
2. sich etwas anschauen; beobachten I **watch TV** fernsehen I **Watch out!** Pass auf! / Vorsicht! I

°**watchdog** ['wɒtʃdɒg] Wächter/in, Aufpasser/in
water ['wɔːtə] Wasser I
waterfall ['wɔːtəfɔːl] Wasserfall II
°**waterfront** ['wɔːtəfrʌnt] Hafenviertel *(oft modernisiert und bewohnt)*
°**waterproofs** *(pl)* ['wɔːtəpruːfs] wasserdichte Kleidung
wave [weɪv] Welle II
way [weɪ]:
1. Weg I **ask sb. the way** jn. nach dem Weg fragen II **No way!** Auf keinen Fall! / Kommt nicht in Frage! III 1 (20) **on the way to ...** auf dem Weg zu/nach ... I **tell sb. the way (to ...)** jm. den Weg (nach ...) beschreiben II °**There's no way you'll ...** Unmöglich, dass du ... **this/that way** hier entlang/dort entlang; in die Richtung II
2. Art und Weise III 3 (51) **in an interesting way** auf eine interessante Art und Weise III 3 (51) **in this way** auf diese Weise III 3 (51) **the way he ...** die Art und Weise, wie er ... III 3 (51) **in some/many ways** in mancher/vielerlei Hinsicht III 3 (51)

▶ S. 185 way
we [wiː] wir I
wear [weə], **wore, worn** tragen *(Kleidung)* I
weather ['weðə] Wetter II
website ['websaɪt] Website I
°**wedding** ['wedɪŋ] Hochzeit
Wednesday ['wenzdeɪ], ['wenzdi] Mittwoch I
wee [wiː] *(Scottish, infml)* klein III 5 (83)
week [wiːk] Woche I **a three-week holiday** ein dreiwöchiger Urlaub III 3 (51)
weekend [ˌwiːk'end] Wochenende I **at the weekend** am Wochenende I
weigh [weɪ] wiegen I
weird [wɪəd] seltsam, komisch III 4 (74)
welcome sb. (to) ['welkəm] jn. begrüßen (in), jn. willkommen heißen (in) III 4 (76) **Welcome to Plymouth.** Willkommen in Plymouth. I
well [wel]:
1. gut II; *(gesundheitlich)* gut, gesund II **I don't feel well** Ich fühle mich nicht gut. / Mir geht's nicht gut. II
2. **Well, ...** Nun, ... / Also, ... / Na ja, ... I

°**wellies** ['weliz] *(pl, infml)* Gummistiefel
well-known [ˌwel'nəʊn], ['welˌnəʊn] bekannt, wohlbekannt III 3 (48)
Welsh [welʃ] Walisisch; walisisch III 1 (10)
went [went] *siehe* **go**
were [wɜː], [wə] *siehe* **be**
west [west] Westen; nach Westen; westlich III 1 (11) **westbound** ['westbaʊnd] Richtung Westen III 1 (18) **western** ['westən] westlich, West- III 1 (10) **western** ['westən] westlich, West- III 4 (66)
wet [wet] nass I
whale [weɪl] Wal I
what? [wɒt] was? I **What about you?** Und du/ihr? / Und was ist mit dir/euch? I **What about ...?** Wie wäre es mit ...? II **What colour ...?** Welche Farbe ...? I **What is the story about?** Wovon handelt die Geschichte? Worum geht es in der Geschichte? I **What programmes ...?** Welche Programme ...? / Welche Art von Programmen ...? I **What size tea would you like?** Wie groß soll der/dein Tee sein? II **What time is it?** Wie spät ist es? I **What would you like to eat?** Was möchtest du essen? I **What's your name?** Wie heißt du? I **What's for lunch?** Was gibt es zum Mittagessen? I **What's for homework?** Was haben wir als Hausaufgabe auf? I **What's she like?** Wie ist sie? / Wie ist sie so? I **What's up?** Was gibt's? / Was ist los? III 4 (78) **I don't know what to do.** Ich weiß nicht, was ich tun soll. III 2 (42)
▶ S. 183 Question words + to-infinitive
whatever [wɒt'evə] was (auch) immer III 5 (91)
▶ S. 195 whenever etc.
wheel [wiːl]: **big wheel** Riesenrad I
when [wen]:
1. wenn I
2. als I
3. **when?** wann? I

whenever [ˌwen'evə] wann (auch) immer; egal, wann III 5 (91)
▶ S. 195 whenever etc.
where? [weə] wo? / wohin? / woher? I **We had no idea where to go.** Wir hatten keine Ahnung, wohin wir gehen sollten. III 2 (42)
▶ S. 183 Question words + to-infinitive
wherever [weər'evə] wo (auch) immer III 5 (91)
▶ S. 195 whenever etc.
which [wɪtʃ]:
1. **which?** welche(r, s)? I
2. der/die/das; die *(Relativpronomen)* II

while [waɪl]:
1. während II
2. eine Weile, einige Zeit III 1 (20) **for a while** eine Weile, eine Zeit lang III 1 (20)

▶ S. 175 German "während"
whisper ['wɪspə] flüstern II
whistle ['wɪsl]:
1. pfeifen II
2. (Triller-)Pfeife III 1 (24) **blow a whistle** pfeifen (auf der Trillerpfeife) III 1 (24)
3. Pfiff III 5 (94)

white [waɪt] weiß I

whiteboard ['waɪtbɔːd] Whiteboard, Weißwandtafel III 2 (37)
who [huː]:
1. Who is there? Wer ist da? I **Who did you tell?** Wem hast du es erzählt? II **Who does he know?** Wen kennt er? II **I don't know who to ask.** Ich weiß nicht, wen ich fragen kann/soll. III 2 (42)
▶ S. 183 Question words + to-infinitive
2. der/die/das; die (Relativpronomen) II
whoever [huː'evə] wer (auch) immer III 5 (91)
▶ S. 195 whenever etc.
whole [həʊl] ganze(r, s), gesamte(r, s) II
whose? [huːz] wessen? II
why [waɪ] warum I **that's why** deshalb, darum II
°**wicked** ['wɪkɪd] böse, schlecht
wide [waɪd] weit; breit III 2 (40)
wild [waɪld] wild II
°**wildlife** ['waɪldlaɪf] Tier- und Pflanzenwelt
will [wɪl]: **we'll miss the girls (= we will miss the girls)** wir werden die Mädchen verpassen II **I'll have a tea.** Ich nehme einen Tee. *(beim Essen, im Restaurant)* II
win [wɪn], **won, won** gewinnen I
wind [wɪnd] Wind II
window ['wɪndəʊ] Fenster I
windy ['wɪndi] windig II
wing [wɪŋ] Flügel III 1 (24)
winner ['wɪnə] Gewinner/in, Sieger/in I
winter ['wɪntə] Winter I
wise [waɪz] weise II
wish [wɪʃ]:
1. Wunsch I **make a wish** sich etwas wünschen I
2. wünschen II **I wish I was there.** Ich wünschte, ich wäre da. II
°**witch** [wɪtʃ] Hexe
with [wɪð]
1. mit I
2. bei I
without [wɪ'ðaʊt] ohne I
woke [wəʊk] *siehe* **wake**
woken [wəʊkən] *siehe* **wake**
woman ['wʊmən], *pl* **women** ['wɪmɪn] Frau I
won [wʌn] *siehe* **win**
wonder ['wʌndə] sich fragen, gern wissen wollen III 2 (34)
°**wonderful** ['wʌndəfl] wunderbar
won't [wəʊnt]: **she won't come (= she will not come)** sie wird nicht kommen II
wood [wʊd] Holz II
wooden ['wʊdn] hölzern; Holz- III 2 (40)
word [wɜːd] Wort I **May I have a word with you?** Kann ich Sie kurz sprechen? II **word order** Wortstellung I
wordbank ['wɜːdˌbæŋk] „Wortspeicher" I
wore [wɔː] *siehe* **wear**
work [wɜːk]:
1. arbeiten I °**work sth. out** etwas herausfinden/herausarbeiten
2. Arbeit I
3. funktionieren III 1 (19)
workbook ['wɜːkbʊk] Arbeitsheft I
worker ['wɜːkə] Arbeiter/in II
worksheet ['wɜːkʃiːt] Arbeitsblatt II
workshop ['wɜːkʃɒp] Werkstatt III 2 (30); Workshop, Lehrgang II
world [wɜːld] Welt II **in the world** auf der Welt II **natural world** (Welt der) Natur III 2 (31) °**take the world by storm** die Welt im Sturm erobern **World Cup** Weltmeisterschaft III 3 (55) °**World Heritage Site** Welterbestätte
worm [wɜːm] Wurm I
worn [wɔːn] *siehe* **wear**
worried ['wʌrid] besorgt, beunruhigt I
worry (about) ['wʌri] sich Sorgen machen (wegen, um) II
worse [wɜːs] schlechter, schlimmer II
worst [wɜːst] der/die/das schlechteste/schlimmste …; am schlechtesten/schlimmsten II
worth [wɜːθ] wert III 1 (16)
would [wʊd]: **I would choose Sam** ich würde Sam wählen II **What would you like to eat?** Was möchtest du essen? I **I'd (= I would) like …** Ich möchte … I
write [raɪt], **wrote, written** schreiben I **write sth. down** etwas aufschreiben II
writer ['raɪtə] Schreiber/in III 4 (69); Schriftsteller/in III 4 (69)
written ['rɪtn] *siehe* **write**
wrong [rɒŋ]:
1. falsch, verkehrt I **No, that's wrong.** Nein, das ist falsch. / Nein, das stimmt nicht. I
2. sb. is wrong jemand irrt sich; jemand hat Unrecht I
3. What's wrong with you? Was fehlt dir?; Was ist los mit dir? II
wrote [rəʊt] *siehe* **write**

Y

yacht [jɒt] Jacht III 5 (83)
year [jɪə]:
1. Jahr I **last/next year's …** das … vom letzten/nächsten Jahr II **this year's …** das diesjährige … II
2. Jahrgang(sstufe) I
yellow ['jeləʊ] gelb I
yes [jes] ja I **Yes, that's right.** Ja, das ist richtig. / Ja, das stimmt. I
yesterday ['jestədeɪ], ['jestədi] gestern I
yet [jet]: **not … yet** noch nicht I **Have you … yet?** Hast du schon …? II
yoga ['jəʊgə] Yoga I
yoghurt ['jɒgət] Joghurt I
you [juː]:
1. du; Sie; ihr; dir; dich; euch; Ihnen I
2. man III 1 (24)
young [jʌŋ] jung I
your [jɔː], [jə] dein/e; euer/eure; Ihr/Ihre I
yours [jɔːz] deiner, deine, deins; eurer, eure, eures II
yourself [jɔː'self] dich, dir; sich (bei „Sie") III 5 (84) **about yourself** über dich selbst I **Enjoy yourself.** Viel Spaß! / Amüsiere dich gut! III 5 (GF/167) **Help yourself.** Greif zu! / Bedien dich! III 5 (GF/167)
yourselves [jɔː'selvz] euch; sich (bei „Sie") III 5 (85)
yummy ['jʌmi] *(infml)* lecker I

Z

zone [zəʊn]: **pedestrian zone** Fußgängerzone II
zoo [zuː] Zoo I

Das **German – English Dictionary** enthält den **Lernwortschatz** der Bände 1 bis 3 von *English G Access*.
Es kann dir eine erste Hilfe sein, wenn du vergessen hast, wie etwas auf Englisch heißt.

Wenn du wissen möchtest, wo das entsprechende englische Wort zum ersten Mal in *English G Access* vorkommt, dann kannst du im **English – German Dictionary** (S. 198–220) nachschlagen.

Im **German – English Dictionary** werden folgende **Abkürzungen** verwendet:

sth. = something (etwas) sb. = somebody (jemand) jn. = jemanden jm. = jemandem
pl = *plural* (Mehrzahl) *infml* = *informal* (umgangssprachlich)

▶ Der Pfeil weist auf Kästen im **Vocabulary** (S.172–197) hin, in denen du weitere Informationen zu diesem Wort findest.

A

ab: auf und ab up and down [ˌʌp‿ən ˈdaʊn] **Ab mit euch jetzt!** Off you go now. [ɒf]
abbauen *(Kohle, Erz)* mine [maɪn]
abbiegen: (nach) links/rechts abbiegen turn left/right [tɜːn]
Abend evening [ˈiːvnɪŋ] **am Abend** in the evening **heute Abend** tonight [təˈnaɪt] **zu Abend essen** have dinner [ˈdɪnə]
Abendbrot, Abendessen dinner [ˈdɪnə]
abends in the evening [ˈiːvnɪŋ]
Abenteuer adventure [ədˈventʃə]
aber but [bʌt], [bət] **Aber egal, …** Anyway, … [ˈeniweɪ]
abfahren leave [liːv]
Abfall rubbish [ˈrʌbɪʃ]
Abfalleimer litter bin [ˈlɪtə bɪn]
abgeben: etwas abgeben *(einreichen)* hand sth. in [ˌhænd‿ˈɪn]
abholen: jn. abholen pick sb. up [ˌpɪk‿ˈʌp]
abkühlen: sich abkühlen cool off
Abkürzung *(Kurzform eines Wortes)* abbreviation [əˌbriːviˈeɪʃn]
Abneigungen: Vorlieben und Abneigungen likes and dislikes *(pl)* [ˌlaɪks‿ən ˈdɪslaɪks]
abräumen *(Tisch, Geschirr)* clear [klɪə]
Absatz *(in einem Text)* paragraph [ˈpærəgrɑːf]
Abschluss ending [ˈendɪŋ]
abschreiben copy [ˈkɒpi]
absetzen: etwas absetzen *(Hut, Helm)* take sth. off [ˌteɪk‿ɒf]
▶ S. 177 off
abspielen *(CD usw.)* play [pleɪ]
absuchen: etwas (nach etwas) absuchen scan sth. (for sth.) [skæn]
abwaschen: das Geschirr abwaschen wash the dishes *(pl)* [ˈdɪʃɪz]
acht eight [eɪt]
achten: darauf achten, dass … make sure that …
Achtung *(Respekt)* respect [rɪˈspekt] **Achtung!** *(Aufgepasst!)* Look out!
Acker field [fiːld]
addieren (zu) add (to) [æd]
Adjektiv adjective [ˈædʒɪktɪv]
adoptiert, Adoptiv- adopted [əˈdɒptɪd]
Adresse address [əˈdres]
Adverb adverb [ˈædvɜːb]
Affe monkey [ˈmʌŋki]
ähnlich: etwas/jm. ähnlich similar to sth./sb. [ˈsɪmələ]
Aktivität activity [ækˈtɪvəti]
Akzent accent [ˈæksənt]
albern silly [ˈsɪli]
alle all [ɔːl]; *(jeder)* everyone [ˈevriwʌn], everybody [ˈevribɒdi] **alle anderen** everybody else
▶ S. 195 … else
allein alone [əˈləʊn]; *(ohne Hilfe)* on my/your/their/… own [əʊn]
alleinstehend *(ledig)* single [ˈsɪŋgl]
alles everything [ˈevriθɪŋ]; all [ɔːl] **alles in allem** *(insgesamt)* altogether [ˌɔːltəˈgeðə] **vor allem** especially [ɪˈspeʃli]
Alltags- everyday [ˈevrideɪ]
als 1. *(zeitlich)* when [wen]; *(während)* as [æz], [əz] **als Erstes** first [fɜːst] **als Nächstes** next [nekst] **2. als ob** as if; like *(infml)* **3. als Kind** as a child **4. älter als** older than [ðæn], [ðən]
also 1. *(deshalb, daher)* so [səʊ] **2. Also, …** Well, … [wel]
alt old [əʊld] **Wie alt bist du?** How old are you? **… ist so alt wie du** … is your age [eɪdʒ]
Alter age [eɪdʒ] **… ist in deinem Alter** … is your age [eɪdʒ]
am 1. *(in Ortsangaben)* at [æ], [ət] **am Meer** by the sea [baɪ] **am Telefon** on the phone **2.** *(in Zeitangaben)* **am Abend** in the evening **am Montag/Dienstag/…** on Monday/Tuesday/… **am Morgen** in the morning **am Nachmittag** in the afternoon **am Samstagmorgen** on Saturday afternoon **am Wochenende** at the weekend
Ameise ant [ænt]
Ampel traffic light [ˈtræfɪk laɪt] *(oft auch Plural:)* traffic lights
amtlich, Amts- official [əˈfɪʃl]
amüsieren: sich amüsieren have fun [fʌn] **Amüsier dich gut!** Enjoy yourself.
an 1. *(in Ortsangaben)* at [æ], [ət] **an britischen Schulen** at British schools **2. an sein** *(Radio, Licht usw.)* be on
anbauen *(anpflanzen)* grow [grəʊ]
anbieten offer [ˈɒfə]
andauern *(im Gang sein)* go on
Andenken souvenir [ˌsuːvəˈnɪə]
andere(r, s) other [ˈʌðə] **ein anderer …/eine andere …/ein anderes …** another … [əˈnʌðə] **einer nach dem anderen** one by one **alle anderen** everybody else
▶ S. 195 … else
ändern; sich ändern change [tʃeɪndʒ]
anders *(verschieden)* different [ˈdɪfrənt]
Anfang beginning [bɪˈgɪnɪŋ]
anfangen start [stɑːt]; begin [bɪˈgɪn]
anfangs at first [ət ˈfɜːst]
anfassen touch [tʌtʃ]
anfühlen: sich gut/kalt/… anfühlen feel good/cold/…
angemalt painted [ˈpeɪntɪd]
angreifen attack [əˈtæk]
Angst: jm. Angst machen scare sb. [skeə]
anhalten stop [stɒp]
Anhaltspunkt *(Hinweis)* clue [kluː]
anhören 1. sich etwas anhören listen to sth. [ˈlɪsn]; *(probehalber)* check sth. out [ˌtʃek‿ˈaʊt] *(infml)* **2. sich gut anhören** *(gut klingen)* sound good [saʊnd]
anklopfen (an etwas) knock (on sth.) [nɒk]
ankommen arrive [əˈraɪv]
Ankunft arrival [əˈraɪvl]
anlächeln: jn. anlächeln smile at sb. [smaɪl]
anmalen paint [peɪnt]
anordnen *(in eine bestimmte Ordnung bringen)* arrange [əˈreɪndʒ]
anpflanzen grow [grəʊ]
Anruf phone call [ˈfəʊn kɔːl], *(kurz auch:)* call
anrufen call [kɔːl]; phone [fəʊn]
Anrufer/in caller [ˈkɔːlə]
Ansage *(Durchsage)* announcement [əˈnaʊnsmənt]
anschauen: sich etwas anschauen watch sth. [wɒtʃ]; look at sth. [lʊk]; *(probehalber)* check sth. out [ˌtʃek‿ˈaʊt] *(infml)*

anschließen: sich einem Klub anschließen join a club [dʒɔɪn]
Anschrift address [ə'dres]
ansehen: sich etwas ansehen watch sth. [wɒtʃ]; look at sth. [lʊk]
Anspannung tension ['tenʃn]
Anspitzer sharpener ['ʃɑːpnə]
anstarren: jn./etwas anstarren stare at sb./sth. [steə]
anstelle von instead of [ɪn'sted_əv]
anstellen: sich anstellen *(Schlange stehen)* queue [kjuː]
Anstieg climb [klaɪm]
anstreichen paint [peɪnt]
Antwort answer ['ɑːnsə]
antworten answer ['ɑːnsə]; reply [rɪ'plaɪ]
Anzahl number ['nʌmbə]
Anzeige *(Inserat)* advert ['ædvɜːt]
anziehen: etwas anziehen *(Kleidung)* put sth. on [ˌpʊt_'ɒn] **sich schick anziehen** dress up [ˌdres_'ʌp]
Anzug suit [suːt]
anzünden light [laɪt]
Apfel apple ['æpl]
Apfelsine orange ['ɒrɪndʒ]
Apparat: Bleib/Bleiben Sie am Apparat. Hold on a minute. [ˌhəʊld_'ɒn], *(oft auch kurz:)* Hold on.
April April ['eɪprəl]
Aquarienhaus aquarium [ə'kweəriəm]
Aquarium aquarium [ə'kweəriəm]
Arbeit work [wɜːk]; job [dʒɒb]
arbeiten work [wɜːk]
Arbeiter/in worker ['wɜːkə]
Arbeitsblatt worksheet ['wɜːkʃiːt]
Arbeitsheft workbook ['wɜːkbʊk]
Architekt/in architect ['ɑːkɪtekt]
Ärger kriegen/haben be in trouble ['trʌbl]; get into trouble
arm poor [pɔː], [pʊə]
Arm arm [ɑːm] **jn. am Arm nehmen** take sb. by the arm
Armbanduhr watch [wɒtʃ]
Art: eine Art (von) … a kind of … [kaɪnd] **Art und Weise** way [weɪ] **auf eine interessante Art und Weise** in an interesting way **die Art und Weise, wie er …** the way he …
▶ S. 185 way ("Art und Weise")
Artikel article ['ɑːtɪkl]
Arzt/Ärztin doctor ['dɒktə]
Asche ash [æʃ]; *(sterbliche Überreste)* ashes *(pl)* ['æʃɪz]
Astronaut/in astronaut ['æstrənɔːt]
Atem, Atemzug breath [breθ]
Atlantik: der Atlantik, der Atlantische Ozean the Atlantic (Ocean) [ət'læntɪk]
Attraktion attraction [ə'trækʃn]
auch too [tuː]; also ['ɔːlsəʊ]; as well [əz 'wel] **auch aus Berlin** from Berlin too; also from Berlin **auch nicht** not … either ['aɪðə], ['iːðə] **Ich auch.** Me too. **Ich auch nicht.** Me neither. ['naɪðə], ['niːðə] **wann auch immer** whenever [ˌwen'evə] **was auch immer** whatever [wɒt'evə] **wer auch immer** whoever [huː'evə] **wo auch immer** wherever [weər'evə]
▶ S. 195 whenever, wherever, whatever, whoever
auf on [ɒn] **auf das Boot (hinauf)** onto the boat ['ɒntʊ] **auf dem Bild/Foto** in the picture/photo **auf dem Dachboden** in the attic **auf dem Weg zu/nach …** on the way to … **auf den Bahnhof/Mr Bell zu** towards the station/Mr Bell [tə'wɔːdz] **auf der Landkarte/dem Stadtplan** on the map **auf der Welt** in the world **auf Englisch** in English **auf einmal** suddenly ['sʌdnli] **auf und ab** up and down **Auf keinen Fall!** No way! [ˌnəʊ 'weɪ] **Auf welcher Seite sind wir?** What page are we on? **Auf Wiedersehen.** Goodbye.
aufbewahren keep [kiːp]
aufbleiben: lange aufbleiben stay up late
aufeinander *(übereinander)* on top of each other [iːtʃ_'ʌðə]
auffordern: jn. auffordern, etwas (nicht) zu tun tell sb. (not) to do sth.
Aufgabe task; exercise ['eksəsaɪz]; job
aufgeben give up
Aufgepasst! Look out!
aufgeregt *(gespannt)* excited [ɪk'saɪtɪd]; *(nervös)* nervous ['nɜːvəs]
aufheben 1. *(aufsparen)* keep [kiːp] **2. etwas aufheben** *(vom Boden)* pick sth. up [ˌpɪk_'ʌp]
aufhören: Hör auf (damit)! Stop it! *(infml)*
auflisten list [lɪst]
aufmachen open ['əʊpən]
aufnehmen: (mit jm.) Kontakt aufnehmen get in touch (with sb.) [tʌtʃ]
aufpassen: auf jn. aufpassen look after sb.
aufragen *(Berge, Säulen, Türme, …)* rise up [ˌraɪz_'ʌp]
aufregend *(spannend)* exciting [ɪk'saɪtɪŋ]
aufrufen: die Namen aufrufen call out the names
aufschauen *(hochsehen)* look up [lʊk_'ʌp]
aufschreiben: etwas aufschreiben write sth. down [ˌraɪt 'daʊn]
aufsetzen: etwas aufsetzen *(Hut, Helm)* put sth. on [ˌpʊt_'ɒn] **sich aufsetzen** sit up
aufsparen *(aufheben)* keep [kiːp]
aufspringen jump up [ˌdʒʌmp_'ʌp]
aufstehen get up [ˌget_'ʌp]; stand up
Aufstieg climb [klaɪm]
aufsuchen *(Arzt)* see
auftauchen *(erscheinen)* appear [ə'pɪə]
auftreten *(Künstler/in)* perform [pə'fɔːm]
aufwachen wake up [ˌweɪk_'ʌp]
aufwachsen grow up [ˌgrəʊ_'ʌp]
aufwecken: jn. aufwecken wake sb. up [ˌweɪk_'ʌp]
aufzeichnen *(Musik, Daten)* record [rɪ'kɔːd]
Aufzug lift [lɪft]
Auge eye [aɪ]
Augenblick moment ['məʊmənt]
August August ['ɔːgəst]
aus from [frɒm], [frəm] **aus … heraus / aus … hinaus** out of … ['aʊt_əv] **aus etwas (gemacht) sein** be made of sth.
ausblasen: etwas ausblasen blow sth. out [ˌbləʊ_'aʊt]
ausbrechen: in Tränen ausbrechen burst into tears [bɜːst]
ausbreiten; sich ausbreiten spread [spred]
ausdenken: sich etwas ausdenken think of sth. [θɪŋk]; *(erfinden)* make sth. up
Ausdruck expression [ɪk'spreʃn]; phrase [freɪz]
Auseinandersetzung argument ['ɑːgjumənt]
Ausflug trip [trɪp]
Ausfuhr export ['ekspɔːt]
ausführen: den Hund ausführen walk the dog
ausgeben: Geld ausgeben (für) spend money (on) [spend]
Ausgehverbot: jm. Ausgehverbot erteilen ground sb. [graʊnd]
auskennen: sich mit etwas auskennen know about sth.
auslachen: jn. auslachen laugh at sb.
auspacken unpack [ˌʌn'pæk]
ausprobieren try [traɪ]; check out [ˌtʃek_'aʊt] *(infml)*
auspusten: etwas auspusten blow sth. out [ˌbləʊ_'aʊt]
Ausritt ride [raɪd]
Ausrufezeichen exclamation mark [ˌekskləˈmeɪʃn mɑːk]
ausruhen: sich ausruhen rest [rest]; *(entspannen)* relax [rɪ'læks]
Ausrüstung equipment [ɪ'kwɪpmənt]; kit
Aussage *(Botschaft)* message ['mesɪdʒ]
ausschalten: etwas ausschalten turn sth. off [ˌtɜːn_'ɒf]
▶ S. 177 off
aussehen: glücklich/wütend/… aussehen look happy/angry/…
Außen- *(im Freien)* outdoor ['aʊtdɔː]
Außenseite: die Außenseite the outside [ˌaʊt'saɪd]
außer *(bis auf)* except [ɪk'sept]
Äußere: das Äußere the outside [ˌaʊt'saɪd]
außergewöhnlich extraordinary [ɪk'strɔːdnri]
außerhalb von … outside … [ˌaʊt'saɪd]
Aussicht, Blick (auf) view (of) [vjuː]
Aussprache pronunciation [prəˌnʌnsi'eɪʃn]
aussteigen get off [ˌget_'ɒf] **aus einem Bus/Boot aussteigen** get off a

bus/boat **aus einem Auto aussteigen** get out of a car
▶ S. 177 off
ausstrecken: die Hand ausstrecken reach over [ˌriːtʃ‿ˈəʊvə]
aussuchen: (sich) etwas aussuchen choose sth. [tʃuːz]
auswählen: etwas auswählen choose sth. [tʃuːz]
auswandern emigrate [ˈemɪgreɪt]
ausziehen: etwas ausziehen *(Kleidung)* take sth. off [ˌteɪk‿ɒf]
▶ S. 177 off
Auto car [kɑː] **mit dem Auto fahren** go by car
Autor/in author [ˈɔːθə]

B

Bach stream [striːm]
Bad bath [bɑːθ]
Badezimmer bathroom [ˈbɑːθruːm]
Bahnhof station [ˈsteɪʃn]
Bahnsteig platform [ˈplætfɔːm]
bald soon [suːn] **Bis bald.** See you. **schon bald** before long
Ball ball [bɔːl]
Banane banana [bəˈnɑːnə]
Band *(Musikgruppe)* band [bænd]
Bank *(Geldinstitut)* bank [bæŋk]
Bär bear [beə]
Barkeeper barman, *pl* barmen [ˈbɑːmən]
Bart beard [bɪəd]
Basketball basketball [ˈbɑːskɪtbɔːl]
bauen build [bɪld]
Bauer/Bäuerin farmer [ˈfɑːmə]
Bauernhaus farmhouse [ˈfɑːmhaʊs]
Bauernhof farm [fɑːm]
Baum tree [triː]
Beamte(r), Beamtin official [əˈfɪʃl]
beantworten answer [ˈɑːnsə]
bearbeiten *(Texte, Videos)* edit [ˈedɪt]
Becher mug [mʌg] **ein Becher …** a mug of …
bedecken *(zudecken)* cover [ˈkʌvə]
bedeuten mean [miːn]
Bedeutung meaning [ˈmiːnɪŋ]
bedienen: Bedien dich! *(Greif zu!)* Help yourself.
Bedingungen *(Verhältnisse)* conditions [kənˈdɪʃnz]
beeilen: sich beeilen hurry (up) [ˌhʌri‿ˈʌp]
beenden: etwas beenden finish sth. [ˈfɪnɪʃ]; end sth.
beerdigen bury [ˈberi]
befördern carry [ˈkæri]
befragen: jn. befragen interview sb. [ˈɪntəvjuː]
begabt talented [ˈtæləntɪd]
Beginn beginning [bɪˈgɪnɪŋ]
beginnen start [stɑːt]; begin [bɪˈgɪn]
begraben *(beerdigen)* bury [ˈberi]
Begründung reason [ˈriːzn]
begrüßen: jn. begrüßen (in) *(willkommen heißen)* welcome sb. (to) [ˈwelkəm]
beheimaten: etwas beheimaten be home to sth.
behutsam *(sanft)* gently [ˈdʒentli]
bei *(in Ortsangaben)* at [æt], [ət] **bei den Blackwells zu Hause** at the Blackwells' house **bei Oma** at Grandma's **bei jm. sein** be with sb.
beibringen: jm. beibringen, etwas zu tun teach sb. to do sth. [tiːtʃ]
beide both [bəʊθ] **eins beide** *(Ergebnis im Sport)* one all [ˌwʌn‿ˈɔːl]
Bein leg [leg]
beinahe almost [ˈɔːlməʊst]; nearly [ˈnɪəli]
Beispiel example [ɪgˈzɑːmpl] **zum Beispiel (z.B.)** for example (e.g.) [ˌiː ˈdʒiː] *(from Latin* exempli gratia*)*
beißen bite [baɪt]
bekämpfen: jn. bekämpfen fight sb. [faɪt]
bekannt well-known [ˌwelˈnəʊn], [ˈwelˌnəʊn]
bekommen get [get] **etwas bekommen** *(Krankheit)* come down with sth.
▶ S. 180 (to) come across/down/over/…
belebt *(Straße, Viertel)* busy [ˈbɪzi]
bellen bark [bɑːk]
Bellen bark [bɑːk]
beliebt (bei) popular (with) [ˈpɒpjələ]
bemalt painted [ˈpeɪntɪd]
benehmen: sich benehmen behave [bɪˈheɪv]
benennen name [neɪm]
benötigen need [niːd]
benutzen use [juːz]
beobachten watch [wɒtʃ]; *(untersuchen, studieren)* study [ˈstʌdi]
Bereich area [ˈeəriə]
bereit ready [ˈredi]
bereits already [ɔːlˈredi]
Berg mountain [ˈmaʊntən]
bergab downhill [ˌdaʊnˈhɪl]
bergauf uphill [ˌʌpˈhɪl]
Bergwerk mine [maɪn]
Bericht report [rɪˈpɔːt]
berichten: jm. etwas berichten tell sb. about sth. [tel]
beruhigen: sich beruhigen calm down [ˌkɑːm ˈdaʊn] **jn. beruhigen** calm sb. down
berühmt (für, wegen) famous (for) [ˈfeɪməs]
berühren touch [tʌtʃ]
beschäftigt sein *(viel zu tun haben)* be busy [ˈbɪzi]
Bescheid: über etwas Bescheid wissen know about sth.
beschließen decide [dɪˈsaɪd]
beschreiben: (jm.) etwas beschreiben describe sth. (to sb.) [dɪˈskraɪb] **jm. den Weg (nach …) beschreiben** tell sb. the way (to …)
Beschreibung description [dɪˈskrɪpʃn]
beschriften *(etikettieren)* label [ˈleɪbl]
Beschriftung *(Etikett)* label [ˈleɪbl]
beschützen: jn./etwas beschützen (vor jm./etwas) protect sb./sth. (from sb./sth.) [prəˈtekt]
Besetzung *(Theaterstück)* cast [kɑːst]
besiegen beat [biːt]
besitzen own [əʊn]
besondere(r, s) special [ˈspeʃl]
besonders *(vor allem)* especially [ɪˈspeʃli]
besorgen: (sich) etwas besorgen get sth.
besorgt worried [ˈwʌrid]
besser better [ˈbetə]
beste(r, s) best [best] **das Beste an …** the best thing about …
bestellen order [ˈɔːdə]
Bestrafung punishment [ˈpʌnɪʃmənt]
Besuch visit [ˈvɪzɪt]
besuchen: jn. besuchen visit sb. [ˈvɪzɪt]; see sb. [siː]
Besucher/in visitor [ˈvɪzɪtə]
Betonung stress [stres]
Betonungszeichen stress mark [ˈstres mɑːk]
betreten *(hineingehen)* enter [ˈentə]
Bett bed [bed]
beunruhigt worried [ˈwʌrid]
Beutel bag [bæg]
Bevölkerung population [ˌpɒpjuˈleɪʃn]
bevor before [bɪˈfɔː]
bewachen guard [gɑːd]
bewegen; sich bewegen move [muːv]
Bewegung movement [ˈmuːvmənt]
bewölkt cloudy [ˈklaʊdi]
bezahlen pay [peɪ] **etwas bezahlen** pay for sth. [peɪ] **bezahlt werden** get paid
Bibliothek library [ˈlaɪbrəri]
Bild picture [ˈpɪktʃə] **auf dem Bild** in the picture
bilden *(formen)* form [fɔːm]
Bildschirm screen [skriːn] **geteilter Bildschirm** split screen [splɪt ˈskriːn]
Bildschirm(auf)teilung split screen [splɪt ˈskriːn]
Bildung education [ˌedʒuˈkeɪʃn]
Bildunterschrift caption [ˈkæpʃn]
billig cheap [tʃiːp]
Bindestrich hyphen [ˈhaɪfən]
Bindewort linking word [ˈlɪŋkɪŋ wɜːd]
bis **1.** till [tɪl]; until [ənˈtɪl] **bis zwölf Uhr** till/until twelve o'clock **bis spätestens 20 Uhr** by 8 pm [baɪ] **bis jetzt** so far **Bis gleich. / Bis bald.** See you. **bis zehn zählen** count to ten **bis (zu)** up to **von … bis …** from … to …
2. bis auf *(außer)* except [ɪkˈsept]
Biss bite [baɪt]
bisschen: ein bisschen a bit [ə ˈbɪt]
Bissen bite [baɪt]
bitte **1.** *(in Fragen und Aufforderungen)* please [pliːz]
2. Bitte sehr. / Hier bitte. Here you are.

bitten: jemanden bitten, etwas zu tun ask sb. to do sth. [ɑːsk] **um etwas bitten** ask for sth.
blau blue [bluː]
bleiben stay [steɪ] **(mit jm.) in Verbindung bleiben** stay in touch (with sb.) [tʌtʃ] **Bleib/Bleiben Sie am Apparat.** Hold on a minute. [ˌhəʊld_ˈɒn], *(oft auch kurz:)* Hold on.
Bleistift pencil [ˈpensl]
Blick (auf) view (of) [vjuː] **einen Blick auf etwas werfen** have a look at sth.
Blitz(e) lightning *(no pl)* [ˈlaɪtnɪŋ] **ein Blitz** a flash of lightning
Blockflöte recorder [rɪˈkɔːdə]
blöd *(albern)* silly [ˈsɪli]; *(dumm)* stupid [ˈstjuːpɪd]
Blog *(Weblog, digitales Tagebuch)* blog [blɒg]
Blogger/in blogger [ˈblɒgə]
blond blond *(bei Frauen oft:* blonde) [blɒnd]
bloß **1.** only [ˈəʊnli]; *(einfach nur)* just [dʒʌst]
2. *(Hände, Arme, Füße)* bare [beə]
Blume flower [ˈflaʊə]
Blut blood [blʌd]
Blüte flower [ˈflaʊə]
Boden ground [graʊnd]
Boot boat [bəʊt]
Bootsfahrt cruise [kruːz]
Bord: an Bord on board [bɔːd]
böse auf jn. angry with sb. [ˈæŋgri]
Botschaft *(Aussage)* message [ˈmesɪdʒ]
brauchen need [niːd]; *(Zeit)* take [teɪk] **du brauchst es nicht zu tun** you needn't do it [ˈniːdnt]
braun brown [braʊn]
brav good
brechen *(kaputt gehen)* break [breɪk]
breit wide [waɪd]
brennen burn [bɜːn]
Brief letter [ˈletə]
Brille glasses *(pl)* [ˈglɑːsɪz]
bringen *(mit-, herbringen)* bring [brɪŋ]; *(weg-, hinbringen)* take [teɪk] **etwas zustande bringen** *(schaffen)* manage sth. [ˈmænɪdʒ]
Brise breeze [briːz]
britisch British [ˈbrɪtɪʃ]
Broschüre brochure [ˈbrəʊʃə]
Brot bread [bred]
Brücke bridge [brɪdʒ]
Bruder brother [ˈbrʌðə]
brüllen roar [rɔː]
Brust(korb) chest [tʃest]
Buch book [bʊk]
buchen *(reservieren)* reserve [rɪˈzɜːv]
Bücherei library [ˈlaɪbrəri]
Buchhandlung bookshop [ˈbʊkʃɒp]
Buchstabe letter [ˈletə]
buchstabieren spell [spel]
bücken: sich bücken bend down [bend]
Bühne stage [steɪdʒ] **hinter der Bühne** backstage [ˌbækˈsteɪdʒ]
Burg castle [ˈkɑːsl]
Bürgermeister/in mayor [meə]
Bürgersteig pavement [ˈpeɪvmənt]
Büro office [ˈɒfɪs]
Bus bus **mit dem Bus fahren** go by bus

C

Café café [ˈkæfeɪ]
Camping camping [ˈkæmpɪŋ]
Cent cent [sent]
▶ S. 189 Pounds and euros
Champion champion [ˈtʃæmpiən]
Chance chance [tʃɑːns]
Chaos chaos [ˈkeɪɒs]
Chat chat [tʃæt]
chatten chat [tʃæt]
Checkliste checklist [ˈtʃeklɪst]
Chor choir [ˈkwaɪə]
Clown clown [klaʊn]
Cola cola [ˈkəʊlə]
Comedyshow comedy [ˈkɒmədi]
Computer computer [kəmˈpjuːtə]
cool cool [kuːl]
Cornflakes cornflakes [ˈkɔːnfleɪks]
Cottage cottage [ˈkɒtɪdʒ]
Cousin, Cousine cousin [ˈkʌzn]
Curry(gericht) curry [ˈkʌri]

D

da, dahin *(dort, dorthin)* there [ðeə] **da sein** *(zu Hause sein)* be in **nicht da sein** *(nicht zu Hause sein)* be out **nicht (mehr) da sein** be gone [gɒn]
Dach roof [ruːf]
Dachboden attic [ˈætɪk] **auf dem Dachboden** in the attic
dagegen: etwas dagegen haben mind [maɪnd]
▶ S. 178 (to) mind
daheim at home [ət ˈhəʊm]
daher *(deshalb)* so [səʊ]
damit so that, *(oft auch kurz:)* so
danach after that
dankbar *(froh)* glad [glæd]
Danke. Thank you. [ˈθæŋk juː]; Thanks. [θæŋks] **dank Maya** thanks to Maya **Danke, gut.** Fine, thanks. **Danke, dass ihr zugehört habt.** Thank you for listening.
danken: jm. danken thank sb. [θæŋk]
dann then [ðen]
darstellende Kunst drama [ˈdrɑːmə]
darum that's why
das *(Artikel)* the [ðə]
das *(Relativpronomen)* **1.** *(für Dinge)* which; that
2. *(für Personen)* who; that
das (dort) *(Singular)* that [ðæt]; *(Plural)* those [ðəʊz] **das Auto dort** that car
dass that [ðæt], [ðət] **es zeigt, dass …** it shows that …
dasselbe wie … the same as … [seɪm]
dauern *(Zeit brauchen)* take [teɪk]
davor *(zeitlich)* before that
Deck deck [dek]
dein(e) … your … [jɔː], [jə]
deiner, deine, deins yours [jɔːz]
Delfin dolphin [ˈdɒlfɪn]
Demonstration demonstration [ˌdemənˈstreɪʃn]
denken think [θɪŋk] **an etwas denken** think of sth.; *(sich merken, nicht vergessen)* remember sth. [rɪˈmembə]
Denkmal memorial [məˈmɔːriəl]; monument [ˈmɒnjumənt]
denn: Was ist denn? What's the matter? [ˈmætə]
dennoch still [stɪl]
der *(Artikel)* the [ðə]
der *(Relativpronomen)* **1.** *(für Personen)* who; that
2. *(für Dinge)* which; that
der … (dort) *(Singular)* that … [ðæt]; *(Plural)* those … [ðəʊz] **der … (hier)** *(Singular)* this … [ðɪs]; *(Plural)* these … [ðiːz]
derselbe wie … the same as … [seɪm]
deshalb so [səʊ]; that's why
Design design [dɪˈzaɪn]
Designer/in designer [dɪˈzaɪnə]
Detail detail [ˈdiːteɪl]
deuten: auf etwas deuten *(zeigen)* point to sth. [pɔɪnt]
deutlich clear(ly) [klɪə], [ˈklɪəli]
Deutsch; deutsch German [ˈdʒɜːmən]
Dezember December [dɪˈsembə]
Dialog dialogue [ˈdaɪəlɒg]
dich you [juː]; *(Reflexivpronomen)* yourself [jɔːˈself]
dick fat [fæt]
die *(Artikel)* the [ðə]
die *(Relativpronomen)* **1.** *(für Personen)* who; that
2. *(für Dinge)* which; that
die … (dort) *(Singular)* that … [ðæt]; *(Plural)* those … [ðəʊz] **die … (hier)** *(Singular)* this … [ðɪs]; *(Plural)* these … [ðiːz]
Dieb/in thief [θiːf], *pl* thieves [θiːvz]
Dienstag Tuesday [ˈtjuːzdeɪ, ˈtjuːzdi]
dies (hier) *(Singular)* this [ðɪs]; *(Plural)* these [ðiːz]
diese(r, s): dieser Ort / diese Pause / dieses Fach this place/break/subject **diese Leute** these people **Diese(r, s) hier.** This one.
dieselbe(n) wie … the same as … [seɪm]
diesjährige(r, s): das diesjährige Musical/Theaterstück/… this year's musical/play/…
Ding thing [θɪŋ]
dir you [juː]; *(Reflexivpronomen)* yourself [jɔːˈself]
direkt direct [dəˈrekt], [daɪˈrekt]

Disko disco ['dɪskəʊ]
Diskussion discussion [dɪ'skʌʃn]
dokumentieren *(Daten festhalten)* record [rɪ'kɔːd]
Dom cathedral [kə'θiːdrəl]
Donner thunder ['θʌndə]
Donnerstag Thursday ['θɜːzdeɪ, -di]
Doppel- double ['dʌbl]
Doppelpunkt colon ['kəʊlən]
Dorf village ['vɪlɪdʒ]
dort(hin) there [ðeə] **dort entlang** that way **dort unten** down there
Dose tin [tɪn]
dran: Ich bin dran. (It's) my turn. [tɜːn]
draußen outside [ˌaʊt'saɪd] **nach draußen** out(side)
drehen: sich im Kreis drehen spin around [ˌspɪn‿ə'raʊnd]
drei three [θriː]
Dreieck triangle ['traɪæŋgl]
drinnen inside [ˌɪn'saɪd] **nach drinnen** inside
dritte(r, s) third [θɜːd]
drittgrößte(r, s) third biggest
drüben: da/dort drüben over there
drücken press [pres]; *(schieben, stoßen)* push [pʊʃ]
du you [juː]
Dudelsack bagpipes *(pl)* ['bægpaɪps]
dumm stupid ['stjuːpɪd]
Dummerchen silly ['sɪli]
dunkel dark [dɑːk]
Dunkelheit dark [dɑːk]; darkness ['dɑːknəs]
Dunst(schleier) mist [mɪst]
durch through [θruː]
Durchsage announcement [ə'naʊnsmənt]
dürfen can [kæn], [kən]; may [meɪ]; be allowed to [ə'laʊd] **du darfst es nicht tun** you mustn't do it ['mʌsnt]
Durst haben be thirsty ['θɜːsti]
durstig sein be thirsty ['θɜːsti]
Dusche shower ['ʃaʊə]
duschen; sich duschen have a shower ['ʃaʊə]
DVD DVD [ˌdiːviː'diː]

E

eben: gerade eben just [dʒʌst]
ebenso as well [əz 'wel]
echt *(wirklich)* real ['riːəl]
Ecke corner ['kɔːnə] **Church Road, Ecke London Road** on the corner of Church Road and London Road **Laden an der Ecke** *(„Tante-Emma-Laden")* corner shop ['kɔːnə ʃɒp]
egal: Geld ist mir egal. I don't care about money. **Aber egal, …** *(Wie dem auch sei)* Anyway, … ['eniweɪ] **egal, wann** whenever [ˌwen'evə]
▶ S. 191 (to) care
▶ S. 195 whenever, wherever, whatever, whoever

Ehre honour ['ɒnə]
Ehrenamtliche(r) volunteer [ˌvɒlən'tɪə]
Ei egg [eg]
Eierkuchen pancake ['pænkeɪk]
eifersüchtig (auf) jealous (of) ['dʒeləs]
eigene(r, s): mein eigener Film / mein eigenes Zimmer / … my own film/room/… [əʊn]
eigentlich in fact [ɪn 'fækt]; actually ['æktʃuəli]
▶ S. 184 actually
Eiland *(kleine Insel)* isle [aɪl]
eilen; sich beeilen hurry (up) ['hʌri]
Eimer bucket ['bʌkɪt]
ein(e) *(Artikel)* a, an [ə], [ən] **ein anderer …/eine andere …/ein anderes …** another … [ə'nʌðə] **einer nach dem anderen** one by one **eines Nachts/Tages** one night/day **ein paar** a few [ə 'fjuː]; some [sʌm], [səm]
einander *(sich gegenseitig)* each other [iːtʃ‿'ʌðə]
einbringen *(Heu)* bring in
Eindruck impression [ɪm'preʃn]
einfach 1. *(nicht schwierig)* easy ['iːzi] 2. **einfach nur** just [dʒʌst]
Einführung *(Einleitung)* introduction [ˌɪntrə'dʌkʃn]
eingeschaltet sein *(Radio, Licht usw.)* be on
einhundert a hundred, one hundred ['hʌndrəd]
einige a few [ə 'fjuː]; some [sʌm], [səm]
einigen: sich auf etwas einigen agree on sth. [ə'griː]
Einkäufe erledigen do the/some shopping ['ʃɒpɪŋ]
einkaufen shop [ʃɒp] **einkaufen gehen** go shopping ['ʃɒpɪŋ]; do the shopping / do some shopping
Einkaufszentrum shopping centre ['ʃɒpɪŋ sentə]; shopping mall ['ʃɒpɪŋ mɔːl], *(kurz auch:)* mall
einladen: jn. einladen (zu) invite sb. (to) [ɪn'vaɪt]
Einladung (zu, nach) invitation (to) [ˌɪnvɪ'teɪʃn]
einlegen: eine Pause einlegen pause [pɔːz]
Einleitung introduction [ˌɪntrə'dʌkʃn]
einmal 1. once [wʌns] **noch einmal** again [ə'gen] 2. **auf einmal** *(plötzlich)* suddenly ['sʌdnli] 3. **(noch) nicht einmal** not even
einmarschieren: in ein Land einmarschieren invade a country [ɪn'veɪd]
einreichen: etwas einreichen hand sth. in [ˌhænd‿'ɪn]
eins one [wʌn] **eins zu eins/eins beide** *(Ergebnis im Sport)* one all [ˌwʌn‿'ɔːl]
einsam lonely ['ləʊnli]
einschalten: etwas einschalten turn sth. on [ˌtɜːn‿'ɒn]
einschlafen fall asleep [ˌfɔːl‿ə'sliːp]

einsilbig *(aus einer Silbe bestehend)* one-syllable ['sɪləbl]
einsteigen: in ein Auto/Taxi einsteigen get in(to) a car/taxi **in einen Bus/einen Zug/ein Flugzeug einsteigen** get on a bus/train/plane
Eintrag, Eintragung *(im Tagebuch, Wörterbuch)* entry ['entri]
eintreffen arrive [ə'raɪv]
eintreten *(in Raum)* enter **in einen Klub eintreten** join a club [dʒɔɪn]
Eintritt entry ['entri]
Eintrittskarte ticket ['tɪkɪt]
Einwohner(zahl) population [ˌpɒpju'leɪʃn]
Einzelheit detail ['diːteɪl]
einziehen move in **in ein Haus einziehen** move into a house
einzige(r, s): der/die/das einzige …; die einzigen… the only … ['əʊnli]
Eis ice [aɪs]; *(Speiseeis)* ice cream [ˌaɪs 'kriːm]
Eistee iced tea
Elefant elephant ['elɪfənt]
elektronisch electronic [ɪˌlek'trɒnɪk]
Element element ['elɪmənt]
elf eleven [ɪ'levn]
Eltern parents ['peərənts]
E-Mail email ['iːmeɪl]; mail
emigrieren *(auswandern)* emigrate ['emɪgreɪt]
emporragen *(Berge, Säulen, Türme, …)* rise up [ˌraɪz‿'ʌp]
Ende end [end]; *(Abschluss)* ending **am oberen Ende (von)** at the top (of) **am unteren Ende (von)** at the bottom (of) ['bɒtəm] **zu Ende sein** be over
enden finish ['fɪnɪʃ]; end
endlich *(schließlich)* at last [ət 'lɑːst]; finally ['faɪnəli]
Endspiel final ['faɪnl]
Energie energy ['enədʒi]
eng *(schmal)* narrow ['nærəʊ]
Engel angel ['eɪndʒl]
Englisch; englisch English ['ɪŋglɪʃ]
entgegnen reply (to) [rɪ'plaɪ]
entlang: die Straße/den Fluss/… entlang along the street/the river/… [ə'lɒŋ] **dort entlang** that way
entscheiden: sich entscheiden decide [dɪ'saɪd]
Entscheidung decision [dɪ'sɪʒn]
Entschuldigung. 1. *(Tut mir leid.)* (I'm) sorry. ['sɒri] 2. **Entschuldigung, … / Entschuldigen Sie, …** *(Darf ich mal stören?)* Excuse me, … [ɪk'skjuːz miː]
entsetzt shocked [ʃɒkt]; in horror ['hɒrə]
entspannen: sich entspannen relax [rɪ'læks]
entwerfen *(konstruieren, entwickeln)* design [dɪ'zaɪn]
entwickeln *(entwerfen, konstruieren)* design [dɪ'zaɪn]
Entwurf draft [drɑːft]

er 1. *(männliche Person)* he [hiː] 2. *(Ding; Tier)* it [ɪt]
Erdbeere strawberry ['strɔːbəri]
Erdboden ground [graʊnd]
Erde *(der Planet)* earth [ɜːθ] *(oft auch:* Earth*)* **auf der Erde** on earth **unter der Erde** underground [ˌʌndə'graʊnd]
Ereignis event [ɪ'vent]
Erfahrung(en) experience *(no pl)* [ɪk'spɪəriəns]
erfinden invent [ɪn'vent]
Erfolg success [sək'ses]
erforschen explore [ɪk'splɔː]
Ergebnis result [rɪ'zʌlt]
erhältlich available [ə'veɪləbl]
erhellen *(aufleuchten lassen)* light up [ˌlaɪt 'ʌp]
erinnern: sich an etwas erinnern remember sth. [rɪ'membə]
Erinnerung memory ['meməri]
erkältet sein have a cold [kəʊld]
Erkältung: eine Erkältung haben have a cold [kəʊld]
erklären: jm. etwas erklären explain sth. to sb. [ɪk'spleɪn]
erkranken: an etwas erkranken come down with sth.
▶ S. 180 (to) come across/down/over/…
erkunden explore [ɪk'splɔː]
erlauben allow [ə'laʊ]
erläutern: jm. etwas erläutern explain sth. to sb. [ɪk'spleɪn]
erraten guess [ges]
erreichbar *(Telefon)* available [ə'veɪləbl]
erreichen reach [riːtʃ]
erröten go red
erscheinen *(auftauchen)* appear [ə'pɪə]
erschrecken: jn. erschrecken scare sb. [skeə]
erst only ['əʊnli] **erst um drei** *(nicht vor drei)* not till three; not until three
erstaunlich amazing [ə'meɪzɪŋ]
erste(r, s) first [fɜːst] **als Erstes** first **der erste Tag** the first day **zum ersten Mal** for the first time
ertrinken drown [draʊn]
erwachsen werden grow up [ˌgrəʊ_'ʌp]
Erwachsene(r) adult ['ædʌlt]
erwarten: etwas erwarten expect sth. [ɪk'spekt] **Ich kann es kaum erwarten, … zu sehen.** I can't wait to see …
erwidern reply (to) [rɪ'plaɪ]
erzählen (von) tell (about) [tel]
Erzählung story ['stɔːri]
Erziehung education [ˌedʒu'keɪʃn]
erzielen: einen Treffer erzielen score [skɔː]
es it [ɪt] **es ist … / es gibt …** there's … **es sind … / es gibt …** there are … **Ach, du bist es.** Oh, it's you. **Bist du es?** Is that you?
essen eat [iːt] **zu Abend/Mittag essen** have dinner/lunch
Essen *(Lebensmittel)* food [fuːd]; *(Mahlzeit)* meal [miːl]
Esszimmer dining room ['daɪnɪŋ ruːm]
Etikett label ['leɪbl]
etikettieren label ['leɪbl]
etwas 1. something ['sʌmθɪŋ]; *(in Fragen)* anything ['eniθɪŋ] **sonst noch etwas** anything else
▶ S. 195 … else
2. *(ein bisschen)* some [sʌm], [səm]; a bit [ə 'bɪt]
euch you [juː]; *(Reflexivpronomen)* yourselves [jɔː'selvz]
euer …/eure … your … [jɔː], [jə]
eurer, eure, eures yours [jɔːz]
Euro euro (€) ['jʊərəʊ]
▶ S. 189 Pounds and euros
Europa Europe ['jʊərəp]
europäisch: die Europäische Union the EU [ˌiː 'juː] (the European Union [ˌjʊərəpiːən 'juːniən])
Eurozone eurozone ['jʊərəʊzəʊn]
ewig *(für immer)* for ever [fər 'evə]
Exemplar copy ['kɒpi]
Export export ['ekspɔːt]

F

Fackel torch [tɔːtʃ]
fähig sein, etwas zu tun be able to do sth. ['eɪbl]
Fahne *(Flagge)* flag [flæg]
Fähre ferry ['feri]
fahren go [gəʊ]; *(ein Auto/mit dem Auto)* drive [draɪv] **in Urlaub fahren** go on holiday **mit dem Bus/Auto/Zug fahren** go by bus/car/train **Rad fahren** ride a bike
Fahrkarte ticket ['tɪkɪt]
Fahrkartenschalter ticket office ['tɪkɪt_ˌɒfɪs]
Fahrplan timetable ['taɪmteɪbl]
Fahrrad bike [baɪk]
Fahrstuhl lift [lɪft]
Fahrt journey ['dʒɜːni]; ride [raɪd]
fair fair [feə]
Fakt fact [fækt]
Fall: Auf keinen Fall! No way! [ˌnəʊ 'weɪ]
fallen fall [fɔːl]; drop [drɒp] **etwas fallen lassen** drop sth. [drɒp]
falls if [ɪf]
falsch wrong [rɒŋ]; false [fɔːls] **Nein, das ist falsch.** No, that's wrong.
Familie family ['fæməli] **eine vierköpfige Familie** a family of four **Familie Blackwell** the Blackwell family
Fan fan [fæn]
fangen catch [kætʃ]
fantastisch fantastic [fæn'tæstɪk]
Farbe colour ['kʌlə]
Farm farm [fɑːm]
Fasching carnival ['kɑːnɪvl]
fast almost ['ɔːlməʊst]; nearly ['nɪəli]
Februar February ['februəri]
Federmäppchen pencil case ['pensl keɪs]
fehlen be missing ['mɪsɪŋ] **die fehlenden Wörter** the missing words **Was fehlt dir?** What's wrong with you?
Fehler mistake [mɪ'steɪk]; *(Schuld)* fault [fɔːlt] **einen Fehler machen** make a mistake
Feier celebration [ˌselɪ'breɪʃn]
feiern celebrate ['selɪbreɪt]
fein fine [faɪn]
Feind/in enemy ['enəmi]
Feld field [fiːld]
Fell coat [kəʊt]
Fels, Felsen rock [rɒk]
felsig rocky ['rɒki]
Fenster window ['wɪndəʊ]
Ferien holidays *(pl)* ['hɒlədeɪz]
Fernbedienung remote control [rɪˌməʊt kən'trəʊl] *(kurz auch:* remote*)*
fernsehen watch TV [ˌwɒtʃ tiː'viː]
Fernsehen, Fernsehgerät TV [ˌtiː'viː] **im Fernsehen** on TV
fertig 1. **mit etwas fertig werden/sein** finish sth. ['fɪnɪʃ] **Wir sind fertig.** *(Wir haben es erledigt.)* We're finished. ['fɪnɪʃt]
2. *(bereit)* ready ['redi] **Wir sind fertig.** *(Wir sind bereit.)* We're ready. **sich fertig machen (für)** get ready (for)
3. **jn. fertig machen** *(zurechtweisen)* give sb. a hard time *(infml)*
Fertigkeit skill [skɪl]
Fest *(Festival)* festival ['festɪvl]
festhalten: sich an etwas festhalten hold onto sth. [həʊld]
Festival festival ['festɪvl]
fett fat [fæt]
Feuer fire ['faɪə]
Feuerwerk fireworks *(pl)* ['faɪəwɜːks]
Feuerwerkskörper firework ['faɪəwɜːk]
Fieber temperature ['temprətʃə] **Fieber haben** have a temperature
Figur *(in Roman, Film, usw.)* character ['kærəktə]; *(Gestalt)* figure ['fɪgə]
Film film [fɪlm]; movie ['muːvi]
filmen film [fɪlm]
Filzstift felt pen [ˌfelt 'pen]
Finale final ['faɪnl]
finden find [faɪnd] **Freunde finden** make friends **Wie findest du …?** How do you like …?
Finger finger ['fɪŋgə]
Finsternis darkness ['dɑːknəs]
Fisch fish [fɪʃ], *pl* fish
Fischerei fishing ['fɪʃɪŋ]
Flagge flag [flæg]
Flasche bottle ['bɒtl]
Fleck spot [spɒt]
Fleisch meat [miːt]
fliegen fly [flaɪ]
fliehen escape [ɪ'skeɪp]
Flosse fin [fɪn]
Flucht escape [ɪ'skeɪp]
Flügel wing [wɪŋ]
Flughafen airport ['eəpɔːt]
Flugzeug plane [pleɪn] **im Flugzeug** on the plane

Fluss river ['rɪvə]
flussabwärts downstream [ˌdaʊn'striːm]
flussaufwärts upstream [ˌʌp'striːm]
flüstern whisper ['wɪspə] **..., sagte er flüsternd.** ..., he said under his breath. [breθ]
folgen follow ['fɒləʊ]
Folie *(für Projektor)* transparency [træns'pærənsi]
Form form [fɔːm]; *(Gestalt)* shape [ʃeɪp]
formen form [fɔːm]
Forschung(en) research *(no pl)* ['riːsɜːtʃ]
fort away [ə'weɪ]
fortfahren *(weiterreden)* go on [ˌgəʊ_'ɒn]
fortsetzen: etwas fortsetzen continue sth. [kən'tɪnjuː] **sich fortsetzen** *(weitergehen)* continue
Foto photo ['fəʊtəʊ] **auf dem Foto** in the photo **Fotos machen** take photos
Fotoapparat camera ['kæmərə]
fotografieren take photos [ˌteɪk 'fəʊtəʊz]; photograph ['fəʊtəgrɑːf]
Foul foul [faʊl]
Frage question ['kwestʃn] **eine Frage stellen** ask a question **Kommt nicht in Frage!** No way! [ˌnəʊ 'weɪ]
fragen ask [ɑːsk] **jn. nach dem Weg fragen** ask sb. the way **sich fragen** *(gern wissen wollen)* wonder ['wʌndə]
Fragezeichen question mark ['kwestʃən mɑːk]
Französisch; französisch French [frentʃ]
Frau 1. woman ['wʊmən], *pl* women ['wɪmɪn] **2. Frau Schwarz** Mrs Schwarz ['mɪsɪz] **3.** *(übliche Anrede von Lehrerinnen)* **Frau Bell** Miss Bell [mɪs]
frei free [friː] **einen Tag frei bekommen/haben** get/have a day off [ɒf]
Freistoß free kick [ˌfriː 'kɪk]
Freitag Friday ['fraɪdeɪ], ['fraɪdi]
Freiwillige(r) volunteer [ˌvɒlən'tɪə]
Freizeit free time [ˌfriː 'taɪm]
Freizeitaktivitäten free-time activities [ˌfriːtaɪm_æk'tɪvətiz]
Fremdenführer/in guide [gaɪd]
freuen: sich auf etwas freuen look forward to sth. ['fɔːwəd] **Freut mich, dich/euch/Sie kennenzulernen.** Nice to meet you.
Freund friend [frend]; *(Partner)* boyfriend ['bɔɪfrend] **Freunde finden** make friends
Freundin friend [frend]; *(Partnerin)* girlfriend ['gɜːlfrend]
freundlich friendly ['frendli]; kind [kaɪnd]
Friede, Frieden peace [piːs]
friedfertig peaceful ['piːsfl]
friedlich peaceful ['piːsfl]
frieren be cold [kəʊld]
frisch fresh [freʃ]
Friseur/in hairdresser ['heədresə]
froh *(glücklich)* happy ['hæpi]; *(dankbar)* glad [glæd]
Frosch frog [frɒg]
Frucht fruit [fruːt]
früh early ['ɜːli]
früher (einmal) in the old days
Frühling spring [sprɪŋ]
Frühstück breakfast ['brekfəst] **Zimmer mit Frühstück** bed & breakfast
frühstücken have breakfast
Frühstückspension bed & breakfast
fühlen; sich fühlen feel [fiːl] **Ich fühle mich nicht gut.** I don't feel well.
führen lead [liːd]
füllen fill [fɪl]
Füller pen [pen]
fünf five [faɪv]
funktionieren work
für for [fɔː], [fə]
furchtbar terrible ['terəbl]; awful ['ɔːfl]
fürchterlich terrible ['terəbl]; awful ['ɔːfl]
Fuß foot [fʊt], *pl* feet [fiːt] **zu Fuß gehen** walk [wɔːk] **jm. auf die Füße treten** *(auch im übertragenen Sinne)* tread on sb.'s toes [tred] *(infml)*
Fußabdruck footprint ['fʊtprɪnt]
Fußball football ['fʊtbɔːl]
Fußboden floor [flɔː]
Fußgänger/in pedestrian [pə'destriən]
Fußgängerzone pedestrian zone [pə'destrɪən zəʊn]
Futter food [fuːd]
füttern feed [fiːd]
Fütterungszeit feeding time ['fiːdɪŋ taɪm]

G

Gabel fork [fɔːk]
Galerie gallery ['gæləri]
Gang 1. *(Korridor)* corridor ['kɒrɪdɔː] **2. im Gang sein** *(andauern)* go on
ganz *(völlig)* quite [kwaɪt] **ganz allein** all alone **ganz Plymouth** all of Plymouth
ganze(r, s) whole [həʊl] **das ganze Plymouth** all of Plymouth **den ganzen Tag** all day **die ganze Zeit** all the time **ganzer Satz** full sentence
gar nichts nothing ['nʌθɪŋ]
Garage garage ['gærɑːʒ], ['gærɪdʒ]
Garten garden ['gɑːdn]
Gartenarbeit gardening ['gɑːdnɪŋ]
Gärtnern gardening ['gɑːdnɪŋ]
Gast guest [gest]
Gastfamilie host family ['həʊst fæməli]
Gatter gate [geɪt]
gebackene Kartoffeln *(im Backofen in Fett gebacken)* roast potatoes [rəʊst pə'teɪtəʊz]
Gebäude building ['bɪldɪŋ]
geben give [gɪv] **Es gibt ...** *(Singular)* There's ...; *(Plural)* There are ... **Gibt es (irgendwelche) ...?** Are there any ...? ['eni] **Was gibt es zum Mittagessen?** What's for lunch? **Was gibt's?** *(Was ist los?)* What's up?
Gebiet area ['eəriə]
geboren sein/werden be born [bɔːn]
gebrochen broken ['brəʊkən]
Geburtstag birthday ['bɜːθdeɪ] **Ich habe am 5. Mai Geburtstag.** My birthday is on 5th May. **Ich habe im Mai Geburtstag.** My birthday is in May. **Wann hast du Geburtstag?** When's your birthday?
Gedanke thought [θɔːt] **jemandes Gedanken lesen** read sb.'s mind [maɪnd]
Gedenk- memorial [mə'mɔːriəl]
Gedicht poem ['pəʊɪm]
Gefahr danger ['deɪndʒə]
gefährlich dangerous ['deɪndʒərəs]
gefallen: Wie gefällt dir ...? How do you like ...?
Gefangene(r) captive ['kæptɪv]
Gefängnis prison ['prɪzn]
Gefäß pot [pɒt]
Gefühl feeling ['fiːlɪŋ]
gegen 1. against [ə'genst] **2. gegen 18 Uhr** around 6 pm [ə'raʊnd]
Gegend area ['eəriə]; *(Landschaft)* countryside ['kʌntrisaɪd] **hier in der Gegend** round here [ˌraʊnd 'hɪə]
gegenüber (von) opposite ['ɒpəzɪt]
Gegenwart present ['preznt]
gehen go [gəʊ]; *(zu Fuß gehen)* walk [wɔːk]; *(weggehen, verlassen)* leave [liːv] **an Land gehen** land **ans Telefon gehen** answer the phone **einkaufen gehen** go shopping **Los geht's. / Jetzt geht's los.** Here we go. **nach Hause gehen** go home **segeln gehen** go sailing ['seɪlɪŋ] **spazieren gehen** go for a walk [wɔːk] **Wie geht's? / Wie geht es dir/euch/Ihnen?** How are you? **Mir geht's nicht gut.** I don't feel well. **Worum geht es in der Geschichte?** What is the story about? **Es geht um eine Möwe.** It's about a seagull.
gehören: zu etwas gehören *(zu etwas passen)* go with sth.
Gehweg *(Bürgersteig)* pavement ['peɪvmənt]
Geist ghost [gəʊst]
Gel gel [dʒel]
Gelächter laughter ['lɑːftə]
gelangen *(hinkommen)* get [get]
gelangweilt sein be/feel bored [bɔːd]
gelb yellow ['jeləʊ]
Geld money ['mʌni] **Geld ausgeben (für)** spend money (on) [spend] **Geld sammeln (für)** raise money (for) [reɪz]
Gelegenheit *(Chance)* chance [tʃɑːns]
gemacht: aus etwas gemacht sein be made of sth.
Gemeinde community [kə'mjuːnəti]

Gemeinschaft community [kə'mju:nəti]
Gemüse vegetables *(pl)* ['vedʒtəblz]
genannt werden *(heißen)* be called [kɔ:ld]
genau **1.** *(Adjektiv)* exact [ɪg'zækt] **2.** *(Adverb)* exactly [ɪg'zæktli] **genau hinschauen** look closely ['kləʊsli] **genau in dem Moment** just then **genau wie ...** just like ... ['dʒʌst laɪk]
genial brilliant ['brɪliənt]
genießen enjoy [ɪn'dʒɔɪ]
genug enough [ɪ'nʌf] **genug von etwas haben** *(etwas satt haben, einer Sache überdrüssig sein)* be tired of sth. ['taɪəd]
geöffnet open ['əʊpən]
Geografie geography [dʒi'ɒgrəfi]
gerade *(im Moment)* at the moment ['məʊmənt] **gerade dann** just then **gerade eben** just [dʒʌst] **jetzt gerade** *(in diesem Moment)* right now
geradeaus weiter straight on [streɪt_'ɒn]
Geräusch sound [saʊnd]; noise [nɔɪz]
gern: Ich tanze/singe/... gern. I like dancing/singing/... **Ich hätte gern ...** I'd like ... [ˌaɪd 'laɪk] (= I would like ...) **Ich würde gern gehen.** I'd like to go. **Ich würde sehr gern bleiben.** I'd love to stay. **Was hättest du gern?** What would you like? [wʊd]
gernhaben like [laɪk]
gesamte(r, s) whole [həʊl]
Gesamtsumme: eine Gesamtsumme von ... a total of ... ['təʊtl]
Geschäft *(Laden)* shop [ʃɒp]
geschäftig *(belebt)* busy ['bɪzi]
geschehen (mit) happen (to) ['hæpən]
Geschenk present ['preznt]
Geschichte **1.** *(vergangene Zeiten)* history ['hɪstri] **2.** *(Erzählung)* story ['stɔ:ri]
geschieden divorced [dɪ'vɔ:st]
Geschirr: das Geschirr abwaschen, spülen wash the dishes *(pl)* ['dɪʃɪz]
Geschwindigkeit speed [spi:d]
Gesicht face [feɪs]
Gesichtsausdruck facial expression [ˌfeɪʃl_ɪk'spreʃn]
gespannt *(aufgeregt)* excited [ɪk'saɪtɪd]
Gespenst ghost [gəʊst]
Gespräch talk; *(Unterhaltung)* conversation [ˌkɒnvə'seɪʃn]
Gestalt *(Figur)* figure ['fɪgə]; *(Form)* shape [ʃeɪp]
Gestaltung *(Design)* design [dɪ'zaɪn]; *(Layout)* layout ['leɪaʊt]
gestern yesterday ['jestədeɪ], [-di]
gesund well [wel] **Ich bin wieder gesund.** I'm well again.
geteilter Bildschirm split screen [splɪt 'skri:n]
Getränk drink [drɪŋk]
gewinnen win [wɪn]
Gewinn *(Preis)* prize [praɪz]
Gewinner/in winner ['wɪnə]
Gewitter storm [stɔ:m]
gewöhnlich **1.** *(Adjektiv: üblich)* usual ['ju:ʒuəl] **2.** *(Adverb: normalerweise)* usually ['ju:ʒuəli]
gießen pour [pɔ:]
Giraffe giraffe [dʒə'rɑ:f]
Gipfel summit ['sʌmɪt]
Gitarre guitar [gɪ'tɑ:] **Gitarre spielen** play the guitar
glänzend *(großartig)* brilliant ['brɪliənt]
Glas glass [glɑ:s] **ein Glas Wasser** a glass of water
glatt *(rutschig)* slippery ['slɪpəri]
glauben believe [bɪ'li:v]; think [θɪŋk]
gleich nachdem ... just after ...
gleichzeitig at one time
Gleis *(Bahnsteig)* platform ['plætfɔ:m]
gliedern *(strukturieren)* structure ['strʌktʃə]
Glocke bell [bel]
Glück: Glück haben be lucky **Viel Glück!** Good luck! [lʌk]
glücklich happy ['hæpi]
Glückspilz: Du Glückspilz. Lucky you. ['lʌki]
Gokart go-kart ['gəʊ kɑ:t]
Gold gold [gəʊld]
golden, Gold- gold ['gəʊld]
Gott God [gɒd]
Gottesdienst service ['sɜ:vɪs]
Grab grave [greɪv]
Graben ditch [dɪtʃ]
Grabstein gravestone ['greɪvstəʊn]
Grafschaft *(in Großbritannien)* county ['kaʊnti]
Gramm gram [græm]
Gras grass [grɑ:s]
grau grey [greɪ]
grausam cruel ['kru:l]
Grenze border ['bɔ:də]
groß big [bɪg]; large [lɑ:dʒ]; *(Person)* tall [tɔ:l] **Wie groß soll der/dein Tee sein?** What size tea would you like?
großartig great [greɪt]; brilliant ['brɪliənt]
Größe size [saɪz]
Großeltern grandparents ['grænpeərənts]
Großmutter grandmother ['grænmʌðə]
Großstadt city ['sɪti]
Großvater grandfather ['grænfɑ:ðə]
grün green [gri:n]
Grund *(Begründung)* reason ['ri:zn]
gründen found [faʊnd]
Gruppe group (of) [gru:p]; *(Band)* band [bænd]
gruselig scary ['skeəri]
Gruß: Liebe Grüße, ... *(Briefschluss)* Love, ...
grüßen: Grüß ... von mir. Say hello to ... for me.
gucken look [lʊk]
▶ S. 180 (to) look after/around/for/...
gut good [gʊd]; *(gesundheitlich)* well; *(Adverb)* well [wel] **gut sein in Kung-Fu / gut Kung-Fu können** be good at kung fu **Danke, gut.** Fine, thanks. **Guten Morgen.** Good morning. [gʊd 'mɔ:nɪŋ] **Guten Tag.** Hello. [hə'ləʊ] **Mir geht's nicht gut. / Ich fühle mich nicht gut.** I don't feel well.
gutaussehend good-looking [ˌgʊd'lʊkɪŋ]
Güter goods *(pl)* [gʊdz]
Gymnastik gymnastics [dʒɪm'næstɪks]

H

Haar, Haare hair [heə]
haben have [hæv], [həv]; have got; *(Idee, Vorschlag auch:)* come up with **Durst haben** be thirsty ['θɜ:sti] **genug von etwas haben** *(etwas satt haben)* be tired of sth. ['taɪəd] **Glück haben** be lucky **Hunger haben** be hungry ['hʌŋgri] **Ich habe im Mai Geburtstag.** My birthday is in May. **jemand hat Recht/Unrecht** someone is right/wrong **viel zu tun haben** *(beschäftigt sein)* be busy ['bɪzi] **Wann hast du Geburtstag?** When's your birthday?
Hafen harbour ['hɑ:bə]
Hai shark [ʃɑ:k]
halb elf (10.30 / 22.30) half past ten ['hɑ:f pɑ:st]
Halbzeit half [hɑ:f], *pl* halves [hɑ:vz] **zur Halbzeit** at half time
Hallo. Hello. [hə'ləʊ]
Hals neck [nek]; *(Kehle)* throat [θrəʊt]
Halsschmerzen haben have a sore throat [ˌsɔ: 'θrəʊt]
Halt stop [stɒp]
halten hold [həʊld] **einen Vortrag/ eine Rede halten (über)** give a talk (about) **(mit jm.) Kontakt halten** stay in touch (with sb.) [tʌtʃ]
Haltestelle stop [stɒp]
Hamburger hamburger ['hæmbɜ:gə]; burger
Hammer hammer ['hæmə]
hämmern hammer
Hamster hamster ['hæmstə]
Hand hand [hænd] **die Hand ausstrecken** reach over [ˌri:tʃ_'əʊvə]
Handel trade [treɪd]
handeln: Es handelt von einer Möwe. It's about a seagull. **Wovon handelt die Geschichte?** What is the story about?
Handout handout ['hændaʊt]
Handpuppe puppet ['pʌpɪt]
Handschuh glove ['glʌv]
Handy mobile phone [ˌməʊbaɪl 'fəʊn], *(kurz auch:)* mobile
Handzettel handout ['hændaʊt]
hängen hang [hæŋ]
hart hard [hɑ:d]; *(knallhart; schwierig)* tough [tʌf] **hart werden** go hard

hassen hate [heɪt]
Haupt- main [meɪn]
Hauptsatz main clause ['meɪn klɔːz]
Hauptteil *(eines Textes)* body ['bɒdi]
Haus house [haʊs] **nach Hause gehen** go home **nach Hause kommen** come home **zu Hause** at home **zu Hause sein** be in **nicht zu Hause sein** be out
Hausarrest: jm. Hausarrest erteilen ground sb. [graʊnd]
Hausaufgabe(n) homework ['həʊmwɜːk] **Hausaufgaben machen** do my / your / … homework **Was haben wir als Hausaufgabe auf?** What's for homework?
Häuschen *(Cottage)* cottage ['kɒtɪdʒ]
Haustier pet [pet]
heftig: heftiger Regen heavy rain ['hevi]
Heftpflaster plaster ['plɑːstə]
Heide(kraut) heather ['heðə]
Heim *(Zuhause)* home [həʊm]
Heimat sein für etwas be home to sth.
Heimatstadt hometown [ˌhəʊm'taʊn]
heiraten: jn. heiraten marry sb. ['mæri]
heiß hot [hɒt]
heißen *(genannt werden)* be called [kɔːld] **Ich heiße …** My name is … **Wie heißt du?** What's your name? **jn. willkommen heißen (in)** welcome sb. (to) ['welkəm]
hektisch *(geschäftig)* busy ['bɪzi]
Held/in hero ['hɪərəʊ], *pl* heroes
helfen help [help]
Helfer/in helper ['helpə]
hell bright [braɪt]
Hemd shirt [ʃɜːt]
herauf up [ʌp]
heraus out [aʊt] **aus … heraus** out of … ['aʊt‿əv]
herausfinden find out
herausfischen fish out
herausfordern: jn. herausfordern (zu etwas) challenge sb. (to sth.) ['tʃælɪndʒ]
Herausforderung challenge ['tʃælɪndʒ]
Herausgeber/in editor ['edɪtə]
herausnehmen take out
herausziehen pull out
Herberge hostel ['hɒstl]
Herbst autumn ['ɔːtəm]
hereinkommen come in [ˌkʌm‿'ɪn]
Herr Schwarz Mr Schwarz ['mɪstə]
herrennen: hinter jm. herrennen run after sb. [ˌrʌn‿'ɑːftə]
herrlich lovely ['lʌvli]
herüberkommen (zu/nach) come over (to)
▶ S. 180 (to) come across/down/over/…
herum: um … herum around … [ə'raʊnd] **überall um sie herum** all around her **um 18 Uhr herum** *(gegen 18 Uhr)* around 6 pm
herumgeben pass around [ˌpɑːs‿ə'raʊnd]
herumhacken: auf jm. herumhacken pick on sb. [pɪk] *(infml)*
herumirren wander ['wɒndə]
herumlaufen walk around; wander
herumreichen pass around
herumrennen run around
herumwirbeln *(sich im Kreis drehen)* spin around [ˌspɪn‿ə'raʊnd]
herunter down [daʊn] **von … herunter** off [ɒf]
▶ S. 177 off
hervorheben *(mit Textmarker)* highlight ['haɪlaɪt]
Herz heart [hɑːt] **Tiere liegen mir am Herzen.** I care about animals.
▶ S. 191 (to) care
Heu hay [heɪ]
heute today [tə'deɪ] **heute Nachmittag/Abend/…** this afternoon/evening/… **heute Nacht, heute Abend** tonight [tə'naɪt]
hier here [hɪə] **Hier bitte.** *(Bitte sehr.)* Here you are. **hier in der Gegend** round here [ˌraʊnd 'hɪə] **hier in der Nähe** near here **hier herüber** over here **hier oben** up here
hierher here [hɪə] **bis hierher** *(bis jetzt)* so far
Hilfe help [help]
Himmel sky [skaɪ]; *(im religiösen Sinn)* heaven ['hevn]
hinauf up [ʌp] **auf das Boot hinauf** onto the boat ['ɒntʊ]
hinaufklettern (auf) climb [klaɪm]
hinaus out [aʊt] **aus … hinaus** out of … ['aʊt‿əv]
hinbringen take [teɪk]
hinein: in die Küche hinein into the kitchen ['ɪntʊ]
hineingehen go in; *(eintreten)* enter ['entə]
hineinspringen dive in [daɪv‿'ɪn]
hinfallen fall [fɔːl]
hinkommen *(gelangen)* get [get]
hinlegen: etwas hinlegen put sth. down **sich hinlegen** lie down [ˌlaɪ 'daʊn]
hinsetzen: sich hinsetzen sit down [ˌsɪt 'daʊn]
Hinsicht: in mancher Hinsicht in some ways **in vielerlei Hinsicht** in many ways
hinstellen: sich hinstellen stand [stænd]
hinten: von hinten from behind [bɪ'haɪnd]
hinter behind [bɪ'haɪnd] **hinter jm. herrennen** run after sb. [ˌrʌn‿'ɑːftə] **aus dem hinteren Teil des Buses** from the back of the bus **hinter der Bühne** backstage [ˌbæk'steɪdʒ]
Hintergrund background ['bækgraʊnd]
hinterlassen: eine Nachricht hinterlassen leave a message [ˌliːv‿ə 'mesɪdʒ]
hinüberrennen (zu/nach …) run over (to) ['əʊvə]
hinunter down [daʊn]
hinunterbeugen: sich hinunterbeugen bend down [bend]
Hinweis *(Anhaltspunkt)* clue [kluː]
hinweisen: (jn.) auf etwas hinweisen point sth. out (to sb.) [ˌpɔɪnt‿'aʊt]
hinzufügen (zu) add (to) [æd]
Hirsch deer, *pl* deer [dɪə]
Hobby hobby ['hɒbi]
hoch high [haɪ]; *(Gebäude, Baum)* tall [tɔːl]
Hochland: das schottische Hochland the Highlands *(pl)* ['haɪləndz]
Hochmoor moor [mɔː], [mʊə]
hochsehen *(aufschauen)* look up [lʊk‿'ʌp]
hochspringen jump up
hoffen hope [həʊp]
höflich polite [pə'laɪt]
Höhle cave [keɪv]
holen: (sich) etwas holen get sth.
Hölle hell [hel]
Holz wood [wʊd]
hölzern wooden ['wʊdn]
horchen listen ['lɪsn]
hören hear [hɪə]
Horn horn [hɔːn]
Hose trousers *(pl)* ['traʊzəz]
Hotel hotel [həʊ'tel]
hübsch pretty ['prɪti]; *(schön, wunderbar)* lovely ['lʌvli]
Hüfte hip [hɪp]
Hügel hill [hɪl]
Hund dog [dɒg]
Hunger haben be hungry ['hʌŋgri]
Hungersnot famine ['fæmɪn]
hungrig sein be hungry ['hʌŋgri]
Husten haben have a cough [kɒf]
Hut hat [hæt]
Hütehund sheepdog ['ʃiːpdɒg]

I

ich I [aɪ] **Ich auch.** Me too.
ideal *(perfekt)* perfect ['pɜːfɪkt]
Idee idea [aɪ'dɪə]
identifizieren: jn./etwas identifizieren (anhand von etwas) identify sb./sth. (by sth.) [aɪ'dentɪfaɪ]
ihm him [hɪm]; *(bei Dingen, Tieren)* it
ihn him [hɪm]; *(bei Dingen, Tieren)* it
ihnen them [ðem], [ðəm]
Ihnen *(höfliche Anredeform)* you [juː]
ihr *(Plural von „du")* you [juː]
ihr: Hilf ihr. Help her. [hɜː]
ihr(e) … *(vor Nomen; besitzanzeigend)*
1. *(zu „she")* her … [hɜː, hə]
2. *(zu „it")* its … [ɪts]
3. *(zu „they")* their … [ðeə]
Ihr(e) … *(vor Nomen; besitzanzeigend)* *(zur höflichen Anredeform „you")* your … [jɔː, jə]

ihrer, ihre, ihrs *(zu „she")* hers [hɜːz]; *(zu „they")* theirs [ðeəz]
Ihrer, Ihre, Ihrs *(höfliche Anredeform)* yours [jɔːz]
im: im Jahr 1580 in 1580 **im Flugzeug** on the plane **im Radio** on the radio
Imbiss snack [snæk]
immer always ['ɔːlweɪz] **für immer** for ever [fər 'evə] **immer noch** still [stɪl] **immer wieder** again and again **etwas immer wieder / immer weiter tun** keep doing sth. [kiːp] **wann (auch) immer** whenever [ˌwen'evə] **was (auch) immer** whatever [wɒt'evə] **wer (auch) immer** whoever [huː'evə] **wo (auch) immer** wherever [weər'evə]
▶ S. 195 whenever, wherever, whatever, whoever
in in [ɪn]; *(in Ortsangaben auch oft:)* at [æt], [ət] **in der Beach Road** in Beach Road **in der Beach Road 8** at 8 Beach Road **in der Dean Street** in Dean Street **in der Dean Street 14** at 14 Dean Street **in der Nacht** at night **in der Nähe von** near **in der Schule** at school **in die Küche (hinein)** into the kitchen **in England** in England **in Ordnung** all right **in Schwierigkeiten sein** be in trouble ['trʌbl]
Inder/in Indian ['ɪndiən]
indirekt indirect [ˌɪndə'rekt], [ˌɪndaɪ'rekt]
indisch Indian ['ɪndiən]
Infinitiv infinitive [ɪn'fɪnətɪv]
Information(en) (über) information (about) *(no pl)* [ˌɪnfə'meɪʃn]
Informations- und Kommunikationstechnologie ICT [ˌaɪ siː 'tiː] (Information and Communication Technology)
Ingenieur/in engineer [ˌendʒɪ'nɪə]
Inhalt content ['kɒntent]
Inlineskaten skating ['skeɪtɪŋ]
Inlineskates skates [skeɪts]
innehalten pause [pɔːz]
Innenhof courtyard ['kɔːtjɑːd]
Innenseite: die Innenseite the inside [ˌɪn'saɪd]
Innere(r, s): im Innern von ... inside ... [ˌɪn'saɪd] **das Innere** the inside
innerhalb von ... inside ... [ˌɪn'saɪd]
Insel island ['aɪlənd]; *(Eiland)* isle [aɪl]
Inserat *(Anzeige)* advert ['ædvɜːt]
insgesamt *(alles in allem)* altogether [ˌɔːltə'geðə]
Instrument instrument ['ɪnstrəmənt]
Interaktion interaction [ˌɪntər'ækʃn]
interessant interesting ['ɪntrəstɪŋ]
interessieren: sich interessieren (für) be interested (in) ['ɪntrəstɪd] **jn. interessieren** interest sb. ['ɪntrəst] **Wen interessiert das?** Who cares?
interessiert sein (an) be interested (in) ['ɪntrəstɪd]
Internat boarding school ['bɔːdɪŋ skuːl]
international international [ˌɪntə'næʃnəl]
Interview interview ['ɪntəvjuː]
interviewen: jn. interviewen interview sb. ['ɪntəvjuː]
irgendetwas? anything? ['eniθɪŋ]
irgendjemand? anybody? / anyone? ['enibɒdi, 'eniwʌn]
irgendwelche: Gibt es irgendwelche ...? Are there any ...? ['eni]
irren: jemand irrt sich *(jemand hat Unrecht)* someone is wrong [rɒŋ]

J

ja yes [jes] **Ja, das ist richtig. / Ja, das stimmt.** Yes, that's right.
Jacht yacht [jɒt]
Jacke, Jackett jacket ['dʒækɪt]
Jahr year [jɪə]
Jahrgang, Jahrgangsstufe year [jɪə]
Jahrhundert century ['sentʃəri]
Januar January ['dʒænjuəri]
je: besser als je zuvor better than ever
Jeans jeans *(pl)* [dʒiːnz]
jede(r, s) ... every ... ['evri]; *(jede(r, s) einzelne)* each ... [iːtʃ]
Jedenfalls, ... *(Wie dem auch sei)* Anyway, ... ['eniweɪ]
jeder *(alle)* everyone ['evriwʌn], everybody ['evribɒdi] **sonst jeder** everybody else
▶ S. 195 ... else
Jeep jeep [dʒiːp]
jemals ever ['evə] **Bist du jemals in ... gewesen?** Have you ever been to ...?
jemand somebody / someone ['sʌmbədi, 'sʌmwʌn]; *(in Fragen)* anybody? / anyone? ['enibɒdi, 'eniwʌn] **jemand anders** someone else **Finde jemanden, der ...** Find someone who ...
▶ S. 195 ... else
jene(r, s): jener Ort / jene Fähre / jenes Kleid that place/ferry/dress **jene Leute** those people
jetzt now [naʊ] **jetzt gerade** right now **bis jetzt** so far **Jetzt, wo du ...** Now that you ...
Job job [dʒɒb]
Joghurt yoghurt ['jɒgət]
Jongleur/in juggler ['dʒʌglə]
jonglieren: mit etwas jonglieren juggle sth. ['dʒʌgl]
jubeln cheer [tʃɪə]
Judo judo ['dʒuːdəʊ]
Jugendliche(r) kid [kɪd] *(infml)*
Juli July [dʒu'laɪ]
jung young [jʌŋ]
Junge boy [bɔɪ]
Juni June [dʒuːn]
Juwelen jewels *(pl)* ['dʒuːəlz]

K

Kaffee coffee ['kɒfi]
Käfig cage [keɪdʒ]
Kajak kayak ['kaɪæk]
Kakao cocoa ['kəʊkəʊ]
Kalender diary ['daɪəri]
kalt cold [kəʊld]
Kamera camera ['kæmərə]
Kameramann cameraman, *pl* -men
Kamin fireplace ['faɪəpleɪs]
Kampf *(Schlägerei)* fight; *(Schlacht)* battle ['bætl]
kämpfen fight [faɪt] **gegen jn. kämpfen** fight sb.
Kämpfer/in fighter ['faɪtə]
Kanal canal [kə'næl]
Kaninchen rabbit ['ræbɪt]
Kante edge [edʒ]
Kantine canteen [kæn'tiːn]
Kapitän/in captain ['kæptɪn]
Kappe cap [cæp]
kaputt broken ['brəʊkən] **kaputt gehen** break [breɪk] **etwas kaputt machen** break sth.
Karneval carnival ['kɑːnɪvl]
Karotte carrot ['kært]
Karren cart [kɑːt]
Karriere career [kə'rɪə]
Karte (an) card (to) [kɑːd]
Kartoffel potato [pə'teɪtəʊ], *pl* potatoes
Käse cheese [tʃiːz]
Kasse *(in Geschäften)* cash desk ['kæʃ desk]; *(für den Verkauf von Eintrittskarten)* ticket office ['tɪkɪt‿ɒfɪs]
Kästchen box [bɒks]
Kasten box [bɒks]
Kathedrale cathedral [kə'θiːdrəl]
Katze cat [kæt]
kaufen buy [baɪ]
Käufer/in shopper ['ʃɒpə]
kaum: Ich kann es kaum erwarten, ... zu sehen I can't wait to see ...
Kehle throat [θrəʊt]
kein(e) no [nəʊ] **keine(r, s) von ...** none of ... [nʌn] **Es gibt/sind keine ...** There aren't any ... ['eni] **Ich bin kein Junge.** I'm not a boy. **Ich mag kein Grün.** I don't like green. **er hat keine Zeit** he doesn't have time
Keks biscuit ['bɪskɪt]
kennen know [nəʊ] **Woher kennst du ...?** How do you know ...?
kennenlernen meet [miːt] **Freut mich, dich/euch/Sie kennenzulernen.** Nice to meet you.
kennzeichnen: etwas kennzeichnen mark sth. up [ˌmɑːk‿'ʌp]
Kerze candle ['kændl]
Kette chain [tʃeɪn]
Kilogramm, Kilo (kg) kilogram ['kɪləgræm], kilo ['kiːləʊ] (kg)
Kilometer (km) kilometre ['kɪləmiːtə], [kɪ'lɒmɪtə] (km)

Kind child [tʃaɪld], *pl* children ['tʃɪldrən]; *(infml auch:)* kid [kɪd]
Kino cinema ['sɪnəmə]
Kirche church [tʃɜːtʃ]
Kiste box [bɒks]
Klang sound [saʊnd]
klar *(deutlich)* clear [klɪə]
Klasse class [klɑːs]
Klassenkamerad/in classmate ['klɑːsmeɪt]
Klassenzimmer classroom ['klɑːsruːm]
klatschen *(Beifall)* clap [klæp] **Klatscht in die Hände.** Clap your hands.
Klavier piano [pi'ænəʊ] **Klavier spielen** play the piano
Klebestift glue stick ['gluː stɪk]
klebrig sticky ['stɪki]
Klebstoff glue [gluː]
Kleid dress [dres]
Kleidung, Kleidungsstücke clothes *(pl)* [kləʊðz]
klein little ['lɪtl]; small [smɔːl]; *(bes. Scottish English, infml:)* wee [wiː]
klettern climb [klaɪm]
Klingel bell [bel]
klingeln ring [rɪŋ]
klingen sound [saʊnd]
Klippe cliff [klɪf]
klopfen knock [nɒk]; *(tippen)* tap [tæp]
Klopfen tap [tæp]
Klub club [klʌb] **in einen Klub eintreten / sich einem Klub anschließen** join a club [dʒɔɪn]
klug clever ['klevə]
Knall bang [bæŋ]
knallhart tough [tʌf]
Kneipe pub [pʌb]
Knie knee [niː]
knien kneel [niːl]
kochen cook [kʊk]
Kohle coal [kəʊl]
Kohlebergwerk coal mine ['kəʊl maɪn]
Komiker/in comedian [kə'miːdiən]
komisch **1.** *(lustig)* funny ['fʌni] **2.** *(seltsam, merkwürdig)* funny; strange [streɪndʒ]; weird [wɪəd]
Komma comma ['kɒmə] **1,6 (eins Komma sechs)** 1.6 (one point six) [pɔɪnt]
▶ S. 181 Numbers
kommen come [kʌm]; *(gelangen, hinkommen)* get [get] **Ich komme aus Plymouth.** I'm from Plymouth. **Komm, Dad!** *(Na los, Dad!)* Come on, Dad. **nach Hause kommen** come home **auf etwas kommen** *(Idee, Vorschlag)* come up with sth. **Kommt nicht in Frage!** No way! [ˌnəʊ 'weɪ]
▶ S. 180 (to) come across/down/over/…
Komödiant/in comedian [kə'miːdiən]
Komödie comedy ['kɒmədi]
König king [kɪŋ]
Königin queen [kwiːn]
königlich royal ['rɔɪəl]
Königreich kingdom ['kɪŋdəm]

können can [kæn], [kən]; be able to ['eɪbl] **ich kann nicht … / du kannst nicht …** *usw.* I can't … / you can't … *etc.* [kɑːnt] **gut Kung-Fu können** be good at kung fu
konnte(n): ich konnte … I could … [kʊd]; I was able to … ['eɪbl] **ich konnte nicht …** I couldn't … [kʊdnt]; I wasn't able to …
könnte(n): Was könnte besser sein? What could be better? [kʊd], [kəd] / What might be better? [maɪt]
▶ S. 188 möglich – wahrscheinlich – sicherlich
Konsonant consonant ['kɒnsənənt]
konstruieren *(entwerfen)* design [dɪ'zaɪn]
Kontakt: (mit jm.) Kontakt aufnehmen get in touch (with sb.) [tʌtʃ] **(mit jm.) Kontakt halten** stay in touch (with sb.)
Kontext *(Text-, Satzzusammenhang)* context ['kɒntekst]
Kontrolle *(Überprüfung)* check [tʃek]
kontrollieren *(überprüfen)* check [tʃek]
konzentrieren: sich konzentrieren (auf etwas) concentrate (on sth.) ['kɒnsntreɪt]
Konzert concert ['kɒnsət]
Koordinator/in coordinator [kəʊ'ɔːdɪneɪtə]
Kopf head [hed]
Kopfschmerzen haben have a headache ['hedeɪk]
Kopie copy ['kɒpi]
kopieren copy ['kɒpi]
Korb basket ['bɑːskɪt]
Körper body ['bɒdi]
Körperteil part of the body
korrekt correct [kə'rekt]
Korridor corridor ['kɒrɪdɔː]
korrigieren correct [kə'rekt]
kosten cost [kɒst] **Die Kamera kostet …** The camera is … **Die DVDs kosten …** The DVDs are … **Was/Wie viel kostet …?** How much is …? **Was/Wie viel kosten …?** How much are …?
kostenlos free
köstlich delicious [dɪ'lɪʃəs]
Kostüm costume ['kɒstjuːm]
Kraft *(Energie)* energy ['enədʒi]
kräftig strong [strɒŋ]
Kram stuff [stʌf] *(infml)*
krank sick [sɪk]; ill [ɪl]
Krankenhaus hospital ['hɒspɪtl]
Krankheit illness ['ɪlnəs]; *(ernsthaft; ansteckend)* disease [dɪ'ziːz]
Krebs *(Tier)* crab [kræb]
Kreis circle ['sɜːkl]
Kreisverkehr roundabout ['raʊndəbaʊt]
kreuzen; sich kreuzen cross [krɒs]
Kreuzfahrt cruise [kruːz]
Kreuzotter adder ['ædə]
Kreuzung *(Straßenkreuzung)* junction ['dʒʌŋkʃn]
Kreuzworträtsel crossword ['krɒswɜːd]

Kricket cricket ['krɪkɪt]
Krieg war [wɔː]
kriegen: Ärger kriegen get into trouble
Krone crown [kraʊn]
Küche kitchen ['kɪtʃɪn]
Kuchen cake [keɪk]
Kugelschreiber pen [pen]
Kuh cow [kaʊ]
kühl cool [kuːl]
kümmern: sich um jn. kümmern look after sb.
Kultur culture ['kʌltʃə]
Kunst art [ɑːt]
Künstler/in artist ['ɑːtɪst]; performer [pə'fɔːmə]
Kunststoff plastic ['plæstɪk]
Kunststück trick [trɪk]
kurz short [ʃɔːt] **kurz nachdem …** just after … **Kann ich Sie kurz sprechen?** May I have a word with you?
küssen; sich küssen kiss [kɪs]
Küste coast [kəʊst]

L

lächeln smile [smaɪl]
Lächeln smile [smaɪl]
lachen laugh [lɑːf] **über jn./etwas lachen** laugh at sb./sth.
Laden shop [ʃɒp] **Laden an der Ecke** *(„Tante-Emma-Laden")* corner shop ['kɔːnə ʃɒp]
Lage: in der Lage sein, etwas zu tun be able to do sth. ['eɪbl]
Lamm lamb [læm]
Lampe lamp [læmp]
Land *(auch als Gegensatz zur Stadt)* country ['kʌntri]; *(Grund und Boden)* land [lænd] **an Land gehen** land
landen land [lænd]
Landkarte map ['mæp] **auf der Landkarte** on the map
Landschaft *(ländliche Gegend)* countryside ['kʌntrisaɪd]
Landwirt/in farmer ['fɑːmə]
lang long [lɒŋ] **eine Zeit lang** for a while **lange aufbleiben** stay up late
langsam slow [sləʊ] **er schüttelte langsam den Kopf** he shook his head slowly ['sləʊli]
langweilen: sich langweilen be/feel bored [bɔːd]
langweilig boring ['bɔːrɪŋ]
Laptop laptop ['læptɒp]
Lärm noise [nɔɪz] **voller Lärm** noisy ['nɔɪzi]
lärmend noisy ['nɔɪzi]
lassen **1.** let **Lass mich dir … zeigen.** Let me show you … **Lass(t) uns …** Let's … **2.** leave [liːv] **Lass bitte das Fenster offen.** Leave the window open, please. **etwas übrig lassen (für jn.)** leave sth. (for sb.) **etwas fallen lassen** drop

sth. [drɒp] **3. Lass das!** *(Hör auf damit)* Stop it! *(infml)*
laufen run [rʌn]; *(im Fernsehen, Radio)* be on
Läufer/in runner ['rʌnə]
laut loud [laʊd]; *(unangenehm laut)* noisy ['nɔɪzi] **laut (vor)lesen** read aloud [ə'laʊd] **mit lauter Stimme** in a loud voice **etwas lauter stellen** turn sth. up [tɜːn]
läuten ring [rɪŋ]
lautlos silently ['saɪləntli]
Lautsprecher loudspeaker [ˌlaʊd'spiːkə]
Layout layout ['leɪaʊt]
Leben life [laɪf], *pl* lives [laɪvz] **am Leben sein** be alive [ə'laɪv]
leben 1. *(wohnen)* live [lɪv] **2.** *(am Leben sein)* be alive [ə'laɪv]
Lebensraum habitat ['hæbɪtæt]
lecker delicious [dɪ'lɪʃəs]; tasty ['teɪsti]; yummy ['jʌmi] *(infml)*
ledig *(alleinstehend)* single ['sɪŋgl]
leer empty ['empti]
legen *(hinlegen, ablegen)* put [pʊt]
Legende legend ['ledʒənd]
Lehm clay [kleɪ]
lehren *(unterrichten)* teach [tiːtʃ]
Lehrer/in teacher ['tiːtʃə]
Lehrgang workshop ['wɜːkʃɒp]
Leiche body ['bɒdi]
leicht *(einfach)* easy ['iːzi]
leid: Es tut mir leid (wegen ...) I'm sorry (about ...)
leiden: nicht leiden können dislike [dɪs'laɪk]
leise quiet ['kwaɪət]; silent ['saɪlənt] **sie sang leise** she sang softly ['sɒftli] **etwas leiser stellen** turn sth. down
leiten lead [liːd]
Leiter/in leader ['liːdə]; *(Orchester, Theater)* director [də'rektə]
lenken steer [stɪə]
lernen learn [lɜːn]; *(studieren)* study ['stʌdi]
Lernposter study poster ['stʌdi pəʊstə]
lesen read [riːd] **jemandes Gedanken lesen** read sb.'s mind [maɪnd]
Leser/in reader ['riːdə]
letzte(r, s) last [lɑːst]; *(Final-, End-)* final ['faɪnl] **letztes Wochenende / letzten Freitag** last weekend/Friday **das Musical/Theaterstück vom letzten Jahr** last year's musical/play
leuchtend bright [braɪt]
Leute people ['piːpl]; folk *(pl)* [fəʊk] *(infml)*
Licht light [laɪt]
Lichtblitz flash [flæʃ]
Liebe: Alles Liebe, ... / Liebe Grüße, ... *(Briefschluss)* Love, ...
liebe(r, s) dear [dɪə]
lieben love [lʌv]
Liebling *(Schatz)* darling ['dɑːlɪŋ]
Lieblings-: mein Lieblingstier my favourite animal ['feɪvərɪt]
Lied song [sɒŋ]
Lieferwagen van [væn]
liegen lie [laɪ] **Tiere liegen mir sehr am Herzen.** I really care about animals. ▶ S. 191 (to) care
lila purple ['pɜːpl]
Lineal ruler ['ruːlə]
Linie *(U-Bahn)* line [laɪn]
linke(r, s) left [left] **auf der linken Seite** on the left **nach links** left **(nach) links abbiegen** turn left
Lippe lip [lɪp]
Liste list [lɪst]
Loch hole [həʊl]
Löffel spoon [spuːn]
Lokal *(Kneipe)* pub [pʌb]
Lokal- *(am/vom Ort)* local ['ləʊkl]
los: Los geht's. / Jetzt geht's los. Here we go. **Los mit euch jetzt!** Off you go now. **Was ist los?** What's the matter? ['mætə]; What's up? **Was ist los mit Justin/dir?** *(Was fehlt Justin/dir?)* What's wrong with Justin/you?
lösen solve [sɒlv]
Löwe lion ['laɪən]
Luchs lynx [lɪŋks], *pl* lynx *or* lynxes
Luft air [eə]
lustig: sich über jn./etwas lustig machen make fun of sb./sth.

M

machen *(tun)* do [duː]; *(herstellen)* make [meɪk] **aus etwas gemacht sein** be made of sth. **einen Fehler machen** make a mistake **einen Spaziergang machen** go for a walk [wɔːk] **Fotos machen** take photos **Hat es Spaß gemacht?** Was it fun? **jn. zu etwas machen** make sb. sth. **sich fertig machen (für)** get ready (for) ['redi]
Mädchen girl [gɜːl]
Magen stomach ['stʌmək]
magisch magic ['mædʒɪk]; magical ['mædʒɪkl]
Mahlzeit meal [miːl]
Mai May [meɪ]
Make-up make-up ['meɪk_ʌp]
mal: (vorher) schon mal before [bɪ'fɔː] **Warst du schon mal hier?** Have you been here before?
Mal time [taɪm] **dieses Mal** this time **zum ersten Mal** for the first time
Malaria malaria [mə'leəriə]
malen paint [peɪnt]
Maler/in painter ['peɪntə]
Mama mum [mʌm]
man you
manchmal sometimes ['sʌmtaɪmz]
Mann man [mæn], *pl* men [men]
Mannschaft team [tiːm]
Mantel coat [kəʊt]
Marine navy ['neɪvi]
Marionette puppet ['pʌpɪt]
markieren mark (up) [mɑːk]; *(mit Textmarker)* highlight ['haɪlaɪt]
Markt market ['mɑːkɪt]
Marmelade jam [dʒæm]
März March [mɑːtʃ]
Maske mask [mɑːsk]
Material material [mə'tɪəriəl]
Mathematik maths [mæθs]
Matrose sailor ['seɪlə]
Matsch mud [mʌd]
Mauer wall [wɔːl]
Maul mouth [maʊθ]
Medien: soziale Medien social media *(pl)* [ˌsəʊʃl 'miːdiə]
Meer sea [siː] **am Meer** by the sea
Meerschweinchen guinea pig ['gɪni pɪg]
Megaphon loudspeaker [ˌlaʊd'spiːkə]
mehr more [mɔː] **nicht mehr** not ... any more **nicht mehr da sein** be gone [gɒn]
mehrere *(verschiedene)* several ['sevrəl]
Meile *(ca. 1,6 km)* mile [maɪl]
meilenweit for miles [maɪlz]
mein(e) ... my ... [maɪ]
meinen *(sagen wollen)* mean [miːn]
meiner, meine, meins mine [maɪn]
Meinung opinion [ə'pɪnjən] **meiner Meinung nach** in my opinion
meisten: die meisten Menschen most people [məʊst] **die meisten von ihnen** most of them
meistens usually ['juːʒuəli]
Meister/in master ['mɑːstə]; *(Champion)* champion ['tʃæmpiən]
melden: sich melden put your hand up
Menge *(Menschenmenge)* crowd [kraʊd]
Mensa *(Kantine)* canteen [kæn'tiːn]
Menschen people ['piːpl]
merken: sich etwas merken remember sth. [rɪ'membə]
Merkzettel crib sheet ['krɪb ʃiːt] *(infml)*
Messer knife [naɪf], *pl* knives [naɪvz]
Meter metre ['miːtə]
mich me [miː]; *(Reflexivpronomen)* myself [maɪ'self]
Milch milk [mɪlk]
Million million ['mɪljən]
Mimik *(Gesichtsausdruck)* facial expression [ˌfeɪʃl_ɪk'spreʃn]
Mine 1. *(Bergwerk)* mine [maɪn] **2.** *(Militär)* mine [maɪn]
Minute minute ['mɪnɪt]
mir me [miː]; *(Reflexivpronomen)* myself [maɪ'self]
mit with [wɪð] **mit dem Bus/Auto fahren** go by bus/car
Mitfahrgelegenheit lift [lɪft]
Mitglied member ['membə]
Mitlaut *(Konsonant)* consonant ['kɒnsənənt]
mitmachen: (bei etwas) mitmachen join in (sth.) [dʒɔɪn]
Mitschüler/in classmate ['klɑːsmeɪt]
mitsingen: (mit jm.) mitsingen sing along (with sb.)

Mittag: zu Mittag essen have lunch [lʌntʃ]
Mittagessen lunch [lʌntʃ]
mittags at lunchtime ['lʌntʃtaɪm]
Mittagszeit lunchtime ['lʌntʃtaɪm]
Mitte middle ['mɪdl]; *(Zentrum)* centre ['sentə]
Mitternacht midnight ['mɪdnaɪt]
Mittwoch Wednesday ['wenzdeɪ, -di]
Mitwirkende *(Besetzung in Theaterstück, Film)* cast [kɑːst]
Möbel furniture *(no pl)* ['fɜːnɪtʃə] **Die Möbel sind neu.** The furniture is new. **ein Möbel(stück)** a piece of furniture [piːs]
Mobiltelefon mobile phone [ˌməʊbaɪl 'fəʊn], *(kurz auch:)* mobile
möchte: Ich möchte … (haben) I'd like … [ˌaɪd 'laɪk] (= I would like …) **Ich möchte gehen.** I'd like to go. **Was möchtest du (haben)?** What would you like? [wʊd] **Was möchtest du essen?** What would you like to eat?
Mode fashion ['fæʃn]
Model model ['mɒdl]
Modell model ['mɒdl]
modern modern ['mɒdən]
mögen like [laɪk]; *(auf etwas stehen)* be into *(infml)* **nicht mögen** dislike [dɪs'laɪk] **Ich mag Grün nicht. / Ich mag kein Grün.** I don't like green.
Möglichkeit *(Chance)* chance [tʃɑːns]
Möhre carrot ['kært]
Moment moment ['məʊmənt] **im Moment** at the moment **Warte einen Moment. / Moment mal.** Wait a minute.
Monat month [mʌnθ]
Mond moon [muːn]
Mondlicht moonlight ['muːnlaɪt]
Monster monster ['mɒnstə]
Montag Monday ['mʌndeɪ, 'mʌndi]
Monument (für/zum Gedenken an) monument (to) ['mɒnjumənt]
morgen tomorrow [tə'mɒrəʊ] **morgen früh, morgen Vormittag** tomorrow morning
Morgen *(Vormittag)* morning ['mɔːnɪŋ] **am Morgen** in the morning
morgens in the morning ['mɔːnɪŋ]
Moschee mosque [mɒsk]
Motorrad motorbike ['məʊtəbaɪk]
Möwe seagull ['siːgʌl]
MP3-Player, MP3-Spieler MP3 player [ˌempiː'θriː ˌpleɪə]
müde tired ['taɪəd]
Müll rubbish ['rʌbɪʃ]
Mund mouth [maʊθ]
Münze coin [kɔɪn]
murmeln: …, murmelte er. …, he said under his breath. [breθ]
Museum museum [mju'ziːəm]
Musical musical ['mjuːzɪkl]
Musik music ['mjuːzɪk]
Musiker/in musician [mju'zɪʃn]
müssen have to ['hæv tə]; need to ['niːd tə]; must [mʌst] **du musst es nicht tun** you don't have to do it; you don't need to do it; you needn't do it ['niːdnt]
▶ S. 188 möglich – wahrscheinlich – sicherlich
Mutter mother ['mʌðə]
Mutti mum [mʌm]

N

Na: Na ja, … Well, … [wel] **Na los, Dad!** *(Komm, Dad!)* Come on, Dad. **Na und?** So? [səʊ]; Who cares?
nach **1.** *(örtlich)* to [tu], [tə] **nach draußen** outside [ˌaʊt'saɪd] **nach drinnen** inside [ˌɪn'saɪd] **nach Hause gehen/kommen** go/come home **nach oben** up; *(im Haus)* upstairs [ˌʌp'steəz] **nach unten** down; *(im Haus)* downstairs [ˌdaʊn'steəz] **nach vorn** to the front **einer nach dem anderen** one by one
2. *(zeitlich)* after ['ɑːftə] **nach dem Frühstück** after breakfast **Viertel nach zehn (10.15 / 22.15)** quarter past ten ['kwɔːtə pɑːst]
Nachbar/in neighbour ['neɪbə]
nachdem after ['ɑːftə] **gleich nachdem / kurz nachdem …** just after …
nachgehen *(Uhr)* be slow
Nachmittag afternoon [ˌɑːftə'nuːn] **am Nachmittag** in the afternoon
nachmittags in the afternoon [ˌɑːftə'nuːn]
Nachricht message ['mesɪdʒ] **eine Nachricht hinterlassen** leave a message [ˌliːv_ə 'mesɪdʒ]
Nachrichten news *(no pl)* [njuːz]
nachschauen have a look
nachschlagen look up
Nachspeise dessert [dɪ'zɜːt]
nächste(r, s) next [nekst] **das nächste Bild / die nächste Frage** the next picture/question **das Musical/Theaterstück/… vom nächsten Jahr** next year's musical/play/… **als Nächstes** next [nekst]
Nacht night [naɪt] **heute Nacht** tonight [tə'naɪt] **in der Nacht** at night
Nachttisch dessert [dɪ'zɜːt]
nachts at night [ət 'naɪt]
nachverfolgen *(überwachen)* monitor ['mɒnɪtə]
nackt *(Hände, Arme, Füße)* bare [beə]
Nähe: in der Nähe von near [nɪə] **hier in der Nähe** near here
nahe (bei) near [nɪə]
nahegelegen: eine nahegelegene Stadt a nearby town ['nɪəbaɪ]
Name name [neɪm] **Mein Name ist Silky.** My name is Silky.
Nase nose [nəʊz]
nass wet [wet] **jn. nass spritzen** splash sb. [splæʃ]
Nation nation ['neɪʃn]
national, National- national ['næʃnəl]
Naturkunde natural history [ˌnætʃrəl 'hɪstri]
natürlich natural ['nætʃrəl]; *(selbstverständlich)* of course [əv 'kɔːs]
Naturwissenschaft science ['saɪəns]
Naturwissenschaftler/in scientist ['saɪəntɪst]
neben next to ['nekst tʊ]
Nebensatz sub-clause ['sʌbklɔːz] **Nebensatz mit if** if-clause ['ɪfklɔːz]
nehmen take [teɪk] **jn. am Arm nehmen** take sb. by the arm **etwas wichtig nehmen** care about sth. [keə]
▶ S. 191 (to) care
neidisch (auf) jealous (of) ['dʒeləs]
nein no [nəʊ] **Nein, das ist falsch. / Nein, das stimmt nicht.** No, that's wrong.
nennen name [neɪm]; *(rufen, bezeichnen)* call [kɔːl]
nervös nervous ['nɜːvəs]
nett nice [naɪs]; kind [kaɪnd]
Netz net [net]
neu new [njuː]
neugierig curious ['kjʊəriəs]
Neuigkeiten news [njuːz]
neun nine [naɪn]
nicht not [nɒt] **auch nicht** not … either ['aɪðə], ['iːðə] **Ich auch nicht.** Me neither. ['naɪðə], ['niːðə] **Geh nicht.** Don't go. [dəʊnt] **Ich mag Grün nicht.** I don't like green. **Ich weiß (es) nicht.** I don't know. **nicht mehr** not … any more **nicht vor drei** not till three; not until three **…, nicht wahr?** …, right? **noch nicht** not … yet [jet] **(noch) nicht einmal** not even
nichts not … anything ['eniθɪŋ]
nicken nod [nɒd]
nie never ['nevə] **(vorher) noch nie** not … before, never … before
niemals never ['nevə]
niemand no one ['nəʊ wʌn], nobody ['nəʊbədi]; not … anybody/anyone ['enibɒdi, 'eniwʌn] **niemand anders / niemand sonst** no one else [els]
▶ S. 195 … else
niesen sneeze [sniːz]
nirgendwo(hin) nowhere ['nəʊweə]
noch: noch ein Foto one more photo [mɔː]; another photo [ə'nʌðə] **noch einmal** again [ə'gen] **noch nicht** not … yet [jet] **noch nicht einmal** not even **immer noch** still [stɪl] **(vorher) noch nie** not/never before **sonst noch etwas?** anything else? **was (sonst) noch?** what else? **wer (sonst) noch?** who else?
▶ S. 195 … else
Nomen noun [naʊn]
Norden north [nɔːθ] **nach Norden** north **Richtung Norden** northbound ['nɔːθbaʊnd]

nördlich north [nɔːθ]; northern ['nɔːðən]
Nordosten north-east [ˌnɔːθ‿'iːst] **nach Nordosten** north-east
nordöstlich north-east [ˌnɔːθ‿'iːst]
Nordwesten north-west [ˌnɔːθ'west] **nach Nordwesten** north-west
nordwestlich north-west [ˌnɔːθ'west]
normal normal ['nɔːməl]
normalerweise usually ['juːʒuəli]
Note *(Musik)* note [nəʊt]
nötig necessary ['nesəsəri]
Notiz note [nəʊt] **(sich) Notizen machen** *(beim Lesen oder Zuhören)* take notes **(sich) Notizen machen (über/zu etwas)** *(zur Vorbereitung)* make notes (on sth.)
notwendig necessary ['nesəsəri]
November November [nəʊ'vembə]
null, Null nil [nɪl]; *(in Telefonnummern)* o [əʊ]
Nummer number ['nʌmbə]
nun now [naʊ] **Nun, …** Well, … [wel] **Nun, da du …** Now that you …
nur only ['əʊnli]; *(einfach nur)* just [dʒʌst]

O

ob if **als ob** as if; like *(infml)*
oben *(an der Spitze, am oberen Ende)* at the top (of); *(darüber)* above [ə'bʌv]; *(im Haus)* upstairs [ˌʌp'steəz] **hier oben** up here **nach oben** up; *(im Haus)* upstairs
Oberfläche surface ['sɜːfɪs]
oberhalb (von) above [ə'bʌv]
Objekt object ['ɒbdʒekt]
Obst fruit [fruːt]
Obstsalat fruit salad [ˌfruːt 'sæləd]
oder or [ɔː]
offen open ['əʊpən]
öffnen; sich öffnen open ['əʊpən]
Öffnungszeiten opening times *(pl)*
oft often ['ɒfn], ['ɒftən]
ohne without [wɪ'ðaʊt]
Ohr ear [ɪə]
Ohrhörer earphones *(pl)* ['ɪəfəʊnz]
Oje! Oh dear! [dɪə]
okay OK [ˌəʊ'keɪ]; all right [ɔːl 'raɪt]
Oktober October [ɒk'təʊbə]
Öl oil [ɔɪl]
Oma grandma ['grænmɑː]
Onkel uncle ['ʌŋkl]
online online [ˌɒn'laɪn]
Opa grandpa ['grænpɑː]
Orange orange ['ɒrɪndʒ]
orange(farben) orange ['ɒrɪndʒ]
ordnen order ['ɔːdə]
Ordnung: in Ordnung *(okay)* all right [ɔːl 'raɪt]; OK [ˌəʊ'keɪ]
organisieren organize ['ɔːgənaɪz]
Ort place [pleɪs] **am/vom Ort** local ['ləʊkl]
örtlich local ['ləʊkl]
Osten east [iːst] **nach Osten** east
Ostern Easter ['iːstə]
östlich east [iːst]; eastern ['iːstən]
Otter otter ['ɒtə]
Ozean ocean ['əʊʃn]

P

paar: ein paar a few [ə 'fjuː]; some [sʌm], [səm]; a couple ['kʌpl]
Paar: ein Paar a pair (of) [peə]; a couple ['kʌpl]
Päckchen packet ['pækɪt]
packen pack [pæk]; *(sich greifen)* grab [græb]
Packung packet ['pækɪt]
Palast palace ['pæləs]
Panik: in Panik geraten panic ['pænɪk]
Papa dad [dæd]
Papier paper ['peɪpə]
Parade parade [pə'reɪd]
Park park [pɑːk]
parken park [pɑːk]
Parlament parliament ['pɑːləmənt]
Partner/in partner ['pɑːtnə]
Party party ['pɑːti]
Pass *(Reisepass)* passport ['pɑːspɔːt]
Pass auf! *(Vorsicht!)* Watch out! [ˌwɒtʃ‿'aʊt]
passen: zu etwas passen *(zu etwas gehören)* go with sth. **zueinander passen** go together
passieren (mit) happen (to) ['hæpən]
Pause break [breɪk] **eine Pause einlegen** pause [pɔːz]
pausieren pause [pɔːz]
Pence pence [pens]
▶ S. 188 Pounds and euros
perfekt perfect ['pɜːfɪkt]
Person person ['pɜːsn]; *(in Roman, Film, Theaterstück usw.)* character ['kærəktə]
Personalausweis ID card [ˌaɪ 'diː kɑːd]
Pfad path [pɑːθ]; trail [treɪl]
Pfannkuchen pancake ['pænkeɪk]
Pfeffer pepper ['pepə]
Pfeife **1.** *(Trillerpfeife)* whistle ['wɪsl] **2.** *(Tabakspfeife)* pipe [paɪp]
pfeifen whistle ['wɪsl]; blow the whistle [bləʊ]
Pferd horse [hɔːs]
Pfiff whistle ['wɪsl]
Pflanze plant [plɑːnt]
pflanzen plant [plɑːnt]
Pflaster *(Heftpflaster)* plaster ['plɑːstə]
Pforte *(Gatter)* gate [geɪt]
Pfote paw [pɔː]
Pfund *(britische Währung)* pound (£) [paʊnd]
▶ S. 189 Pounds and euros
Piano piano [pi'ænəʊ]
Picknick picnic ['pɪknɪk]
piepen beep [biːp]
pink pink [pɪŋk]
Pizza pizza ['piːtsə]
Plan plan [plæn]; *(Zeitplan, Programm)* schedule ['ʃedjuːl]
planen plan [plæn]
Planet planet ['plænɪt]
Plantage plantation [plɑːn'teɪʃn]
Plastik plastic ['plæstɪk]
Plattform platform ['plætfɔːm]
Platz place [pleɪs]; *(Position)* position [pə'zɪʃn]; *(freier Raum)* room [ruːm]; *(Sportplatz, Spielfeld)* pitch [pɪtʃ] **auf dem zweiten Platz** in second place
Plätzchen *(Keks)* biscuit ['bɪskɪt]
plaudern chat [tʃæt]
plötzlich suddenly ['sʌdnli]
Pokal *(Trophäe)* trophy ['trəʊfi]
Polizei police *(pl)* [pə'liːs]
Polizeiwache, -revier police station [pə'liːs steɪʃn]
Polizist police officer [pə'liːs‿ˌɒfɪsə]; policeman [pə'liːsmən]
Polizistin police officer [pə'liːs‿ˌɒfɪsə]; policewoman [pə'liːswʊmən]
Pommes frites chips *(pl)* [tʃɪps]; *(American English)* fries *(pl)* [fraɪz]
Pony pony ['pəʊni]
populär (bei) popular (with) ['pɒpjələ]
Porträt *(Personenbeschreibung)* profile ['prəʊfaɪl]
Position position [pə'zɪʃn]; *(Standort)* location [ləʊ'keɪʃn]
Postamt post office ['pəʊst‿ɒfɪs]
Poster poster ['pəʊstə]
Posting *(auf Blog)* post [pəʊst]
Postkarte postcard ['pəʊstkɑːd]
praktisch practical ['præktɪkl]
Praline chocolate ['tʃɒklət]
prallen: gegen etwas prallen hit sth. [hɪt]
Präsentation presentation [ˌprezn'teɪʃn]
präsentieren: (jm.) etwas präsentieren present sth. (to sb.) [prɪ'zent]
Präsident/in president ['prezɪdənt]
Preis **1.** *(Kaufpreis)* price [praɪs] **2.** *(Gewinn)* prize [praɪz]
preiswert *(billig)* cheap [tʃiːp]
Prinz prince [prɪns]
Prinzessin princess [ˌprɪn'ses], ['prɪnses]
pro: einmal/zweimal pro Woche/Jahr once/twice a week/year
Probe *(Theater)* rehearsal [rɪ'hɜːsl]
probieren try [traɪ]
Problem problem ['prɒbləm]
Profil *(Personenbeschreibung, Porträt)* profile ['prəʊfaɪl]
Programm programme ['prəʊgræm]; *(Zeitplan)* schedule ['ʃedjuːl]
Projekt project ['prɒdʒekt]
Prospekt *(Broschüre)* brochure ['brəʊʃə]
Protest protest ['prəʊtest]
protestieren protest [prə'test]
prüfen *(testen)* test [test]; *(überprüfen)* check [tʃek]; *(untersuchen)* look into
Publikum audience ['ɔːdiəns]
Pullover pullover ['pʊləʊvə]

Punkt point [pɔɪnt]; *(Satzzeichen)* full stop [ˌfʊl ˈstɒp]; *(Fleck)* spot [spɒt]
▶ S. 181 Numbers
Punktestand *(Spielstand)* score [skɔː]
putzen clean [kliːn]
Puzzle jigsaw [ˈdʒɪɡsɔː]

Q

Quadratkilometer (km²) square kilometre (sq km) [ˌskweə kɪˈlɒmɪtə]
Quiz quiz [kwɪz]

R

Rabe raven [ˈreɪvn]
Rad *(Fahrrad)* bike [baɪk] **Rad fahren** ride a bike [ˌraɪd‿ə ˈbaɪk]
Radiergummi rubber [ˈrʌbə]
Radio radio [ˈreɪdiəʊ] **im Radio** on the radio
Rallye rally [ˈræli]
Rand edge [edʒ]
rasen race [reɪs]
Rasen grass [ɡrɑːs]
raten guess [ɡes]
Rathaus town hall [ˌtaʊn ˈhɔːl]
Ratte rat [ræt]
rau *(See)* rough [rʌf]
Raubtier predator [ˈpredətə]
rauchen smoke [sməʊk]
rauf und runter up and down [ˌʌp‿ən ˈdaʊn]
räumen *(frei machen)* clear [klɪə]
rausgehen: mit dem Hund rausgehen walk the dog
reagieren (auf) react (to) [riˈækt]
Recherche research *(no pl)* [ˈriːsɜːtʃ]
Recht: jemand hat Recht someone is right
rechte(r, s) right [raɪt] **auf der rechten Seite** on the right **nach rechts** right **(nach) rechts abbiegen** turn right
Rechtschreibung spelling [ˈspelɪŋ]
Redakteur/in editor [ˈedɪtə]
Rede talk [tɔːk]; *(offiziell)* speech [spiːtʃ] **eine Rede halten (über)** give a talk (about)
reden talk [tɔːk]; speak [spiːk]
Redner/in speaker [ˈspiːkə]
Referat talk [tɔːk] **ein Referat halten (über)** give a talk (about)
Refrain chorus [ˈkɔːrəs]
Regal shelf [ʃelf], *pl* shelves [ʃelvz]
Regel rule [ruːl]
regelmäßig regular [ˈreɡjələ]
Regen rain [reɪn]
Regenbogen rainbow [ˈreɪnbəʊ]
Regenmantel raincoat [ˈreɪnkəʊt]
Regenschirm umbrella [ʌmˈbrelə]
Regenwald rainforest [ˈreɪnfɒrɪst]
Regierung government [ˈɡʌvənmənt]
regional regional [ˈriːdʒənl]
Regisseur/in director [dəˈrektə]
regnen rain [reɪn]
regnerisch rainy [ˈreɪni]
Reh deer, *pl* deer [dɪə]
reich rich [rɪtʃ]
Reihe **1.** line [laɪn] **2.** *(wartende Menschen)* queue [kjuː] **3. Ich bin an der Reihe.** (It's) my turn. [tɜːn]
Reihenfolge order [ˈɔːdə]
Reim rhyme [raɪm]
Reise trip [trɪp]; journey [ˈdʒɜːni]
Reiseführer guidebook [ˈɡaɪdbʊk]
Reiseleiter/in guide [ɡaɪd]
reisen travel [ˈtrævl]
Reisende(r) traveller [ˈtrævələ]
Reisepass passport [ˈpɑːspɔːt]
reiten ride [raɪd]
Reiten riding [ˈraɪdɪŋ]
Religion religion [rɪˈlɪdʒən]
rennen run [rʌn]
Rennen race [reɪs]
Reportage report [rɪˈpɔːt]
Republik republic [rɪˈpʌblɪk]
reservieren reserve [rɪˈzɜːv]
Respekt respect [rɪˈspekt]
Rest rest [rest]
Restaurant restaurant [ˈrestrɒnt]
Resultat result [rɪˈzʌlt]
retten save [seɪv]; *(in Sicherheit bringen)* rescue [ˈreskjuː]
Revier *(Territorium)* territory [ˈterətri]
Rezept *(Kochrezept)* recipe [ˈresəpi]
Rhythmus rhythm [ˈrɪðəm]
richten: etwas auf jn. richten point sth. at sb. [pɔɪnt]
richtig right [raɪt]; correct [kəˈrekt] **Ja, das ist richtig.** Yes, that's right.
Richtung: in die Richtung that way **in Richtung Bahnhof/Mr Bell** towards the station/Mr Bell [təˈwɔːdz] **Richtung Norden** northbound [ˈnɔːθbaʊnd]
riechen smell [smel] **an etwas riechen** smell sth. **gut riechen** smell good
Riegel *(Schokolade, Müsli)* bar [bɑː]
Riese giant [ˈdʒaɪənt]
Riesenhunger: einen Riesenhunger haben be starving [ˈstɑːvɪŋ]
Riesenrad big wheel [bɪɡ ˈwiːl]
riesig huge [hjuːdʒ]
Rinderbraten roast beef [ˌrəʊst ˈbiːf]
Ring ring [rɪŋ]
Ritt ride [raɪd]
Ritter knight [naɪt]
Robbe seal [siːl]
Rock skirt [skɜːt]
Rockmusik rock (music) [rɒk]
Rolle *(in einem Theaterstück, Film)* role [rəʊl]
rollen roll [rəʊl]
rosa pink [pɪŋk]
rot red [red] **rot werden** go red
Route route [ruːt]
Rücken back [bæk]
Rückenflosse dorsal fin [ˌdɔːsl ˈfɪn]
Rückmeldung feedback [ˈfiːdbæk]
Rucksack rucksack [ˈrʌksæk]
rufen call [kɔːl]; shout [ʃaʊt]
ruhen *(sich ausruhen)* rest [rest]
ruhig calm [kɑːm]; *(leise)* quiet [ˈkwaɪət]
Ruine ruin [ˈruːɪn]
Rundgang, Rundfahrt (durch) tour (of) [ˈtʊər‿əv]
runter: rauf und runter up and down [ˌʌp‿ən ˈdaʊn]
runzeln: die Stirn runzeln frown [fraʊn]
rutschig slippery [ˈslɪpəri]

S

Sache thing [θɪŋ]
Saft juice [dʒuːs]
Sage *(Legende)* legend [ˈledʒənd]
sagen say [seɪ] **jm. sagen, dass er/sie etwas (nicht) tun soll** tell sb. (not) to do sth.
Sahne cream [kriːm]
Salat *(Gericht, Beilage)* salad [ˈsæləd]
Samba samba [ˈsæmbə]
sammeln collect [kəˈlekt] **Geld sammeln (für etwas)** raise money (for sth.) [reɪz]
Samstag Saturday [ˈsætədeɪ, ˈsætədi]
Sand sand [sænd]
Sandwich sandwich [ˈsænwɪtʃ], [-wɪdʒ]
sanft softly [ˈsɒftli]; *(behutsam)* gently [ˈdʒentli] **mit sanfter Stimme** in a soft voice
Sänger/in singer [ˈsɪŋə]
satt: etwas satt haben be tired of sth. [ˈtaɪəd]
Satz sentence [ˈsentəns] **Satz, der in das Thema eines Absatzes einführt** topic sentence [ˌtɒpɪk ˈsentəns]
sauber clean [cliːn] **sauber machen** clean [kliːn]
Säugetier mammal [ˈmæml]
Säule column [ˈkɒləm]
Schach chess [tʃes]
schade: Es war schade, dass … It was a pity that … [ˈpɪti]
Schaf sheep, *pl* sheep [ʃiːp]
Schäfer/in shepherd [ˈʃepəd]
schaffen: etwas schaffen *(zustande bringen)* manage sth. [ˈmænɪdʒ]
Schafhirte/-hirtin shepherd [ˈʃepəd]
Schal scarf [skɑːf], *pl* scarves [skɑːvz]
Schatten *(einer Person, eines Gegenstandes)* shadow [ˈʃædəʊ]
Schatz *(Liebling)* darling [ˈdɑːlɪŋ]
schauen look [lʊk]
▶ S. 180 (to) look after/around/for/…
Schauspiel *(darstellende Kunst)* drama [ˈdrɑːmə]

Schauspieler/in actor ['æktə]
schauspielern act [ækt]
scheinen **1.** *(Sonne)* shine [ʃaɪn] **2. (zu sein/zu tun) scheinen** seem (to be/do) [siːm]
scheu shy [ʃaɪ]
Scheune barn [bɑːn]
schick: sich schick anziehen dress up [ˌdres‿'ʌp]
schicken: jm. etwas schicken send sth. to sb. [send] **einem Freund/einer Freundin eine SMS schicken** text a friend [tekst]
schieben push [pʊʃ]
Schiedsrichter/in referee [ˌrefə'riː]
schießen: ein Tor schießen score [skɔː]
Schiff ship [ʃɪp]
Schiffsreise cruise [kruːz]
Schild sign [saɪn]; *(Etikett)* label
Schildkröte tortoise ['tɔːtəs]
Schinkenspeck bacon ['beɪkən]
Schirm umbrella [ʌm'brelə]
Schlacht battle ['bætl]
Schlaf sleep [sliːp]
schlafen sleep [sliːp]; *(nicht wach sein)* be asleep [ə'sliːp]
Schlafparty sleepover ['sliːpəʊvə]
Schlafzimmer bedroom ['bedruːm]
schlagen hit [hɪt]; *(besiegen)* beat [biːt]
Schlägerei fight
Schlagzeug drums *(pl)* [drʌmz] **Schlagzeug spielen** play the drums
Schlagzeuger/in drummer ['drʌmə]
Schlamm mud [mʌd]
Schlange **1.** snake [sneɪk] **2.** *(wartende Menschen)* queue [kjuː] **Schlange stehen** queue [kjuː]
schlau clever ['klevə]
schlecht bad [bæd] **schlechter** worse [wɜːs] **der/die/das schlechteste ...; am schlechtesten** worst [wɜːst] **schlecht werden** *(Lebensmittel)* go bad **Mir ist schlecht.** I feel sick.
schließen *(zumachen)* close [kləʊz]
schließlich at last [ət 'lɑːst]; finally ['faɪnəli]
schlimm bad [bæd] **schlimmer** worse [wɜːs] **der/die/das schlimmste ...; am schlimmsten** worst [wɜːst]
Schloss castle ['kɑːsl]
Schluss end [end]; *(Abschluss)* ending ['endɪŋ]
Schlussfolgerung conclusion [kən'kluːʒn]
Schlüssel key [kiː]
Schlüsselwort keyword ['kiːwɜːd]
schmal narrow ['nærəʊ]
schmecken taste [teɪst]
schmelzen melt [melt]
schmerzen hurt [hɜːt]
Schmetterling butterfly ['bʌtəflaɪ]
Schmuggel; das Schmuggeln smuggling ['smʌglɪŋ]
schmuggeln smuggle ['smʌgl]
Schmuggler/in smuggler ['smʌglə]
schmutzig dirty ['dɜːti]
schnappen *(sich greifen)* grab [græb]
Schnee snow [snəʊ]
schneiden cut [kʌt]; *(Film, Video bearbeiten)* edit ['edɪt]
schnell fast [fɑːst]; quick [kwɪk]
Schnitt! *(beim Filmen)* Cut! [kʌt]
schockiert shocked [ʃɒkt]
Schokolade chocolate ['tʃɒklət]
schön beautiful ['bjuːtɪfl]; *(nett)* nice [naɪs]; *(herrlich, wunderbar)* lovely ['lʌvli]
schon already [ɔːl'redi] **schon bald** before long **Hast du schon ...?** Have you ... yet? [jet] **(vorher) schon mal** before
schottisch: das schottische Hochland the Highlands *(pl)* ['haɪləndz]
Schrank cupboard ['kʌbəd]
schrecklich terrible ['terəbl]; awful ['ɔːfl]
Schrei scream [skriːm]
schreiben write [raɪt]
Schreiber/in writer ['raɪtə]
Schreibtisch desk [desk]
Schreibweise spelling ['spelɪŋ]
schreien shout [ʃaʊt]; cry [kraɪ]; scream [skriːm]
Schriftsteller/in writer ['raɪtə]
Schritt step [step]
schüchtern shy [ʃaɪ]
Schuh shoe [ʃuː]
Schuld *(Fehler)* fault [fɔːlt]
Schule school [skuːl] **in der Schule** at school
Schüler/in student ['stjuːdənt]
Schulfach (school) subject ['sʌbdʒɪkt]
Schulheft *(Übungsheft)* exercise book ['eksəsaɪz bʊk]
Schulleiter/in head teacher [ˌhed 'tiːtʃə]
Schultasche school bag ['skuːl bæg]
Schulter shoulder ['ʃəʊldə]
Schultyrann bully ['bʊli]
Schüssel bowl [bəʊl]
schütteln shake [ʃeɪk] **er schüttelte den Kopf** he shook his head
schützen: jn./etwas schützen (vor jm./etwas) protect sb./sth. (from sb./sth.) [prə'tekt]
schwarz black [blæk]
schweigend silently ['saɪləntli]
Schwein pig [pɪg]
schwer **1.** *(von Gewicht)* heavy ['hevi] **2.** *(schwierig)* difficult ['dɪfɪkəlt]; hard [hɑːd] **jm. das Leben schwer machen** give sb. a hard time *(infml)*
Schwert sword [sɔːd]
Schwester sister ['sɪstə]
schwierig difficult ['dɪfɪkəlt]; hard [hɑːd]; tough [tʌf]
Schwierigkeit: in Schwierigkeiten geraten get into trouble
Schwimmbad, Schwimmbecken (swimming) pool [puːl]
schwimmen swim [swɪm]
Schwimmer/in swimmer ['swɪmə]
Schwimmweste life jacket ['laɪf dʒækɪt]
schwindlig dizzy ['dɪzi]
sechs six [sɪks]
See **1.** *(Binnensee)* lake [leɪk] **2.** *(die See, das Meer)* sea [siː]
seekrank seasick ['siːsɪk]
Seemann sailor ['seɪlə]
Segelboot sailing boat ['seɪlɪŋ bəʊt]
segeln sail [seɪl] **segeln gehen** go sailing ['seɪlɪŋ]
sehen see [siː]
Sehenswürdigkeiten sights *(pl)* [saɪts]
sehr very ['veri] **Das hat uns sehr geholfen.** That helped us a lot.
seidig silky ['sɪlki]
Seil rope [rəʊp]
sein *(Verb)* be [biː]
sein(e) ... *(vor Nomen; besitzanzeigend)* **1.** *(zu „he")* his ... [hɪz] **2.** *(zu „it")* its ... [ɪts]
seiner, seine, seins his [hɪz
seit **1. seit 10 Uhr/letzter Woche/2012/...** since 10 o'clock/last week/2012/... [sɪns] **2. seit Stunden/Wochen/Jahren/...** for hours/weeks/years/...
Seite **1.** side [saɪd] **auf der linken Seite** on the left **auf der rechten Seite** on the right **2.** *(Buchseite)* page [peɪdʒ] **Auf welcher Seite sind wir?** What page are we on?
Sekunde second ['sekənd]
selbst wenn even if ['iːvn‿ɪf]
Selbstlaut *(Vokal)* vowel ['vaʊəl]
selbstverständlich of course [əv 'kɔːs]
seltsam strange [streɪndʒ]; weird [wɪəd]
senden: jm. etwas senden send sth. to sb. [send]
Sendung *(im Radio, Fernsehen)* programme ['prəʊgræm]
September September [sep'tembə]
Sessel armchair ['ɑːmtʃeə]
Set set [set]
setzen: sich setzen sit [sɪt] **sich (mit jm.) in Verbindung setzen** get in touch (with sb.) [tʌtʃ]
seufzen sigh [saɪ]
Shorts *(kurze Hose)* shorts *(pl)* [ʃɔːts]
Show show [ʃəʊ]
sich **1.** *(Reflexivpronomen)* herself [hɜː'self]; himself [hɪm'self]; itself [ɪt'self]; themselves [ðəm'selvz]; *(zur höflichen Anrede „Sie")* yourself [jɔː'self]; yourselves [jɔː'selvz] **2. sich (gegenseitig)** *(einander)* each other [iːtʃ‿'ʌðə]
sicher sure [ʃʊə], [ʃɔː]
Sicht: aus meiner Sicht from my point of view [ˌpɔɪnt‿əv 'vjuː]
Sichtung sighting ['saɪtɪŋ]
sie **1.** *(Einzahl; weibliche Person)* she [ʃiː] **Frag sie.** Ask her. [hɜː] **2.** *(Einzahl; Ding, Tier)* it [ɪt] **3.** *(Mehrzahl)* they [ðeɪ] **Frag sie.** Ask them. [ðem, ðəm]
Sie *(höfliche Anredeform)* you [juː, ju]

sieben seven ['sevn]
Sieger/in winner ['wɪnə]
Signal *(Stichwort, am Theater)* cue [kjuː]
Silbe syllable ['sɪləbl]
Silvester New Year's Eve [ˌnjuː jɪəz‿'iːv]
singen sing [sɪŋ]
Sirene siren ['saɪrən]
Situation situation [ˌsɪtʃu'eɪʃn]
Sitz seat [siːt]
sitzen sit [sɪt]
Sklave, Sklavin slave [sleɪv]
Sklaverei slavery ['sleɪvəri]
Skyline skyline ['skaɪlaɪn]
Smalltalk *(spontan geführtes Gespräch in umgangssprachlichem Ton)* small talk
SMS text message ['tekst mesɪdʒ], *(kurz auch:)* text **einem Freund/einer Freundin eine SMS schicken** text a friend
Snack snack [snæk]
so **1.** *(auf diese Weise)* like that / like this **Und er so: „Stop …"** He was like: "Stop …" *(infml)*
2. (nicht) so groß wie (not) as big as [æz], [əz]
3. so cool/nett/leise/… so cool/ nice/quiet/… [səʊ] **so ein/e …** such a … [sʌtʃ]
▶ S. 182 such a + noun / so + adjective
4. so tun, als ob pretend [prɪ'tend]
sobald as soon as [əz 'suːn‿əz]
Socke sock [sɒk]
sodass so that, *(oft auch kurz:)* so
soeben just [dʒʌst]
Sofa sofa ['səʊfə]
sofort immediately [ɪ'miːdiətli]
sogar even ['iːvn]
Sohn son [sʌn]
Soldat/in soldier ['səʊldʒə]
sollen: Soll ich …? Shall I … ? [ʃæl] **Du solltest … / Ihr solltet …** You should … [ʃʊd], [ʃəd]
▶ S. 188 möglich – wahrscheinlich – sicherlich
Solo- solo ['səʊləʊ]
Sommer summer ['sʌmə]
Sonnabend Saturday ['sætədeɪ, -di]
Sonne sun [sʌn]
Sonnenbrille sunglasses *(pl)* ['sʌnglɑːsɪz]
Sonnenschein sunshine ['sʌnʃaɪn]
sonnig sunny ['sʌni]
Sonntag Sunday ['sʌndeɪ, 'sʌndi]
sonst: sonst noch etwas? anything else? [els] **sonst jeder** everybody else **niemand sonst** no one else **was sonst noch?** what else? **wer sonst noch?** who else?
▶ S. 195 … else
Sorge: sich Sorgen machen (wegen, um) worry (about) ['wʌri]
sorgen: dafür sorgen, dass … make sure that …
Souvenir souvenir [ˌsuːvə'nɪə]
sowie *(sobald)* as soon as [əz 'suːn‿əz]
soziale Medien social media *(pl)* [ˌsəʊʃl 'miːdiə]

Spagetti spaghetti [spə'geti]
spanisch Spanish ['spænɪʃ]
spannend *(aufregend)* exciting [ɪk'saɪtɪŋ]
Spannung *(Anspannung)* tension ['tenʃn]
Spaß fun [fʌn] **Spaß haben** have fun [fʌn] **Hat es Spaß gemacht?** Was it fun? **Viel Spaß!** Enjoy yourself.
spät late [leɪt] **Du bist spät dran. / Du bist zu spät.** You're late. **Wie spät ist es?** What time is it?
später later ['leɪtə]
spazieren gehen go for a walk [wɔːk]
Spaziergang walk [wɔːk] **einen Spaziergang machen** go for a walk
Spickzettel crib sheet ['krɪb ʃiːt] *(infml)*
Spiegel mirror ['mɪrə]
Spiel game [geɪm]; *(Wettkampf, Match)* match [mætʃ]
spielen play [pleɪ] **Gitarre spielen** play the guitar **Klavier spielen** play the piano **Schlagzeug spielen** play the drums
Spieler/in player ['pleɪə]
Spielfeld pitch [pɪtʃ]
Spielstand *(Punktestand)* score [skɔː]
Spielzeug toy [tɔɪ]
Spitze top [tɒp] **an der Spitze (von)** at the top (of)
Sport; Sportart sport [spɔːt] **Sport treiben** do sport
Sportler/in sportsperson ['spɔːtspɜːsn]
Sportunterricht PE [ˌpiː‿'iː] (Physical Education)
Sprache language ['læŋgwɪdʒ]
sprechen (mit jm.) speak (to sb.) [spiːk] **Kann ich Sie kurz sprechen?** May I have a word with you?
Sprecher/in speaker ['spiːkə]
springen jump [dʒʌmp]
spritzen: jn. nass spritzen splash sb. [splæʃ]
Sprung jump [dʒʌmp]
spülen: das Geschirr spülen wash the dishes *(pl)* [ˌwɒʃ ðə 'dɪʃɪz]
Spur: keine Spur von … no sign of … [saɪn]
Staat state [steɪt]
Stadion stadium ['steɪdiəm]
Stadt town [taʊn]; *(Großstadt)* city ['sɪti]
Stadtplan map [mæp] **auf dem Stadtplan** on the map
Stammbaum family tree ['fæməli triː]
Stand *(Marktstand)* stall [stɔːl]
Standard; Standard- standard ['stændəd]
ständig: etwas ständig tun *(immer wieder)* keep doing sth. [kiːp]
Standort location [ləʊ'keɪʃn]
Standpunkt point of view [ˌpɔɪnt‿əv 'vjuː]
Star star [stɑː]
stark strong [strɒŋ] **starker Regen** heavy rain ['hevi]

starren stare [steə]
Station *(Haltestelle)* stop [stɒp]
statt *(anstelle von)* instead of [ɪn'sted‿əv]
stattdessen instead [ɪn'sted]
stattfinden take place [teɪk 'pleɪs]
stechen: etwas in etwas stechen stick sth. into sth. [stɪk]
stecken: etwas in etwas stecken stick sth. into sth. [stɪk]
stehen stand [stænd] **auf etwas stehen** be into sth. *(infml)* **Schlange stehen** queue [kjuː] **Wie steht es?** *(Sport)* What's the score? [skɔː]
stehlen steal [stiːl]
steil steep [stiːp]
Stein stone [stəʊn]
steinig rocky ['rɒki]
Stelle place [pleɪs]; *(Job, Arbeitsstelle)* job [dʒɒb] **an zweiter Stelle** in second place
stellen *(hinstellen, abstellen)* put [pʊt] **eine Frage stellen** ask a question **etwas lauter/leiser stellen** turn sth. up/down [tɜːn]
Stempel stamp [stæmp]
sterben die [daɪ]
Stern star [stɑː]
steuern steer [stɪə]
Stichwort *(im Wörterbuch)* headword ['hedwɜːd]; *(am Theater)* cue [kjuː]
Stiefel boot [buːt]
Stift *(zum Schreiben)* pen [pen]
still quiet ['kwaɪət]; silent ['saɪlənt]
Stimme voice [vɔɪs] **mit lauter Stimme** in a loud voice
stimmen: Ja, das stimmt. Yes, that's right. [raɪt] **Nein, das stimmt nicht.** No, that's wrong. [rɒŋ]
Stirn: die Stirn runzeln frown [fraʊn]
Stock stick [stɪk]
Stock(werk) floor [flɔː]
stöhnen groan [grəʊn]
Stöhnen groan [grəʊn]
stolz (auf) proud (of) [praʊd]
stoppen stop [stɒp]
stoßen push [pʊʃ] **gegen etwas stoßen** hit sth. [hɪt] **auf etwas stoßen** *(zufällig)* come across sth.
▶ S. 180 (to) come across/down/over/…
Strafe punishment ['pʌnɪʃmənt]
strahlend *(leuchtend hell)* bright [braɪt]
Strand beach [biːtʃ]
Straße street [striːt]; road [rəʊd]
Straßenkreuzung junction ['dʒʌŋkʃn]
Straßenkünstler/in street artist
Strecke *(Route)* route [ruːt]
Streit argument ['ɑːgjumənt]
streiten; sich streiten argue ['ɑːgjuː]
Strophe verse [vɜːs]
strukturieren structure ['strʌktʃə]
Stück: ein Stück … a piece of … [piːs]
Student/in student ['stjuːdənt]
studieren study ['stʌdi]
Studio studio ['stjuːdiəʊ]
Stufe step [step]

Stuhl chair [tʃeə]
Stunde hour ['aʊə]; *(Unterrichtsstunde)* lesson ['lesn] **ein einstündiges Konzert** a one-hour concert
Stundenplan timetable ['taɪmteɪbl]
Sturm storm [stɔːm]
stürmisch *(rau, See)* rough [rʌf]
stürzen fall [fɔːl]
Subjekt subject ['sʌbdʒekt]
Substantiv noun [naʊn]
suchen: etwas suchen look for sth. ['lʊk fɔː]
Süden south [saʊθ] **nach Süden** south
südlich south [saʊθ]; southern ['sʌðən]
Südosten south-east [ˌsaʊθ‿'iːst] **nach Südosten** south-east
südöstlich south-east [ˌsaʊθ‿'iːst]
Südwesten south-west [ˌsaʊθ'west] **nach Südwesten** south-west
südwestlich south-west [ˌsaʊθ'west]
Suppe soup [suːp]
süß sweet [swiːt]
Süßigkeiten sweets *(pl)* [swiːts]
Symbol symbol ['sɪmbl]
Szene scene [siːn]

T

Tabelle table ['teɪbl]
Tafel **1.** *(Schultafel)* board [bɔːd] **2.** *(Schokolade)* bar [bɑː]
Tag day [deɪ]
Tagebuch diary ['daɪəri]
Tagesausflüge machen go on day trips [trɪps]
Taille waist [weɪst]
Tal valley ['væli]
talentiert talented ['tæləntɪd]
Tante aunt [ɑːnt]
Tante-Emma-Laden corner shop ['kɔːnə ʃɒp]
Tanz dance [dɑːns]
tanzen dance [dɑːns]
Tänzer/in dancer ['dɑːnsə]
Tanzfläche dance floor ['dɑːns flɔː]
Tasche bag [bæg]; *(Manteltasche, Hosentasche usw.)* pocket ['pɒkɪt]
Taschenlampe torch [tɔːtʃ]
Tasse: eine Tasse ... a cup of ... [kʌp]
Tatsache fact [fækt]
tatsächlich actually ['æktʃuəli]
▶ S. 184 actually
Tatze paw [pɔː]
Team team [tiːm]
Technik, Technologie technology [tek'nɒlədʒi]
Tee tea [tiː]
Teelöffel teaspoon ['tiːspuːn]
Teil part [pɑːt] **aus dem hinteren Teil des Buses** from the back of the bus
teilnehmen: an etwas teilnehmen take part in sth. [ˌteɪk 'pɑːt]; *(Wettkampf)* compete in sth. [kəm'piːt]
Telefon telephone ['telɪfəʊn], *(kurz auch:)* phone **am Telefon** on the phone **ans Telefon gehen** answer the phone
Telefonat call [kɔːl]
Telefongespräch *(Anruf)* phone call ['fəʊn kɔːl], *(kurz auch:)* call
Telefonzelle telephone box
Teller: ein Teller ... a plate of ... [pleɪt]
Temperatur temperature ['temprətʃə]
Tempus *(grammatische Zeit)* tense [tens]
Tennis tennis ['tenɪs]
Termin appointment [ə'pɔɪntmənt]
Territorium territory ['terətri]
Test test [test]
testen test [test]
teuer expensive [ɪk'spensɪv]
Text text [tekst] **einen Text schnell nach bestimmten Wörtern/Informationen absuchen** scan a text [skæn]
Theater theatre ['θɪətə]
Theaterstück play [pleɪ]
Thema theme [θiːm]; topic ['tɒpɪk]
Thermometer thermometer [θə'mɒmɪtə]
tief deep [diːp]
Tier animal ['ænɪml]
Tipp tip [tɪp]
tippen *(vorsichtig klopfen)* tap [tæp]
Tisch table ['teɪbl]
Tischler/in carpenter ['kɑːpəntə]
Tischtennis table tennis
Titel title ['taɪtl]
Toast(brot) toast [təʊst]
Tochter daughter ['dɔːtə]
Tod death [deθ]
Toilette toilet ['tɔɪlət]
Tomate tomato [tə'mɑːtəʊ], *pl* tomatoes
Ton *(Lehm)* clay [kleɪ]
Top *(Oberteil)* top [tɒp]
Topf pot [pɒt]
Tor **1.** *(Pforte, Gatter)* gate [geɪt] **2.** *(Sport)* goal [gəʊl] **ein Tor schießen** score (a goal) [skɔː]
Torfrau goalkeeper ['gəʊlkiːpə]
Tornetz goal net ['gəʊl net]
Torwart goalkeeper ['gəʊlkiːpə]
tot dead [ded]
töten kill [kɪl]
Tourist/in tourist ['tʊərɪst]
traditionell traditional [trə'dɪʃənl]
tragen **1.** carry ['kæri] **2.** *(Kleidung)* wear [weə]
Trainer/in *(von Sportmannschaften)* manager ['mænɪdʒə]
trainieren practise ['præktɪs]; train [treɪn]
Training training ['treɪnɪŋ]
Traktor tractor ['træktə]
Träne tear [tɪə] **in Tränen ausbrechen** burst into tears [bɜːst]
Transporter *(Lieferwagen)* van [væn]
Trauerfeier funeral ['fjuːnərəl]
Traum dream [driːm]
traurig sad [sæd]
treffen; sich treffen meet [miːt] **etwas treffen** hit sth. **jn. treffen** *(zufällig)* come across sb.
▶ S. 180 (to) come across/down/over/...
Treffer: einen Treffer erzielen score [skɔː]
Treppe; Treppenstufen stairs *(pl)* [steəz]
treten kick [kɪk] **jm. auf die Füße/Zehen treten** *(auch im übertragenen Sinne)* tread on sb.'s toes [tred] *(infml)*
Trick trick [trɪk]
Trimester term [tɜːm]
trinken drink [drɪŋk]
trocken dry [draɪ]
Trommel drum [drʌm]
Trommler/in drummer ['drʌmə]
Trophäe trophy ['trəʊfi]
trotzdem still [stɪl]
Tschüs. Bye. [baɪ]
T-Shirt T-shirt ['tiːʃɜːt]
Tulpe tulip ['tjuːlɪp]
tun do [duː] **etwas tun müssen** have to do sth.; need to do sth. **etwas tun wollen** want to do sth. [wɒnt] **Tut mir leid.** (I'm) sorry. **viel zu tun haben** be busy ['bɪzi]
Tunnel tunnel ['tʌnl]
Tür door [dɔː]
Türklingel doorbell ['dɔːbel]
Turm tower ['taʊə]
Turnen gymnastics [dʒɪm'næstɪks]; *(Sportunterricht)* PE [ˌpiː‿'iː] (Physical Education)
Turnhalle gym [dʒɪm]
Turnier *(Wettkampf)* trials *(pl)* ['traɪəlz]
Turnschuh trainer ['treɪnə]
Tyrann *(in der Schule)* bully ['bʊli]

U

U-Bahn: die U-Bahn the underground *(no pl)* ['ʌndəgraʊnd]; *(in London)* the Tube *(no pl)* [tjuːb]
üben practise ['præktɪs]
über **1.** *(räumlich)* over ['əʊvə]; *(oberhalb von)* above [ə'bʌv] **(quer) über das Moor/die Straße** across the moor/the street [ə'krɒs] **2.** *(mehr als)* over ['əʊvə] **über 400 Jahre** over 400 years **3. über mich/dich/...** about me/you/... [ə'baʊt] **über dich selbst** about yourself [jɔː'self]
überall everywhere ['evriweə] **überall um sie herum** all around her
überarbeiten *(Text u.Ä.)* revise [rɪ'vaɪz]
übereinander *(aufeinander)* on top of each other [iːtʃ‿'ʌðə]
überfüllt *(voller Menschen)* crowded ['kraʊdɪd]
übergeben: Ich muss mich übergeben. I'm going to be sick.

überhaupt: Und überhaupt, ... And anyway, ... ['eniweɪ]
überleben survive [sə'vaɪv]
übernachten (in/bei) *(vorübergehend wohnen)* stay (at/with) [steɪ]
überprüfen check [tʃek]
Überprüfung check [tʃek]
überqueren cross [krɒs]
überrascht surprised [sə'praɪzd]
Überraschung surprise [sə'praɪz]
Überschrift title ['taɪtl]
übersetzen translate [træns'leɪt]
Übersetzung translation [træns'leɪʃn]
übertragen werden *(Programm, Sendung)* be on
überwachen *(nachverfolgen)* monitor ['mɒnɪtə]
üblich usual ['ju:ʒuəl]
übrig: übrig sein be left [left] **etwas übrig lassen (für jn.)** leave sth. (for sb.) [li:v]
übrigens by the way [ˌbaɪ ðə 'weɪ]; actually ['æktʃuəli]
▶ S. 184 actually
Übung exercise ['eksəsaɪz]
Übungsheft exercise book ['eksəsaɪz bʊk]
Ufer *(eines Sees)* shore [ʃɔ:]
Uhr **1.** *(Armbanduhr)* watch [wɒtʃ]; *(Wand-, Stand-, Turmuhr)* clock [klɒk]
2. 4 Uhr morgens 4 am [ˌeɪ‿'em]
4 Uhr nachmittags / 16 Uhr 4 pm [ˌpi:‿'em] **um 1 Uhr / 13 Uhr** at 1 o'clock [ə'klɒk]
Uhrzeit time [taɪm]
um **1.** *(örtlich)* **um ... (herum)** around ... [ə'raʊnd] **um die Welt** round the world [raʊnd]
2. *(zeitlich)* **um 1 Uhr / 13 Uhr** at 1 o'clock [ə'klɒk] **um 18 Uhr herum** *(gegen 18 Uhr)* around 6 pm
3. um zu to [tu], [tə]
umarmen: jn. umarmen hug sb. [hʌg]; give sb. a hug [hʌg]
umdrehen *(wenden)* turn around [ˌtɜ:n‿ə'raʊnd] **sich umdrehen** turn (around/round)
▶ S. 177 (to) turn
umher: in der Bücherei / auf dem Strand umher around the library/the beach [ə'raʊnd]
umher-: umherrennen run around [ˌrʌn‿ə'raʊnd] **umherspazieren** walk around
umsehen: sich (auf der Farm) umsehen look around (the farm)
umsteigen change [tʃeɪndʒ]
umtauschen *(Geld wechseln)* change [tʃeɪndʒ]
Umweltverschmutzung pollution [pə'lu:ʃn]
umziehen (nach) move (to) [mu:v]
Umzug *(Parade)* parade [pə'reɪd]
und and [ænd, ənd] **Und du? / Und was ist mit dir?** What about you? **Und? / Na und?** So? [səʊ] **Und er**

so: „Stop ..." He was like: "Stop ..." *(infml)*
unfair unfair [ʌn'feə]
Unfall: einen Unfall haben crash [kræʃ]
ungefähr about [ə'baʊt]
ungerecht unfair [ʌn'feə]
ungewöhnlich unusual [ʌn'ju:ʒuəl]
unglaublich *(erstaunlich)* amazing [ə'meɪzɪŋ]
unglücklich unhappy [ʌn'hæpi]
unheimlich scary ['skeəri]
unhöflich impolite [ˌɪmpə'laɪt]
Uniform uniform ['ju:nɪfɔ:m]
Union: die Europäische Union the EU [ˌi: 'ju:] (the European Union [ˌjʊərəpi:ən 'ju:niən])
unmöglich impossible [ɪm'pɒsəbl]
Unrecht: jemand hat Unrecht someone is wrong [rɒŋ]
unregelmäßig irregular [ɪ'regjələ]
uns us [ʌs], [əs]; *(Reflexivpronomen)* ourselves [ɑ:'selvz], [aʊə'selvz]
unser(e) ... our ... ['aʊə]
unserer, unsere, unseres ours ['aʊəz]
unten *(am unteren Ende)* at the bottom (of) ['bɒtəm]; *(darunter)* below [bɪ'ləʊ]; *(im Haus)* downstairs [ˌdaʊn'steəz] **dort unten** down there **nach unten** down; *(im Haus)* downstairs
unter under ['ʌndə]; *(unterhalb von)* below [bɪ'ləʊ] **unter der Erde** underground [ˌʌndə'graʊnd]
unterbrechen interrupt [ˌɪntə'rʌpt]
untergehen *(Sonne)* go down [daʊn]
unterhalb (von) below [bɪ'ləʊ]
unterhalten: sich unterhalten (mit) talk (to) [tɔ:k]
Unterhaltung **1.** *(Gespräch)* conversation [ˌkɒnvə'seɪʃn]
2. *(Vergnügen)* entertainment [ˌentə'teɪnmənt]
unterirdisch underground [ˌʌndə'graʊnd]
unterrichten teach [ti:tʃ]
unterstreichen underline [ˌʌndə'laɪn]
untersuchen *(prüfen)* look into; *(studieren)* study ['stʌdi]
Untertitel subtitle ['sʌbtaɪtl]
unterwegs out and about
Unwetter storm [stɔ:m]
Urlaub holiday ['hɒlədeɪ] **in Urlaub fahren** go on holiday **in Urlaub sein** be on holiday
usw. (und so weiter) etc. (et cetera) [et'setərə]

V

Vater father ['fɑ:ðə]
Vati dad [dæd]
Vegetarier/in vegetarian [ˌvedʒə'teəriən]
vegetarisch vegetarian [ˌvedʒə'teəriən]

Verabredung appointment [ə'pɔɪntmənt]
verändern; sich verändern change [tʃeɪndʒ]
verängstigt scared [skeəd]
verantwortlich responsible [rɪ'spɒnsəbl]
Verb verb [vɜ:b]
verbessern; sich verbessern improve [ɪm'pru:v] **etwas verbessern** *(korrigieren)* correct sth. [kə'rekt]
verbeugen: sich verbeugen bow [baʊ]
verbinden connect [kə'nekt]; link [lɪŋk]
Verbindung: sich (mit jm.) in Verbindung setzen get in touch (with sb.) [tʌtʃ] **(mit jm.) in Verbindung bleiben** stay in touch (with sb.)
verbreiten; sich verbreiten spread [spred]
verbrennen burn [bɜ:n]
verbringen: Zeit verbringen (mit) spend time (on) [spend]
verbunden sein be connected [kə'nektɪd]
verdienen *(Geld)* earn [ɜ:n]
vereinigt: das Vereinigte Königreich the UK (the United Kingdom) [ˌju: 'keɪ], [juˌnaɪtɪd 'kɪŋdəm]
verfügbar available [ə'veɪləbl]
Vergangenheit past [pɑ:st]
vergehen *(Zeit)* go by; pass [pɑ:s]
vergessen forget [fə'get]
vergewissern: sich vergewissern, dass ... make sure that ...
Vergnügungspark fun park
verhalten: sich verhalten behave [bɪ'heɪv]
Verhältnisse *(Bedingungen)* conditions *(pl)* [kən'dɪʃnz]
verheiratet (mit) married (to) ['mærɪd]
verkaufen sell [sel]
Verkäufer/in shop assistant ['ʃɒp‿əˌsɪstənt], *(kurz auch:)* assistant
Verkehr traffic ['træfɪk]
Verkehrsampel traffic light ['træfɪk laɪt] *(oft auch Plural:)* traffic lights
verkehrt wrong [rɒŋ]
verkleiden: sich verkleiden dress up [ˌdres‿'ʌp]
Verkleidung costume ['kɒstju:m]
verknüpfen connect [kə'nekt]; link [lɪŋk]
verlassen leave [li:v]
verletzen hurt [hɜ:t]
verletzt hurt [hɜ:t]
verlieren lose [lu:z]
vermissen miss [mɪs]
vermisst *(verschollen)* missing ['mɪsɪŋ]
verneigen: sich verneigen bow [baʊ]
verpassen miss [mɪs]
verrückt mad [mæd] **verrückt werden** go mad
Vers *(Reim)* rhyme [raɪm]; *(Strophe)* verse [vɜ:s]
verschieden different ['dɪfrənt]
verschiedene *(mehrere)* several ['sevrəl]

Verschmutzung *(der Umwelt)* pollution [pə'lu:ʃn]
verschollen missing ['mɪsɪŋ]
verschwinden disappear [ˌdɪsə'pɪə]
versprechen promise ['prɒmɪs]
verstecken; sich verstecken hide [haɪd]
verstehen understand [ˌʌndə'stænd] **Hast du es verstanden?** Did you get it? *(infml)* **Verstehe.** I see.
Versuch try [traɪ]
versuchen try [traɪ] **Versuch's mal.** Have a go.
verteidigen: jn./etwas verteidigen (gegen) defend sb./sth. (against) [dɪ'fend]
verwenden use [ju:z]
Video video ['vɪdiəʊ]
Videokamera video camera ['vɪdiəʊ kæmrə]
viel a lot (of); lots (of); much [mʌtʃ] **Viel Glück!** Good luck! [lʌk] **viel zu tun haben** be busy ['bɪzi] **Wie viel kosten ...?** How much are ...? **Wie viel kostet ...?** How much is ...?
viele a lot (of); lots (of); many ['meni]
vielleicht maybe ['meɪbi] **sie sind vielleicht zu Hause** they may be at home [meɪ]
▶ S. 188 möglich – wahrscheinlich – sicherlich
vier four [fɔ:]
Viertel: Viertel nach zehn (10.15/22.15) quarter past ten ['kwɔ:tə pɑ:st] **Viertel vor elf (10.45/22.45)** quarter to eleven ['kwɔ:tə tʊ]
violett purple ['pɜ:pl]
Visum visa ['vi:zə]
Vogel bird [bɜ:d]
Vokal vowel ['vaʊəl]
Volk people ['pi:pl]; nation ['neɪʃn]
voll full (of) [fʊl] **voller Menschen** crowded ['kraʊdɪd]
Volleyball volleyball ['vɒlibɔ:l]
völlig quite [kwaɪt]
Vollmond full moon [fʊl 'mu:n]
von of [ɒv], [əv]; from [frɒm], [frəm] **ein Lied von ...** a song by ... [baɪ] **von ... bis ...** from ... to ... **von ... herunter** off [ɒf]
▶ S. 177 off
vor **1.** *(örtlich)* in front of [ɪn 'frʌnt‿əv] **vor der Schule** *(vorm Gebäude)* in front of the school; *(außerhalb der Schule)* outside the school [ˌaʊt'saɪd] **2.** *(zeitlich)* before [bɪ'fɔ:] **vor der Schule** *(vor Schulbeginn)* before school **vorm Unterricht** before lessons **vor zwei Tagen** two days ago [ə'gəʊ] **Viertel vor elf (10.45/22.45)** quarter to eleven ['kwɔ:tə tʊ] **nicht vor drei** not till three; not until three
vorankommen *(zurechtkommen)* get on [ˌget‿'ɒn]
vorbei (an) past [pɑ:st]
vorbei sein *(zu Ende sein)* be over
vorbei-: an etwas/jm. vorbeigehen/vorbeifahren pass sth./sb. [pɑ:s] **vorbeikommen (bei)** *(besuchen)* come over (to)
▶ S. 180 (to) come across/down/over/...
vorbereiten: etwas vorbereiten prepare sth. [prɪ'peə] **sich vorbereiten (auf)** get ready (for) ['redi]
Vordergrund foreground ['fɔ:graʊnd]
Vorderseite front [frʌnt]
Vorfahr/in ancestor ['ænsestə]
Vorführung *(Demonstration)* demonstration [ˌdemən'streɪʃn]
vorgehen *(Uhr)* be fast
vorhaben: Ich habe vor ein Lied zu singen. I'm going to sing a song.
vorher: vorher schon mal before **vorher noch nie** not ... before, never ... before
Vorlieben und Abneigungen likes and dislikes *(pl)* [ˌlaɪks‿ən 'dɪslaɪks]
Vormittag morning ['mɔ:nɪŋ]
vorn: nach vorn to the front [frʌnt]
vorschlagen: (jm.) etwas vorschlagen suggest sth. (to sb.) [sə'dʒest]
Vorschrift *(Regel)* rule [ru:l]
Vorsicht! Watch out! [ˌwɒtʃ‿'aʊt]
vorsichtig careful ['keəfl]
vorspielen: etwas vorspielen act sth. out [ˌækt‿'aʊt]
Vorspielen *(Theater)* audition [ɔ:'dɪʃn]
Vorsprechen *(Theater)* audition
vorstellen **1. (jm.) etwas vorstellen** *(präsentieren)* present sth. (to sb.) [prɪ'zent] **2. jn. (jm.) vorstellen** introduce sb. (to sb.) [ˌɪntrə'dju:s] **3. sich etwas vorstellen** imagine sth. [ɪ'mædʒɪn] **Stell dir vor, Dad ...** Guess what, Dad ...
Vorstellung **1.** *(Idee)* idea [aɪ'dɪə] **2.** *(Präsentation)* presentation [ˌprezn'teɪʃn] **3.** *(Show)* show [ʃəʊ]
Vortrag talk [tɔ:k] **einen Vortrag halten (über)** give a talk (about)
vorüber: vorbei (an), vorüber (an) past [pɑ:st]
vorübergehen *(Zeit)* go by; pass [pɑ:s]

W

wach awake [ə'weɪk]
Wache, Wachposten guard [gɑ:d]
wachsen grow [grəʊ]
wählen *(aussuchen)* choose [tʃu:z]
wahr true [tru:] **..., nicht wahr?** ..., right?
während **1. während des Spiels** during the match ['djʊərɪŋ] **2. während wir spielten** while we were playing [waɪl]; as we were playing
▶ S. 175 German "während"
Wahrheit truth [tru:θ]
wahrscheinlich probably ['prɒbəbli]
Währung currency ['kʌrənsi]
Wal whale [weɪl]
Wald forest ['fɒrɪst]
Walisisch; walisisch Welsh [welʃ]
Wand wall [wɔ:l]
wann? when? [wen] **Wann hast du Geburtstag?** When's your birthday. **wann (auch) immer / egal, wann** whenever [ˌwen'evə]
▶ S. 195 whenever, wherever, whatever, whoever
Waren *(Güter)* goods *(pl)* [gʊdz]
warm warm [wɔ:m]
Warnung warning ['wɔ:nɪŋ]
warten (auf) wait (for) [weɪt] **Warte einen Moment.** Wait a minute.
warum? why? [waɪ]
was what [wɒt] **Was gibt es zum Mittagessen?** What's for lunch? **Was haben wir als Hausaufgabe auf?** What's for homework? **Was hättest du gern? / Was möchtest du?** What would you like? **Was ist denn? / Was ist los?** What's the matter? / What's up? **Und was ist mit dir?** What about you? **was (auch) immer** whatever [wɒt'evə] **was (sonst) noch?** what else?
▶ S. 195 whenever, wherever, whatever, whoever
▶ S. 195 ... else
waschen wash [wɒʃ]
Wasser water ['wɔ:tə]
Wasserfall waterfall ['wɔ:təfɔ:l]
Website website ['websaɪt]
Wechselgeld change [tʃeɪndʒ]
wechseln *(Geld)* change [tʃeɪndʒ]
wecken: jn. wecken wake sb. up [ˌweɪk‿'ʌp]
weg away [ə'weɪ] **weg sein** *(nicht mehr da sein)* be gone [gɒn]
Weg way [weɪ]; *(Pfad)* path [pɑ:θ]; trail [treɪl] **auf dem Weg zu/nach ...** on the way to ... **jm. den Weg (nach ...) beschreiben** tell sb. the way (to ...) **jn. nach dem Weg fragen** ask sb. the way
wegen: Es tut mir leid wegen ... I'm sorry about ...
weggehen leave [li:v]
wehtun hurt [hɜ:t]
weich soft [sɒft]
Weide field [fi:ld]
Weihnachten Christmas ['krɪsməs] **1. Weihnachtstag** *(25. Dezember)* Christmas Day
weil because [bɪ'kɒz]
Weile: eine Weile (for) a while [waɪl]
weinen cry [kraɪ]
weise wise [waɪz]
Weise: auf diese Weise in this way
weiß white [waɪt]
Weißwandtafel whiteboard ['waɪtbɔ:d]
weit **1.** *(breit)* wide [waɪd] **2. weit (entfernt)** far [fɑ:] **weiter** further ['fɜ:ðə] **am weitesten** furthest ['fɜ:ðɪst]

weiter **1. geradeaus weiter** straight on [streɪt‿'ɒn] **2. etwas immer weiter tun** keep doing sth. [ki:p]
weiter-: weitergehen *(sich fortsetzen)* continue **weitergehen/-laufen/-segeln/...** walk/run/sail/... on **weitermachen** go on **weiterreden** go on
welche(r, s) **1. Auf welcher Seite sind wir?** What page are we on? **Welche Farbe ...?** What colour ...? **2.** *(aus einer begrenzten Anzahl)* which [wɪtʃ] **Welche Klubs ...?** *(= Welche von diesen Klubs ...?)* Which clubs ...?
Welle wave [weɪv]
Welt world [wɜ:ld] **auf der Welt** in the world **Welt der Natur** natural world
Weltmeisterschaft World Cup [ˌwɜ:ld 'kʌp]
wem? who? **Wem hast du es erzählt?** Who did you tell?
wen? who? **Wen kennt Sam?** Who does Sam know?
wenden **1.** *(umkehren)* turn around [ˌtɜ:n‿ə'raʊnd] **2. sich an jn. wenden** turn to sb.
▶ S. 177 (to) turn
weniger (als) less (than) [les]
wenigstens at least [ət 'li:st]
wenn **1.** *(zeitlich)* when [wen] **2.** *(falls)* if [ɪf] **selbst wenn** even if ['i:vn‿ɪf]
wer? who? [hu:] **Wer kennt Sam?** Who knows Sam? **wer (auch) immer** whoever [hu:'evə] **wer (sonst) noch?** who else?
▶ S. 195 whenever, wherever, whatever, whoever
▶ S. 195 ... else
Werbespot advert ['ædvɜ:t]
Werbung *(Werbespot)* advert ['ædvɜ:t] **Werbung machen für etwas** promote sth. [prə'məʊt]
werden become [bɪ'kʌm] **rot werden** go red / turn red **wütend/kalt werden** get angry/cold **hart/schlecht/verrückt werden** go hard/bad/mad
werfen throw [θrəʊ] **einen Blick auf etwas werfen** have a look (at sth.)
Werkstatt workshop ['wɜ:kʃɒp]
wert worth [wɜ:θ]
wessen? whose? [hu:z]
Westen west [west] **nach Westen** west
westlich west [west]; western ['westən]
Wettbewerb competition [ˌkɒmpə'tɪʃn]; contest ['kɒntest]
Wetter weather ['weðə]
Wettkampf *(Match)* match [mætʃ]; *(Turnier)* trials *(pl)* ['traɪəlz]
wichtig important [ɪm'pɔ:tnt] **etwas wichtig nehmen** care about sth. [keə] **Tiere sind mir sehr wichtig.** I really care about animals.
▶ S. 191 (to) care

wie **1.** *(Fragewort)* how [haʊ] **Wie alt bist du?** How old are you? **Wie findest du ...? / Wie gefällt dir ...?** How do you like ...? **Wie geht's? / Wie geht es dir/euch?** How are you? **Wie heißt du?** What's your name? **Wie ist sie (so)?** What's she like? **Wie spät ist es?** What time is it? **Wie viel kosten ...?** How much are ...? **Wie viel kostet ...?** How much is ...? **Wie war es?** What was it like? **Wie wäre es mit ...?** What about ...? **Wie dem auch sei, ...** Anyway, ... ['eniweɪ] **2. wie Jungen** like boys [laɪk] **genau wie ...** just like ... **3. der-/die-/dasselbe wie ...** the same as ... [æz], [əz] **(nicht) so groß wie** (not) as big as **4. Wie John Lennon (einmal) sagte ...** As John Lennon said ...
wieder again [ə'gen] **immer wieder** again and again **etwas immer wieder tun** keep doing sth. [ki:p]
wiederholen **1.** repeat [rɪ'pi:t] **2.** *(Lernstoff)* revise [rɪ'vaɪz]
Wiederholung *(des Lernstoffs)* revision [rɪ'vɪʒn]
wiegen weigh [weɪ]
wild wild [waɪld]
willkommen: jn. willkommen heißen (in) welcome sb. (to) ['welkəm] **Willkommen in Plymouth.** Welcome to Plymouth. ['welkəm]
Wind wind [wɪnd]
windig windy ['wɪndi]
Winter winter ['wɪntə]
wir we [wi:]
wirklich really ['rɪəli]
Wirklichkeit: in Wirklichkeit *(eigentlich)* in fact [ɪn 'fækt]
wischen *(Fußboden)* mop [mɒp]
Wischmopp mop [mɒp]
wissbegierig *(neugierig)* curious ['kjʊəriəs]
wissen know [nəʊ] **..., weißt du. / ..., wissen Sie.** ..., you know. [nəʊ]; ..., you see. **über etwas Bescheid wissen** know about sth. **gern wissen wollen** wonder ['wʌndə] **Woher weißt du ...?** How do you know ...? **Weißt du was, Dad ...** Guess what, Dad ...
Witz joke [dʒəʊk]
witzig funny ['fʌni]
wo where [weə] **wo (auch) immer** wherever [weər'evə]
▶ S. 195 whenever, wherever, whatever, whoever
Woche week [wi:k]
Wochenende weekend [ˌwi:k'end] **am Wochenende** at the weekend
Wochentag day of the week
Woher kommst du? Where are you from? **Woher weißt/kennst du ...?** How do you know ...?
wohin? where? [weə]

wohlbekannt well-known [ˌwel'nəʊn], ['welˌnəʊn]
Wohlfahrtsorganisation charity ['tʃærəti]
Wohltätigkeit, wohltätige Zwecke charity ['tʃærəti]
wohnen *(leben)* live [lɪv]; *(vorübergehend)* stay [steɪ]
Wohnheim hostel ['hɒstl]
Wohnung flat [flæt]; apartment [ə'pɑ:tmənt]
Wohnwagen caravan ['kærəvæn]
Wohnzimmer living room ['lɪvɪŋ ru:m]
Wolke cloud [klaʊd]
wollen: etwas haben wollen want sth. [wɒnt] **etwas tun wollen** want to do sth.
Workshop workshop ['wɜ:kʃɒp]
Wort word [wɜ:d]
Wortart part of speech [ˌpɑ:t‿əv 'spi:tʃ]
Wortstellung word order ['wɜ:d‿ɔ:də]
Wovon handelt die Geschichte? What is the story about?
wund sore [sɔ:]
wundervoll magical ['mædʒɪkl]
Wunsch wish [wɪʃ]
wünschen wish [wɪʃ] **Ich wünschte, ich wäre da.** I wish I was there. **sich etwas wünschen** make a wish
würde: Ich würde gern ... I'd like to ... **Ich würde sehr gern ...** I'd love to ...
Wurm worm [wɜ:m]
wütend (auf jn.) angry (with sb.) ['æŋgri]

Y

Yoga yoga ['jəʊgə]

Z

Zahl number ['nʌmbə]; figure ['fɪgə]
zählen count [kaʊnt] **bis zehn zählen** count to ten
zauberhaft magical ['mædʒɪkl]
z.B. (zum Beispiel) e.g. [ˌi: 'dʒi:] *(from Latin* exempli gratia*)*
Zahn tooth [tu:θ], *pl* teeth [ti:θ]
Zahnarzt/-ärztin dentist ['dentɪst]
Zahnschmerzen haben have a toothache ['tu:θeɪk]
Zauber- magic ['mædʒɪk]
Zaun fence [fens]
Zeh toe [təʊ] **jm. auf die Zehen treten** *(auch im übertragenen Sinne)* tread on sb.'s toes [tred] *(infml)*
zehn ten [ten]
Zeichen sign [saɪn]
Zeichensetzung punctuation [ˌpʌŋktʃu'eɪʃn]
zeichnen draw [drɔ:]
Zeichnung drawing ['drɔ:ɪŋ]

zeigen show [ʃəʊ] **auf etwas zeigen** point to sth. [pɔɪnt] **es zeigt, dass …** it shows that …
Zeile line [laɪn]
Zeit time [taɪm]; *(Tempus, grammatische Zeit)* tense [tens] **die ganze Zeit** all the time **eine Zeit lang** (for) a while **Zeit verbringen (mit)** spend time (on) [spend]
Zeitlupe slow motion [ˌsləʊ 'məʊʃn]
Zeitschrift magazine [ˌmæɡə'ziːn]
Zeitung paper ['peɪpə]
Zelt tent [tent]
zelten gehen go camping ['kæmpɪŋ]
Zeltplatz campsite ['kæmpsaɪt]
Zentrum centre ['sentə]
zerbrechen break [breɪk]
zerbrochen broken ['brəʊkən]
zerstören destroy [dɪ'strɔɪ]
Zeug *(Kram)* stuff [stʌf] *(infml)*
Ziege goat [ɡəʊt]
ziehen pull [pʊl]
ziemlich quite [kwaɪt]
Ziffer number ['nʌmbə]; figure ['fɪɡə]
Zimmer mit Frühstück bed & breakfast
Zimmerer/Zimmerin carpenter ['kɑːpəntə]
zischen hiss [hɪs]
Zoo zoo [zuː]
zu **1.** *(örtlich)* to [tu], [tə] **auf den Bahnhof zu** towards the station [tə'wɔːdz] **auf Mr Bell zu** towards Mr Bell
2. zu spät/kalt/groß/… too late/cold/big/… [tuː]
3. Es ist Zeit zu gehen. It's time to go. **Nice to meet you.** Freut mich, dich/euch/Sie kennenzulernen.
zubereiten *(kochen)* cook [kʊk]
zudecken cover ['kʌvə]
zuerst first [fɜːst]; *(anfangs)* at first [ət 'fɜːst]
Zug train [treɪn]
Zugabe encore ['ɒŋkɔː]
zugehen: auf etwas zugehen head for sth. [hed]
zugreifen: Greif zu! *(Bedien dich!)* Help yourself.
Zuhause home [həʊm]
zuhören listen ['lɪsn] **Hör(t) mir zu.** Listen to me.
Zuhörer/in listener ['lɪsənə]
Zukunft future ['fjuːtʃə]
zukünftige(r, s) future ['fjuːtʃə]
zum Beispiel for example [fər‿ɪɡ'zɑːmpl]
zulassen *(erlauben)* allow [ə'laʊ]
zumachen close [kləʊz]
zumindest at least [ət 'liːst]
Zunge tongue [tʌŋ]
Zungenbrecher tongue-twister ['tʌŋˌtwɪstə]
zurechtkommen get on [ˌget‿'ɒn]
zurück back [bæk]
zurücklassen leave [liːv]
zusammen together [tə'ɡeðə]
Zusammenhang *(Text-, Satzzusammenhang)* context ['kɒntekst]
zusammenpassen *(zueinander passen)* go together
Zuschauer/innen *(Publikum)* audience ['ɔːdiəns]
zustande: etwas zustande bringen manage sth. ['mænɪdʒ]
zusteuern: auf etwas zusteuern head for sth. [hed]
zustimmen: jm. zustimmen agree with sb. [ə'ɡriː]
Zutritt entry ['entri]
zuvor: besser als je zuvor better than ever
zuwenden: sich jm. zuwenden turn to sb. ['tɜːn]
zwei two [tuː]
zweimal twice [twaɪs]
zweisilbig two-syllable ['sɪləbl]
zweite(r, s) second ['sekənd] **auf dem zweiten Platz / an zweiter Stelle** in second place
zweitgrößte(r, s) second biggest
Zwillinge twins *(pl)* [twɪnz]
zwischen between [bɪ'twiːn]
zwölf twelve [twelv]

English sounds

[iː]	**gree**n, h**e**, s**ea**
[i]	happ**y**, monk**ey**
[ɪ]	b**i**g, **i**n, expens**i**ve
[e]	r**e**d, y**e**s, ag**ai**n, br**ea**kfast
[æ]	c**a**t, **a**nimal, **a**pple, bl**a**ck
[ɑː]	cl**a**ss, **a**sk, c**ar**, p**ar**k
[ɒ]	s**o**ng, **o**n, d**o**g, wh**a**t
[ɔː]	d**oor**, **or**, b**a**ll, f**our**, m**or**ning
[uː]	bl**ue**, r**u**ler, t**oo**, tw**o**, y**ou**
[ʊ]	b**oo**k, g**oo**d, p**u**llover
[ʌ]	m**u**m, b**u**s, c**o**lour
[ɜː]	g**ir**l, **ear**ly, h**er**, w**or**k, T-sh**ir**t
[ə]	**a** partn**er**, **a**gain, tod**a**y
[eɪ]	n**a**me, **eigh**t, pl**ay**, gr**ea**t
[aɪ]	t**i**me, r**igh**t, m**y**, **I**
[ɔɪ]	b**oy**, t**oi**let, n**oi**se
[əʊ]	**o**ld, n**o**, r**oa**d, yell**ow**
[aʊ]	t**ow**n, n**ow**, h**ou**se
[ɪə]	h**ere**, y**ear**, id**ea**
[eə]	wh**ere**, p**air**, sh**are**, th**eir**
[ʊə]	t**our**

[b]	**b**oat, ta**b**le, ver**b**
[p]	**p**ool, **p**a**p**er, sho**p**
[d]	**d**a**d**, win**d**ow, goo**d**
[t]	**t**en, le**tt**er, a**t**
[ɡ]	**g**ood, a**g**ain, ba**g**
[k]	**c**at, **k**itchen, ba**ck**
[m]	**m**u**m**, **m**an, re**m**e**m**ber
[n]	**n**o, o**n**e, te**n**
[ŋ]	so**ng**, you**ng**, u**n**cle, tha**n**ks
[l]	he**ll**o, **l**ike, o**l**d, sma**ll**
[r]	**r**ed, **r**uler, f**r**iend, so**rr**y
[w]	**w**e, **wh**ere, **o**ne
[j]	**y**ou, **y**es, **u**niform
[f]	**f**amily, a**f**ter, lau**gh**
[v]	ri**v**er, **v**ery, se**v**en, ha**v**e
[s]	**s**i**s**ter, po**s**ter, ye**s**
[z]	plea**s**e, **z**oo, qui**z**, hi**s**, mu**s**ic
[ʃ]	**sh**op, sta**t**ion, Engli**sh**
[ʒ]	televi**s**ion, u**s**ually
[tʃ]	tea**ch**er, **ch**ild, wa**tch**
[dʒ]	**G**ermany, **j**ob, pro**j**ect, oran**ge**
[θ]	**th**anks, **th**ree, ba**th**room
[ð]	**th**e, **th**is, fa**th**er, wi**th**
[h]	**h**ere, **wh**o, be**h**ind
[x]	lo**ch**

Am besten kannst du dir die Aussprache der einzelnen Lautzeichen einprägen, wenn du dir zu jedem Zeichen ein einfaches Wort merkst – das [iː] ist der **green**-Laut, das [eɪ] ist der **name**-Laut usw.

First names
(Vornamen)

Adam ['ædəm]
Adrian ['eidriən]
Albert ['ælbət]
Amelia [ə'mi:liə]
Angus ['æŋgəs]
Ashling ['æʃlɪŋ]
Benandonner [ˌbenən'dɒnə]
Beth [beθ]
Beyoncé [bɪ'jɒnseɪ]
Brian ['braɪən]
Callum ['kæləm]
Cate [keɪt]
Charles [tʃɑ:lz]
Charlie ['tʃɑ:li]
Chloe ['kləʊi]
Clementine ['kleməntaɪn]
Dylan ['dɪlən]
Edward ['edwəd]
Emily ['eməli]
Finn [fɪn]
Frank [fræŋk]
Gareth ['gærəθ]
Gemima [dʒə'meɪmə]
George [dʒɔ:dʒ]
Giles [dʒaɪlz]
Gordon ['gɔ:dn]
Grace [greɪs]
Gwen [gwen]
Hadrian ['heɪdriən]
Harry ['hæri]
Iain ['i:ən]
Jack [dʒæk]
James [dʒeɪmz]
Jerry ['dʒeri]
Jimmy ['dʒɪmi]
John [dʒɒn]
Katie ['keɪti]
Khan [kɑ:n]
Knuckles ['nʌkəlz]
Lauren ['lɒrən]
Lewis ['lu:ɪs]
Luke [lu:k]
Mary ['meəri]
Maxine [mæk'si:n]
Mishal ['mɪʃəl]
Mo [məʊ]
Morgan ['mɔ:gən]
Norman ['nɔ:mən]
Oliver ['ɒlɪvə]
Oonagh ['u:nə]
Paige [peɪdʒ]
Paul [pɔ:l]
Philip ['fɪlɪp]
Ray [reɪ]
Ringo ['rɪŋgeʊ]
Robert ['rɒbət]
Roger ['rɒdʒə]
Ronald ['rɒnəld]
Ross [rɒs]
Ruscaire ['rʌskərə]
Sandra ['sændrə], ['sɑ:ndrə]
Sandy ['sændi]
Sherlock ['ʃɜ:lɒk]
Skye [skaɪ]
Tom [tɒm]
Willy ['wɪli]

Family names / Surnames
(Familiennamen)

Abrams ['eibrəmz]
Baden-Powell [ˌbeɪdn'pəʊəl]
Barnes [bɑ:nz]
Bates [beɪts]
Beedle ['bi:dl]
Blanchett ['blɑ:ntʃət]
Bond [bɒnd]
Boyd [bɔɪd]
Carr [kɑ:]
Clarke [klɑ:k]
Dickens ['dɪkɪnz]
Edwards ['edwədz]
Evans ['evənz]
Ferguson ['fɜ:gəsən]
Foster ['fɒstə]
Fraser ['freɪzə]
Grant [grɑ:nt]
Grimble ['grɪmbl]
Hammerstein ['hæməstaɪn]
Harrison ['hærɪsən]
Henri ['henri]
Hill [hɪl]
Holmes [həʊmz]
Hunter ['hʌntə]
Jezzard ['dʒezɑ:d]
Kirk [kɜ:k]
Lennon ['lenən]
Macdonald [mək'dɒnəld]
MacLeod [mə'klaʊd]
MacNeil [mək'ni:l]
McCartney [mə'kɑ:tni]
McCool [mə'ku:l]
McCray [mə'kreɪ]
McGough [mə'gɒf]
Nash [næʃ]
Nobel [nəʊ'bel]
Oscar ['ɒskə]
Patten ['pætən]
Potter ['pɒtə]
Reid [ri:d]
Rogers ['rɒdʒəz]
Ross [rɒs]
Scott [skɒt]
Seeger ['si:gə]
Skeefe [ski:f]
Smart [smɑ:t]
Smith [smɪθ]
Starr [stɑ:]
Twist [twɪst]

Place names
(Ortsnamen)

Bangor ['bæŋgə]
Bannockburn ['bænəkbɜ:n]
the **Beat Museum** ['bi:t]
Belfast [ˌbel'fɑ:st, 'belfɑ:st]
Birkenhead [ˌbɜ:kən'hed]
Blackfriars [ˌblæk'fraɪəz]
Brandenburg ['brændnbɜ:g]
Buckingham Palace [ˌbʌkɪŋəm 'pæləs]
the **Burren** ['bʌrən]
Caerdydd [kaɪə'di:ð]
Caernarfon [kə'nɑ:vən]
Cardiff ['kɑ:dɪf]
Carlingford ['kɑ:lɪŋfəd]
Castlebay [ˌkɑ:sl'beɪ]
the **Cavern Club** ['kævən]
Chelsea ['tʃelsi]
Chinatown ['tʃaɪnətaʊn]
Dublin ['dʌblɪn]
Edinburgh ['edɪnbərə]
Euston ['ju:stən]
Everton ['evətən]
Fulham ['fʊləm]
Georgetown ['dʒɔ:dʒtaʊn]
the **Giant's Causeway** [ˌdʒaɪənts 'kɔ:zweɪ]
Glasgow ['glɑ:zgəʊ]
Great Homer Street [ˌgreɪt 'həʊmə stri:t]
Hamburg ['hæmbɜ:g]
Hammersmith ['hæməsmɪθ]
Hampstead Heath [ˌhæmpstɪd 'hi:θ]
Hyde Park [ˌhaɪd 'pɑ:k]
Isle of Barra [ˌaɪl‿əv 'bærə]
King's Cross [ˌkɪŋz 'krɒs]
Lambeth ['læmbəθ]
Leeds [li:dz]
Liverpool ['lɪvəpu:l]
Loch Ness [ˌlɒx 'nes]
London ['lʌndən]
Marble Arch [ˌmɑ:bl‿'ɑ:tʃ]
Mathew Street ['mæθju:]
Merseyside ['mɜ:zisaɪd]
Moscow ['mɒskəʊ]
Notting Hill [ˌnɒtɪŋ 'hɪl]
One New Change [ˌwʌn nju: 'tʃeɪndʒ]
Oxford Street ['ɒksfəd stri:t]
Richmond ['rɪtʃmənd]
the **River Clyde** [klaɪd]
the **River Mersey** ['mɜ:zi]
the **River Thames** ['temz]
Russell Square [ˌrʌsl 'skweə]
Saint Patrick's Cathedral [sənt ˌpætrɪks kə'θi:drəl]
Saint Paul's Cathedral [sənt ˌpɔ:lz kə'θi:drəl]
the **Shard** [ʃɑ:d]
Snowdon ['snəʊdn]
Snowdonia [snəʊ'dəʊniə]
Southampton [ˌsaʊθ'hæmptən]
Temple Bar [ˌtempl 'bɑ:]
Urquhart Castle ['ɜ:kət]
Vauxhall ['vɒksɔ:l]
the **Watkin Path** ['wɒtkɪn]
Wavertree ['weɪvətri:]
Westbourne Grove [ˌwestbɔ:n 'grəʊv]
Westminster ['westmɪnstə]
Wimbledon ['wɪmbldən]

Other names

Bamana [bæ'mɑ:nə]
Beatle ['bi:tl]
Big Ben [ˌbɪg 'ben]
djembe ['dʒembeɪ]
Doctor Who [ˌdɒktə 'hu:]
Dracula ['drækjʊlə]
Eisteddfod [ə'steðvɒd]
Google ['gu:gl]
Greaty ['greɪti]
Hobbit ['hɒbɪt]
Igbo ['i:bəʊ]
the **Jubilee line** ['dʒu:bəli]
leprechaun ['leprəkɔ:n]
Ogoni [əʊ'gəʊni]
Raven ['reɪvn]
the **Rosetta Stone** [rəʊ'zetə]
Shadow ['ʃædəʊ]
the **Titanic** [taɪ'tænɪk]
udu ['u:du:]
UNESCO [ju:'neskəʊ]

Countries and continents

Country/Continent	Adjective	Person	People
Marco is from ***Italy****.*	*Pizza is* ***Italian****.*	*Marco is* ***an Italian****.*	***The Italians*** *invented pizza.*
Africa ['æfrɪkə] *Afrika*	African ['æfrɪkən]	an African	the Africans
Albania [æl'beɪniə] *Albanien*	Albanian [æl'beɪniən]	an Albanian	the Albanians
Asia ['eɪʒə, 'eɪʃə] *Asien*	Asian ['eɪʃn, 'eɪʒn]	an Asian	the Asians
Australia [ɒ'streɪliə] *Australien*	Australian [ɒ'streɪliən]	an Australian	the Australians
Austria ['ɒstriə] *Österreich*	Austrian ['ɒstriən]	an Austrian	the Austrians
Belarus [ˌbel'ru:s] *Weißrussland*	Belarusian [ˌbel'ru:siən]	a Belarusian	the Belarusians
Belgium ['beldʒəm] *Belgien*	Belgian ['beldʒən]	a Belgian	the Belgians
Bosnia and Herzegovina ['bɒzniə ən ˌhɜ:tsəgə'vi:nə] *Bosnien und Herzegowina*	Bosnian ['bɒzniən]; Herzegovinian [ˌhɜ:tsəgə'vɪniən]	a Bosnian; a Herzegovinian	the Bosnians; the Herzegovinians
Bulgaria [bʌl'geəriə] *Bulgarien*	Bulgarian [bʌl'geəriən]	a Bulgarian	the Bulgarians
China ['tʃaɪnə] *China*	Chinese [ˌtʃaɪ'ni:z]	a Chinese	the Chinese
Croatia [krəʊ'eɪʃə] *Kroatien*	Croatian [krəʊ'eɪʃn]	a Croatian	the Croatians
Cyprus ['saɪprəs] *Zypern*	Cypriot ['sɪpriət]	a Cypriot	the Cypriots
the **Czech Republic** [ˌtʃek rɪ'pʌblɪk] *Tschechien, die Tschechische Republik*	Czech [tʃek]	a Czech	the Czechs
Denmark ['denmɑ:k] *Dänemark*	Danish ['deɪnɪʃ]	a Dane [deɪn]	the Danes
England ['ɪŋglənd] *England*	English ['ɪŋglɪʃ]	an Englishman / an Englishwoman	the English
Estonia [e'stəʊniə] *Estland*	Estonian [e'stəʊniən]	an Estonian	the Estonians
Europe ['jʊərəp] *Europa*	European [ˌjʊərə'pi:ən]	a European	the Europeans
Finland ['fɪnlənd] *Finnland*	Finnish ['fɪnɪʃ]	a Finn [fɪn]	the Finns
France [frɑ:ns] *Frankreich*	French [frentʃ]	a Frenchman / a Frenchwoman	the French
Germany ['dʒɜ:məni] *Deutschland*	German ['dʒɜ:mən]	a German	the Germans
(Great) Britain ['brɪtn] *Großbritannien*	British ['brɪtɪʃ]	a Briton ['brɪtn]	the British
Greece [gri:s] *Griechenland*	Greek [gri:k]	a Greek	the Greeks
Greenland ['gri:nlənd]	Greenlandic [gri:n'lændɪk]	a Greenlander ['gri:nləndə]	the Greenlanders
Guyana [gaɪ'ænə] *Guyana (früher: British Guyana)*	Guyanese [gaɪ'əni:z]	a Guyanese	the Guyanese
Hungary ['hʌŋgəri] *Ungarn*	Hungarian [hʌŋ'geəriən]	a Hungarian	the Hungarians
Iceland ['aɪslənd] *Island*	Icelandic [aɪs'lændɪk]	an Icelander ['aɪsləndə]	the Icelanders
India ['ɪndiə] *Indien*	Indian ['ɪndiən]	an Indian	the Indians
Ireland ['aɪələnd] *Irland*	Irish ['aɪrɪʃ]	an Irishman / an Irishwoman	the Irish
Italy ['ɪtəli] *Italien*	Italian [ɪ'tæliən]	an Italian	the Italians
Kosovo ['kɒsəvəʊ] *Kosovo*	Kosovan ['kɒsəvən]	a Kosovan	the Kosovans

Country/Continent	Adjective	Person	People
*Marco is from **Italy**.*	*Pizza is **Italian**.*	*Marco is **an Italian**.*	***The Italians** invented pizza.*
Latvia ['lætviə] *Lettland*	Latvian ['lætviən]	a Latvian	the Latvians
Lithuania [ˌlɪθju'eɪniə] *Litauen*	Lithuanian [ˌlɪθju'eɪniən]	a Lithuanian	the Lithuanians
Luxembourg ['lʌksəmbɜːg] *Luxemburg*	Luxembourg	a Luxembourger ['lʌksəmbɜːgə]	the Luxembourgers
Macedonia [ˌmæsə'dəʊniə] *Mazedonien*	Macedonian [ˌmæsə'dəʊniən]	a Macedonian	the Macedonians
Malta ['mɔːltə] *Malta*	Maltese [mɔːl'tiːz]	a Maltese	the Maltese
Moldova [mɒl'dəʊvə] *Moldawien*	Moldovan [mɒl'dəʊvən]	a Moldovan	the Moldovans
Montenegro [ˌmɒntɪ'niːgrəʊ] *Montenegro*	Montenegrin [ˌmɒntɪ'niːgrɪn]	a Montenegrin	the Montenegrins
the **Netherlands** ['neðələndz] *die Niederlande*	Dutch [dʌtʃ]	a Dutchman / a Dutchwoman	the Dutch
Nigeria [naɪ'dʒɪəriə] *Nigeria*	Nigerian [naɪ'dʒɪəriən]	a Nigerian	the Nigerians
North America [ˌnɔːθ‿ə'merɪkə] *Nordamerika*	North American [ˌnɔːθ‿ə'merɪkən]	a North American	the North Americans
Northern Ireland [ˌnɔːðən‿'aɪələnd] *Nordirland*	Northern Irish [ˌnɔːðən‿'aɪrɪʃ]	a Northern Irishman / a Northern Irishwoman	the Northern Irish
Norway ['nɔːweɪ] *Norwegen*	Norwegian [nɔː'wiːdʒən]	a Norwegian	the Norwegians
Poland ['pəʊlənd] *Polen*	Polish ['pəʊlɪʃ]	a Pole [pəʊl]	the Poles
Portugal ['pɔːtʃʊgl] *Portugal*	Portuguese [ˌpɔːtʃu'giːz]	a Portuguese	the Portuguese
Romania [ru'meɪniə] *Rumänien*	Romanian [ru'meɪniən]	a Romanian	the Romanians
Russia ['rʌʃə] *Russland*	Russian ['rʌʃn]	a Russian	the Russians
Scotland ['skɒtlənd] *Schottland*	Scottish ['skɒtɪʃ]	a Scot [skɒt]; a Scotsman / a Scotswoman	the Scots, the Scottish
Serbia ['sɜːbiə] *Serbien*	Serbian ['sɜːbiən]	a Serbian	the Serbians
Slovakia [sləʊ'vækiə] *die Slowakei*	Slovak ['sləʊvæk]	a Slovak	the Slovaks
Slovenia [sləʊ'viːniə] *Slowenien*	Slovenian [sləʊ'viːniən]	a Slovenian	the Slovenians
South America [ˌsaʊθ‿ə'merɪkə] *Südamerika*	South American [ˌsaʊθ‿ə'merɪkən]	a South American	the South Americans
Spain [speɪn] *Spanien*	Spanish ['spænɪʃ]	a Spaniard ['spænɪəd]	the Spanish
Sweden ['swiːdn] *Schweden*	Swedish ['swiːdɪʃ]	a Swede [swiːd]	the Swedes
Switzerland ['swɪtsələnd] *die Schweiz*	Swiss [swɪs]	a Swiss	the Swiss
Turkey ['tɜːki] *die Türkei*	Turkish ['tɜːkɪʃ]	a Turk [tɜːk]	the Turks
Ukraine [juː'kreɪn] *die Ukraine*	Ukrainian [juː'kreɪniən]	a Ukrainian	the Ukrainians
the **United Kingdom** [juˌnaɪtɪd 'kɪŋdəm] *das Vereinigte Königreich*	British ['brɪtɪʃ]	a Briton ['brɪtn]	the British
the **United States of America** [juˌnaɪtɪd ˌsteɪts‿əv‿ə'merɪkə] *die Vereinigten Staaten von Amerika*	American [ə'merɪkən]	an American	the Americans
Wales [weɪlz] *Wales*	Welsh [welʃ]	a Welshman/-woman	the Welsh

x = nicht lernen

infinitive	simple past	past participle	
(to) **be**	*I/he/she/it* **was**; *you/we/you/they* **were**	**been**	sein
(to) **beat**	**beat**	**beaten**	schlagen; besiegen
(to) **become**	**became**	**become**	werden
(to) **begin**	**began**	**begun**	beginnen, anfangen
x (to) **bend**	**bent**	**bent**	sich bücken, sich beugen
x (to) **bite** [aɪ]	**bit** [ɪ]	**bitten** [ɪ]	beißen
(to) **blow** sth. **out**	**blew**	**blown**	etwas auspusten, ausblasen
(to) **break** [eɪ]	**broke**	**broken**	brechen; zerbrechen
(to) **bring**	**brought**	**brought**	(mit-, her)bringen
(to) **build**	**built**	**built**	bauen
x (to) **burst** into tears	**burst**	**burst**	in Tränen ausbrechen
(to) **buy**	**bought**	**bought**	kaufen
(to) **catch**	**caught**	**caught**	fangen
(to) **choose** [uː]	**chose** [əʊ]	**chosen** [əʊ]	aussuchen, (aus)wählen; sich aussuchen
(to) **come**	**came**	**come**	kommen
(to) **cost**	**cost**	**cost**	kosten
(to) **cut**	**cut**	**cut**	schneiden
(to) **do**	**did**	**done** [ʌ]	tun, machen
(to) **draw**	**drew**	**drawn**	zeichnen
(to) **drive** [aɪ]	**drove** [əʊ]	**driven** [ɪ]	*(mit dem Auto)* fahren
(to) **drink**	**drank**	**drunk**	trinken
(to) **eat**	**ate** [et, eɪt]	**eaten**	essen
(to) **fall**	**fell**	**fallen**	fallen, stürzen; hinfallen
(to) **feed**	**fed**	**fed**	füttern
(to) **feel**	**felt**	**felt**	fühlen; sich fühlen
(to) **fight**	**fought**	**fought**	(be)kämpfen
(to) **find**	**found**	**found**	finden
(to) **fly**	**flew**	**flown**	fliegen
(to) **forget**	**forgot**	**forgotten**	vergessen
(to) **get**	**got**	**got**	bekommen; holen, besorgen; werden; gelangen, (hin)kommen
(to) **give**	**gave**	**given**	geben
(to) **go**	**went**	**gone** [ɒ]	gehen
(to) **grow**	**grew**	**grown**	wachsen; anbauen, anpflanzen
(to) **hang**	**hung**	**hung**	hängen
(to) **have**	**had**	**had**	haben
(to) **hear** [ɪə]	**heard** [ɜː]	**heard** [ɜː]	hören
(to) **hide** [aɪ]	**hid** [ɪ]	**hidden** [ɪ]	verstecken; sich verstecken
(to) **hit**	**hit**	**hit**	schlagen
(to) **hold**	**held**	**held**	halten
(to) **hurt**	**hurt**	**hurt**	schmerzen, wehtun; verletzen
(to) **keep**	**kept**	**kept**	aufheben, aufsparen; aufbewahren
x (to) **kneel** [niːl]	**knelt** [nelt]	**knelt** [nelt]	knien
(to) **know** [nəʊ]	**knew** [njuː]	**known** [nəʊn]	wissen; kennen

infinitive	simple past	past participle	
(to) **lead** [iː]	**led**	**led**	führen, leiten
(to) **leave** [iː]	**left**	**left**	(weg)gehen; abfahren; (zurück)lassen; verlassen
(to) **let**	**let**	**let**	lassen
(to) **lie**	**lay**	**lain**	liegen
(to) **light** [aɪ]	**lit** [ɪ]	**lit** [ɪ]	anzünden
(to) **lose** [uː]	**lost** [ɒ]	**lost** [ɒ]	verlieren
(to) **make**	**made**	**made**	machen; herstellen
(to) **mean** [iː]	**meant** [e]	**meant** [e]	bedeuten; meinen
(to) **meet** [iː]	**met** [e]	**met**	treffen; sich treffen; kennenlernen
(to) **pay**	**paid**	**paid**	bezahlen
(to) **put**	**put**	**put**	*(etwas wohin)* tun, legen, stellen
(to) **read** [iː]	**read** [e]	**read** [e]	lesen
(to) **ride** [aɪ]	**rode**	**ridden** [ɪ]	reiten; *(Rad)* fahren
(to) **ring**	**rang**	**rung**	klingeln, läuten
(to) **rise up** [aɪ]	**rose**	**risen** [ɪ]	aufragen, emporragen
(to) **run**	**ran**	**run**	rennen, laufen
(to) **say** [eɪ]	**said** [e]	**said** [e]	sagen
(to) **see**	**saw**	**seen**	sehen
(to) **sell**	**sold**	**sold**	verkaufen
(to) **send**	**sent**	**sent**	schicken, senden
(to) **shake**	**shook**	**shaken**	schütteln
(to) **shine**	**shone** [ɒ]	**shone** [ɒ]	scheinen *(Sonne)*
(to) **sing**	**sang**	**sung**	singen
(to) **sit**	**sat**	**sat**	sitzen; sich setzen
(to) **sleep**	**slept**	**slept**	schlafen
(to) **speak** [iː]	**spoke**	**spoken**	sprechen
(to) **spend**	**spent**	**spent**	*(Zeit)* verbringen; *(Geld)* ausgeben
(to) **spin around**	**spun**	**spun**	sich (im Kreis) drehen; herumwirbeln
(to) **spread** [e]	**spread** [e]	**spread** [e]	ausbreiten, verbreiten; sich ausbreiten, verbreiten
(to) **stand**	**stood**	**stood**	stehen; sich (hin)stellen
(to) **steal**	**stole**	**stolen**	stehlen
(to) **stick**	**stuck**	**stuck**	stechen, stecken
(to) **swim**	**swam**	**swum**	schwimmen
(to) **take**	**took**	**taken**	nehmen, mitnehmen; (weg-, hin)bringen; dauern, *(Zeit)* brauchen
(to) **teach**	**taught**	**taught**	unterrichten, lehren
(to) **tell**	**told**	**told**	erzählen, berichten
(to) **think**	**thought**	**thought**	denken, glauben
(to) **throw**	**threw**	**thrown**	werfen
(to) **tread** [e]	**trod**	**trodden**	treten
(to) **understand**	**understood**	**understood**	verstehen
(to) **wake up**	**woke up**	**woken up**	aufwachen; (auf)wecken
(to) **wear** [eə]	**wore** [ɔː]	**worn** [ɔː]	tragen *(Kleidung)*
(to) **win**	**won** [ʌ]	**won** [ʌ]	gewinnen
(to) **write**	**wrote**	**written**	schreiben

True and false friends

True friends (Wahre Freunde)

Es gibt viele Wörter, die im Englischen und im Deutschen sehr ähnlich sind – das sind die „wahren Freunde“. Manchmal gibt es allerdings Unterschiede in der Schreibung oder der Aussprache, die man beachten muss.

action ['ækʃn] Aktion
activity [æk'tɪvəti] Aktivität
address [ə'dres] Adresse
April ['eɪprəl] April
aquarium [ə'kweəriəm] Aquarium
arm [ɑːm] Arm
article ['ɑːtɪkl] Artikel
August ['ɔːgəst] August
ball [bɔːl] Ball
band [bænd] Band, Musikgruppe
basketball ['bɑːskɪtbɔːl] Basketball
before [bɪ'fɔː] bevor
begin [bɪ'gɪn] beginnen
blond [blɒnd] blond
bring [brɪŋ] bringen
burger ['bɜːgə] Hamburger
bus [bʌs] Bus
café ['kæfeɪ] Café
camera ['kæmərə] Kamera
camping ['kæmpɪŋ] Camping, Zelten
clown [klaʊn] Clown
club [klʌb] Klub
cola ['kəʊlə] Cola
comedy ['kɒmədi] Comedyshow
comma ['kɒmə] Komma
computer [kəm'pjuːtə] Computer
concert ['kɒnsət] Konzert
consonant ['kɒnsənənt] Konsonant
context ['kɒntekst] Kontext
cool [kuːl] cool
copy ['kɒpi] Kopie
cornflakes ['kɔːnfleɪks] Cornflakes
correct [kə'rekt] korrekt
cost [kɒst] kosten
costume ['kɒstjuːm] Kostüm
cousin ['kʌzn] Cousin, Cousine
crash [kræʃ] crashen
cricket ['krɪkɪt] Cricket
deck [dek] Deck (eines Schiffes)
demonstration [ˌdemən'streɪʃn] Demonstration
designer [dɪ'zaɪnə] Designer/in
dialogue ['daɪəlɒg] Dialog
disco ['dɪskəʊ] Disko
doctor ['dɒktə] Doktor
DVD [diːviː'diː] DVD
elephant ['elɪfənt] Elefant
email ['iːmeɪl] E-Mail
end [end] Ende
fair [feə] fair, gerecht
fall [fɔːl] fallen
family ['fæməli] Familie
fan [fæn] Fan, Anhänger/in
farm [fɑːm] Farm, Bauernhof
film [fɪlm] Film
final ['faɪnl] Finale
find [faɪnd] finden
fine [faɪn] fein
finger ['fɪŋgə] Finger
fish [fɪʃ] Fisch
flag [flæg] Flagge
form [fɔːm] Form
garage ['gærɑːʒ, 'gærɪdʒ] Garage
garden ['gɑːdn] Garten
gel [dʒel] Gel
giraffe [dʒə'rɑːf] Giraffe
glass [glɑːs] Glas
go-kart ['gəʊ kɑːt] Gokart
gold [gəʊld] Gold
gram [græm] Gramm
grass [grɑːs] Gras
guitar [gɪ'tɑː] Gitarre
gymnastics [dʒɪm'næstɪks] Gymnastik
hamburger ['hæmbɜːgə] Hamburger
hamster ['hæmstə] Hamster
hand [hænd] Hand
hobby ['hɒbi] Hobby
hotel [həʊ'tel] Hotel
house [haʊs] Haus
instrument ['ɪnstrəmənt] Instrument
interview ['ɪntəvjuː] Interview
jeans [dʒiːnz] Jeans
job [dʒɒb] Job, Arbeitsstelle
judo ['dʒuːdəʊ] Judo
kilogram ['kɪləgræm] Kilogramm
kilometre ['kɪləmiːtə] Kilometer
kung fu [ˌkʌŋ 'fuː] Kung Fu
lamp [læmp] Lampe
land [lænd] Land
legend ['ledʒənd] Legende
lip [lɪp] Lippe
list [lɪst] Liste
make-up ['meɪk‿ʌp] Make-up
man [mæn] Mann
mediation [ˌmiːdi'eɪʃn] Mediation
metre ['miːtə] Meter
million ['mɪljən] Million
minute ['mɪnɪt] Minute
model ['mɒdl] Model
moment ['məʊmənt] Moment
monster ['mɒnstə] Monster
museum [mju'ziːəm] Museum
music ['mjuːzɪk] Musik
musical ['mjuːzɪkl] Musical
name [neɪm] Name
object ['ɒbdʒekt] Objekt
ocean ['əʊʃn] Ozean

online [ˌɒn'laɪn] online
orange ['ɒrɪndʒ] orange
otter ['ɒtə] Otter
parade [pə'reɪd] Parade
park [pɑːk] Park
partner ['pɑːtnə] Partner/in
party ['pɑːti] Party
perfect ['pɜːfɪkt] perfekt
person ['pɜːsn] Person
photo ['fəʊtəʊ] Foto
picnic ['pɪknɪk] Picknick
pink [pɪŋk] pink, rosa
pizza ['piːtsə] Pizza
plan [plæn] Plan
planet ['plænɪt] Planet
pony ['pəʊni] Pony
poster ['pəʊstə] Poster
prince [prɪns] Prinz
problem ['prɒbləm] Problem
programme ['prəʊgræm] Programm
project ['prɒdʒekt] Projekt
quiz [kwɪz] Quiz, Ratespiel
radio ['reɪdiəʊ] Radio
rally ['ræli] Rallye
religion [rɪ'lɪgʒən] Religion
ring [rɪŋ] Ring
rock (music) [rɒk] Rockmusik
roll [rəʊl] rollen
rucksack ['rʌksæk] Rucksack
ruin ['ruːɪn] Ruine
samba ['sæmbə] Samba
sand [sænd] Sand
sandwich ['sænwɪtʃ] Sandwich
scene [siːn] Szene
second ['sekənd] Sekunde
set [set] Set, Satz
shorts [ʃɔːts] Shorts, kurze Hose
show [ʃəʊ] Show, Vorstellung
sing [sɪŋ] singen
snack [snæk] Snack, Imbiss
sofa ['səʊfə] Sofa
solo ['səʊləʊ] Solo-
song [sɒŋ] Lied, Song
sport [spɔːt] Sport
star [stɑː] (Film-, Pop-)Star
stop [stɒp] anhalten, stoppen
student ['stjuːdənt] Student/in
studio ['stjuːdiəʊ] Studio
subject ['sʌbdʒekt] Subjekt
symbol ['sɪmbl] Symbol
tea [tiː] Tee
team [tiːm] Team, Mannschaft
telephone ['telɪfəʊn] Telefon
tennis ['tenɪs] Tennis
theatre ['θɪətə] Theater
theme [θiːm] Thema
thermometer [θə'mɒmɪtə] Thermometer
title ['taɪtl] Titel
toilet ['tɔɪlət] Toilette
tomato [tə'mɑːtəʊ] Tomate
top [tɒp] Top, Oberteil
tourist ['tʊərɪst] Tourist/in
tractor ['træktə] Traktor
traditional [trə'dɪʃənl] traditionell
train [treɪn] trainieren
trick [trɪk] Trick, Kunststück
T-shirt ['tiːʃɜːt] T-Shirt
tunnel ['tʌnl] Tunnel
uniform ['juːnɪfɔːm] Uniform
vegetarian [ˌvedʒə'teəriən] Vegetarier/in
video ['vɪdiəʊ] Video
volleyball ['vɒlibɔːl] Volleyball
warm [wɔːm] warm
website ['websaɪt] Website
wild [waɪld] wild
wind [wɪnd] Wind
winter ['wɪntə] Winter
workshop ['wɜːkʃɒp] Workshop
yoga ['jəʊgə] Yoga
yoghurt ['jɒgət] Joghurt
zoo [zuː] Zoo

False friends (Falsche Freunde)

! Leider gibt es auch einige Wörter, die im Englischen und Deutschen ähnlich klingen oder aussehen, aber eine ganz andere Bedeutung haben.
Hier sind einige Beispiele für *false friends*:

English	German	German	English
also	= auch	also	= **so; Well ...**
become	= werden	bekommen	= **get**
boot	= Stiefel	Boot	= **boat**
build	= bauen	bilden	= **make, form**
chips	= Pommes frites	Kartoffelchips	= **crisps**
fire	= Feuer	Feier	= **celebration**
kind	= freundlich	Kind	= **child**
handy	= praktisch	Handy	= **mobile**
listen	= zuhören	Listen	= **lists**
map	= Landkarte	Mappe	= **folder**
mist	= Nebel	Mist *(Unsinn)*	= **rubbish**

English	German	German	English
snake	= Schlange	Schnecke	= **snail**
stay	= bleiben	stehen	= **stand**
where	= wo	wer	= **who**
while	= während	weil	= **because**

TIP
Wenn du nicht sicher bist, ob du *true friends* oder *false friends* vor dir hast, dann schau in einem guten Wörterbuch nach.

Unit 1

a)

1	B	E	G	A	N
2	C	H	O	S	E
3	D	R	O	V	E
4	H	E	A	R	D
5	T	H	R	E	W

BEGAN
CHOSE
DROVE
HEARD
THREW

Famous London building

SHARD

b)

1	A	G	R	E	E	D
2	B	E	C	O	M	E
3	C	H	O	S	E	N
4	D	R	I	V	E	N
5	J	U	M	P	E	D
6	P	L	A	Y	E	D

AGREED
BECOME
CHOSEN
DRIVEN
JUMPED
PLAYED

Game

MEMORY

1 a) *False. Our neighbours have been living here since 2011.*
b) *True.*
c) *False. Our neighbours have been living here for xx years. (In 2015 xx = 4 years. In 2016 xx = 5 years, etc.)*

2 a) *False. It's been raining for just under 7 hours.*
b) *False. It's been raining since just after 8 o'clock.*
c) *True.*

3 a) *True.*
b) *False. Mrs Bell has been waiting since 10:05.*
c) *False. Mrs Crown has been waiting for 20 minutes.*

Unit 2

a) 1 *scientist* 2 *furniture* 3 *rock*
4 *school* 5 *fly* 6 *painter*
7 *dentist* 8 *autumn* 9 *glove*

b) *a, I*
an, in
air, all, ill, lip, paw, ran, win
fair, fall, fill, pair, plan, rain, will, wall

2	*the walk through the forest in hours*
2	*the time the students reached the summit*
6	*the time they arrived at the hostel*
10	*the time they started the walk*
13	*the walk in kilometres*
24	*the number of students in the class*
59	*the number of chocolate bars they ate*
1,085	*the climb to the summit in metres*

Unit 3

1 *Gareth thinks Morgan said:* "Who is your favourite teacher?"
2 *Gareth thinks Gwen said:* "Where are we meeting the others?"
3 *Gareth thinks Gwen said:* "Do you live here?"
4 *Gareth thinks Morgan said:* "I'm thirty."
5 *Gareth thinks Gwen said:* "(Please) don't shout."

1 *E post office*
2 *D short*
3 *B phone*
4 *F age*
5 *A egg*
6 *C bottle*

Unit 4

a)
coast	*cliff*
currency	*pound*
mayor	*city*
navy	*ship*
queen	*crown*
president	*republic*
travel	*passport*

b) … *it's important to be* polite *and friendly.*

1 a) *1 point,* b) *2 points,* c) *3 points*
2 a) *3 points,* b) *1 point,* c) *1 point*
3 a) *0 points,* b) *2 points,* c) *3 points* / a) *0 points,* b) *3 points,* c) *0 points*
4 a) *1 point,* b) *3 points,* c) *0 points* / a) *3 points,* b) *0 points,* c) *1 point*
5 a) *0 points,* b) *3 points,* c) *0 points*
6 a) *0 points,* b) *2 points,* c) *3 points*

How many points did you get?
20–24 points: You are a very polite person. Well done!
14–19 points: You are normally polite, but sometimes you forget.
less than 14 points: You should think before you speak. Don't forget to say 'please' and 'thank you'. And smile!

a) 1 *listen,* 2 *take,* 3 *do,* 4 *carry,* 5 *ride,* 6 *take,* 7 *tell,* 8 *wash*
b) *N, T, O, C, D, A, L, S* = *Scotland*

1 *in,* 2 *in,* 3 *in,* 4 *on,* 5 *on,* 6 *at,* 7 *on,* 8 *on,* 9 *on,* 10 *at,* 11 *in,* 12 *at,* 13 *at,* 14 *in,* 15 *on*
Tina's birthday is on the 6th June.

Unit 5

1 *see,* 2 *remember,* 3 *speak,* 4 *phone … text,* 5 *buy … presents*

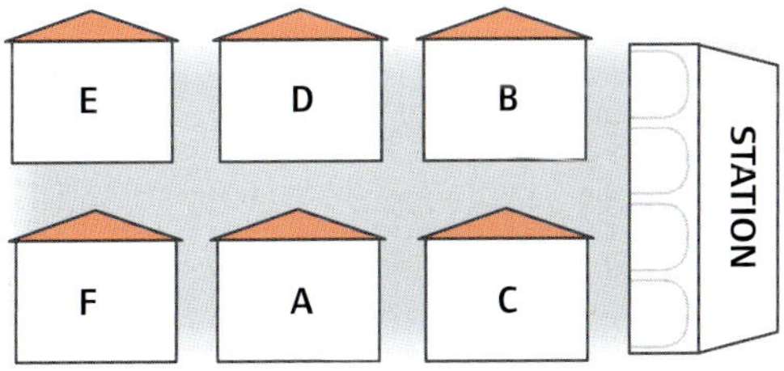

Classroom English

Zu Beginn und am Ende des Unterrichts

Guten Morgen, Frau ...	**Good morning, Mrs/Miss ...** *(bis 12 Uhr)*
Guten Tag, Herr ...	**Good afternoon, Mr ...** *(ab 12 Uhr)*
Entschuldigung, dass ich zu spät komme.	**Sorry I'm late.**
Auf Wiedersehen! / Bis morgen.	**Goodbye. / See you tomorrow.**

Du brauchst Hilfe

Können Sie/Kannst du mir bitte helfen?	**Can you help me, please?**
Auf welcher Seite sind wir, bitte?	**What page are we on, please?**
Was heißt ... auf Englisch/Deutsch?	**What's ... in English/German?**
Können Sie/Kannst du mir bitte ... buchstabieren?	**Can you spell ..., please?**
Können Sie es bitte an die Tafel schreiben?	**Can you write it on the board, please?**

Hausaufgaben und Übungen

Tut mir leid, ich habe mein Schulheft nicht dabei.	**Sorry, I don't have my exercise book.**
Kann ich bitte vorlesen?	**Can I read, please?**
Ich verstehe diese Übung nicht.	**I don't understand this exercise.**
Ich kann Nummer 3 nicht lösen.	**I can't do number 3.**
Entschuldigung, ich bin noch nicht fertig.	**Sorry, I haven't finished.**
Ich habe ... Ist das auch richtig?	**I have ... Is that right too?**
Tut mir leid, das weiß ich nicht.	**Sorry, I don't know.**
Was haben wir (als Hausaufgabe) auf?	**What's for homework?**

Wenn es Probleme gibt

Kann ich es auf Deutsch sagen?	**Can I say it in German?**
Können Sie/Kannst du bitte lauter sprechen?	**Can you speak louder, please?**
Können Sie/Kannst du das bitte noch einmal sagen?	**Can you say that again, please?**
Kann ich bitte das Fenster öffnen/zumachen?	**Can I open/close the window, please?**
Kann ich bitte zur Toilette gehen?	**Can I go to the toilet, please?**

Partnerarbeit

Kann ich mit Julian arbeiten?	**Can I work with Julian?**
Kann ich bitte dein Lineal/deinen Filzstift/... haben?	**Can I have your ruler/felt tip/..., please?**
Danke. / Vielen Dank.	**Thank you. / Thanks a lot.**
Du bist dran.	**It's your turn.**

Diese Arbeitsanweisungen findest du häufig im Schülerbuch.

Act out the song.	Spiel das Lied vor.
Add more words to the table.	Füge weitere Wörter zur Tabelle hinzu.
Ask/Answer the questions.	Stelle/Beantworte die Fragen.
Check/Compare with a partner.	Prüfe/Vergleiche mit einem Partner/einer Partnerin.
Choose the correct/right words.	Wähle die richtigen Wörter.
Copy the words from the box.	Schreibe die Wörter aus dem Kästchen ab.
Correct the sentences.	Verbessere/Korrigiere die Sätze.
Find this information.	Finde/Suche diese Informationen.
Find out about cities in Britain.	Informiere dich über Großstädte in Großbritannien.
Finish/Complete the table below.	Vervollständige die Tabelle unten.
Get more words from page 44.	Hole zusätzliche Wörter von Seite 44.
Give reasons.	Gib Gründe an.
Give your text to another pair.	Gebt euren Text einem anderen Paar.
Go on with new ideas.	Mach weiter mit neuen Ideen.
Hang the poster up in your classroom.	Hänge das Poster im Klassenzimmer auf.
Hold up the card.	Halte die Karte hoch.
Imagine you're Silky.	Stell dir vor, du bist Silky.
Label your drawing.	Beschrifte deine Zeichnung.
Learn the rhyme.	Lerne den Reim/Vers auswendig.
Leave space for your answers.	Lass Platz für deine Antworten.
Listen to Morph.	Hör Morph zu.
Look at page 10.	Sieh auf Seite 10 nach. / Sieh dir Seite 10 an.
Look at the picture.	Schau dir das Bild an.
Look up the word if you don't understand it.	Schlag das Wort nach, wenn du es nicht verstehst.
Make appointments with three partners.	Verabrede dich mit drei Partnern/Partnerinnen.
Make groups of three.	Bildet Dreiergruppen.
Match the words to the pictures.	Ordne die Wörter den Bildern zu.
Practise the words.	Übe die Wörter.
Put all the verbs in the right place.	Setze alle Verben an der richtigen Stelle ein.
Put the card into your MyBook.	Lege die Karte in dein MyBook.
Put up your hand.	Melde dich.
Read the dialogue out loud to your group.	Lies deiner Gruppe den Dialog laut vor.
Rewrite the text.	Schreibe den Text neu.
Scan the text to find these words.	Überfliege den Text und versuche, diese Wörter zu finden.
Sing along with the chorus.	Sing den Refrain mit.
Start a profile for Sam.	Fang ein Profil für Sam an.
Swap cards with another team.	Tauscht Karten mit einem anderen Team.
Take turns.	Wechselt euch ab.
Talk to different partners about the photo.	Rede mit verschiedenen Partnern/Partnerinnen über das Foto.
Talk to your partner like this: ...	Rede so mit deinem Partner/deiner Partnerin: ...
Think of a sentence.	Denk dir einen Satz aus.
Use these words: ...	Verwende diese Wörter: ...
Walk around the classroom.	Geh im Klassenzimmer herum.
Write down the letters in the right order.	Schreibe die Buchstaben in der richtigen Reihenfolge auf.

Quellenverzeichnis

Titelbild

F1online digitale Bildagentur, Frankfurt/Main (The Shard (M); **mauritius images**, Mittenwald (Big Ben (M): ImageBROKER)

Illustrationen

Stefan Bachmann, Wiesbaden (S. 101; S 102); **Christian Bartz**, Berlin (S. 98; S. 99); **Roland Beier**, Berlin (S. 141; S. 142; S. 143; S. 144; S. 148; S. 149; S. 150; S. 157 unten li.; S. 158 Bild 1-3; S. 159 Bild 1-4; S. 168 Finn, Asif taking pictures, unten re. Bild 1-4; S. 173 oben; S. 174; S. 175; S. 177; S. 178; S. 179; S. 180; S. 181; S. 182; S. 183; S. 186; S. 187; S. 190; S. 192; S. 193; S. 194; S. 196); **Carlos Borrell**, Berlin (S. 8 oben United Kingdom inset (u. Hintergrund United Kingdom u. S. 4/5 u. 26/27); S. 8/9); S. 44 map; S. 64); S. 139; S. 140 oben u. unten); **Tobias Dahmen**, Utrecht/NL (S. 12; S. 19; S. 35; S. 36; S. 39; S. 43; S. 58 oben; S. 63; S. 68; S. 70; S. 75; S. 76; S. 81; S. 106-109; S. 112; S. 113; S. 114; S. 115; S. 116; S. 119; S. 123; S. 127; S. 130 oben; S. 154 unten; S. 155 unten; S. 157 oben, unten re.; S. 158 Morph; S. 159 Morph; S. 160 Morph; S. 161; S. 162 Morph; S. 163 Morph; S. 164; S. 165 Morph; S. 167; S. 168 unten li. Morph; S. 169 Morph; S. 248; S. 249); **Datavis Geografik**, **Thomas Klein**, Stegen (Umschlaginnenseite 2); **Jeongsook Lee**, Heidelberg (S. 110 unten; S. 111 Mitte Position of the Titanic; S. 172 unten); **M. B. Schulz**, Düsseldorf (S. 10 (M); S. 20 Pub (M); S. 24/25 (M); S. 30 (M); S. 34 (M); S. 41 (M); S. 56-57 Bild A-E (M); S. 60; S. 66 (M); S. 78 (M); S. 88 Bild 1-6 (M); S. 95 (M))

Bildquellen

A1PIX – YOUR PHOTO TODAY, Taufkirchen (S. 104 oben: YourPhotoToday/PM); **akg images**, Berlin (S. 111 Edward Smith: Universal Images Group; S. 132 (u. 135) Mona Lisa: IAM, Beethoven (u. 135): De Agostini Picture Lib.); **BBC** (S. 87 film stills); **Bridgeman Art Library**, Berlin (S. 67 Titanic: © BRIDGEMANART. COM; S. 134 unten: © BRIDGEMANART.COM; S. 111 oben: © BRIDGEMANART. COM/colour litho by Wong, Raymond; National Geographic Image Collection); **Clipdealer** (S. 33 Cardiff castle: Andres Rodriguez; S. 46 Bild 4 Liverpool Cathedral (M) (u. 132): ArTo; S. 80 yellow house: ArTo; S. 151: Robert Kneschke); **Colourbox.com** (S. 71 pot of gold); S. 110 oben ship, plane); **Corbis**, Düsseldorf (S. 6 oben li. (u. 66 (M)): Ric Ergenbright; S. 9 Bild B (u. 27): Rob Newell/ActionPlus, Bild C: Matt Gibson/LOOP IMAGES/Loop Images, Bild D: Rune Hellestad; S. 10 Hintergrund London (M): (c) Atlantide Phototravel; S. 14 unten re.: (c) English Heritage/Arcaid; S. 15 unten crown jewels: Jonathan Blair; S. 25 female dancer with eyes closed (M): Santino Pani/Demotix, group of dancers in the background (M): Olivia Harris/Reuters, S. 24/25 speactators: Eugenie Absalom/Demotix; S. 27 (u. 50): Bettmann; S. 30 workshop (M): (c) Jetta Productions/ Blend Images; S. 46 Bild 1 Mathew Street (M): LOOP IMAGES; S. 47 Bild 3 Chinese Arch (M): (c) Atlantide Phototravel; S. 56/57 Hintergrund fans: RUSSELL CHEYNE/ Reuters; S. 103: Robert Wallis; S. 111 unten: © The Mariners' Museum); **Cornelsen Schulverlage** (S. 22 film stills oben, Mitte, unten; S. 33 unten li. film still: Tellusvision; S. 70 Mitte; S. 85 unten; culture-images, Köln (S. 132 Tresure Island (u. 135) The digital file and its content are the property of **culture-images**/Lebrecht Music & Arts and protected by intellectual property); **Philip Devlin**, Berlin (S. 65 Bild H; S. 69 Dublin for kids poster stadium; S. 71 chocolate; S. 80 passports); **Dough Productions** (S. 73: Daniel Ò Hara) **dpa Picture-Alliance**, Frankfurt/Main (S. 9 Bild A: dpa; S. 13: dpa; S. 45 Käthe Kollwitz Schule (u. 62): dpa; S. 62 Werner-von-Siemens-Straße: dpa; S. 64 Bild D: C. Bämke/Ar; S. 80 girl looking at train schedule: dpa/Wolfgang Kumm; S. 86 Bannockburn celebration: empics; S. 91 unten: ZB); **F1online digitale Bildagentur**, Frankfurt/Main (S. 9 Bild E: RM Fotosearch; S. 33 Eisteddfod festival: Morris/AGE/ F1online; S. 67 oben re.: Martin Siepmann; S. 105 oben: AGEFOTOSTOCK); **Fotolia** (S. 8 Bild F: zefart; S. 9 Bild M: metropolitana (copyright) cla' #1782447; S. 15 Mitte Tower of London: ian woolcock #55566662; S. 23 Bild 3: mohsinjamil #61003655; S. 55 re.: Claudio Divizia #49632794; S. 27 Bild 4 (u. 65): morrbyte; S. 67 map of Europe: Tanja Bagusat; S. 69 Irish writers brochure Oliver Goldsmith: Georgios Kollidas #55480724; S. 78 oben girls riding horses (M): aleksandrn #33490313; S. 80 timetable: drx #27961856; S. 83 Bild 4 sheep (M): Hugh Shaw; S. 84: Triple Jump; S. 85 oben: martin2014; S. 92 oben: lightpoet #67480800; S. 93 treasure chest (M): Cginspiration); **Foundlight Productions** (S. 82 unten); **Stefanie Gira**, Berlin (S. 31 oben); **Glow Images**, München (S. 64 u. 65 Bild B oben Belfast, Dublin signs (M): Designpics; S. 64 Bild E: Irish Images Collection RM; S. 70 oben re.: Irish Images, S. 78 ruins (M): First Light; S. 80 ImageBROKER RM; S. 83 Bild 5: ImageBROKER RM; S. 85 Mitte bird: ScienceFaction; S. 104 Mitte: ImageZoo); **Stefan Höhne**, Berlin (S. 34 bottle (M)); **INTERFOTO**, München (S. 14 oben li.: Mary Evans/Natural History Museum, oben re.: Mary Evans/Natural History Museum; S. 48: Brown; S. 134: Mary Evans); **LAIF Agentur für Photos & Reportagen**, Köln (S. 9 Bild R: Gehard Westrich; S. 15 Bild C re. (M): Riachard Bowden/Loop Images; S. 23 Bild 5: Andrea Artz; S. 53 museum (M): MAISANT Ludovic/hemis.fr/laif; S. 57 Bild D stadium (M): Xavier DESMIER/RAPHO); **mauritius images**, Mittenwald (S. 4 Mitte li. (u. 28/29): Alamy/Alan Novelli, unten (u. 27 u. 44/45): Alamy/John Davidson Photos; S. 8 Bild I: Carlos Sánchez Pereyra; S. 9 Bild O: Alamy/Greg Balfour Evans, Bild P: United Archives; S. 15 unten li.: Alamy/Richard Green, unten re. signs: Alamy/Simon Montgomery; S. 23 Bild 1: Steve Vidler; S. 24 male dancer with red trousers and mask (M): Alamy/Renato Granieri; S. 27 Bild 3 (u. 65): Alamy/Rick Strange; S. 33 oben Mitte: Alamy/Jeff Morgan 01, oben re. signs: Alamy/Richard Naude; S. 41 oben sign (M): Alamy/Pat Shearman; S. 45 John Lennon Platz (u. 62), Martin-Gropius-Bau (u. 62): Josefine; S. 47 Bild 2 promenade (M) (PRÜFEN): Alamy/Bjanka Kadic, Bild 5 street (M): Alamy/Dave Ellison, Bild 6 bananas (M): Alamy/ Jan Wlodarczyk, market (M): Alamy/Janine Wiedel Photolibrary; S. 51: Bildagentur Hamburg; S. 52 oben: © Sabena Jane Blackbird/Alamy; S. 54: Alamy/Sabena Jane

Blackbird; S. 56 Bild A stadium (M): Alamy/Radharc Images; S. 64 Bild A: Alamy/Eye Ubiquitous; S. 65 Bild G: Alamy/Striking Images; S. 67 unten re.: Alamy/kp; S. 70 unten re.: Alamy/Kevin Foy; S. 71 museum: Alamy/Tim E White; S. 78 field (M): Alamy/Hon F. Lau; S. 80 Stadtinformation: Alamy/Premium Stock Photography GmbH, DJH logo: Steffen Beuthan; S. 82/83 tartan: Alamy/Victor Watts; S. 82 Bild 1 Fringe Festival (M): Alamy/Colin Woodbridge, Bild 2: Alamy/ROBIN MCKELVIE; S. 86 Urquhart Castle: Alamy/John McKenna, National Gallery: Alamy/malcolm sewell; S. 95 police officers (M): Alamy/ RTimages, path (M): Alamy/Peter Paterson; S. 96 Hintergrund field (M): Alamy/ simon evans; S. 104 unten: Alamy/ Rafael Ben-Ari; S. 105 unten: Alamy/Jeff Morgan 09; S. 132 Oliver Twist (u. 135): Alamy/DWD-Media; S. 136 oben: Alamy/VIEW Pictures Ltd); **Tony Morrissey** (S. 61 oben re.); **Nigel Wilson Photography**, Bristol (S. 4 Mo, Emily; S. 5 Dylan, Gwen, Morgan, Gareth; S. 6 Lewis (u. 70 u. 71 chat icon u. 74 chat icon); S. 7; S. 10 teenagers (M); S. 11 oben li. Mo; S. 20 people (M); S. 21; S. 24 girl running away (M); S. 30 girl, man (M); S. 34 boy, girl (M); S. 41 teenagers; S. 42; S. 46 teenagers looking at book, Bild 1 teenagers (M), Bild 4 teenagers (M); S. 47 Bild 2 teenagers (M), Bild 3 teenagers (M), Bild 5 teenagers (M), Bild 6 teenagers (M); S. 49 oben, unten; S. 53 teenagers (M); S. 56 Bild A, B, C teenagers (M); S. 57 Bild D, E teenagers (M); S. 64 boy (u. 124); S. 66 boy (M); S. 74 unten (u. 124), S. 78 teenagers (M); S. 82 oben li. Lewis and Skye (M); S. 83 Bild 4 Lauren (M); S. 88 Bild 1 boy (M), Bild 2 woman (2), Bild 3 boy and girl (M) Bild 4 woman and girl (M), Bild 5 boy and girl (M), Bild 6 boy and girl and woman (M); S. 90 Skye (u. 125), Sandra (u. 125); S. 94 girl (M); S. 95 girl li. (M); S. 96 girl (M); S. 117; S. 128); **Paramount Pictures Corp** (S. 11 London skyline: STAR TREK INTO DARKNESS © Paramount Pictures Corp. All Rights Reserved.); **Pathé** (S. 59 oben li., re., Mitte, unten: Stills and Footage from „There's Only One Jimmy Grimble" courtesy of Pathe); **Photoshot**, Hamburg (S. 23 Bild 4: Alpha-Jeff Spicer; S. 55 li.; S. 65 Bild C: Imagesbroker.net; S. 67 unten li.; S. 86 shop window); **Sapna Richter**, Berlin (S. 17 oben, unten; S. 37 oben li., re.; S. 39 two teenagers talking; S. 44 choir; S. 69 Bild 1, 2, 3, 4; S. 71 unten li. u. re.; S. 91 oben li., Mitte, re.; S. 92 unten; S. 93 folder (M); S. 97 Step 1 three teenagers talking; S. 150; S. 152; S. 153; Umschlaginnenseite 3); **Adam Roach**, Blaneau Gwent (S. 39 oben); **Shutterstock** (S. 4 oben li.: pisaphotography; S. 6 unten li.: Jane Rix; S. 8 Bild J: Bikeworldtravel; S. 9 Bild G: Monkey Business Images, Bild H: Kiev. Victor, Bild K: AdStock RF, Bild L: Cedric Weber, Bild N: Chris Jenner, Bild Q (u. 27): Peter Nadolski; S. 11 unten: DavidYoung; S. 14 unten li: lullabi; S. 15 Bild C li. London Eye (M): Anshar, unten raven: Anna Kucherova; S. 23 Bild 2: Nick Hawkes; S. 24 smiling female dancer behind male dancer (M): Gold Stock Images; S. 27 Bild 7: Joe Gough, Bild 8: chrisdorney; S. 33 oben li.: image4stock; S. 34 Vordergrund waterfall (M), Hintergrund waterfall (M): DJTaylor; S. 37 unten: Luminis; S. 52 Mitte: Bethan Collins, unten: Nikuwka; S. 58 umbrella: Tatiana Popova; S. 64 coins: Asaf Eliason; S. 65 coins: Claudio Divizia; S. 69 Dublin for kids brochure flag of Dublin: e X p o s e, Dublin at night: Bartkowski, Irish writers brochure Bernhard Shaw: Sergey Goryachev, William Yeates: Brendan Howard, Oscar Wilde statue: M Reel; S. 70 Chloe (u. 71 u. 74): BestPhotoPlus, Jack (u. 71): Aschindl; S. 71 Luke: Arina P Habich; S. 74 oben re.: frescomovie; S. 78 sky (M): S.Borisov; S. 80 money (M): Pelfophoto; S. 83 Bild 4 dog (M): Eric Isselee; S. 86 Cycle Arc Bridge: Targn Pleiades, street piper: Gyvafoto; S. 90 Mr. McCray (u. 125): ostill; S. 93 paper (M): DuH; S. 94 rock (M): Martin M303, dog (M): Mackland, bed (M): hxdbzxy; S. 95 beach (M): Spumador, S. 96 dog (M): Eric Isselee; S. 97 Step 4 li.: Anneka, Step 4 re.: Alexander Trinitatov; S. 132 (u. 135) Berlin Underground: PHOTOCREO Michal Bednarek, lift: Carsten Reisinger, Cologne Cathedral (u. 135): Taras Vyshnya, London Underground (u. 132): Stephen Bures, escalator (u. 135): Ekkachai; S. 133 oben: RAEVSKY; S. 136 Mitte re. boys playing basketball: Alexander Raths, unten li.: James Peragine, unten re.: Kenneth Sponsler; S. 137 oben: dotshock, unten: Kruglov_Orda; S. 172 oben (u. 173: Yulia Glam); S. 175: Anna Kucherova; S. 178: optimarc); **Transport for London** (S. 18 Tube map: used by permission of Pulse Creative Limited)

Textquellen

S. 32 u. S. 141 u. S. 142 Wörterbucheintrag, Schulwörterbuch English G 21, Cornelsen Verlag, Berlin 2011; S. 104 *When you are called names, remember, Mr Ifonly, The Panther's Heart* und. S. 105 *My Neighbour's Rabbit* taken from Brian Patten: "Juggling with gerbils". Puffin Books, London 2002; S. 112-115 The Off-side Trap by Mary Colson: in: "Scripts and Sketches". Heinemann Educational Publishers, Oxford 2001, S. 89 ff.

Liedquellen

S. 36 *If I had a hammer*. Text: Lee Hayes und Pete Seeger/ Copyright by Ludlow Music, Inc. D/A/CH: Essex Musikvertrieb GmbH, Hamburg; S. 57 *You'll never walk alone*, Text: Oscar Hammerstein/WILLIAMSON-MUSIC-INC/Boosey & HawkeS. Bote & Bock, Berlin

S. 103 *Penny Lane*, Text: John Lennon, Paul McCartney/ Sony-ATV Tunes LLC/Sony/ATV Music Publishing (Germany GmbH), Berlin

Giving feedback to your classmates

TEXT — PRESENTATION

	CONTENT
✓	You covered the important points in the task.
✓	The information was interesting/new.
✓	You gave examples/details.
✓	You gave your opinion.
✓	You gave arguments for your opinion.
✎	*Your story had a plot.*[2]
	You described the characters.
	...

✓ Choose criteria[1] for your feedback.

✎ Add other criteria you need, e.g. for feedback on a story.

TEXT

	STRUCTURE
✓	Your introduction said what the text is about.
✓	You used paragraphs.
✓	Each paragraph had a new idea.
✓	You had a conclusion.
✎	...

	LANGUAGE
✓	You used different adjectives and adverbs.
✓	You joined sentences with linking words.
✓	You used special vocabulary for the topic.
✓	Your spelling was correct.
✓	Your grammar was correct.
✎	...

PRESENTATION

	STRUCTURE
✓	You introduced the topic.
✓	Your presentation had a clear structure.
✓	You showed your main points on a poster/...
✓	You summed up at the end.
✓	You invited us to ask questions.
✎	...

	COMMUNICATION
✓	You seemed relaxed.
✓	You made eye contact.
✓	You used notes.
✓	You spoke clearly.
✓	You explained your pictures.
✎	...

TIPS

1 Use the criteria you chose to assess[3] your classmate's work.

2 Give details when you say what a classmate did/didn't do well.
Always start with something positive.

Where	What
In the first paragraph you	*wrote a good introduction ....*
At the end of your presentation you	*didn't ask if we had questions /...*

3 Suggest how the classmate could do better.
You could try to *use more linking words like **and** or **because** /use more pictures / ...*

[1] **criteria** *(pl)* [kraɪˈtɪəriə] Kriterien [2]**plot** [plɒt] Handlung [3](to) **assess** [əˈses] einschätzen